Washington & Oregon

Gardener's Guide

Proven Plants for Inspired Gardens

Published by Cool Springs Press, 101 Forrest Crossing Boulevard, Suite 100, Franklin, Tennessee, 37064

Prinzing, Debra.
    Washington & Oregon gardener's guide : proven plants for inspired gardens /
Debra Prinzing & Mary Robson.
        p. cm.
    Includes bibliographical references (p.   ) and index.
    ISBN 1-59186-112-8 (pbk.)
    1. Landscape plants--Washington (State) 2. Landscape plants--Oregon.
    3. Landscape gardening--Washington (State) 4. Landscape gardening--Oregon.
    I. Title: Washington and Oregon gardener's guide. II. Robson, Mary. III. Title.
    SB407.P74 2005
    635.9'09797--dc22
                            2004018171

First printing 2005
Printed in the United States of America
10 9 8 7 6 5 4 3

Managing Editor: Billie Brownell
Designer: Sheri Ferguson, Ferguson Design
Horticulture Editor: Christina Pfeiffer, ISA Certified Arborist, M.S. Urban Horticulture,
        University of Washington
Illustrator: Bill Kersey, Kersey Graphics
Production Artist: S.E. Anderson

On the Cover: *Rhododendron yakushima* photographed by Mark Turner, Turner Photographics®

Visit the Cool Springs Press website at **www.coolspringspress.net**

Washington & Oregon
Gardener's Guide

Proven Plants for Inspired Gardens

Debra Prinzing & Mary Robson

COOL SPRINGS PRESS
Franklin, Tennessee

Dedication

For Master Gardener volunteers throughout the Northwest. The national program started in Washington, in 1973 with Washington State University, and continues today, through hundreds of dedicated and energetic gardening volunteers, learning and sharing horticultural knowledge with others.

Acknowledgments

Any of us who gradually gather knowledge about gardening and enjoying our region have many influences and people to thank—horticulture's a connected world! For George Pinyuh, Washington State University Extension Horticulture agent (retired), who taught me more about growing plants than he will ever know; Dr. Art Kruckeberg, for wisdom on natives of the Northwest; Eric Nelson, WSU Master Gardener, for his encyclopedic knowledge of ornamental grasses; Sue Thompson, for touring me through the grasses of Harstine Heirloom Nursery, Harstine Island; Neil Burkhardt and Jane Stewart of McComb Road Nursery, Sequim, for shrub evaluation; Sharon Collman for insight on IPM, and Wendy Wells and the staff of Wells-Medina Nursery for rhododendrons. Don Morrow, Consulting Rosarian and WSU Master Gardener on roses. Brent Heath, owner of Brent and Becky's Bulbs, Virginia, helped with bulb questions.

Colleagues at Washington State University Extension whose bulletins and writings on general horticulture in the Northwest improved this book: Dr. Gwen Stahnke on turf; Dr. Ray Maleike, Tonie Fitzgerald, Dr. Craig Cogger on soil and fertilizers; and Dr. Tom Cook, turf specialist, Oregon State University.

To my mother, Winifred Sanders, and her mother Olive, who knew the world of gardens from roots to bloom, and in their lifetimes gave me both inspiration and encouragement. My son Nathan delights me with new attentiveness now that he's in his 30s and has discovered growing vegetables!

—*Mary Robson*

I am grateful for the education I've received from countless friends and advisors in the horticultural world, including nursery experts and landscape designers who have shared their enthusiasm about favorite—and proven—plants with me. Thank you to my two garden muses, Jean Zaputil and Karen Page, who each in her own way has infused my life with a love of garden design and plants. I'm extremely grateful to those who have taught me horticulture, including my co-author Mary Robson, under whose leadership I became a Master Gardener in 1998, and the fabulous volunteers at the WSU-King County Master Gardener Urban Demonstration Garden in Bellevue.

Many thanks to my instructors and advisors at South Seattle Community College's Landscape Horticulture program, including Sarah Skamser, Van Bobbit, Penny McCormick, Ann Lantz, and the late and legendary Bud Merrill. My nursery friends, including Marlis Korber and Emery Rhodes of Emery's Garden in Lynnwood; Gillian Mathews, Teresa Malmanger, Todd Waddell, and Ed Poquette of Ravenna Gardens in Seattle and Portland; Alice Schroder of Swans Trail Gardens in Snohomish, Washington; Laine McLaughlin of Steamboat Island Nursery in Olympia, Washington; and many others.

A very special thank you to my parents, Fred and Anita Prinzing, for their lifelong support of me as a writer and speaker. Their love of new experiences and of God's beauty has always inspired me to learn more and share my knowledge with others.

And much, much love to my three guys, Alexander (7), Benjamin (12), and Bruce Brooks, my husband and partner.

—*Debra Prinzing*

We gratefully acknowledge the visionary behind this series, Hank McBride of Cool Springs Press, who offered us the wonderful opportunity to create this useful, relevant guide to plants for Northwest gardens. We also extend our thanks to editor Billie Brownell of Cool Springs Press and Chris Pfeiffer, ISA arborist and consulting horticulturalist, who answered questions patiently and served as horticultural reviewer.

—*DP & MR*

Table of Contents

Featured Plants *for Washington & Oregon*

Welcome to Gardening *in*

Washington & Oregon

Images of cornucopias spilling beauty and variety come to mind when we visualize gardens in Washington and Oregon. Blessed with a very long, though cool, growing season, gardeners in mild western parts of the region often gather rosebuds along with their holly on Christmas Eve. Hardy bananas (gorgeous, though fruitless) overwinter in the warm spots of Seattle and Portland. Gardeners east of the Cascades have perfect growing conditions for succulent apricots and vivid dahlias in the backyard during summer, with sun and warmth ideal for maturing flowers and fruit, despite a short growing season and certainly no December roses. Our region is blessed in agriculture: cherries, pears, apples, and peaches pour from eastern Washington and Oregon's idyllic Hood River valley, while berries thrive in western Washington.

Known for the beauty of its natural landscape, the Pacific Northwest offers some of the most superb growing conditions in the United States, and some considerable challenges. Successful gardening in Washington and Oregon means, first, understanding the geography and its effect on garden climate.

Know Where You Are

The region is roughly bisected by mountains running north to south, with differing climate realities within those areas. The Coastal Northwest extends from British Columbia south through Oregon to California, lying west of the Cascade Mountains, with mild, rainy winters and cool, dry summers. The Inland Northwest, east of the Cascades and west of the Rocky Mountains, copes with frigid winters and sunny, hot, arid summers.

Gardening zones range from warm, nearly tropical zone 9 on the southern Oregon coast, to zone 4, inland near the Rockies. West of the Cascades, the influence of ocean air keeps winter temperatures moderate, seldom dipping below 20 degrees Fahrenheit, though locations along the mountains and in the Willamette Valley regularly turn colder. Most of the Inland Northwest lies in USDA zones 5 (lows of minus 10 to minus 20 degrees Fahrenheit) and 6 (lows of 0 to minus 10 degrees F), but deep winter cold may fall to 30 degrees below zero in eastern Oregon's high desert country.

Winter cold alone makes a difference, but the other factor is available rainfall. A few areas on and near the Olympic Peninsula in western Washington form a genuine temperate rainforest with more than 100 inches of rain per year, but spots where rain is measured in feet rather than inches are the exceptions.

The common impression that Coastal Pacific Northwest areas are soggy with rain year-round isn't accurate; certainly the annual 40-inch average in Seattle would be ideal for plants, but most of it falls during winter, leaving the summer growing season quite dry. Rainfall of less than 5 inches from May through September is common in Seattle and Portland.

East of the Cascades, the total year-round rainfall during winter and summer can be less than 12 inches. Referring to the "high desert" country of Oregon may seem strange, but summer heat and dry winter cold, with little moisture, make the term accurate. For gardeners in all parts of Washington and Oregon, summer water management for landscapes is a major necessity, with water stress on gardens a constant reality. Our driest seasons coincide with the major growth needs of plants.

Once aware of the general USDA hardiness zones of the landscape (check the map on page 21) gardeners also need to adjust for individual conditions caused by *microclimates*. Elevation is a major consideration: The higher the garden, the colder the climate. Fall frosts come earlier; spring frosts stay later as elevations rise.

Temperature moderates at lower elevations, particularly with proximity to water, whether a river, lake, or the ocean. Within the garden, slope and terrain also affect temperature, with the lowest spots colder than slopes. A plant that survives midway up a south-facing slope may expire at the bottom where cold air sinks and settles.

Zonal realities may be defined by "playing" with plants specified for a region that's one zone higher (warmer) than yours. This can mean siting a tender plant in the warmest spot in your garden or providing it with extra winter protection. Against a south-facing stone wall, retained warmth can allow the gardener to leap a zone. In zone 4 it may mean being able to use a plant rated to hardiness zone 5. Gardeners, particularly those west of the Cascades, delight in stretching their zonal limits, recognizing that gardening

In the Garden of Janie and Billie Fowler, Snohomish, Washington

is an adventure. But even with apparent moderation of winter temperatures through gradual climate change, sudden freezes can descend at any time throughout the coldest months, nipping experiments.

Design a Landscape You Enjoy

Selecting plants for the new Northwest landscape means making many choices: Do you want play areas, shrubs to frame a home or a view, trees for afternoon shade, bright leaves for color in fall? A landscape architect or garden designer can help you clarify the needs and possibilities of your landscape. With a professional design, you can do the work yourself or get help with installation. You needn't install the whole plan at once; proceeding in sections reduces the immediate expense and lets you enjoy the developing landscape.

Once you've decided to create a garden, whether to grow vegetables or landscape a home, you'll need to manage the basics of soil preparation, plant installation, fertilization, and watering. Each of these has specific techniques for Washington and Oregon gardeners.

What's Underfoot

Linked together, soil conditions, fertilizer methods, and watering techniques support plant life in your garden. Soils in Washington and Oregon vary, from deep loam in the Willamette and Puyallup River Valleys to places where, thousands of years ago, receding glaciers left shallow mixed gravel, rock, and clay soils. One gardener described her western Washington soil as "Clay, except for the rocks." Whatever your particular soil texture, amendments and careful management can help improve it to provide better plant growth.

When starting a new garden, determine your soil texture, which affects all aspects of planting and growing. Pick up a small, damp handful. Squeeze it, then force out a "ribbon" with your thumb, pressing the soil into a narrow band. Clay soil will hold together, allowing several inches of ribbon to develop, and it will also show the imprints of your fingers. Loam soil, a balance of clay and sand, will form a short but breakable ribbon. Sandy or gravelly soil won't hold together, crumbling as you press.

Clay soils can hold too much water. They do not drain well and are hard to dampen if they dry out. Their advantage is that they hold mineral nutrients well, requiring less fertilizer than sandy soils. Loamy soils strike a good balance, holding water but draining well. Sandy soils allow plenty of air and oxygen to the roots, but drain too fast, being difficult to water in summer and hard to keep fertilized.

Plant roots need both air and water in the soil; both clay and sandy soils can gradually be improved by using organic materials such as compost, manures, or biosolids (composted sewage sludge) as mulch. If an area is to stay bare for a season, plant "green manure" crops such as rye, buckwheat, or crimson clover. These plants help reduce weed invasions on bare ground, and will improve soil when dug in at maturity where they then compost.

How should an older landscape be managed? Adding organic material to an established planted area is best done by mulching. Choose well-composted material and add two inches a year in early spring and late fall. The mulch will slowly improve soil texture as it breaks down but mulch needs regular renewal because it will disappear into the soil as it decomposes.

Soil acidity or alkalinity, measured as pH, also affects plant growth. Most landscape plants grow well in a pH range between 6.0 and 7.0, with 7 being "neutral." At these pH ranges, plants receive and can take in the widest variety of nutrients. Soils west of the Cascades tend to be acidic with pH levels from 5.0 to 6.0 while soils in the eastern areas of Oregon and Washington are often alkaline, with pH levels up to 7.5 or 8.0. Washington State University soil experts point out that soils with a pH of 5.5 to 7.0 do not need soil amendments to adjust the pH level. Check with a nursery or your local Washington State or Oregon State University Extension Office for information on soil testing.

Planting Trees and Shrubs

In the coldest areas, plant in spring; in milder sections, plant in fall or early spring. Careful assessment of soil drainage and conditions contributes to the long-term health and growth of the trees and shrubs. Check the soil drainage by digging a hole 12 inches deep and filling it with water. The water should drain out of the hole at a rate of at least $1/2$ inch an hour, leaving the hole empty after twenty-four hours. If it doesn't or if winter storms leave areas of the landscape soggy and puddled, check with a landscape professional about possible drainage installation to correct the problem. Or choose plants adapted to soggy conditions, such as red alder and redtwig dogwood. Most trees and shrubs do not grow well in heavy, water-retentive soils, and some, like rhododendrons and azaleas, will die.

When planting trees and shrubs—woody plants that will have decades of landscape presence—it's best to prepare the entire large planting bed at once. You may be familiar with old advice to add lots of peat moss or compost to one hole before planting, but this has been discounted by research; woody plant roots tend not to grow out of that localized, enriched spot into native soils.

A better method is to loosen the soil by hand or with a tiller at least down to 8 inches throughout the planting area, removing larger rocks, and then adding organic materials. Be sure that the material has been fully composted; fresh manure or decomposing sawdust may burn new plant roots or reduce available nitrogen in the soil. Add 3 to 4 inches, spread over the planting area, then till or dig it in again. Rake the area smooth, and water it or allow rain to help it settle for a week or so before planting.

Plants will be available in containers, or balled and burlapped, or bare root (only in earliest spring before growth starts.) Proper planting means caring for the plant's roots while installing, and not placing the plant too deep in the ground. Overdeep planting can cause eventual plant decline. Protect all roots from drying while planting by keeping them covered with damp burlap or soil before installation.

For all trees and shrubs, no matter how they are packaged, dig a hole 2 to 3 times wider than the plant's width, and as deep as the plant's root depth (10 inches for a plant in a 10 inch pot). Rest the rootball on firm ground so the plant doesn't go in too deep. For plants in containers, slide the plant out and check its root condition. Matted or circling root systems often follow the outline of the pot. Untangle, unwind, and pull out these circling roots; then reduce their length by cutting them with pruning shears. If left to circle, they will reduce plant growth or kill the plant. If tangled roots are cut off, this will rejuvenate the plant. Make two or three vertical slices through the matted root mass and spread out the roots to allow them to make firm contact with the soil.

What if you are planting only one tree or shrub? If you cannot prepare the entire area, dig the hole only to the existing plant depth so it sits on firm ground, but 2 to 3 times wider than the rootball, loosening the soil thoroughly to provide oxygen to the roots. Do not add any organic material to the planting hole.

Lavender, Hardy Geranium, and Fleabane

Recommendations for trees, shrubs, vines, and woody ground covers are identical: either amend the entire soil area or plant in well loosened native soil if you are landscaping one small area at a time. You're preparing these sturdy woody plants for a long life in the landscape.

Balled-and-burlapped plants come wrapped in fabric, with twine securing it to the rootball. These fabrics aren't always traditional "burlap." Check with the nursery if you have concerns about whether the material should be removed before planting. In general, if it's plastic or other nondegradable fiber, the wrapping should be pulled off the rootball, along with the twine, before planting.

Moisten the rootball thoroughly before disturbing the packing material. Settle the rootball into the hole, being sure the top of the ball rests level with the ground, or an inch higher; avoid planting too deeply. After the plant is in the hole, remove and fold down all the packing and pull it away, cutting it loose and taking it out of the hole. Do not allow any of the material to remain above the soil surface, or it will wick water out of the hole. In general, it's best to cut off all the loose wrappings before covering it. Fill in the hole with native soil, tamp it down, and water well.

Bare-root plants require care to keep roots moist before planting. They may be packed in sawdust to keep the roots damp. When ready to plant, soak the roots 4 to 6 hours in plain water. Soaking longer than this can damage the roots. Fill the hole gradually, holding the plant with one hand, keeping the roots spread, and placing soil carefully to avoid leaving air pockets around roots. Water thoroughly after planting.

All plants need water when they are first installed. After planting, make sure the plant remains level with—or even slightly higher than—the ground; do not pile soil up over the roots or crown of the plant near the trunk. Form a shallow "water saucer" outside the roots, raising or mounding soil up about 2 inches to allow water to remain above the roots and penetrate them. Fill it two or three times, allowing the water to drain into the roots.

Finally, mulch lightly over the new planting, placing 2 inches of composted material over the surface (this won't result in the plant becoming too deep if it's been installed correctly). Choose lightweight but fertile material such as composted bark or manure.

The most important part of plant installation—other than selecting the best plant for the spot—is planting at the proper depth, not too deep.

Water To Keep Them Growing!

Water management is vital in all parts of Washington and Oregon. Newcomers to the region react with surprise to discover that all sections of both states can be extremely dry during the summer months, with insufficient rainfall to assure plant growth during summer. Most nonnative plants in Washington and Oregon require supplemental moisture in addition to rainfall from May through September.

As population grows, efficient water use is crucial because water becomes both scarcer and more expensive. Living with limited summer water is a condition that affects every gardener here. Dry conditions challenge the gardener but need not result in either wasted water or a boring, desiccated landscape.

Garden planning can help deal with the limitations. Select plants that will manage during dry times, although it's certainly not necessary to avoid using water-lovers. Prepare the soil properly, use mulches to help with water retention, and group plants according to their water needs. A gathering of ferns, hostas, and rhododendrons tucked into a shady corner can thrive with a well-placed soaker hose and regular irrigation. Roses, perennial delphinium, and annuals make brilliant summer color, but need sufficient water.

A few basic principles help. Plants need not only water, but air in the soil to give roots oxygen. If the soil doesn't drain well, or plants get overwatered, they can die from lack of air. Too little water causes roots to die, then the whole plant. The roots, not the leaves, need the water. Speedy sprinkling, even if it's fun to wave the hose on a bright summer day, doesn't provide enough water to reach the roots. One reality of Northwest gardening is the presence of brief showers that cloud the sky and dampen the ground but don't offer much real root-quenching water.

Plants lose water by releasing it from their leaves, a process called *transpiration*, normal and necessary for plant health. But when the soil is too dry for the roots to replace water lost through the leaves, the plant wilts. Overcast days with misty rain may not provide much measurable rainfall, but they do reduce a plant's regular water loss.

Knowing your soil type will help. Sandy soils won't hold water and will require more frequent irrigation than clay or loamy soils. WSU soil scientist Dr. Craig Cogger, Ph.D., reminds us that "soil type or texture is a major determining factor of how much water a soil will hold, or how quickly a soil can be irrigated. For example, 1 inch of water applied to a sandy soil will penetrate 12 inches. It will move anywhere from 6 to 10 inches into a good loam soil, and in a clay soil it will percolate down only 4 to 5 inches." Clay soils are difficult to moisten if they dry out.

Adding organic soil amendments to the entire area helps both clay and sandy soil types, because amendments act like little sponges to hold moisture, allowing clay soils to accept water faster and sandy soils to retain it. If you are planting vegetables, flowering perennials, or annuals in separate beds away from woody plants, amend the soil carefully as you plant, providing them with extra organic materials, even when planting one at a time. This differs from the planting management for woody plants.

Since roots need the water, a good principle is to fill the entire root zone with water and then let the soil dry partially before rewatering. Probing the root zone with a trowel or shovel will help demonstrate how efficient the watering is. Whether you use an irrigation system or a soaker hose, or hand water with a garden hose, the objective is the same for all plants: Fill the root zone with water. The smaller the root

'Explorer' Roses Against Rock Wall

Winter Architecture

zone, the more quickly it will dry and the more often it will require water. Seedlings just sprouting have no reserve with which to deal with dry soil.

Trees and shrubs, even those that will eventually tolerate drought, require deep watering in their first two to three summers of growth. For most newly planted trees and shrubs, irrigating to the 12- to 18-inch root level will keep them healthy as they establish. If you have a drip irrigation system, you should include piping that will deliver water deeply.

Many landscapes do include irrigation systems. When well designed, the system preserves the beauty of the landscape, conserves water, and reduces the effort of garden maintenance. Stay aware of the weather and turn off your system during our occasional summer rainy spells. Water spewing from an irrigation system while rain is falling can be a humorous sight, but this too-frequent occurrence wastes resources. Override the automatic timing when rain is predicted. Work with a landscape professional to check, repair, and install efficient up-to-date irrigation systems.

Another effective way to get water to the 12-inch level is to apply water from a hose, allowing it to fill the planting saucer, sink in, and then fill and drain twice more. The objective is to get several gallons of water into the root zone at each watering. Check the time it takes for water to penetrate to root depth. Allow the soil to dry 2 to 3 inches down before rewatering.

The plant's location, as well as the length of time it has been installed, affects its water needs. Shrubs and trees located in southern or western exposures require more water because they experience stronger sunlight and heat. Plants won't get much water from rainfall if grown next to a home's foundation, under overhangs, or under eaves. You will need to watch them carefully for supplemental water needs.

Roots move into moist soils, and if plants have been recently set out (either balled and burlapped or from containers), the original soil in which the plants have been grown is sometimes different from the soil into which they are being planted. To ensure that roots move out into the garden soil, keep both the original rootball and the soil around it moist while plants become established.

What Are "Established Plants?"

Plant descriptions in the *Gardener's Guide* often refer to "established plants," those that have settled into their garden spots. The term generally means trees, shrubs, vines, ground covers and often herbaceous perennials, all plants that have a long life in the landscape. It doesn't refer to most vegetables, annuals, tender perennials, bulbs (especially summer-blooming bulbs), or other short-term plants.

"Establishment" means that the plant's roots have penetrated the surrounding soil, and that emerging root growth has replaced roots lost from transplanting. Established plants put on healthy new branch and foliage growth. If you were to compare an established plant with a newly installed one of the same variety, the established one will have longer and more prolific shoot growth. The process requires at least two to three years of attentive watering and plant observation. After establishment, drought-tolerant plants may get along with relatively little or no extra summer irrigation. But even though established, plants requiring supplementary water, such as azaleas, rhododendrons, and hydrangeas, will continue to need irrigation for the duration of their time in the landscape.

Be particularly aware of the need of native woody plants such as madrona (*Arbutus menziesii*) and western dogwood (*Cornus nutallii*) for summer dryness. Dampness at their crown or over their roots in summer can cause root rot. Don't site native woody plants in the middle of lawns where regular watering is necessary.

Once plants become established, many slow their growth as summer progresses, settling down to ripen seeds. Leaves often turn color during the dry months of July and August. If you look at the landscape as if you were choosing colors to paint it, you'll notice the fresh blue-green of early summer becomes khaki as tree leaves become more and more brown. Many of these "early autumn" symptoms are normal and predictable in our region.

Feed With Fertilizer—In Moderation

Think of fertilizer as one element in the entire cycle of plant life, while recognizing the complex photo-synthesis process that allows green plants to flourish. Fertilizer must partner with water, soil life and soil organisms, light, and healthy plant roots in order to function. Without any one of these elements, fertilizer can't serve the plant. It can't compensate for poor soil or for plants installed in the wrong exposure (a shade loving skimmia that turns yellow in sun won't be improved by adding nitrogen.) Roots suffering from rot can't be helped by fertilizer. Declining or diseased plants shouldn't be fertilized.

Fertilizer supplies plant nutrients that contribute to plant health and allow normal, moderate growth; these nutrients are generally mineral. The primary needs, after the carbon, hydrogen, and oxygen supplied by air and water, are for nitrogen (N), phosphorous (P), and potassium (K), with the most critical nutrient for all plants being nitrogen. Fertilizer packages list the N-P-K ratio and may include 10 other "trace" elements that plants also need. The numbers refer to the nutrients expressed as a percent of the total weight of the package: a 5-10-10 contains 5 percent N, 10 percent P, and 10 percent K. Look for fertilizers with moderate amounts of nitrogen, primarily those such as 4-2-2, 12-0-0, 5-1-1, or 10-6-4.

Plant nutrients come in many different forms, from the organic (derived from living or previously living sources) such as fallen leaves in a forest, to the synthetic (manufactured, generally from non-living sources). Both sources provide the same nutrients, but many gardeners choose organic fertilizers that recycle materials and can benefit soil Before planting, add organic materials if appropriate such as compost, leaves, or aged animal manures to soil. After planting, apply mulch. These amendments help retain water, and as they gradually break down, they host billions of soil microorganisms that convert fertilizers, both organic and synthetic, into forms that plant roots can absorb.

Sensible fertilizer application can protect water resources; stream surveys show that nutrients are washed into streams and rivers by tons yearly. Phosphorous, a necessary nutrient, pollutes fresh water by causing excessive algae growth and should never be overapplied. Learn where the fertilizer you apply will travel during rain or irrigation. Water must partner with all fertilizers to move the nutrients into plant roots. Don't apply granular fertilizers to dry soil; they'll be ineffective and may burn roots. Fertilize moderately rather than overdoing it, because new growth stimulated by nitrogen requires water for support. Keep fertilizer off any area of the garden that won't be irrigated during summer.

What does *not* need to be fertilized? Established landscapes with trees and shrubs growing well can get along with fertile mulch applications but do not need extra fertilizer. If the plants appear normal in color and they grow blossoms, leaves, and branches of sufficient length, fertilizer is not needed. Landscapes installed longer than 10 years should have trees and shrubs that will grow well without fertilizer. (Check with a nursery or a WSU or OSU Master Gardener if trees and shrubs are off-color, because many causes other than fertilizer deficiency can produce such symptoms.)

When should the garden be fertilized? If trees and shrubs are established and growing well, no supplementary fertilizer will be needed. Do not fertilize newly installed trees and shrubs; wait until their roots have grown one season. Then, fertilize as growth starts in the second year.

Apply fertilizer to the garden in late winter or earliest spring, just as plants move into active growth. For trees, shrubs, and most herbaceous perennials, fertilizing once a season using a moderate nitrogen formula such as 4-2-2, will generally be adequate unless a soil test reveals further needs. Spread the fertilizer over the root zone and water it in.

Other plants require more frequent fertilization, especially those that continue to put on fresh growth throughout the summer season, including annuals both in-ground and in containers. Container plants—annuals or perennials that are being kept in pots—should be fertilized twice a month until frost, to keep them growing well. These plants, such as petunias, marigolds, and impatiens, require a low-nitrogen fertilizer (such as a 3-2-2 or 4-2-2) to keep them blooming.

Roses need a regular monthly feeding up to the middle or end of July, but no later. Overfertilized roses are susceptible to winterkill, if temperatures fall abruptly to arctic levels, as seems to happen every few years. That's when vulnerable new foliage produced by late fertilization is killed.

For best plant health, don't overfertilize. Disease and insect difficulties can be worse on plants that have received too much fertilizer, especially those that have too much nitrogen applied. Tender, new overfertilized growth attracts more aphid attacks, aphids being sucking insects that enjoy the plant juices loaded with carbohydrates. Powdery mildew, a common late-summer shrub problem, will also be more serious on overfertilized plants, since it generally attacks the newest, most succulent foliage first.

Enjoy Your Garden!

With all these guidelines to follow, you may be wondering how to enjoy and have *fun* in your garden. The good news is that the more time you spend in the garden, the more quickly you'll become acquainted, informed, and equipped with the knowledge of your own corner of the Northwest.

As you spend time observing your own backyard conditions, watching how your favorite plants respond to climate conditions and seasonal changes, you'll gain a unique understanding of what it means to be a Northwest gardener. In this book, we provide you with an excellent introduction to some of the plants proven to grow here in Washington and Oregon. The resources offered in our reference section suggest great public gardens to visit, plant sources, and local experts who can continue to inspire you.

Enjoy the journey. Whether you're a beginner or an experienced gardener new to the Northwest, you'll have a splendid time discovering how rewarding it is to grow a garden here.

—*Debra Prinzing and Mary Robson*

Pine in Bed of Sea Drift (*Armeria maritima*)

How to Use the *Washington & Oregon Gardener's Guide*

Although we are coauthors, we have each written most chapters independently. Check the end of each chapter introduction to discover by our initials which of us is the author of a chapter. We sometimes collaborated on a chapter; in that case, you'll see our initials at the end of each plant profile. Each entry in this guide provides you with information about a plant's particular characteristics, its habits, and its basic requirements for growth, as well as our personal experience and knowledge of the plant. We have included the information you need to help you achieve success growing each plant. You will find pertinent information including mature height and spread, bloom period and seasonal colors (if any), sun and soil preferences, planting tips, water requirements, fertilizing needs, pruning and care, and pest information. Each section is clearly marked for easy reference.

Sun Preferences

For quick reference, we include symbols to represent the range of sunlight suitable for each plant. "Full Sun" means a site receiving six or more hours of direct sun daily. "Part Sun" means a site that receives direct sun about four to six hours a day or partial sun all day. "Part Shade" designates plants for sites receiving fewer than four hours per day or that have afternoon shade. "Shade" means a plant may need protection from direct sunlight or that it can grow in dappled or even deep shade all day. Some plants grow successfully in more than one range of sun; those are indicated by more than one sun symbol. Note: Afternoon sun is stronger than morning sun; a site in afternoon sun is more apt to stress certain plants.

Full Sun   **Part Sun**   **Part Shade**   **Shade**

Additional Benefits

Many plants offer benefits that further enhance their appeal. These symbols indicate some of the more notable benefits:

 Attracts Butterflies

 Attracts Hummingbirds

 Produces Edible Fruit

 Has Fragrance

 Produces Food for Birds and Wildlife

 Drought Resistant

 Suitable for Cut Flowers or Arrangements

 Long Bloom Period

 Native Plant

 Supports Bees

 Provides Shelter for Birds

 Good Fall Color

Companion Planting and Design

In this section, we offer landscape design ideas and suggestions for companion plantings and different ways to showcase your plants. This is where many people find the most enjoyment and creative expression from gardening.

We Recommend

This section describes those specific cultivars or varieties that we have found to be particularly noteworthy. Here we sometimes suggest other species that are also good choices. Give them a try. These are some of the best plants to grow in Washington and Oregon—and soon you'll find your own personal favorites.

USDA Cold Hardiness Zones

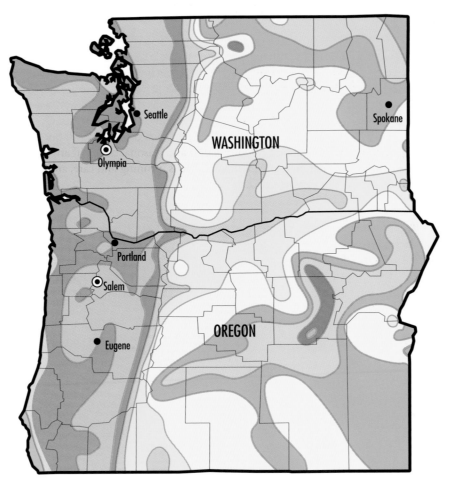

ZONE	Average Annual Min. Temperature (°F)		ZONE	Average Annual Min. Temperature (°F)		ZONE	Average Annual Min. Temperature (°F)
4A	-25 to -30		6A	-5 to -10		8A	15 to 10
4B	-20 to -25		6B	0 to -5		8B	20 to 15
5A	-15 to -20		7A	5 to 0		9A	25 to 20
5B	-10 to -15		7B	10 to 5		9B	30 to 25

USDA Cold Hardiness Zones

The United States Department of Agriculture (USDA) developed the cold-hardiness zone designations to indicate the minimum average temperatures for each region. Each variation of 10 degrees Fahrenheit represents a different zone, indicated by colored bands on a zone map. A zone assigned to a plant indicates the lowest temperature at which the plant can be expected to survive. We have followed the common practice established by the USDA and the American Horticultural Society of listing a plant's "zone range," such as *Zones 5 to 7.* You'll also see these ranges printed on nursery tags. When you know the zone range for each plant, you can understand how it may adapt to climate extremes on either end of the range. For example, in colder climates, the lower zone range tells you a plant's tolerance to low temperatures without protection. In hot climates, the upper zone may indicate a plant's resistance to the stress of drought or extreme heat.

It is important to choose plants suitable for your region of the Northwest. Consult this map to learn in which zone you live. Most of the plants in this book will perform well throughout the area. Though a plant may grow (and grow well) in zones other than its recommended cold-hardiness zone, it is best to select plants labeled for your zone or warmer. All hardiness zone ranges are intended to serve as approximate guides and are not meant to be definitive.

Annuals
for Washington & Oregon

Cosmos

As much as we rely on majestic trees, ornamental shrubs, and flowering perennials to give stature to the landscape, there's something quite wonderful about growing annuals. They provide that instant gratification of brilliant color or delicate blooms just when our gardens need a burst of joy.

An annual germinates from seed, matures, blooms, and sets new seeds in one growing season, before dying with the arrival of winter frost. In the Northwest, tender perennials are also treated as annuals (one-season plants), because they will not survive winter frosts. Because of their short lifespan, annuals may be dismissed as insignificant garden plants, but nothing could be further from the truth. Annuals are an affordable way to incorporate beauty into containers, window boxes, hanging baskets, and bedding areas, giving your garden continual blooms from spring through autumn.

Getting Started with Annuals

While starting seeds indoors is an early spring ritual for many gardeners, the seeds of flowering annuals can often be planted directly into the soil after the date of your area's last expected frost (generally April 1 or later west of the Cascades and May 1 or later east). Consult your county's extension office to check the local last-frost date. You'll enjoy the most success by planting seeds from one of the Northwest seed companies that specialize in cool-season varieties.

Florescent Lights

Follow the seed-planting directions printed on the packet. Annuals require fertile, well-drained soil, but because most annuals need only a small amount of healthy soil for their roots (about 8 inches), even the poorest soil conditions can be readied for seed. Amend sandy or clay soil by incorporating at least one-third organic compost throughout the top 12 inches of the planting bed. Or create an ideal home for annuals by building raised bedding areas with rocks, bricks, or boards. The raised beds can be filled with 8 to 12 inches of fresh topsoil, providing a receptive medium for your seeds.

Seed-Starter Tray in in 10×20 Flat Tray

If you have started seed indoors using a seed-starting soil mix, begin moving seedlings outdoors after the last frost. You will need to harden off transplants (bring them outside for gradually longer periods) for several days. Generally, this means placing flats of seedlings in a protected spot outdoors during the daytime and returning them inside at night.

Plant seed-grown transplants or cell-pack annual starts directly into prepared soil after the last frost. Follow the spacing suggestions noted in this chapter for

Sowing Seeds in a Row

specific annuals, or the guidelines on the plant tag. If you want to fill a window box, hanging basket, or flowerpot with an explosion of annuals, disregard the spacing guidelines and, as one of my garden designer friends would say, "cram 'em in." There's nothing more appealing than an abundantly filled summer container. As long as you keep the plants deadheaded, lightly fertilized, and watered, they'll look great.

Annual Care

This chapter uses several watering terms. In general, the surface of the soil can be allowed to dry out before you need to water your annuals. Infrequent, deep watering (to moisten the root area—approximately 8 inches deep) is preferred for most annuals. Take care not to bruise or damage plants with strong bursts of water from a wand or spray gun. Instead, water at the base of the plants. This technique keeps moisture away from foliage, which is one cause of powdery mildew. If your annuals are container-planted, summer's heat may require you to water daily (containers tend to dry out quickly, especially when situated in full sun). Irrigate plants during the early morning

Sunflower 'Flore Pleno'

hours or after sunset when it's cooler and there's less likelihood for evaporation.

Annuals have rapidly growing root systems that are more sensitive to water needs than established trees, shrubs, or perennials. Learn about your annuals and their water needs by watching their performance after you irrigate. If the plants look vigorous and healthy and if the foliage is plump and green, you've irrigated appropriately. If they flop over and lie in soggy soil, you've probably watered too much. If the foliage looks wilted, it's time to water! This is an imperfect science that requires a bit of experimentation.

Familiar Terms

Terms used throughout this chapter include:

Moist soil: Cool, slightly damp soil in the top 6 to 8 inches or through the root area.

Regular or moderate water: Weekly or twice weekly watering. The soil is not allowed to thoroughly dry out between waterings.

Dry periods: When a plant needs water during "excessive dry spells," this refers to a typical Northwest summer where there is no significant precipitation for two weeks or longer. When you irrigate, water deeply, to at least 12 inches or through the root area.

Planting and Maintenance

Help establish annuals by incorporating an organic fertilizer into the planting bed (work 8 cups of fertilizer, such as 2-4-2, into a 100-square-foot area or follow the recommendation on the package). Once seeds or transplants are established, you can sprinkle slow-release granular fertilizer throughout the bedding area; take note that slow-release fertilizers require temperatures of 60 degrees

Cutting Back

Fahrenheit or higher to activate. If annuals are combined with herbs or perennials in containers, feed with a diluted (one-half or one-quarter strength) liquid fertilizer once a week.

Specific grooming is discussed for each annual featured in this chapter. Trim away or pinch off spent blooms. If a plant begins to look leggy, try cutting it back by one-third to one-half to stimulate new growth. The plants selected for this book generally resist serious pests and diseases, but any annuals that grow in healthy conditions are less likely to succumb to pests and diseases.

Annuals are typically not ranked by zones, mainly because the USDA hardiness zones designate the average minimum temperatures that a plant can tolerate. By the time cold weather arrives, your annuals have died back anyway! Therefore, zones will not be noted in this chapter.

As you try growing the annuals featured here, experiment with the new hybrids that bring a bit of zest into the landscape. Or draw from your childhood memories of Grandmother's garden and grow nostalgic favorites.

—DP

Deadheading

Impatiens Border

Bacopa
Sutera cordata

What did we do before bacopa arrived in nursery green-houses? No other plant matches bacopa's fabulous trailing qualities, not to mention its nearly nonstop spring-to-autumn blooms. This cheery annual is a favorite addition to containers and windowboxes, where its small, rounded, toothed, green leaves softly cascade over the edges, densely hiding even the worst chip on the rim of a pot. It also does well as an informal ground cover paired with other bedding plants. The tiny five-petal flowers blanket the foliage with dots of color, adding fresh highlights against the green foliage. In addition to the white-flowering form, breeders have recently unveiled other lovely hybrids, including mauve, lilac, pink, and pale blue. Bacopa may survive a mild winter and bloom again in spring.

Bloom Period and Seasonal Color
Late spring to frost; white, pink, mauve, lilac, and pale-blue blooms

Mature Height × Spread
4 inches × 18 inches

When, Where, and How to Plant
Plant bacopa after the last frost, along the front of a windowbox or around the edge of a container, encouraging it to trail over the rim. Bacopa can grow in nearly every light condition as an annual, although it will bloom more profusely in a sunnier location. In containers, use fresh, organic potting soil. Bacopa prefers moist, well-drained soil. In the garden, ensure good drainage and air circulation to avoid susceptibility to whitefly. Consult page 23 for planting tips.

Growing Tips
Water bacopa regularly until established, and keep it moist throughout the growing season. Don't allow it to dry out in containers; the leaves and blooms will quickly die. Regular feeding with a liquid fertilizer (such as a half-strength dose every time you water) through the growing season will ensure ongoing blooms.

Care
Encourage bacopa to bloom profusely by giving it adequate moisture, food, and grooming. Given a place to spread, trail, or creep, this plant will reward you with fresh green foliage that's nearly covered by $1/4$-inch blooms. Pinch back older flowers and foliage tips to encourage new growth. If sections dry out or become matted, remove them by cutting away from the under side of the plant. This technique also improves air circulation. Bacopa generally resists pests and diseases.

Companion Planting and Design
Rather than mixing various colors of bacopa in a single windowbox or pot, choose one variety per container and allow it to make an impact with all-over cascading blooms. White forms of bacopa add a dazzling glow at the base of variegated plants such as coleus and fancy-leaf geraniums. The pastel forms are perfect for romantic-style containers, pairing well with old-fashioned annuals and perennials.

We Recommend
Sutera cordata 'Snowflake' is the gold standard that started the bacopa craze. The more vigorous *S. cordata* 'Giant Snowflake' features larger blooms in white. The foliage of *S. cordata* 'Olympic Gold' has yellow splashes; its blooms are white. *S. cordata* 'Lavender Showers' has pale blue-lavender flowers.

Begonia

Begonia species and cultivars

When, Where, and How to Plant

Plant begonias outdoors in late spring once the soil warms and nighttime temperatures exceed 50 degrees Fahrenheit. Begonias need warm, moist, well-drained soil to thrive, but roots will rot if planted in excessively soggy soil. Wax begonias perform best in partial shade, although dark-leafed varieties can handle full sun. See page 23 for planting tips.

Growing Tips

When given the right conditions, begonias are easy-care annuals. They require regular water, especially when grown in full sun. You can keep begonia's roots cool by adding a thin layer of fine mulch (1/2-inch) around the base. Feed with a balanced liquid fertilizer throughout the growing season (such as a half-strength dose every time you water).

Care

Typically low-maintenance annuals, begonias rarely require deadheading other than to tidy up their appearance. They're not prone to pests or diseases; their biggest enemy is overwatering. Pinch off any leaves with white mildew spots. You can dig and pot up begonias in late summer or early autumn, bringing them indoors during the cooler months; return them to the garden the following spring.

Companion Planting and Design

A visit to any municipal park will introduce you to a favorite landscaping use for begonias—mass plantings of pink, white, or red wax begonias are often seen in lavish displays. In the residential garden, try this technique on a smaller scale, and fill in an area beneath a Japanese maple or other small ornamental tree that will provide dappled light. Begonias are an excellent choice for covered porches (such as planter boxes and hanging baskets) because they bloom profusely even in shade. Because their foliage and flowers are fleshy in nature, begonias bruise easily if bumped or trampled. Plant away from high-traffic areas or where pets are likely to venture.

We Recommend

There are countless cultivars of wax begonia (*B. semperflorens*), with pink, red, white, or bicolored blooms. The foliage varies from green to bronze or maroon-tinged. Tuberous begonias (*B. × tuberhybrida*) come in nearly every flower color but blue and purple.

Begonias bring a sultry, exotic style to the garden. With intensely colored flowers and dark-green or maroon-tinged "waxy" leaves, this is a stunning choice for many areas of the annual garden. Begonias grow in nearly every light level, but are especially useful in shady spots where their yellow-centered blooms will shine. You can incorporate begonias into hanging baskets, windowboxes, and bedding areas. Often thought of as houseplants, begonias are perennials typically grown as warm-season annuals. Wax begonias, also called fibrous begonias because of their root structure, have shiny rounded foliage and will blanket the garden with colorful mounds of 1-inch blooms. Tuberous begonias (which grow from tubers) come in trailing or upright forms and will wow you with their enormous, almost roselike blossoms.

Bloom Period and Seasonal Color

Early summer to frost; white, pink, red, yellow, orange, and bicolored blooms, with green, bronze, or maroon foliage

Mature Height × Spread

6 to 24 inches × 6 to 10 inches

Calendula
Calendula officinalis

The sunny orange face of carefree calendula is a favorite addition to the cottage garden. Herbalists appreciate this old-fashioned marigold for its edible and cosmetic qualities, not to mention the delightful way its daisylike flowers punctuate a border. Use the edible petals as a salad garnish or in egg dishes. When added to homemade soaps and lotions, the essential oils of calendula have healing qualities. Easy to grow from seed, this is one of those reliable annuals that fills in empty pockets of soil in kitchen gardens. If you deadhead calendula throughout the summer, it will continue to bloom. Snip off spent seedheads, and shake them around your herb and vegetable beds. The following spring, you'll be enchanted with new calendula blooms in surprising places.

Other Common Names
Pot marigold, English marigold

Bloom Period and Seasonal Color
Early summer to frost; orange, yellow, and cream blooms

Mature Height × Spread
1 to 2 feet × 8 to 12 inches

When, Where, and How to Plant
Place young calendulas outside in spring after the risk of frost. You can also spread calendula seeds directly onto the soil in spring before the frost-free date; they tolerate cooler temperatures. Germination takes seven to fourteen days. This annual prefers full to partial sun and requires moist, well-drained soil, which means it will be happy where most of your vegetables and herbs are planted. Consult page 23 for planting tips

Growing Tips
Water regularly until established. Calendula requires regular watering during dry spells. To keep the roots cool and to retain moisture, add a thin layer of mulch around the base of each plant. If the soil in your garden has good fertility, calendula doesn't require additional feeding; otherwise, you may want to apply a liquid fertilizer, following the directions on page 17.

Care
Generally free of pests and diseases, calendula performs best in the garden when it is regularly deadheaded to prolong blooming. This annual likes cooler summers, making it ideal for some Northwest climates (it is half-hardy to about 25 degrees Fahrenheit). If temperatures climb, cut back languishing blooms and wait for calendula to rebloom in early autumn. This annual will self-sow in the landscape.

Companion Planting and Design
Calendula's gold and orange blooms brighten a "hot" border. For more dramatic contrast, plant these tangerine-colored flowers with blue and purple companions, such as purple-flowering salvias or blue-flowered borages. I visited one herb garden where the owner had planted clusters of calendula as a color accent at the end of each vegetable bed—wow!

We Recommend
Calendula officinalis (pot marigold) has a classic single-petaled orange flower. Numerous cultivars have been introduced by seed companies, including *C. officinalis* 'Pink Surprise' (orange blooms with a tinge of pink). Have fun with a mix like *C. officinalis* 'Pacific Beauty Mix' or 'Touch of Red Mix', and you'll enjoy a variety of warm blooms in the cutting garden.

Coleus
Solenostemon scutellarioides

When, Where, and How to Plant
Plant young nursery starts of coleus outdoors once the weather warms. Coleus is sensitive to frost, so wait until late April or early May to be safe. After planting, feed with a transplant fertilizer such as 3-10-3. Coleus grows best in moist, well-drained soil and prefers light levels from partial sun to shade. Select sun-tolerant cultivars if planting coleus in brighter areas of the garden. Coleus thrives in containers filled with organic potting soil. Consult page 23 for planting tips.

Growing Tips
Water regularly until established. Coleus requires regular watering during dry spells. Add a thin layer of mulch around the base of plants to keep the soil cool. For lush growth, feed with a diluted liquid fertilizer every few weeks.

Care
Generally free of pests and diseases, coleus performs best in the garden when regularly pinched back to keep it tidy. If it gets too tall or spindly, pinch back the flower spikes and the top few leaf pairs. This encourages a fuller, bushier plant. Coleus is easy to propagate from stem cuttings in late summer or early autumn before the frost arrives. Once the plant is rooted, transplant it into potting soil and bring small containers indoors to enjoy the fabulous foliage during winter. Keep the plants in a cool place with bright light. Repeat the process in spring to return your favorite coleus varieties to the garden.

Companion Planting and Design
Take advantage of the deeper tones of coleus and pair them with lime-colored hostas, licorice plants, and potato vines in containers or the shade border. Plant coleus at the base of taller annuals and perennials such as astilbes or nicotiana. Use several coleus plants alone in windowboxes for a kaleidoscope of color.

We Recommend
The newer *Solenostemon scutellarioides* 'Coleus Apricot' is a stunning peachy selection that looks great when paired with dark-plum heuchera. *S. scutellarioides* 'Black Magic' features velvety merlot leaves with a scalloped lime edge. *S. scutellarioides* 'Coleus Volcano' offers alternating splashes of ruby red and maroon.

The richly variegated foliage of coleus has been charming gardeners since the Victorian era, when potted displays filled 19th century conservatories and greenhouses. After a long hiatus as a houseplant, coleus has moved to the front of the border, offering its dramatic velvety tapestry to complement design styles from tropical to romantic. Its foliage palette ranges from lime and bright-yellow to deep-purple and maroon, each of which is unsurpassed for awesome color combinations. Marbled, streaked, splotched, and ruffled, coleus is grown for its foliage rather than the purple flowering spikes—which are typically pinched off to encourage lavish leaf displays. While coleus has traditionally been used in shady areas, several lighter toned cultivars can be grown in containers, baskets, or beds in partial sun.

Bloom Period and Seasonal Color
Spring to fall; multicolored foliage

Mature Height × Spread
1 to 2 feet × 8 to 12 inches

Cosmos

Cosmos bipinnatus

I first fell in love with carefree cosmos in the Seattle garden of a friend who grew up in the Midwest. She planted dozens of cosmos along a sunny fence, instantly bringing a country cottage feeling to a suburban backyard. A native of Mexico, the daisylike cosmos is an easy-to-grow choice for any landscape, preferring average to lean well-drained soil. With a round yellow center disk, the flower seems to float above fringy green foliage, especially when mass planted. Easy to grow from seed and widely available in nursery six-packs, you can find both tall and dwarf varieties in a range of shades from white to dark-magenta. Give your garden an informal look with cosmos—and enjoy cutting it for bouquets come mid- to late summer.

Bloom Period and Seasonal Color
Midsummer to frost; pink, white, and magenta blooms, with newer varieties in yellow and orange

Mature Height × Spread
2 to 5 feet × 18 inches

When, Where, and How to Plant
Young plants started from seed or in nursery packs transplant easily. Move them to the garden after the last frost, but don't plant on a hot day. In early summer, you can sow cosmos directly into warm soil (cover seeds with 1/4-inch soil). A location with full sun is ideal, and since cosmos have a tendency to "flop," try planting them against a fence or shed for added support. In well-drained soil, cosmos will thrive in most fertility conditions. Pinch back the first bud at transplant time to encourage fuller branching. Consult page 23 for planting tips.

Growing Tips
Water cosmos regularly until established; then irrigate only twice monthly. Follow the general feeding guidelines on page 17. If you overwater or overfertilize, you'll likely get a tall plant with fewer flowers.

Care
Cosmos is not prone to diseases or pests, although powdery mildew may appear on the foliage later in the growing season. To avoid this, be sure to space plants so there is good air circulation, thinning transplants to 12 inches apart when the plants are 2 to 3 inches tall. Water only at the base of the plant; wet foliage can also encourage mildew. You may need to stake or otherwise provide support for the taller varieties of cosmos. Cosmos may reseed itself.

Companion Planting and Design
Pair varying sizes and colors of cosmos with other daisylike perennials and annuals, using its cheery presence to soften the design. A mass of shorter cosmos looks charming at the base of a row of tall sunflowers, helping to hide the ragged foliage and bare stems. You can also toss cosmos seeds into any opening in the mixed border, allowing blooms to perk up a bare spot.

We Recommend
New varieties continue to delight Northwest gardeners, including 'Bright Lights', which grows 2 1/2 to 3 feet and offers a mix of yellow, orange, and reddish flowers. *Cosmos* 'Sea Shells' features pink and white flower petals that curl into long, narrow tubes on plants 4 to 5 feet tall.

Garden Verbena
Verbena × hybrida

When, Where, and How to Plant
Plant nursery starts of garden verbena in spring, after the last frost, or in early summer. This annual tolerates a wide range of soils, as long as drainage is adequate. Garden verbena performs best in full sun, although partial sun is also acceptable. Space garden verbena plants 6 to 12 inches apart in containers to allow flowering stems to mingle with companions. This annual can also be grown as a ground cover when situated across a rockery or on mounded soil. Water well. Consult page 23 for planting tips.

Growing Tips
Garden verbena requires moderate water, but is susceptible to root rot if allowed to sit in soggy soil. You can allow the soil to dry out between waterings. Garden verbena generally tolerates heat and drought. Follow the fertilization tips on page 17. If your plants are incorporated into a mixed container with other annuals and perennials, feed weekly with a diluted liquid fertilizer (one-quarter to one-half strength).

Care
Extend this long-blooming summer annual by cutting back garden verbena to half its size in midsummer—you'll soon enjoy early autumn blooms. If stems appear leggy, you can pinch them back to encourage bushy growth. Prevent mildew by watering moderately and allowing good air circulation between plants. Garden verbena is generally pest free.

Companion Planting and Design
Pair garden verbena with other bright annuals and perennials. Create a July 4 celebration container by pairing red and bluish purple garden verbena with white zonal geraniums and white lobelia. Garden verbena mixes well with all sizes of petunia, preferring many of the same conditions.

We Recommend
A vibrant rainbow of *Verbena × hybrida* has been introduced by breeders. 'Homestead Purple' resists mildew and has deep-purple blooms. 'Peaches and Cream' has pale-apricot and white blooms. The tender perennial Brazilian verbena (*V. bonariensis*), often grown as an annual, gets to 6 feet tall, with open, branching stems and tiny purple flowers.

Intense jewel-colored flowers and a lovely cascading habit are two reasons to admire the annual garden verbena. This is a relative of the towering Brazilian verbena, known throughout Northwest landscapes for its exuberant self-sowing. Garden verbena is a bit better behaved, providing a much-needed punch of brilliance in hot locations. The flat flower heads are 2 to 3 inches across, cascading from multibranched trailing stems. The toothed foliage is typically green or gray-green. Use the purple, hot-pink, red, and white-centered flowers to soften the edges of windowboxes or terracotta planters. Softer hues of peach and white are ideal for Victorian-inspired hanging baskets. You can also plant garden verbena at the top of a rockery, where it will appreciate the warm sun and good drainage.

Bloom Period and Seasonal Color
Early summer to frost; white, peach, hot pink, red, purple, and bicolored blooms

Mature Height × Spread
8 to 12 inches × 20 inches

Geranium

Pelargonium species

Terracotta pots filled with red-blooming geraniums, lining front porch steps, symbolize the sheer joy of summer. Many gardeners get their start with this easy-to-grow perennial treated as an annual. Often called zonal geraniums, *to distinguish them from true hardy geraniums, these plants have green, bicolored, variegated or ivylike foliage above which grow clusters of single- or double-petaled flowers on sturdy stems. Geraniums require nominal grooming to maintain their white, pink, orange, red, and deep-maroon blooms that continue until the first frost. They range from the classic seed-grown single-flower forms, usually sold in flats for bedding, to unusual cultivars, propagated from cuttings by specialty nurseries. Wildly popular are the fancy-leaf forms, grown more for their multicolored and patterned foliage than for the floral display.*

Bloom Period and Seasonal Color
Early summer to frost; red, pink, orange, white, and maroon blooms

Mature Height × Spread
1 to 2 feet × 12 to 18 inches

When, Where, and How to Plant
Purchase geranium starts in late spring, and transplant them outdoors once the weather warms. Look for healthy plants with vibrant foliage, good bud formation, and strong stems. Geraniums prefer full or partial sun and well-drained, fertile soil. Set them in the garden, container, or windowbox at the same depth as in the nursery container. Pinch off the first flower of new plants to stimulate foliage growth. Water well, and feed with a dilute liquid fertilizer. Consult page 23 for planting tips.

Growing Tips
Overwatering and overfertilizing make geraniums susceptible to diseases and pests. If you water to saturate the root zone only when the soil is dry and feed with a diluted liquid fertilizer every fourteen days, your geraniums will thrive. Yellowing foliage may indicate overwatering. Add fertilizer when the soil is damp. A thin layer of mulch can help keep the soil cool.

Care
Good grooming is the secret to long-blooming, attractive geraniums. The flowers are displayed on slender, long stalks, which can be easily removed at the base when the bloom is spent. Pinch back leggy stems to encourage fuller growth. If a geranium appears leggy, move it to full sun. Pick off any dried or browning leaves as they appear. To remove occasional aphid infestation, spray with water.

Companion Planting and Design
Place terracotta pots filled with red geraniums around the edge of a patio or along the top of a fence to evoke picture-perfect images of European balconies. Geraniums are traditional choices for Victorian-inspired bedding schemes and mixed borders, where you can use their brilliant blooms to add a punch of color against lighter annuals. Make fancy-leaf and ivy geraniums the stars of your summer containers.

We Recommend
A geranium renaissance has inspired countless new varieties each year. 'Black Velvet Rose', an award-winning selection, features rosy-pink flower clusters and green-edged black foliage. 'Big Red Hybrid' is a large-flowering form of the classic red geranium. For foliage lovers, a favorite is 'Mrs. Quilter', with bronze, green, and gold variegated leaves.

Heliotrope
Heliotropium arborescens

When, Where, and How to Plant

Heliotrope can be grown from seed but must be started indoors two to three months before the last frost. The most fragrant and richly colored forms tend to come from cutting-grown nursery starts. Transplant from nursery pots to your garden beds or containers in early summer once the weather warms (nighttime temperatures above 50 degrees Fahrenheit). Heliotrope prefers full sun and thrives in rich, well-drained soil. Water well, and feed with a dilute liquid fertilizer. Consult page 23 for planting tips.

Growing Tips

Overwatering is a danger, so water the root zone only when the soil's surface is dry. Feed with a diluted (one-quarter to one-half strength) liquid fertilizer every fourteen days to encourage vigorous blooms and leaf growth. A thin layer of mulch can help keep the soil cool.

Care

If given appropriate light, soil, and water conditions, heliotrope requires little care. Pinch off spent blooms to encourage repeat flowering. This woody plant can eventually be trained to a standard. Trim the lower leaves along a central stem for a topiary form. Move this tender annual from the garden to a pot; cut it back, and it regrows while wintering on a sunny windowsill. Aphids can sometimes be a problem. For management, see page 249.

Companion Planting and Design

Design a planting scheme that plays off heliotrope's black-green foliage and dark-purple blooms by pairing clusters of this fragrant annual with lime-colored potato vine or the creamy white splashes of variegated licorice plant. Go for an explosion of fragrance, and plant heliotrope with other aromatic flowers, such as the flowering tobacco plant (*Nicotiana alata*). Use 1-gallon pots of heliotrope as color accents in the border, tucking the containers into bare spots.

We Recommend

Heliotropium 'Marine' grows to 18 inches, with large, deep-purple blooms, a pleasing scent, and fabulous textured foliage. For a shorter heliotrope, try 'Mini Marine' or 'Dwarf Marine' (8-12 inches). Both prove to be a good scale for window-box gardens.

Infuse your life with the perfume of heliotrope, a delightful old-fashioned annual. Tiny florets form clusters of violet to purple blooms, which look sumptuous against deeply veined dark-green foliage. In its native South American habitat, heliotrope is a woody shrub that grows to 10 feet tall. In northern climates like ours, it's treated as an annual, offering gardeners a knockout combination of dark blooms and unforgettable scents. Heliotrope combines well with other aromatic plants, which gives you a perfect excuse to plant them in bedding schemes or containers near the front porch or back door where you'll enjoy the fragrance all summer long. Pamper this jewel of an annual by giving it full sun; rich, well-drained soil; and moderate feedings—your nose will thank you!

Other Common Name
Cherry-pie

Bloom Period and Seasonal Color
Early summer to frost; deep-purple and lavender blooms

Mature Height × Spread
14 to 18 inches × 1 to 2 feet

Impatiens

Impatiens walleriana

Here's the quintessential bedding plant, the ideal annual for painting color into the darker corners of your garden or gracing a woodland setting with sweet blooms. Fresh-looking in lush mounds of white and bright colors, impatiens makes an impact when planted en masse. Add color blocks of impatiens beneath shade trees, or suspend them from a low branch in a hanging basket to enjoy at eye level. This popular annual has glossy foliage and constant blooms. While relied on for their great performance in the shade, newer varieties tolerate some sunlight. Plant breeders have developed varying heights, as well as impatiens with double or ruffled flower petals. The New Guinea types have bolder flowers and foliage, while the Elfin series offers dwarf forms.

Other Common Name
Busy Lizzie

Bloom Period and Seasonal Color
Early summer to frost; pink, coral, red, mauve, white, and bicolored blooms

Mature Height × Spread
6 to 18 inches × 6 to 24 inches

When, Where, and How to Plant
Transfer impatiens to garden beds or containers in early summer once the weather warms. Impatiens prefer average to rich, moist, well-drained soil. Most thrive in shade or filtered sunlight. For waves of flower color, space 4-inch nursery plants 6 to 10 inches apart. They soon grow together to cover the area. Water well, and and feed with a dilute liquid fertilizer. Consult page 23 for planting tips.

Growing Tips
While impatiens require moisture, be careful not to overwater them so that the soil is soggy. The more sun they receive, the more irrigation impatiens need—watch for wilting plants and you'll know it's time to water them. Feed with a diluted (one-quarter to one-half strength) liquid fertilizer every fourteen days to encourage vigorous blooms and leaf growth. A thin layer of mulch can help keep the soil cool.

Care
Generally free of pests and diseases, impatiens are reliably low-maintenance annuals. Pinch back young plants to encourage dense growth. Dig up plants to bring indoors as cold-season houseplants, or take late-summer stem cuttings of a favorite variety to root in water. Once they produce a cluster of roots, transplant the starts into a good potting soil. Overwintered plants need bright light but not direct sun, with reduced watering (allowing the soil to dry out between waterings) for the winter rest period.

Companion Planting and Design
Impatiens offer the garden such a burst of color that you need to think carefully about grouping their varying hues. Some gardeners enjoy the patchwork quilt effect, mixing and matching purples, apricots, oranges, and pinks. If you like a more subtle approach, partner one color of impatiens with white-blooming ones. Plant at least three of the same color impatiens together to establish an eye-catching block of color. Impatiens pair well with other shade lovers, such as ferns and hostas.

We Recommend
Impatiens walleriana Super Elfin series is reliably the best choice for bedding gardens. For containers, try New Guinea impatiens, with an upright, shrubbier habit and rich leaf variegation.

Licorice Plant
Helichrysum petiolare

When, Where, and How to Plant

Add licorice plant to your garden or containers in early summer once the weather warms. This heat-loving plant originates from South Africa, so don't be afraid to situate it in your sunniest location. To make the most of licorice plant's wonderful features, provide it a place to drape or trail, such as along the front of a windowbox or at the top of a rock wall. As long as there's good drainage, licorice plants can grow in most types of soil. Water well, and feed with a dilute liquid fertilizer. Consult page 23 for planting tips.

Growing Tips

Licorice plant requires moderate moisture and feeding. If you've planted it in a mixed pot of perennials and annuals, you can fertilize the container with a diluted (one-quarter to one-half strength) liquid fertilizer every fourteen days; otherwise, fertilizing is unnecessary.

Care

Since this is a woody plant, its trailing stems are stiffer than a vine, but they appear soft. Trim stems as necessary to retain the desired form. You can also trim back ragged-looking stems to rejuvenate a leggy plant. Though licorice plant is generally free of pests and diseases, watch for an occasional bout of powdery mildew (usually worsened by overwatering). Variegated forms may revert. Should this occur, trim out the stems with the solid leaf color.

Companion Planting and Design

Licorice plant has a woolly nature that encourages its stems to knit together with the foliage and branches of nearby plants. The results are as lovely as a hand-woven tapestry. Most varieties of licorice plant feature a light tone, making them ideal as an embroidered accent for plants with purple, burgundy, and bronze foliage. For a dramatic hot-season container, pair silver or lime licorice plants with purple fountain grasses, *Persicaria microcephala* 'Red Dragon', or wine-colored ornamental millet.

We Recommend

Helichrysum petiolare is a great choice that blends its silvery foliage with both bold and pastel companions. 'Limelight' offers chartreuse foliage. 'Variegatum' features creamy-white markings, while 'Splash' has a flashy yellow-green variegation.

Once I discovered the downy-leafed licorice plant, I knew my profuse containers would look wonderful with its trailing stems draped over the edges. While this semiwoody plant with a slight licorice aroma does not resist frost, it often survives mild Northwest winters. Grown primarily for its 1-inch velvety oval leaves on draping stems (the flowers are insignificant), licorice plant is a reliable addition to windowboxes, containers, and urns. It can also be trained as a ground cover. After years of edging pots with the classic silvery and lime varieties, I was ready for a change. Thankfully, the nursery trade has introduced interesting variegated forms. With two-toned green leaves or cream-and-green foliage, the newer varieties are personable companions for plants with bold flowers and foliage.

Bloom Period and Seasonal Color
Spring to frost; two-toned green or cream and green foliage; may survive mild winters

Mature Height × Spread
18 inches × 4 feet

Lobelia
Lobelia erinus

Blue, that most elusive flower color, is abundantly available if you grow lobelia. An indispensable choice for hanging baskets, containers, and borders, lobelia is a delicate, lacy plant whose tubular, lipped flowers range from white and pale-blue to sapphire and dark-purple—even bicolored and rosy selections. You can find varying forms that are compact or trailing, offering a lovely, informal charm to the summer garden. Bronze-foliage forms, with tiny, notched 1/2-inch leaves, add great contrast to the bluish three-lobed blooms. Use lobelia to define and soften the edges of a sunny walkway. Plant the trailing form to cascade over the edges of a windowbox or a traditional terracotta pot. Take note: you should use gloves when handling lobelia, as it can cause skin irritation.

Bloom Period and Seasonal Color
Spring to summer; blue, lilac, white, and
rosy-pink blooms

Mature Height × Spread
3 to 8 inches × 6 to 12 inches

When, Where, and How to Plant
Start lobelia from seed indoors before the last frost. Expect them to reach planting size in two months. Transplant outdoors when daytime temperatures warm to 50 degrees Fahrenheit. You can also plant nursery starts (lobelia is frequently sold in affordable six-packs) at this time, spacing them 4 to 6 inches apart in bedding areas. Lobelia performs best in partial sun, although it can be grown in brighter or shadier locations. It prefers a moist, fertile, well-drained soil, which is why it also performs well in hanging baskets, windowboxes, and containers. Water well, and feed with a dilute liquid fertilizer. Consult page 23 for planting tips.

Growing Tips
Keep this annual moist, especially when grown in full sun. Lobelia loses steam in hot weather, but it rebounds once temperatures cool in autumn. Feed lobelia with a diluted (one-quarter to one-half strength) liquid fertilizer every fourteen days to promote profuse blooms.

Care
Lobelia flowers profusely in cooler environments. To promote flowering, shear back the plant approximately 1 inch after first bloom. Generally free of disease, lobelia occasionally attracts slugs (which is one reason to elevate it above ground level in a container). For treatment, see page 248. Lobelia may self-sow, but it is not aggressive.

Companion Planting and Design
Lobelia makes an excellent filler plant. Use tufted forms to fill in spaces between other bedding annuals where the green or bronzy foliage and masses of tiny flowers will help unify the design. Lobelia is a classic edging plant for the summer garden. The trailing forms of lobelia are ideal for any container design. Not only will the cascading stems gracefully enhance your windowbox or urn, they also help hide the leggy stems of taller companion plants.

We Recommend
Lobelia erinus 'Sapphire', a trailing form, offers tiny true-blue flowers with a white eye. Other trailing lobelias are part of the Cascade series—with flowers ranging from light to dark. Compact 'Crystal Palace' features deep-blue flowers with bronzy-green foliage.

Love-in-a-Mist

Nigella damascena

When, Where, and How to Plant

Love-in-a-mist is best sown directly into the garden once daytime temperatures warm to 50 degrees Fahrenheit. Sow in a full or partial sun location into well-prepared soil that has good drainage. Choose mixed flower colors or buy a single hue—both options will delight you. After sowing, cover with 1/4 inch of soil and water lightly. Seedlings will emerge in two to three weeks. After about eight weeks, you can thin seedlings 6 to 8 inches. Love-in-a-mist has a short bloom time, so you may want to plant successive sowings from early spring to early summer. Love-in-a-mist dislikes its roots to be disturbed, so do not aggressively separate roots when transplanting.

Growing Tips

Water during extended dry periods. In average garden soil, fertilizing is unnecessary.

Care

Love-in-a-mist is typically free of pests and diseases. It will likely self-sow but not aggressively. As unwanted seedlings appear, they are easily removed by hand or with a cultivator. You can let the flowers go to seed; they'll form attractive balloon pods streaked with maroon. To dry, harvest after the maroon stripes appear. Each pod contains many black seeds, which are easy to save or share.

Companion Planting and Design

Romantic gardens are ideal for this annual, which has an old-fashioned sensibility. Wildflower and cottage gardens welcome love-in-a-mist for its fragile, yet carefree form. Sow where the lacy foliage and enchanting blue flowers will add a touch of character, such as at the base of your mailbox post or filling an old galvanized tub. Since these are undemanding plants that won't compete much for water or fertilizer, you can also sow them among roses or in the perennial border.

We Recommend

When sold in seed packages, *Nigella damascena* is typically available in a mix. To obtain a specific color bloom, you may need to purchase starts or order seeds from a specialty mail-order seed source. There are taller selections; 'Oxford Blue' grows to 30 inches. The Persian Jewel series is an excellent cultivar with mixed-color blooms.

I first became enamored with love-in-a-mist in a bouquet of everlasting flowers. Even when dried, its delicate, lacy form catches the eye. Easy to grow, love-in-a-mist makes an even more delightful garden flower, contributing its many unusual qualities to the mixed border. Its multi-petaled lavender, white, pink, and pale-blue flowers represent "love," while the fernlike foliage surrounding the bloom is the "mist." This nostalgic annual thrives in a sunny cutting garden. Love-in-a-mist may be short-lived, but once it has gone to seed, the attractive oval pods remain in the garden until you cut the spent blooms and shake the seedheads around empty spaces to reseed. But even if you don't, love-in-a-mist will return, earning your affection by showing up in unexpected places next summer.

Bloom Period and Seasonal Color
Summer; pale-blue, rose, lavender, and white blooms

Mature Height × Spread
12 to 18 inches × 6 to 8 inches

Marigold
Tagetes species and cultivars

Beginning gardeners embrace the joyful charm of marigolds, which spread their sunny goodwill around the garden. More experienced gardeners continue to grow many varieties of marigolds for brilliant orange, yellow, and vermillion shades. The pompom and carnationlike blooms of marigolds are ideal for defining a sunny border or filling a redwood planter. Their strongly aromatic fragrance is synonymous with summer. Easy to grow from seed, marigolds are fun for children to grow and give as gifts on Mother's Day. Enhance a country garden with them, pairing their intense blooms with other warm-colored flowers like daylilies and black-eyed Susans. The light-yellow forms portray a calmer attitude, acting as a lovely partner to purple- and blue-flowered companions. French marigold cultivars have single and double varieties.

Bloom Period and Seasonal Color
Early summer to frost; yellow, orange, red-orange, and bicolored blooms

Mature Height × Spread
6 to 18 inches × 6 to 12 inches

When, Where, and How to Plant
Start marigolds indoors, six to eight weeks before the last frost. Lightly cover the seeds with soil—they germinate quickly. After the last frost, sow marigolds directly into the garden or transplant nursery starts into full or partial sun. Set them deep into the planting hole, stripping off the bottom leaves to place the plant *below* the soil level (this helps keep taller varieties from flopping). The soil should be moist and well drained, although marigolds can grow in most types of garden soil. Water well, and feed with a dilute liquid fertilizer.

Growing Tips
Give your marigolds a deep soaking during extended dry periods (water at the base of the plant to avoid knocking over tender stems with a strong spray). Feed with a fertilizer low in nitrogen to encourage bloom production rather than aggressive foliage growth. Fertilizers made especially for tomatoes are ideal for marigolds. Apply the fertilizer in liquid form a few times before the plant's maturity. Once blooming, marigolds should not require feeding.

Care
Protect seedlings from slugs and snails by removing lower foliage. Deadhead blooms as they fade. Marigolds are generally disease free. These tender plants may need some protection as early autumn frosts arrive (cover them overnight with landscaping cloth). Clip off any frost-damaged leaves.

Companion Planting and Design
Marigold's vibrant tones appear on the warm end of the color spectrum. Play to their strength, pairing golden marigold with other hot annuals, such as zinnia and cosmos. Use a primary-color scheme, incorporating marigolds with red geraniums and dark-blue lobelia. Or go for high contrast, and pair orange and yellow marigolds with purple salvia.

We Recommend
French marigold (*Tagetes patula*) grows 6 to 18 inches tall and is bushy with smaller single or double flowers. African marigold (*T. erecta*) brings height to the garden, with 1- to 3-foot plants bearing carnationlike blooms. Signet marigold (*T. tenuifolia*) grows to 8 inches, with lacy foliage and tiny, edible flowers.

Nasturtium
Tropaeolum majus

When, Where, and How to Plant

Start nasturtiums indoors in late winter in individual peat pots that can be transplanted into the garden (seedlings resent root disturbance). Or sow the brownish, round seeds outdoors in midspring, covering seeds with 1/4-inch soil. Transplant nursery starts after the last frost. Nasturtiums grow in most types of average to infertile soil, but they prefer moist, well-drained locations in full or partial sun (sandy soil is ideal). Water well. See page 23 for general planting tips.

Growing Tips

Nasturtiums prefer moderate water. Don't fertilize, or you'll have large leaves and wimpy flowers. Cooler summer temperatures are better for nasturtiums than high heat or humidity.

Care

As seedlings germinate, thin to 6 inches for mass effect. Nasturtiums are susceptible to slugs, aphids, and cabbageworms; groom away damaged foliage to keep the plants healthy. For other tips on coping with pests, see page 248. One deterrent is to grow nasturtiums in an elevated location such as a windowbox or hanging basket, which keeps their tasty flowers, petals, and stems away from slugs. Use only organically derived sprays if you plan on eating nasturtium flowers; wait several days after treating them before harvesting your flowers—and rinse them thoroughly.

Companion Planting and Design

Let a mix of nasturtiums spill over the edges of a rockery, brick wall, or sunny path. Try to emulate the famous paintings of Monet's garden in Giverny, where the pathways are nearly obscured by a brilliant carpet of scrambling nasturtium. Pair these cheerful annuals with other edibles in the raised garden beds, allowing their bright flowers and cartoonish leaves to embellish otherwise tidy vegetable rows.

We Recommend

Garden nasturtium (*Tropaeolum majus*) is sold in seed packs as a mix or single varieties. Enjoy one of the unusual hues, such as 'Dwarf Cherry Rose', a clumping form with magenta flowers, or 'Peach Melba', with apricot flowers. 'Alaska' is a dwarf single-flowering form with variegated foliage.

Here's the classic free spirit for kitchen and herb gardens, or a colorful trailing plant in the cutting garden. Nasturtiums are fast-growing, tender perennials grown as annuals. They produce masses of colorful flowers from seed within a few weeks. A traditional favorite for the vegetable patch, thanks to its flowers' edible qualities (won't those peppery petals enhance your next salad?), nasturtiums can be sown directly into the soil in spring or autumn. They grow in full sun, but will tolerate shadier areas. Self-sowers, nasturtium volunteers will emerge in most types of soil, although they do best in well-drained locations. Enjoy their circular leaves, green or splashed with creamy streaks. The five-petaled blooms come in warm shades of deep-orange, red, gold, and pale-yellow.

Bloom Period and Seasonal Color
Early summer to frost; yellow, orange, red, yellow, and bicolored blooms

Mature Height × Spread
1 foot × 1 to 1 1/2 feet (to 8 feet for trailing varieties)

Nicotiana

Nicotiana alata

The old-fashioned charm of nicotiana, or flowering tobacco, belongs in the summer garden, especially as a taller beauty near the back of a border. This lightly fragrant annual adds a feminine touch to borders and containers alike, with graceful stems and lovely blooms in dusky shades of mauve and pale-green. First cultivated for its scent, nicotiana is a favorite for nighttime gardens (early varieties opened their flowers at night, releasing appealing scents). Newer cultivars offer other must-have features, including a wide array of colors, heights, and bloom shapes. Leaves are typically sticky. This is an easy-to-grow, low-maintenance annual. Its flowers fall free after blooming, eliminating deadheading duties. The starlike blooms are displayed on tubular necks, making it easy for hummingbirds to feed on the nectar.

Other Common Name
Flowering tobacco

Bloom Period and Seasonal Color
Early summer to frost; white, crimson, pink, and green blooms

Mature Height × Spread
10 to 24 inches × 12 inches

When, Where, and How to Plant
Nicotiana tolerates cold and can be planted earlier than other tender annuals, just after the last frost. Most garden centers carry cell-packs of nicotiana before the flowers have opened, so choose your starts by looking for healthy rosettes of foliage (plant tags should indicate the bloom color). Plant in moderately rich, moist, well-drained garden soil. Space plants 8-12 inches apart. Nicotiana grows equally well in full or partial sun (the plants respond well to afternoon shade). Water well, and feed with a dilute liquid fertilizer. Consult page 23 for planting tips.

Growing Tips
Water the root zone regularly during hot, dry weather. Otherwise, weekly watering is acceptable. A thin layer of organic mulch will help keep the roots cool and retain moisture. Feeding is usually not required if the plants receive adequate moisture and sunlight.

Care
Generally free of pests and diseases, nicotiana may occasionally suffer from powdery mildew; water only at the base of plants to keep moisture off the foliage. Keep this plant away from tomatoes (which are related) to prevent possible disease sharing. While nicotiana flowers generally fall off on their own, you can tidy your plants by removing blooms as they begin to fade. Taller varieties may require light staking.

Companion Planting and Design
The tall elegance of nicotiana provides much-needed height for low-growing companions like petunia, lobelia, and impatiens. Use the white-flowering cultivars in a moon garden; the blooms practically glow in the dark, perfuming the air. Place nicotiana near a patio or doorway, where its fragrance can be enjoyed as you come and go in the garden.

We Recommend
Nicotiana alata 'Nicki' series has excellent flower production with profuse, colorful blooms that stay open all day. The aptly named cultivar *N. sanderae* 'Fragrant Cloud' climbs to nearly 3 feet and features a strong, sweet fragrance. The 3- to 4-foot *N. sylvestris* offers candelabralike clusters of fragrant, white flowers.

Petunia

Petunia × hybrida

When, Where, and How to Plant

Petunias are best grown from nursery starts; plant them in garden beds or containers after the last frost, although their cold-tolerant nature is good insurance against a sudden temperature drop. Pinch back young plants to encourage more compact growth. Petunias prefer full or partial sun. Give them well-drained soil (this annual suffers in heavy clay soil). Space petunias 6 to 12 inches apart for mass plantings. Water well, and feed with a dilute liquid fertilizer. See page 23 for planting tips.

Growing Tips

Water regularly during hot, dry weather. While petunias tolerate wet weather conditions, avoid fungal disease by providing good drainage and irrigating early in the day (allowing time for moisture to dry off the foliage). A thin layer of organic mulch helps to keep roots cool and to retain moisture. In poor to average soil, you can feed with a liquid fertilizer monthly.

Care

These pest- and disease-free, low-maintenance annuals look attractive even when neglected. But keep them tidy by removing spent blooms. You can shear the entire plant of its blooms in midsummer to encourage more vigorous blooming and to keep it from looking leggy. Fertilize after shearing.

Companion Planting and Design

Combine petunias with other trailing plants like lobelia and potato vine, encouraging all those lovely stems to weave together for an abundant display in a container or windowbox. Most forms of petunias serve as excellent "pillow" plants, filling in spaces at the base of taller annuals and perennials to hide ragged foliage or bare stems. Combine rosy and pale-pink petunias with hot-pink zonal geraniums for a country garden display.

We Recommend

Choose from among the many numerous categories of hybrid petunias—grandifloras, with flowers up to 4 inches (try the Cascade trailing series); multifloras, which bloom more profusely than grandifloras with flowers about half their size (try the Wave series); and millifloras, whose 1-inch miniature blooms blanket the entire plant.

Petunias have a way of filling any spot in which they're planted with an amiable exuberance all season long. Seeing a cascading explosion of funnel-shaped petunias makes me want to slow down and savor the moment in my garden. Froths of petunia flowers enhance your garden just where you need a splash of color and charm. This dependable and versatile long-blooming annual comes in many forms, with varieties hybridized for trailing and mounding habits. Choose single or double, smooth or ruffled, striped or veined—in nearly every color but bright-orange. Petunias are lightly fragrant and can be combined with countless other annuals or planted for a singular sensation. The Wave series is suitable for ground covers. 'Supertunias' are noteworthy for long-blooming performance and easy care.

Bloom Period and Seasonal Color

Early summer to frost; pink, red, purple, blue, rose, and yellow blooms; may be veined or striped

Mature Height × Spread

8 to 12 inches × 12 to 18 inches

Snapdragon
Antirrhinum majus

Children young and old delight in this storybook annual; snapdragon features a profusion of small vivid blooms, each of which resembles a dragon's head. Pinch the sides of its flowers to see the "snapping" of the dragon's not-so-ferocious mouth. When grown along a picket fence or in a mixed cottage border, snapdragon's long-blooming, colorful spires add a casual style to the landscape. Cherished by the Victorians, this sun-loving annual has a many-hued palette and varying heights. It's a timeless addition to the cutting garden, borders, and containers. Plant the compact forms along the front of a border, using them as edging. Pair the taller ones—some of which reach heights of nearly 4 feet—with sunflowers and cosmos for a flower-packed wall of blooms.

Bloom Period and Seasonal Color
Early summer to frost; pink, yellow, peach, purple, plum, and multicolored blooms

Mature Height × Spread
6 to 36 inches × 8 to 15 inches

When, Where, and How to Plant
Choose from among the numerous rust-resistant varieties of seeds or young plants. Start snapdragon seeds indoors six to eight weeks before planting out; the seeds may also be directly sown into the garden once nighttime temperatures reach 50 degrees Fahrenheit. Light is required for germination, so don't cover the seeds. Transplant seedlings or nursery cell-packs into rich, well-drained soil (avoid heavy clay sites) in full to partial sun. This is one annual that can tolerate your garden's hottest locations. Water well, and feed with a dilute liquid fertilizer. Thin seedlings to 6 to 12 inches.

Growing Tips
Snapdragons are happiest in consistently moist soil. A light layer of mulch helps retain moisture at the root level. Water at the base of the plants to ensure you don't knock over taller blooms. To stimulate blooms, feed snapdragons with a balanced fertilizer as they reach peak bloom. You can hold off feeding them again until after the plants have finished blooming.

Care
To encourage a second flush of blooms, cut back after the first bloom and feed them again. Rust, a brownish fungus, is a menace to snapdragons. Avoid this problem by selecting rust-free varieties and providing adequate space between plants for good air circulation. Taller forms may require light staking. Cut back spent blooms to encourage new flower production. Snapdragons may self-sow in your garden.

Companion Planting and Design
Taller snapdragons are good companions for other lofty annuals, such as nicotiana. For drama, pair a deep-purple snapdragon with the pale-green nicotiana. Plant multicolored snapdragon seed mixes to create a vibrant backdrop for other bedding plants like lobelia or impatiens. Shorter forms pair cheerfully with petunia and cosmos.

We Recommend
Antirrhinum majus cultivars vary widely, from dwarf types like 'Tahiti', 'Bells', and 'Chimes' (to 12 inches) to mid-range forms, including 'Liberty' and 'Sonnet' (12 to 24 inches). Taller types include 'Rocket', which can grow 3 to 4 feet tall.

Sunflower
Helianthus species

When, Where, and How to Plant
Start sunflowers after the danger of frost has passed, planting seeds $1/4$ inch deep. Seeds can also be started indoors in peat pots, three to four weeks before setting out. Sunflower seeds germinate quickly, often producing their first sets of leaves in a week's time. This classic, easy-to-grow annual thrives in full sun and most soil types. Carefully thin young seedlings to about 1 foot apart in all directions. Water seedlings well to establish. See page 23 for planting tips.

Growing Tips
Sunflowers generally tolerate drought, although they appreciate deep watering during dry spells. Keep the soil weed free and moderately moist while plants are young. This is an annual that flowers brilliantly with little or no fertilization.

Care
These easy-care annuals are generally free of pests and diseases. But critters in the garden do like to feed on them. Squirrels have been observed jumping from the top of a fence and grabbing onto the seedhead for a late-summer snack. There's little you can do but appreciate the many birds that thrive on the nutritious seedheads. Stake taller varieties to keep them upright, particularly in windy spots or after a surprise summer rainfall. Cut sunflowers and bring them indoors—both to fill your vases and to stimulate more flower growth.

Companion Planting and Design
Sunflowers satisfy our desire for vertical interest in the garden. Dwarf forms, such as 'Incredible', are well suited for container plantings, with heights of 15 to 20 inches. Grow a variety of tall annuals, such as cosmos or snapdragons, in front of sunflowers to hide their fading foliage. A sunflower "fence," planted around the edges of a front yard, creates a cheerful entry garden.

We Recommend
Helianthus 'Autumn Beauty' is a classic mix of bright, warm-colored flowers in oranges and reds—great for your cutting garden. 'Mammoth' is known for reaching fairytale proportions of up to 10 feet tall, perfect for impressing youngsters. For pure drama, try 'Red Sun', a vibrant crimson flower with dark centers that grows to 6 feet.

The quintessential summer annual, sunflowers define the country garden's happy profile. While we can't always replicate the alluring look of a sunflower-filled field, we can use these giant annuals to add stature and character to the garden. Sunflowers turn their enormous faces to the light, adding a delightful charm to the vegetable patch, meadow, and cutting garden. The classic golden sunflower has a giant seed-filled center surrounded by a crown of petals. For variety, choose cultivars from short to tall, with multiple stems or single stalks. Blooms range from pure-yellow to deep-bronze. Young gardeners begin a love affair when they plant enormous sunflower seeds in the children's garden. Older gardeners value sunflowers for infusing height, bold blooms, and happy-go-lucky allure to the border.

Bloom Period and Seasonal Color
Late summer to frost; yellow, gold, bronze, creamy white, and chocolate blooms

Mature Height × Spread
2 to 12 feet × 1 to 2 feet

Sweet Pea
Lathyrus odoratus

Romance is summed up in a bouquet of fresh-cut sweet peas, one of the garden's most profusely fragrant flowers. A whiff of sweet peas recalls our best garden memories. Grow them for their lighthearted, romantic spirit as they scramble onto a latticework fence. You'll enjoy cutting bunches of their flowers to fill vases. Typically a vine that climbs with tendrils, sweet peas are also available in dwarf forms, producing delicate, pealike blooms in watercolor washes of pink, bluish purple, magenta, and cream. Train climbers onto bamboo stakes or open trellises, encouraging their random habit to bloom at will. If you add sweet peas to the vegetable garden, take caution not to mix them with edible pea vines. All parts of sweet pea are toxic.

Bloom Period and Seasonal Color
Summer to frost; pink, red, purple, lavender, blue, apricot, peach, white, and bicolored blooms

Mature Height × Spread
4 to 6 feet × 6 to 12 inches

When, Where, and How to Plant
A well-prepared site and proper seed handling pays off when growing this reputedly difficult plant. Begin with rich soil, well worked to at least 8 inches deep to allow oxygen into the medium. If you have clay soil, amend the site thoroughly with organic compost. Plant in early spring, choosing a site in full or partial sun. Soak the pelletlike seeds in water for twenty-four hours before planting; you can also nick them with a paring knife to enhance germination. Place seeds 1 to 2 inches deep into the soil to protect them from birds. Nursery starts are also available; site as above, following the planting tips on page 23. To extend the bloom season, sow a second crop of sweet peas a month after the first. They grow best in early summer, when temperatures are cooler.

Growing Tips
Don't let the root area dry out; water at the base of plants to keep moisture off leaves and flowers. Feed lightly during the growing season with weekly doses of diluted (one-quarter strength) liquid fertilizer.

Care
Protect seedlings from slugs until established (remove slugs by hand). Pinch back the first few leaf sets at the base to encourage branching. Provide support, such as a lattice, trellis, or garden twine tied to a fence. Sweet peas can succumb to root rot and mildew if overwatered or rooted in heavy soil. To prevent disease from spreading, rotate your sweet pea location each season.

Companion Planting and Design
Sweet peas create an ideal floral screen to blanket an unattractive fence or post. If the support doesn't offer something for the vines to twine around, use string or chicken wire. Plant color-friendly companions that play to the sweet pea's palette of pinks, purples, and maroons—both heliotrope and love-in-a-mist blend beautifully with these charming plants.

We Recommend
Heirloom gardeners have revived many old-fashioned varieties of *Lathyrus odoratus*. 'Cupani' is a strain of the first cultivated sweet pea, with beautiful bicolored deep-maroon and violet flowers.

Sweet Potato Vine

Ipomoea batatas

When, Where, and How to Plant

Sweet potato vine is best grown from nursery starts; plant them in containers, hanging baskets, or windowboxes after the last frost. Place several plants 6 inches apart to line the edge of a container. As with many annuals suitable for containers, it's fine to place them closer together. These ornamental vines perform well in conditions ranging from full sun to partial shade. Use fresh, well-drained potting soil. Water well, and and feed with a dilute liquid fertilizer. Some varieties of sweet potato vine can be used as a seasonal ground cover; follow the planting tips on page 23. In the garden, this plant prefers moist, well-drained soil.

Growing Tips

Water regularly during hot, dry weather. Irrigate when the foliage shows signs of wilting. If your sweet potato vines are part of a mixed container planting with other annuals and perennials, feed weekly with a dilute liquid fertilizer (one-quarter to one-half strength). Follow the general fertilizing tips on page 17.

Care

This low-maintenance addition to ornamental containers and beds is generally free of pests and diseases. Unlike its twining relative, moonflower, sweet potato vine needs no support, cascading nicely over the edge of a container. Pinch or cut back to control growth as needed.

Companion Planting and Design

Go for impact with this plant's colorful choices and bold leaf forms. The deep-burgundy and maroon varieties in a light-colored urn make a brilliant backdrop for maple or multilobed leaf shapes. Combine lime and purple vines in a single pot, allowing them to trail below taller ornamental grasses, gold- and green-streaked carex or plum-colored New Zealand flax. Pastel perennials look lovely when accented by a variegated pink-cream-and-green sweet potato vine.

We Recommend

Ipomoea batatas 'Blackie' features darkish purple, deeply lobed foliage. 'Margarita' offers large, chartreuse, heart-shaped leaves. Variegated forms of sweet potato vine include 'Tricolor' and 'Pink Frost'.

Sweet potato vine delivers two of the most fashionable new shades to the well-designed garden: deep-purple and bright-chartreuse. Thanks to this ornamental member of the sweet potato family, we grow sweet potato vines for their trailing stems of architectural foliage. The shapes and colors vary, but you can count on this cascading vine to enhance any summer container or windowbox, serving as a graphic counterpoint to the blooms towering above it. Sweet potato vine will extend its reach up to 7 feet, sharing either dark or bright foliage, as well as several variegated choices. If it gets too long, just trim it back. When it's time to pull up old annuals, don't be surprised to find sizeable sweet potato tubers in your soil.

Bloom Period and Seasonal Color
Summer to frost; burgundy, chartreuse, and variegated green-white-pink foliage

Mature Height × Spread
6 inches × 7 feet

Bulbs, Corms, Rhizomes, & Tubers *for Washington & Oregon*

Gardens in Washington and Oregon benefit nearly year-round from the colorful flowering of bulbs, corms, tubers, and rhizomes. The earliest snowdrop bulbs will open the season in midwinter, with color right through to the small, hardy cyclamen of late November. Adaptable, able to manage weather extremes, and often water-wise, these plants provide fascination and garden pleasure.

Their suitability for the Pacific Northwest shows in commercial enterprise: the Skagit Valley in western Washington grows more acreage in tulips than anywhere else in the nation, indeed more than almost anywhere outside Holland. Summer-blooming dahlias fill hundreds of acres, to be shipped all over the United States. Iris and lily breeding have famously occupied western Oregon and Washington for decades, with some of the most noted lilies of the 20th century hybridized here. The long, cool springs and mild summers of the western region suit these perfectly. Their tough hardiness makes the spring bulbs also useful for the coldest areas.

Two distinct planting times distinguish these. Fall-planted bulbs and corms (crocus, daffodils, tulips, hyacinths, lilies, and others) can cope with winter cold; they must be settled into the ground after summer and before hard freezes come. Mulched over after autumn planting, they emerge in early and midspring, long before most perennial flowers start growing. The second group, summer bloomers, are seldom able to cope with winter freezes; they are instead planted in late spring as the soils warm, about the time summer vegetables go in. These, often the most brilliant of the summer flowers, include gladioli, dahlias, cannas, and crocosmias. (Some of these may winter over in the milder coastal areas of Oregon and Washington, returning to bloom the following summer.)

Fringed Tulip

Identifying, Selecting, and Storing These Plants

Gardeners take a verbal shortcut by calling all these plants "bulbs." Some are true bulbs, like lilies, tulips, and daffodils (as well as onions!). Evolved from modified leaves, true bulbs have distinct fleshy layers. "Corms," including crocus, cyclamen, crocosmia, and gladiolus, are firm and solid, derived from stems. Tubers and rhizomes, both modified roots, may be dahlias, irises, or cannas. What they have in common is the ability to store nutrients for long periods.

When selecting, look for the most firm and solid. Especially with the bulbs, like daffodils and tulips, small "bargain" types often bloom poorly or fail to bloom at all. Buying large, well-developed bulbs, tubers, and corms pays off in garden excellence.

Proper storage helps these grow best. Even though, as a group, they're adapted to life out of soil and in storage, they should be planted the same season they're purchased. (All these plants decline if left in storage for months.) Do not store bulb-type plants in closed plastic bags.

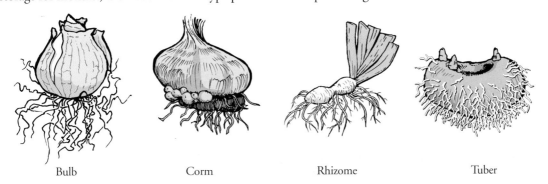

| Bulb | Corm | Rhizome | Tuber |

Hardy bulbs, for fall planting, require cool but not refrigerated storage. Remove them from the plastic bags they may be packaged in and store them in brown paper bags. A cool, dark spot with good air circulation, such as a garage or basement or even an airy cupboard, will keep them healthy until planting time. Spring-planted bulbs such as dahlias and gladioli need darkness above freezing temperatures (many of them start sending up shoots even before they're planted, so check them when in storage).

Soil Preparation and Planting Technique

Choose the spot, in sun or shade, according to the needs of the specific plant. Most spring bloomers need full or partial sun; most summer bloomers definitely enjoy sun (see plant descriptions for specifics on

Crocosmia and Dahlias

this). Well-drained organically amended soil is best for most bulbs; few of them can endure soggy winter soil or standing water. Work in composted material.

Most are easily handled and planted, making them excellent plants to use in projects with young gardeners. Fall bloomers such as crocuses, narcissuses, and tulips can be planted at three times their own height: If the crocus is 1 inch tall, set it 3 inches down.

Space them twice their depth apart; for instance, plant those crocuses 2 inches apart. Plant with the roots pointing down and the shoots facing up. Plant in multiples; all these spring bloomers look better in groups. They can be set in one at a time, making individual holes, but it's easier to dig a larger hole, remove the soil, set bulbs, and cover the entire planting.

All these spring bloomers contain their first-year flower embryo within. Many will perennialize (come up year after year) or naturalize (seed themselves through the area). Fertilizing when planting helps them remain healthy year after year. Place bulb fertilizer at the bottom of the planting hole or area, using the recommended amount on the package. Mix it in so that emerging roots don't touch the fertilizer.

After planting, water thoroughly, allowing moisture to soak down to bulb level. Autumn rains may be late, and soils are often dry when it's planting time for spring bloomers. Apply 2 inches of any mulch after watering.

Keep the planting watered until rains become regular, which may be as late as November. Spring rains supply sufficient water for hardy bulbs, which need moisture until leaves fade. In summer, the plants are dormant and require no water.

Summer bloomers, planted in warm late-spring soils, also require systematic watering and fertilizing. Fertilize when planting, and keep plants moist throughout the blooming season. They need deep soaking once a week until late summer.

Care After Bloom

Spring-blooming plants that will perennialize, such as snowdrops, crocuses, and daffodils, must have foliage completely ripened (browned) before it's removed. When bulb foliage is up about 1 inch, before blooming, spread bulb fertilizer over the plantings, at about 5 pounds per 100 square feet. After blooming, remove the flowers only, leaving the stems, but allow all leaves to die back naturally, often six to seven weeks following bloom. Don't braid or otherwise fold them because that retards ripening.

Summer-blooming foliage will stop growing with fall frosts. Lift the plants gently, allow the foliage to turn brown for a few days, and then store the tubers or corms dry, in sawdust or peat moss, in darkness where temperatures stay above freezing. Replant in spring.

Pest Problems

Generally carefree, these plants universally suffer from problems with garden slugs, which chew emerging new leaves and eat buds. See page 250 of Plant Health Care for details about slug control. Their other common pest is aphids, which is also covered in the Plant Health Care section.

Container Planting

Almost all bulbs, corms, and tubers thrive in containers. Use a well-drained potting mix, or add $1/4$ pumice by volume if further drainage is needed. Check the container for adequate drain holes. Plant at the same time as garden installation, allowing spring-blooming bulbs to experience the normal outdoor winter chill. (Protect pots from freezing by sinking them in the ground or surrounding them with a mulch, such as sawdust or leaves.)

Fill the pot $3/4$ with potting mix, watering it thoroughly. Then install the bulbs. Set the bulbs and corms closer together than you would in the ground, 1 to 2 inches apart. Cover with soil to within 1 inch of the container top, then water again. This method allows for plenty of root room beneath the plants as they grow.

Summer-blooming bulbs, which may grow much larger, require big containers, sufficient to plant about 8 inches down and 6 to 8 inches apart (for lilies, tall dahlias, and cannas).

Color, beautiful form, and fascination come with choosing bulb-type plants—the only dilemma they present is selection from their amazing variety.

— MR

Mixed Glads

Calla Lily

Zantedeschia aethiopica and cultivars

If you love flower arranging, you probably associate calla lilies with creamy elegance that has an Art Deco feel in the huge rolled petals (spathe) with protruding yellow center (spadix). Gardeners in mild areas may be surprised to find these thriving in summer gardens and surviving winter to multiply well year after year. Suited to container growth in colder areas, they need room to expand to their full size, since their deep-green (often white-spotted), broad leaves are nearly as decorative as the flowers. Native to wet areas in South Africa, they've been hybridized to offer a range of sunset colors, as well as the familiar creamy white, and they give a natural grace to the summer garden featuring a "tropical" theme.

Bloom Period and Seasonal Color
Summer; creamy-white, yellow, gold, apricot, and pink blooms

Flower Height × Width
2 to 6 feet × 1/2 to 2 feet

Zones
7 to 8

When, Where, and How to Plant
Calla lily rhizomes will be shipped from catalogs or are available in nurseries during spring. Soak the rhizomes for a few hours before planting (they're very dry when stored). These plants emerge as the soils warm, so plant in late April or May west of the Cascades; they are not hardy east of the Cascades. They'll bloom in full sun or partial shade (even under deciduous trees). Calla lilies require organically amended soil and should be set about 2 inches down and 18 inches apart. If planting in pots, set them as close as 5 inches apart but choose a pot with plenty of root room. See page 47 for more planting tips.

Growing Tips
Calla lilies produce abundant leaves and flowers, and need ample fertilization to keep up the show. Fertilize when planting and then monthly throughout summer. Regular water is vital; they die if they dry out. A soaker hose tucked around the plants will help keep them growing. These plants thrive on the edges of ponds, with their roots in water in situations resembling those of their native sites.

Care
Pests don't bother calla lilies, but drought will. Leaves die back with cold weather and should be clipped off when brown; follow with 2 to 3 inches of organic mulch over the rhizome for winter protection. In cold-winter areas, lift and store the plants after the first frost kills the leaves. Where weather allows, plantings left in the ground expand and multiply more readily than those brought inside for winter.

Companion Planting and Design
Edge a shady patio in company with ferns or planted behind perennials with similar needs, such as astilbe and hosta. They're at their best tucked along small water features and backing up *Iris spuria*, the water-loving Japanese iris, or plumy *Filipendula purpurea*.

We Recommend
The most common—and most elegant—calla lily, white *Zantedeschia aethiopica*, is hardy in zones 7 to 8. Colorful newer hybrids such as 'Flame' and 'Scarlet Pimpernel' (18 inches) suit container culture, blending well with summer flowers.

Crocosmia
Crocosmia species and hybrids

When, Where, and How to Plant
Plant crocosmia in spring after the soil warms, setting corms 3 to 5 inches deep and about 6 inches apart, depending on the ultimate size of the cultivar. Well-drained, organically amended soil in full or partial sun helps these corms develop good root systems. In hot-weather summer areas, they prefer partial shade. (Remove perennial weeds before setting corms.) Mulch over the corms after planting. Crocosmia isn't hardy as a perennial in the coldest sections east of the mountains.

Growing Tips
Moisture's needed; even though they look as if they'd bounce along without water, they require regular watering before and during bloom. After bloom, the plant's dormancy often coincides with the return of fall rains west of the Cascades. Fertilize when growth resumes in spring, using a low-nitrogen formula such as a 5-10-10 or 6-1-1.

Care
Generally pest free, crocosmia can mildew without good air circulation. In areas colder than zone 6, lift the corms out of the ground after the first frost. Shake the soil away, and tuck the roots into dry sand or perlite, keeping them dry and cool (40 degrees Fahrenheit). Replant in spring; crocosmia may often bloom sparsely because they don't have time to establish large corms. In some very cold areas, buy new corms each spring rather than storing them. In mild areas, divide every four years when bloom slows and corms become crowded. Some growers report 'Lucifer' stays hardy to zone 5.

Companion Planting and Design
Gardeners usually grow cultivars of *Crocosmia* × *crocosmiiflora*, red 'Lucifer', yellow 'Citronella', and soft-yellow 'Jenny Bloom'. They work in containers (allow enough room for growth), and develop into effective clumps for color with dahlias and summer daisies. Plant in groups to maximize the show.

We Recommend
For a quiet feeling, we like the soft yellows and pale oranges, and if you're able to find apricot 'Star of the East' or 'Solfatare', you'll have a plant that blends well with pastel dahlias.

Brilliance in late summer bursts forth from crocosmia, a South African native that perks along slowly, growing handsome sword-shaped leaves before opening stalks of flowers. Crocosmias excite the garden when earlier perennials have faded. Before opening, the buds have intriguing sculptural form, almost like large compressed feathers. Flower stalks often carry over thirty open blooms, making excellent cut flowers. These plants grow from corms, expanding well when happy in the garden to produce lots of tiny sets clinging to the larger ones. They can grow into large, permanent clumps in milder areas like zones 6 to 7, their presence reminiscent of New Zealand flax (Phormium) but with the bonus of flowers. They attract hummingbirds, particularly the best-known red cultivar, 'Lucifer', making an unforgettable garden show.

Other Common Name
Montbretia

Bloom Period and Seasonal Color
Mid- to late summer; yellow, red, and orange blooms

Flower Height × Width
1 to 3 feet × 1/2 to 1 foot

Zones
6 to 9

Crocus
Crocus species and hybrids

Sprigs of early color, crocuses adorn both containers and the open garden, bringing thoughts of spring to the garden as readily as early bird song. These adaptable corms multiply and spread generously once settled. First to light the garden is the small 'snow crocus' (Crocus chrysanthus and hybrids), often blooming several weeks before the larger familiar Dutch hybrids (Crocus vernus), with their crayon-box colors of yellow, blue, and purple. You'll also find autumn blooming crocus (blue Crocus specious) and Crocus sativus, the saffron crocus, growing well in the Northwest and allowing you to harvest culinary saffron in October. Loved for thousands of years, crocuses suit walkways and entries, where you'll enjoy their flashes of color. Plant by the dozens for best landscape effect.

Bloom Period and Seasonal Color
Late winter into early spring: yellow, white, purple, lavender, and striped blooms; fall-blooming species: blue and lavender blooms

Flower Height × Width
3 to 5 inches × 1 to 2 inches

Zones
3 to 8

When, Where, and How to Plant
Plant spring- and fall-blooming crocuses in autumn, before the ground freezes (November or even December in western Washington). Well-drained soil and full to partial sun is important; amend clay soils with organic compost, or plant in containers. (See page 47 of this chapter.) Settle smaller corms about 3 inches deep and an inch apart in groupings of at least a dozen to increase garden impact; larger "Dutch flowered" corms can go 2 to 3 inches apart. Autumn-bloomers, requiring the same sun and soil conditions, must be planted between August and September (they're available in early fall).

Growing Tips
Fertilize when planting with a balanced bulb fertilizer (see page 47 of this chapter). Avoid touching the fertilizer to the corm. Water well after planting; continue watering plantings until fall rains commence. Fertilize again in spring when corms emerge with 1 inch of foliage. If planting in pots, add pumice or perlite to ensure good soil drainage.

Care
Crocuses are free from most insect and disease problems; soggy soils induce root rot or corms that simply won't grow. Enemy #1 is the squirrel, which will excavate and munch corms or even yank out emerging foliage. Cover plantings or containers with 1/2-inch mesh hardware cloth to deter them. In badly squirrel-afflicted locations, make wire "cages" to completely surround the crocuses. Let the foliage turn completely brown in spring before removing it; this happens early, allowing crocuses to clear the way for later spring plantings. Protect pots from winter freezes by burying them in soil up to the rim.

Companion Planting and Design
Every garden has spots for crocuses—tuck them in front of small conifers and broadleaf evergreens; use in groups along pathways; or combine with early perennials such as vinca.

We Recommend
Crocus chrysanthus 'Blue Pearl' brings the earliest beauty. The larger *Crocus vernus* 'Remembrance' shines in deep purple. All herb gardens need *Crocus sativus* for an exciting (even if tiny) autumn harvest of saffron.

Daffodil
Narcissus species and hybrids

When, Where, and How to Plant
Plant in fall, before the soil freezes, as late as Thanksgiving in western Washington. Sun exposures range from full to partial shade. Bulbs require well-drained soil, amended with organic materials. Put the bulbs in cool, dry storage before planting, removing them from plastic and placing them in brown paper bags to prevent mold. (See page 47.) Planting depth varies with bulb size; install at three times the length of the bulb and 3 to 6 inches apart, wider for larger bulbs. Mulch with 2 to 3 inches of compost or leaf mold after planting.

Growing Tips
Fertilize at planting with a balanced bulb fertilizer (see page 47). Fertilize again in spring when bulbs emerge to about 1 inch. Water after planting, even in rainy weather, to settle the bulbs and encourage rooting. Most do not require moisture after they've gone dormant, making them great partners in "water-wise" gardening.

Care
Narcissus grows easily and resists most pests, including the four-footed ones. Bulbs may occasionally be ruined by narcissus bulb fly; if they fail to grow, discard them (you'll see the internal damage from the fly larvae). Slugs will do in the new stems and buds (see page 250 of Plant Health Care). Allow spent foliage to "ripen" after bloom; Dutch bulb experts recommend about seven weeks of growth for daffodils following bloom; then the foliage can be cut off when it's beginning to turn brown. Cool summers west of the Cascades sometimes leave daffodil foliage still green on July 4. Don't fold, knot, or otherwise mutilate the ripening foliage no matter how tidy you wish to be.

Companion Planting and Design
Try narcissus with perennial heuchera, for emerging leaf contrast; plant them among low-growing shrub nandina or native mahonia for color interest. Add them to perennial gardens, next to daylilies, whose emerging foliage will cover daffodil's dormancy.

We Recommend
Try *Narcissus* 'Quail', a brilliant yellow with long-lived blooms; 'Ice Follies' for creamy elegance; and 'Cheerfulness' for powerful late-season fragrance.

Graceful, varied, and sturdy, narcissus bulbs bring the first substantial blooming color to the Northwest spring garden. Often called daffodils or jonquils, they're all part of the narcissus family. Thanks to plant hybridizers, gardeners will find varied colors and forms from simple elegant single yellow flowers to deeply ruffled pink doubles, suiting all landscape schemes from country cottage to elaborately formal. Many narcissus, especially the later-bloomers, offer distinctive long-lasting fragrance. By choosing varieties carefully, you'll welcome blooms for more than two months of spring in the cool maritime Northwest. They naturalize well, returning year after year in widening clumps, safe from munching deer or chomping squirrels because the bulbs carry a natural toxin. They make good container specimens with perennials; daffodils launch the flower garden.

Other Common Names
Jonquil, narcissus

Bloom Period and Seasonal Color
February to April; yellow, orange, pink, rose, cream, and white blooms

Flower Height × Width
4 to 24 inches × $^1/_2$ to 3 inches

Zones
3 to 8

Dahlia

Dahlia species and cultivars

Dahlias start slowly in spring but work up to late summer and early fall fireworks, providing varied flower color when other ornamental plants slow down. Native to central Mexico, they proclaim their heritage by appreciating warm weather and moist growing conditions. Their range of size and color astonishes gardeners, from the tiny 12-inch types suitable for window boxes and patio containers to "giant decorative," whose flowers exceed 10 inches in diameter. Fascinating flower shapes include tight, formal balls and shaggy mopheads, making them great additions to the cutting garden. In spring, you'll find dahlias in nursery packs, already started, or as tuberous roots resembling small yams. Some feature bronzy or dark leaves that further set off the flower show, combining happily with perennials and grasses.

Bloom Period and Seasonal Color
Summer; red, orange, pink, rose, purple, cream, white, and bicolored blooms

Flower Height × Width
10 inches to 8 feet × 2 to 14 inches

Zones
7 to 10

When, Where, and How to Plant
Warm soil encourages sprouting; start dahlia tubers indoors with bottom heat in flats, or wait until the soil warms to plant outside in full sun. Plant in well-drained, amended garden soil with a pH of 6 to 6.5. Plant 5 to 8 inches deep depending on the tuber size; set stakes when planting to support the heavy growth of the tall ones (if you wait until growth emerges to put stakes in, it's easy to damage the buried tuber).

Growing Tips
These rambunctious plants require fertilizer to support their leaves and flowers; use a 10-10-10 at planting, and fertilize at least monthly during active growth. Never let them go completely dry, which reduces bud set and can kill the plant outright.

Care
To encourage bushier branching, pinch the shoots back when they have three sets of leaves. Generally easy to grow when they receive the sun, water, and nutrients they require, dahlias can suffer late in the season from powdery mildew, managed by removing all foliage after frost. Watch for slugs on emerging plants. Aphids like the foliage, and earwigs sometimes inhabit the tight curls of petals; neither pest is seriously damaging, though you will want to shake earwigs out of the flowers before arranging! When frost browns the top growth, remove that growth. Lift the tubers in cold climates, and store them in sand or vermiculite. Check tubers in midwinter, and water the storage medium very lightly if they have shriveled severely. In western Washington and Oregon, dahlias often overwinter in the ground, especially if deeply mulched.

Companion Planting and Design
Color variety makes dahlias useful companions for perennial garden flowers; reds and yellows comport well with brilliant crocosmia 'Lucifer'; pinks and whites complement gray-leaved foliage like artemisia and lavender.

We Recommend
The informal shapes on the "waterlily" dahlias look great in the garden, and they stay at about 4 feet; a peach-colored beauty is 'Jean Enersen'. Also try bright 'Mignon' dahlias in pots where their small cheerful flowers can shine up close.

Daylily
Hemerocallis species

When, Where, and How to Plant

Daylilies may be planted in early spring or fall, spring being more suitable in colder areas. They're sold either bare-root or in containers. Daylilies prefer sun (although they do well in partial sun) and well-drained soil amended with organic material. They bloom in shade, but the colors often appear faded, so this isn't ideal. Prepare the soil deeply, and settle the tuberous roots carefully; avoid twisting them, and keep the emerging foliage level (the crown) close to the soil surface. Work the soil down between the roots, and water them well to avoid pockets of air around the roots.

Growing Tips

Generally carefree, daylilies grow easily and do well with moderate amounts of summer water, but they do need moisture for the buds to set properly. Irrigate weekly before bloom and during bloom. Daylilies are often listed as water-wise plants, but they can't go without summer irrigation. In well-enriched soil, fertilizer isn't often needed, but a spring application can increase the plants' general vigor.

Care

Few pests bother daylilies, but thrips can affect both foliage and flowers. Deer eat the buds and leave the foliage alone (which does the gardener no good!). Slugs, the persistent enemy of flower gardens, eat holes in the leaves. Many daylilies stay evergreen in western Washington and Oregon; others need the dead foliage removed in fall. Trim evergreen types in early spring. Clumps can expand for three to four years before needing division but will cease blooming if they get too crowded. Divide after bloom in fall or in early spring.

Companion Planting and Design

Mass plantings of daylilies can cover troublesome moderate slopes or edge walkways and drive areas. They combine beautifully with other summer perennials, especially alliums, grasses, and rudbeckias, and feature mounds of soft chartreuse leaves.

We Recommend

Both 'Joan Senior', a 36-inch-tall creamy white, featuring petals with a heavy velvety texture, and 'Stella d'Oro', a reblooming yellow, blend well with other summer colors.

Summer favorites, daylilies get their popularity from handsome grasslike leaves and arching bloom stems. They've been hybridized steadily, and the brilliant color combinations can boggle the mind. Named because individual flowers stay open for only one day, the plant's effectiveness depends on having many flowers on each stalk—thirty to seventy over several weeks—making them invaluable color producers in the summer garden. They aren't true lilies, which are bulbs, but grow a mass of storage roots that help them multiply and fill space rapidly. Many cultivars rebloom after the early summer show, adding to their value as border edgers and companions for shrubs. They make good company for sunny areas where spring-blooming bulbs are naturalized, as the daylilies' emerging foliage disguises the fading bulb leaves.

Bloom Period and Seasonal Color

Summer; all rainbow colors except true-blue blooms, vivid combinations often with three colors

Flower Height × Width

1 to 6 feet × 2 to 6 inches

Zones

3 to 9

Frittilaria
Frittilaria species and hybrids

Fascinating shapes and varied colors make spring-blooming frittilarias a definite plus in the early garden. Small chequer lilies (F. meleagris) resemble old-fashioned purple and white gingham dresses, providing interest on meadow edges. The crown imperial (F. imperialis) soars up to 3 feet, with brilliant primary reds and yellows backing up plantings of tulips and daffodils. All frittilarias have hanging, bell-shaped flowers, with petals showing color outside to make the plants more vivid. Leaves on smaller frittilarias resemble those on grape hyacinth; on the bigger ones, they look like lily leaves. Frittilarias multiply well once settled in the garden, coming back spring after spring to add interest and color to perennial borders and bulb plantings, providing a "collector's garden" touch to your spring selection.

Bloom Period and Seasonal Color
Midspring; yellow, red, purple, gold, and white blooms

Flower Height × Width
5 to 36 inches × 2 to 8 inches

Zones
3 to 9

When, Where, and How to Plant
Select and plant frittilaria bulbs in fall (container plants are not available). Choose spots that receive sun and that will stay sunny through summer to ripen the foliage. (The smaller frittilarias can grow in light shade at the edge of deciduous trees.) Planting depth depends on bulb size; dig the hole three times as deep as the height of the bulb. (See page 47.) Crown imperial frittilarias are among the largest bulbs and require extremely well-drained soil to avoid rot. Some recommendations suggest "tipping" the bulb on its side, but this isn't necessary if the soil is draining well.

Growing Tips
Frittilarias adapt to the alkaline soils of eastern Washington and Oregon; they benefit from lime applications west of the Cascades. Water these plants well when planting, and then provide moisture until the foliage dies down.

Care
Allow the foliage to ripen completely. Frittalarias go completely dormant in summer, making them useful for water-wise gardens. If smaller types are planted in grass edges, allow the foliage to turn brown before mowing, just as you would do with crocuses planted in lawns. The chequer lily (*Frittilaria meleagris*) is the hardiest type in cold locations. Like snowdrops, smaller frittilarias may be divided when the foliage is still green in spring (but not the crown imperial).

Companion Planting and Design
Large crown imperial frittilarias with their primary reds and yellows soar above spring bulbs; choose similar tulip colors and bright-yellow daffodils for a bright scene. Chequer lilies resemble grape hyacinths in stature, and a small group of them provides good contrast to those midseason purples and blues, since they bloom at the same time.

We Recommend
The charm of smaller frittilarias adds to walkway edges and looks good near emerging perennial foliage. The dramatic deep purple-black *Frittilaria persica* offers a long-lived 2-foot stalk of dangling mysterious dark bells that set off midseason pink tulips such as 'Elizabeth Arden' or Triumph tulip 'Apricot Beauty'.

Gladiolus
Gladiolus species and cultivars

When, Where, and How to Plant

Gladiolus grows best in warm sunny spots, so pick a full or partly sunny location. Plant in spring once the soil begins to warm—about the time deciduous trees begin sprouting new foliage. You'll see a pointed end on the corm where the new shoot will emerge; plant this point up, about 5 inches apart and three times the depth of the corm. The soil should be amended with compost and well drained. Plant at two-week intervals May through June to ensure a continuous color show. (Each corm generally produces one blooming stalk.) Mulch lightly over the planting area using compost or other fine textured materials. Some glads, those with stalks up to 4 feet tall, will need staking. If your garden experiences wind frequently, plant the shorter gladiolus.

Growing Tips

Regular water helps quick and vigorous growth. Fertilize every two weeks with a liquid fertilizer low in nitrogen (such as a fish fertilizer).

Care

Glads occasionally have problems with thrips, which attack foliage and flowers, causing them to brown. You can remove affected plants, but thrips are difficult to manage with insecticides, and they seem to have no natural enemies. Lift and store corms before the first killing frost, allowing the foliage and roots to dry thoroughly (spread the plants out before storing firm bulbs in a dry cool spot). Glads overwinter in milder areas, but are often lifted and stored to clean off multiplying corms and old leaves. Label the corms when storing unless you like a multicolored planting next summer!

Companion Planting and Design

Smaller glads work well tucked in the middle of perennial borders, providing color behind low candytuft or heucheras, or with white Shasta daisies and herbs. Line them up in a cutting garden or on the edge of a vegetable garden for a summer-long supply of cut flowers.

We Recommend

Small glads, particularly those sold as 'nanus', grow well in containers and on the edge of my perennial garden. A beautiful one is the shell-pink 'Peach Blossom'.

Once considered a rather clunky florist flower, gladiolus provides reliable summer color in forms and heights much more graceful than you might expect. Like crocosmia, another summer flower with sword-shaped leaves, glads are corms, easy to plant and, because they are generally easy to propagate, quite affordable. Their paintbox-colored flowers have more impact than their leaves, so they aren't useful for foliage effect. They're all about bloom: Each stalk carries dozens of flowers. Some species (such as G. callianthus) bear only one flower. They can soar to 4 feet, but the easiest types to work into the garden scene stay at about 18 inches. Sometimes called baby or nanus glads, many of the shorter ones are hybrids of G. tristis. All glads love hot weather.

Bloom Period and Seasonal Color
Summer; red, yellow, orange, pink, purple, cream, green, and bicolored blooms

Flower Height × Width
1 to 5 feet × 2 to 6 inches

Zones
7 to 10

Grape Hyacinth
Muscari species

Vivid blue contrasts beautifully with daffodils and tulips in sunny spots. Grape hyacinths offer one of spring's best blues, blooming in sky- and deep-water blues unmatched until summer iris. They're named for their clustered individual oval flowers forming a densely clothed spike. Their small, 6-inch stature shows best when they're grouped by dozens—simple to do because they're affordable and multiply well. They naturalize happily, returning year after year. Dutch gardeners famously plant them in decorative "rivers" flowing through other spring plantings, unlikely in our gardens but showing mass color to best effect. Plant them where you'll enjoy their subtle fragrance, which blends with air and daffodils for a spring sensation. Grape hyacinths enhance container bulb plantings, performing beautifully when tucked into pots.

Bloom Period and Seasonal Color
Midspring; blue, purple, and white blooms

Flower Height × Width
4 to 8 inches × 1 to 2 inches

Zones
3 to 8

When, Where, and How to Plant
Plant grape hyacinths in fall with other spring-blooming bulbs. True bulbs, they appreciate well-drained soil in full sun or light shade under deciduous trees before full leaf. Plant 2 inches apart at a depth of three times the bulb size (about 4 inches down). Remove all perennial weed roots from these plantings because they'll be long-lived in the garden. Because grape hyacinths send up extra flower spikes as they grow, the period of bloom is longer. Some species, notably *Muscari neglectum*, grow rapidly and spread by seed; they become invasive if planted around better mannered plants such as trillium. Plant this type when it can ramble unimpeded, not in perennial borders. Older gardens may have the invasive type; dig them up and don't allow the flowers to go to seed (not easy if you have many!). *M. armeniacum* and *M. latifolium* don't spread unreasonably, so these are the species to order when planning the spring garden.

Growing Tips
Fertilize when planting. Water when planting, and then keep the plants watered if fall rains come late. Also see the chapter introduction for more bulb watering advice.

Care
Allow the foliage to die down completely in spring. This progresses quickly, and leaves can be removed without becoming unsightly. Some species send up early leaves in autumn, creating patches of odd-looking green spikes. Let them be; they're cold hardy and they will be followed by midspring flowers at the normal time. There are no pests or diseases to worry about.

Companion Planting and Design
M. armeniacum blends beautifully in front of smaller midspring tulips, such as 'Apricot Beauty', dark-purple 'Negrita', and white 'Hiberia'. They contrast with later daffodils and shine with pink-flowered 'Accent'.

We Recommend
Try *M. latifolium* for color interest. The flower spike, taller than most muscari, shades from black-purple to light-blue at the top, great for a visible spot such as a rock wall. 'Valeris Finnis' wears pale blue, light as a robin's egg, a rare color.

When, Where, and How to Plant

Plant irises in fall or spring in milder areas, and in spring in colder zones. Choose full sun in milder, cooler areas and partial shade where summers bake. They'll do well in neutral or acidic soil, not in soil that's considerably alkaline (though if you do have such soil, *Iris germanica* will thrive). Rhizomes should be planted 1 to 2 inches down, about 2 feet apart, though it will take them two or three seasons to fill in fully. Mulch over the site to keep weeds at bay.

Growing Tips

Regular water helps the Siberian and other irises grow well. Irises can tolerate dry spells after bloom ceases, but not while in bud and bloom. Many Siberian irises can stand occasional flooding or wetter soils than most irises. Fertilize when planting; it's seldom necessary to fertilize after that if the soil is well amended.

Care

In the first two years, irises don't appreciate disturbance, so do not cultivate heavily over the roots. Siberian iris grows free of leaf spot or other disease problems that affect German (bearded) iris. Older clumps develop "hollow" open centers surrounded by a circle of younger, more vigorous plants. Digging and dividing Siberian iris takes definite persistence because they resist being separated and require sturdy tools. Clip off flowering stems after bloom. (Some gardeners like the handsome seed-heads that form in autumn if some of the spent flowers are left on the plant.) Deer eat all members of the iris family.

Companion Planting and Design

Great color, including glorious blues, and persistent grassy clumps of leaves make irises great perennial border plants. They bloom with herbaceous peonies and roses, and add height behind hardy geraniums.

We Recommend

Siberian iris 'Flight of Butterflies', hybridized several decades ago by Seattle grower Jean Witt, remains an awesome standard. Also look for 'Caesar's Brother', a dark—almost cobalt—blue with ample flowers, and 'Butter and Sugar', soft-white and yellow. These are good flowers for cutting if gathered in the bud.

Perhaps no single plant family has as many different botanical types as the iris. The bulbs (such as the spring Iris reticulata and the early-summer Dutch iris) are planted in fall with other hardy bulbs like tulips. Drought-tolerant rhizomes of German iris are available in dozens of colors for summer bloom. Some irises are even comfortable living in bogs and on pond edges (I. spuria). One of the most useful, adaptable, and beautiful types is the Siberian iris, a rhizome that also forms roots, which gradually develop large grasslike clumps of easy-to-grow, reliable plants for perennial and shrub borders. The leaves add dimension to the border, and the flowers grow gracefully above the permanent leaf clumps. They're rock hardy and multiply well over the years.

Bloom Period and Seasonal Color

Early summer; white, yellow, blue, purple, and lavender blooms

Flower Height × Width

1 1/2 to 2 feet × 2 to 4 inches

Zones

2 to 9

Lily

Lilium species and cultivars

Many plants borrow the name lily, but the only true lilies grow from bulbs. Bright Asiatics bloom first, followed by tall fragrant Trumpets and Orientals. Over centuries, collectors have gathered many species from the wild. Using these, growers in western Washington and Oregon developed breeding programs that yield new colors and types of these hardy plants, including new interspecific hybrids like Orienpet or OTs (a combination of Orientals and Trumpets). Cool summers and mild winters west of the Cascades suit lily production admirably. Lilies enliven container gardens, tuck beautifully into perennial borders, make wonderful long-lasting cut flowers, and add summer interest to the water-wise shrub border. They multiply well once established. For color, graceful pendant flower form, fragrance, and sheer glamour, lilies adorn the garden all summer.

Bloom Period and Seasonal Color
Summer; white, peach, pink, red, orange, purple, yellow, and bicolored blooms

Flower Height × Width
1 1/2 to 6 feet × 4 to 12 inches

Zones
3 to 8

When, Where, and How to Plant
Lilies never go dormant, even when they're harvested. Buy high-quality bulbs, avoiding those with shoots longer than 2 inches inside their store wrappings. In cold areas, plant in fall when the bulbs arrive. In Western Washington and Oregon, plant in fall or spring. Choose a site in full sun to dappled shade. Well-drained soil's a must; if you have clay, amend with perlite and compost or build raised beds. The better the soil drainage and quality, the more successful the lily. Plant at three times the depth of the bulb, 8 to 12 inches apart. Water well after planting. Lilies thrive in containers; choose one that allows plenty of root room below and above the bulbs. Set the bulbs 4 inches apart in containers; cover them with 6 inches of soil.

Growing Tips
Fertilize when planting with a balanced bulb fertilizer; if the soil is amended with compost and the site is mulched, the bulbs may not require further fertilizing during growth. Many lilies produce "stem roots" above the bulb to bring in water and nutrient supplies. This makes soil preparation vital so that roots can penetrate. Water before bud set and after bloom.

Care
The foliage must turn completely brown before you remove lilies in fall. When cutting them for flower arrangements, don't take more than a third of any stem. Protect these plants from slugs, which can destroy lilies, as they do many tender bulbs. (See page 250 in Plant Health Care.) Protect containers from freezing by moving them into an unheated garage or sinking them into the ground.

Companion Planting and Design
Early-blooming Asiatic lilies complement summer daisies, cosmos, and bachelor's buttons. Tall fragrant Trumpet and Aurelian lilies, mid- and late-summer bloomers, shine with roses, lavender, and hardy geraniums. Experiment with some of the newer Orienpet or OT hybrids, which grow to 4 feet, are somewhat more cold hardy and more drought tolerant, and suit containers.

We Recommend
'Early Sorbet', with raspberry tones, and later, 'Black Beauty', maroon with white petal edges, add elegance to perennial borders.

Ornamental Onion

Allium species

When, Where, and How to Plant

Plant when installing other fall-planted hardy bulbs. They require sun and well-drained soil but can handle either slightly acidic or slightly alkaline areas; soggy ground causes bulb rot. (See page 48 for planting tips.) Ornamental onions are excellent in cold-weather spots. Mark the area where you plant them; they emerge at the same time as spring bulbs but bloom much later. Bulbs increase best where sun strikes the soil in summer.

Growing Tips

Supply water through the bloom period. They can manage drought afterward as the stalks die back in mid- to late summer. Fertilize with a bulb formula when planting in fall.

Care

Flowers can be dried by harvesting them at peak color and standing them upright in a cool spot. If you want to allow seeds to form, when cutting for dried flowers, allow the stalks to ripen first. Seeds sprout liberally and can form blooming-sized plants in three years if set into a nursery bed. They generally resist pests, but are subject to white rot if planted near affected edible onions. Animals avoid them!

Companion Planting and Design

Ornamental onions make wonderful additions to early perennial gardens, along with peonies, *Rosa rugosa,* and catmint (*Nepeta mussini*). They are naturals in herb gardens; the edible alliums, such as chives (*A. schoenoprasum*), provide both color and cooking greens, while the ornamentals add height and vividness. Many of the larger types develop yellowed leaves before blooming (this is normal) and need plantings in front of them to disguise their bare knees. Artemisia, stachys, or dusty miller contrast well, their soft-gray leaves hiding the feet of alliums.

We Recommend

Standouts for vivid garden presences include *A. christophii* and *A. schubertii* for vigorous globe forms and handsome seedheads resembling fireworks. Colorful *A. aflatunense* shines in purple splendor. Drumstick allium (*A. sphaerocephalon*) looks good in masses of twelve bulbs among grasses and annual cosmos; it produces excellent pale-green seedheads and masses of new bulbs for the following year.

Purple globes rising from straight stalks, ornamental onions bring unusual design distinction into the early-summer perennial garden. Members of the family that gives us culinary garlic, chives, and onions, bulbs carry a whiff of their relationship, but are seldom strong enough to be annoying. Easy to grow, they look best grouped in irregular numbers from three to dozens, depending on their stature. A. giganteum, at nearly 5 feet with 6-inch globes, can act as living sculpture, with some cultivars getting even larger. Ornamental onions make good cut flowers, with handsome seedheads adding visual interest even after the brilliant purples and pinks fade. Allium species return reliably, increasing their stands year after year as the bulbs multiply; these sturdy garden producers resist rodent and deer attacks.

Bloom Period and Seasonal Color
Early and midsummer; purple, pink, soft-blue, white, and yellow blooms

Flower Height × Width
4 inches to 5 feet × 1 to 8 inches

Zones
3 to 8

Snowdrop
Galanthus nivalis

Subtle and miniature, snowdrops hail the beginning of spring and indicate the presence of a caring gardener. Their flowers dangle like small lanterns from arched stems with three clear-white petals surrounding three smaller petals shaded green. They offer a crisp, white look to perennial garden edges, pathways, and rockeries where their flowers can be best admired. English gardens feature "snowdrop woods" in spring, and it's possible to achieve gradually expanding layers of snowdrops where trees are limbed up and early winter sunlight penetrates. If you're a fan of the children's book The Secret Garden by Frances Hodgson Burnett, you'll remember that the first emerging bulbs in the old neglected garden were snowdrops. They manage freezing temperatures, often emerging through light snow and persisting for decades.

Bloom Period and Seasonal Color
Late winter to early spring; crisp white and green blooms

Flower Height × Width
5 to 10 inches × 1 to 2 inches

Zones
3 to 8

When, Where, and How to Plant
Snowdrops thrive best in well-drained, humus-enriched soil (see page 48), placed where they receive some early spring sun but are sheltered from baking sun in midsummer once they go dormant. Plant as early in fall as bulbs can be received; they establish slowly from bulbs and will fail if allowed to dry out in storage. Set about 3 inches apart to allow for bulb multiplication. Water well when planting, and don't allow the newly planted area to go dry before fall rains arrive. The most successful way to plant is with plants "in the green" from gardens in spring where they've just finished bloom (unlike nearly all other spring bulbs, they like being moved before the leaves die back). European nurseries carry snowdrops for sale in spring, but this is rare in the United States. You'll have to speak to a gardening friend about sharing!

Growing Tips
Reliable moisture levels from fall and winter rains help the bulbs establish. If you like, sprinkle balanced bulb fertilizer over them in fall. Mulch with compost or leaf mold.

Care
Snowdrops live for years once in place, but require lifting and dividing about every three to four years when clumps become crowded and bloom lessens. Divide in spring immediately after bloom, setting the bulbs about 3 inches apart and planting even the tiniest bulb, because all will rapidly grow to blooming size. Squirrels and deer avoid them. They're free of pest problems.

Companion Planting and Design
Tucked next to perennial hellebores and ferns, snowdrops sing of spring and lighten shady spots under deciduous trees such as Japanese maple and flowering cherries long before leaves emerge. They're best planted in ample clumps.

We Recommend
Early spring gardens need these tiny perfect flowers, delightfully nicknamed "fair Maids of Spring." If you can find the giant snowdrop (*Galanthus elwesii*), you'll have a distinct turquoise tint to larger leaves (up to 10 inches tall) that emerge and bloom even earlier than the common snowdrop. Select nursery-propagated rather than wild-collected bulbs.

Tulip
Tulipa species and hybrids

When, Where, and How to Plant
Tulips need full-sun spots. Plant in fall before the ground freezes; tulips can be planted up until mid-December, though finishing by November gives best results. These plants grow best in well-drained soil, with a pH of 6 to 7. Set bulbs three times their own depth; space them to allow for the wide leaf expanse on the taller types, up to 5 inches apart. Protect the plantings from squirrels and deer, which will eliminate all traces of your tulips if they're able. (In deer country, plant in containers and move them to protected patios, or build a fence.) Use a bulb fertilizer at planting, water well, and mulch after planting.

Growing Tips
See pages 48 for fertilizing and watering tips.

Care
Tulips can be fussy. They're susceptible (like almost all bulbs) to slug attacks that can ruin the emerging or blooming plant, and they get difficult disease problems in wet soils. A fungal disease called tulip botrytis, or tulip fire, persists in soil; remove affected bulbs and rotate plantings, avoiding repeat plantings of tulips in the same spot year after year. Plant in clean soil in containers, if necessary. Larger tulips often provide one to two seasons of bloom and then disappear when the bulbs split. Choose the small species types for the longest garden life. Set those where you won't be watering in summer; they like dry times when dormant.

Companion Planting and Design
Perennial alyssum, annual forget-me-nots, and pansies set off tulips, as do bulbous scillas, grape hyacinths, and true hyacinths. Match the companion to the size of the tulip, choosing taller ground covers with the tall tulips.

We Recommend
For length of bloom and naturalizing, we like the species *Tulipa tarda*. A larger tulip, *T. fosteriana* (Emperor tulips), often lasts three to four years and features early blooms in bright yellow, red, and orange. For sheer spectacle, go with the tall Darwins, especially 'Ivory Floradale', and for cut flowers, select a parrot tulip, such as 'Salmon Parrot'.

Tulips, rightfully, hold pride of place as flower fascinators for generations of spring gardeners. From early miniature species blooms to late-season hybrids with terrific garden stature and presence, they're loved for their shining colors and fascinating shapes. These bulbs, many of them short-lived in the garden, offer design impact that few other hardy spring flowers possess. A group of tall Darwin hybrids can soar 30 inches, with vivid color, such as that of 'Elizabeth Arden', a sharp pink justifying one writer's description of tulips as "the lipstick of the garden." A handful of the creamy yellow species Tulipa tarda tucked into a rock wall brings intimate pleasure. Change through the seasons marks the best-planned gardens, and tulips punctuate your garden, bringing the scene to life.

Bloom Period and Seasonal Color
Late winter to mid-May; all colors but true-blue blooms

Flower Height × Width
4 to 30 inches × 1 to 5 inches

Zones
3 to 8

Conifers *for Washington & Oregon*

Conifers so dominate the native plant communities of Washington and Oregon that travelers can identify their location by the differences in the conifer population, from giant western red cedar in the west coast rain forests to Douglas fir and western larch throughout the Cascade Mountains, with ponderosa and lodgepole pines on the drier inland side. Ancient plants botanically, all conifers indeed do bear cones, though not all resemble the familiar pinecone. They spread by seeds in native populations but are also often grafted for nursery cultivars. Foliage can be the form of the familiar needled type as with pines, or as scales like on cedars and junipers, resembling flattened green feathers. Colors vary, with foliage shining in deep green-blue tones or yellows (or even in fall tones such as on cryptomeria and larch when they change color).

Selecting Conifers

This chapter suggests some of the most useful conifers for gardens in Washington and Oregon. Some, like Douglas fir, grow vigorously and rapidly, and will overwhelm a small landscape. Where space allows, the native conifers suit local terrain and style perfectly. But be sure to check the ultimate height and

width of a conifer before planting it. Fortunately, the fascination for these plants makes many of them available in smaller cultivars; check with a nursery about the availability of conifers that will complement and enhance smaller garden spaces. A smaller species, such as mountain hemlock (*Tsuga mertensiana*), grown separately as a specimen, will add dignity and elegance to any landscape.

Soil Preparation and Planting

Nearly all conifers require full sun to grow their best. Site the plant where the soil is well drained, a vital necessity for most conifers. Once established, they generally tolerate drought, but check the individual plant requirements for specifics.

See page 12 for tree and shrub planting details. If you are planting a large balled-and-burlapped tree, set the plant into the hole and

Mixed Conifer Collection

Weeping Larch 'Pendula'

then remove the wrappings, cutting back as much of the rope and wrappings as possible. If any can't be removed, such as the material deep in the hole, poke and cut through the burlap to allow root growth. Removal is necessary because many trees and shrubs are packed in non-biodegradable plastic-based wrappers that won't break down in the soil to allow roots to grow out.

Fertilizer is not necessary for the first growing season while the roots reestablish themselves. Keep the trees and shrubs watered when they feel dry at about the 5-inch level (dig a small soil section out with a trowel and check).

Pest and Problems

Despite being evergreens, conifers do lose older needles and scale leaves; don't be surprised by yellowing or browning. Pines often lose their three- or four-year-old needles, which turn brown in late summer and drop off through winter; this is quite normal. What would be of concern is the browning or yellowing of new shoots and growth. This seldom happens, but if it does, it indicates the possibility of disease or drought problems.

We haven't recommended the spruce (*Picea* species) because it suffers from severe and recurring insect problems in western sections, but it does better in cold inland areas, so if Colorado blue spruce (*Picea pungens* 'Glauca') is a favorite, you'll find it does better in eastern Washington or eastern Oregon.

Establishing a Framework

Conifers offer amazing variety—from the smallest ground cover to soaring trees, with heat and cold hardiness that gives them terrific usefulness. Unequalled for low-maintenance landscaping when properly chosen and planted, conifers help establish the year-round structure of the garden, coming into their best interest in winter when other plants lose leaves or die to the ground. Some grow in familiar conical form, but many will cascade down slopes, form perfect rounded balls, or shoot narrowly skyward in a pencil shape. Check out the following profiles to find one for your garden.

—MR

American Arborvitae

Thuja occidentalis species and cultivars

Gardeners choose Thuja occidentalis *cultivars for the tidy and sculptural shapes of the evergreen plants, since they naturally grow in upright cylindrical or low globular forms. Foliage, soft to touch, and pungently fragrant when crushed, stays flattened and featherlike, in rich green that sometimes turns slightly copper or bronzed in winter. Often overused or thoughtlessly sited in landscapes, arborvitae offer far more than common landscape beauty, because hybridizers have developed exciting shapes and colors The straight species is seldom planted, since cultivars offer far better choices. Plant as a small tree for a vertical specimen accent, in a group to give the suggestion of a forest, or as a screening hedge. Globe forms, often in bright yellow, like T. occidentalis 'Rheingold', add interest to foundation plantings.*

Other Common Names
Pyramidalis, eastern arborvitae, white cedar

Bloom Period and Seasonal Color
Evergreen; yellow, blue-green, or variegated foliage

Mature Height × Spread
2 to 10 feet × 2 to 25 feet

Zones
2 to 9

When, Where, and How to Plant
Install during fall or spring, either from containers or balled and burlapped. American arborvitae can be planted through winter in the milder areas of western Washington. Good drainage, as with most conifers, is essential. Root difficulties resulting from soggy soils can kill arborvitae. If clay soils cannot be amended, plant on a raised berm. They suit either acidic or slightly alkaline soils. Full sun is best, though in very cold regions partial shade can help prevent winter injury. If sited as foundation plants under roof overhangs, be sure to set soaker hoses or other means of watering for difficult-to-reach areas. See page 64 for planting tips.

Growing Tips
Drought tolerant once settled, arborvitae will take cold temperatures but are not suited to dry, hot exposed or windy spots. In very cold areas, protect this plant from the wind and keep it mulched with 2 to 3 inches of composted material. Fertilize once in spring with a moderate nitrogen formula such as 5-10-10 or 6-2-2.

Care
Foliage may brown in winter from freezing but will often outgrow this damage in spring. Snow and ice storms can bend or break branches and affect shape, especially on the upright vertical types. Some gardeners tie branches back in autumn to keep them from breaking, circling the plants with twine. As soon as possible after a storm, brush snow off with a broom. Prune in earliest spring before new growth emerges to best enjoy the varied colors on new foliage. Do not prune past the live growth on the branches; American arborvitae will not fill in or break growth from old wood. Root problems from wet soil are their worst difficulty. Deer menace them and must be fenced out!

Landscape Merit
Anchoring an island bed or forming an attractive hedge, this plant blends with either casual or formal landscapes.

We Recommend
Try 'Umbraculifera' or 'Globosa' as rounded accents. For hedging, 'Emerald' (also sold as 'Smaragd') forms a narrow pyramid, 30 inches wide and 8 feet high, growing to 15 feet when mature.

Douglas Fir
Pseudotsuga menziesii

When, Where, and How to Plant

Plant container-grown or balled-and-burlapped trees in spring or fall in full sun to partial shade. Douglas firs are also sold bare root from conservation districts to reforest native landscapes in spring; see page 256 for nursery contacts. Soak bare-root plants in water four to eight hours before planting. Tolerant of acidic or neutral soils, Douglas firs don't manage alkaline soils well. Well-drained soil and proper spacing, at least 20 feet apart for specimens, help their growth. Turn to page 64 for planting tips.

Growing Tips

Douglas fir requires moist soil for establishment and needs irrigation for three to four years before it's able to manage dry summers; also see page 64 for more details. Surround trees with soaker hoses to help with summer watering. They require little fertilization after planting, though a moderate nitrogen formula in an organic or slow-release form applied in spring for the first several years helps the tree grow. Once you cease summer watering after three or four years, stop fertilizing.

Care

Douglas firs respond to mulching—2 to 3 inches of composted bark is the perfect choice. Established plants may require no care at all unless branches receive storm damage. Douglas fir-Cooley spruce gall adelgid insect can damage new growth, causing needles to yellow, but trees often endure this without much setback. If trees are planted too close together, the lower branches will die off, requiring that the tree be limbed up to get rid of the dead branches. Where a house is surrounded by mature Douglas firs, gardeners often remove lower limbs for about 30 feet up the trunk to allow more light and garden space for landscaping.

Landscape Merit

Douglas fir is valuable as a specimen tree or forested untrimmed screening. They can be planted 6 feet apart as hedging, and will tolerate shearing, although shearing must be done faithfully before spring growth begins in order to maintain the hedge form.

We Recommend

In the coldest areas, choose the Rocky Mountain Douglas fir, *Pseudotsuga menziesii*. 'Fletcheri' grows more slowly and stays smaller.

Native to western North America, Douglas fir is renowned for both timber production and landscape contributions. Gardeners may more often coexist with Douglas firs on their landscape than plant them, because housing developments are often sited within areas of cleared Douglas fir forests. Soft, short green needles grow densely, and handsome medium-brown pendant cones cover mature trees. Immature cones enliven the scene by staying chartreuse most of the summer. The bark develops a rust-brown attractive woven pattern as trees mature. They're sometimes planted as "living Christmas trees," which is fine if the space allowed for them will accommodate a tree that gets to 40 feet tall in 30 years. Where they have sufficient space, mature Douglas firs develop a conical form with sweeping lower branches.

Bloom Period and Seasonal Color
Evergreen; new growth, young cones lime-green

Mature Height × Spread
50 to 200 feet × 20 to 40 feet

Zones
3 to 9

Fir

Abies species

Firs, including Spanish fir (Abies pinsapo) and noble fir (A. procera), offer year-round landscape elegance. A classic northwestern Christmas tree, native noble fir develops a clear conical outline that persists throughout its life. Its branches, arranged in tiers that form a pyramid, rise spaced on the trunk, emphasizing the tree's form. The small, close-set, bluish green needles are soft when touched; the needles are the most fragrant of any evergreen, emitting a citrusy aroma when crushed. Spanish fir, native to southern Spain, carries distinctly prominent needles, stiffer and more prickly than other firs, earning it the nickname "hedgehog fir." Like noble fir, its blue-green tints shine in contrast to flowering plants when used as an anchor for a perennial border.

Bloom Period and Seasonal Color
Evergreen; tints of blue and silver

Mature Height × Spread
60 feet × 30 feet

Zones
4 to 9

When, Where, and How to Plant
Spanish fir or noble fir may be planted in either spring or fall in milder areas, but in spring where winters get fierce. As with all woody plants, they're sold either balled and burlapped or in containers, seldom bare root. An acidic or neutral soil suits it, but must have excellent drainage. Give any fir plenty of space in full sun. Though the ultimate forest size is large, these firs will grow slowly in the landscape and stay manageable for decades. Choose a small plant to install, rather than a larger specimen, to allow the roots to develop successfully in garden soil.

Growing Tips
Noble fir prefers cool summer temperatures and may require extra water east of the Cascades. Water regularly in summer throughout the tree's life. Make sure the water goes deep, to the plant's roots. Form a basin around the tree with a raised earth edge to keep water in as you soak the plant. Alpine fir and Spanish fir endure hot, dry, exposed conditions better than noble fir but need careful watering at least twice a month until established.

Care
If the soil is well amended, very little fertilizer will be needed. Maintain composted material as a 2- to 3-inch mulch. Root rot can kill fir trees, affecting them where soils drain poorly. Slow growth or the dying of lower and crown branches may signify this. Firs are also susceptible to balsam woolly adelgid, white cottony masses obvious on bark and branches.

Landscape Merit
Noble fir sets off an island planting and can thrive on raised, bermed soil. Its bluish needle color shines year-round and is particularly stunning when contrasted with the fall reds and oranges of vine maples and tree sumac.

We Recommend
Firs make excellent landscape specimens. Their distinct shapely symmetry recommends them as accent plants. Try Spanish fir combined with rosemary, lavender, and rockrose (*Cistus*) for a water-wise planting with a Mediterranean style.

Mugo Pine
Pinus mugo and cultivars

When, Where, and How to Plant

Plant from containers in spring in the coldest areas or almost anytime in milder regions. Mulch over rootballs after planting. Mugo pines can adapt to either acidic or alkaline soils but need excellent drainage. Plant on a raised berm if the soil drains poorly. Full sun is necessary. Although winter hardy to zone 2, mugos do not grow well in shade even in the coldest climates. Refer to page 64 for planting advice.

Growing Tips

Fertilize once lightly in spring as growth starts; use a low-nitrogen fertilizer such as a 6-2-2. Summer irrigation is needed only for the first three or four dry summers.

Care

Mugo pines establish slowly, putting on little growth for the first two or three years. Most of the newer cultivars remain small, but can vary because many are seed grown. You'll see variations in size and color even in nursery plants with identical names. Pines will not resprout from old wood; when pruning, cut back to a live-needled growth point on a branch. Don't leave stubs. Or control their size by cutting emerging spring candles in half before they open. Such trimming reduces the plant's dimensions while maintaining a natural look. Older needles persist for up to five years without shedding. Very few problems bother pines. They suffer root rot in soggy soils, which can be avoided by correcting the drainage before planting. Deer won't munch them.

Landscape Merit

Effective as accent plants or in containers, the smallest types suit rockeries and foundation plantings. They're good textural companions for ornamental grasses and sun-loving perennials such as rudbeckia and potentilla, as well as brilliant-red fall maples.

We Recommend

'Mops' grows about 3 feet by 3 feet, a compact mound when young and spreading more with age (after 10 years or so). *Pinus mugo* var. *pumilo* makes a handsome landscape specimen with slightly shorter needles. 'Winter Gold' carries long green needles that turn deep gold in fall, remaining gold until spring growth.

Mugo pines serve marvelously as handsome shrubs in the toughest conditions. Though related to taller pines, they're stocky and small, many reaching only 5 feet by 5 feet at maturity—even after twenty years of growth. Often overlooked because of their familiarity and frequency in landscape use, these pines offer plenty of visual interest when sited properly. Expanding spring growth contrasts in soft-cream and tan to dark-green older needles. The new growth, called candles, resembles tapers on an old-fashioned Christmas tree. All pine needles grow bundled in a "sheath" where the needle expands from the branch. Mugos have two soft needles per bundle. Drought tolerant, mugo pines also work in seaside plantings because they can tolerate wind and salt spray in full sun.

Other Common Name
Swiss mountain pine

Bloom Period and Seasonal Color
Evergreen; possible blue or yellow tones

Mature Height × Spread
2 to 10 feet × 2 to 5 feet

Zones
2 to 7

Ponderosa Pine

Pinus ponderosa

The familiar three-needled tree, ponderosa pine grows extensively in eastern Washington and Oregon. Hikers in ponderosa pine forests throughout the Cascades respond happily to these sun lovers, whose scent in hot air delights. Long prickly needles carpet the ground under the tree, and their length, 6 to 10 inches, allows their use for pine needle baskets. Mature trees drop large woody cones appreciated for home decoration. While valued for lumber, ponderosa pines are common and successful landscape trees, quite long lived, with decades of garden value once established. They require both sun and space, settling comfortably in the driest areas. Though uncommon in natural stands west of the Cascades, they're well suited to water-wise gardens where an open-form conical tall pine fits the design.

Other Common Name
Western yellow pine, yellow pine

Bloom Period and Seasonal Color
Evergreen

Mature Height × Spread
50 to 100 feet × 30 to 40 feet

Zones
3 to 7

When, Where, and How to Plant
Plant container-grown or balled-and-burlapped ponderosa pines in spring. This drought-resistant tree won't compromise with wet soils or shady areas. Plant in full sun, choosing well-drained, light, porous sandy or gravelly soil. Acidic or neutral soil is fine. Set trees at least 20 feet apart. When planting for screening, stagger the trees in triangular patterns to allow maximum light to reach each tree. Unlike many other conifers that tolerate being used as hedges, ponderosa pines won't grow well if planted too close together. Page 64 provides more details on planting.

Growing Tips
Don't fertilize newly planted trees the first season; the roots need time to recover from being moved. Like all pines, ponderosa requires very little fertilizer once established. In the second season, fertilize with a nitrogen formula such as a 6-2-2 before growth starts in spring. Water deeply for the first two years, soaking roots at least twice a month during the driest part of summer (July to September). Keep 2 to 3 inches of mulch over the roots throughout the year.

Care
Pruning is not usually needed. Ponderosa pines have few pest problems.

Landscape Merit
The best known of all the native western pines, ponderosa pine is not an ordinary garden tree for small landscapes, but rather for revitalizing native areas or planting as a specimen tree or in well-spaced groups for screening, where space allows. Ponderosa pine reaches 60 feet in fifty years, growing rather slowly into a shapely straight-trunked tree. Homes often have sections of these trees remaining on acreage as part of the clearing process for building. They're common as accent trees in parks and municipal areas on both sides of the Cascades.

We Recommend
Pinus ponderosa can be kept in a container when small, where it makes a handsome miniature or even bonsai. Move it out into the landscape after three years, or root prune it to keep the plant small enough for a container. *P. ponderosa* var. *scopulorum* from the Rocky Mountains grows shorter needles and offers a more graceful landscape form.

Shore Pine

Pinus contorta

When, Where, and How to Plant

Shore pine grows on several different soil types—more than most pines—from bogs to poor, dry soils. Choose a sunny spot, and plant in spring from containers or balled and burlapped. Bare-root shore pine may be available bundled in spring from local conservation districts; see a list of nurseries on page 256. Bare-root planting is a great way to fill in a native area. Soak the roots in water for four to eight hours before planting—never leave bare roots exposed to the air. Lodgepole pines must have well-drained soil and full sun. High fertility isn't needed for either pine. Mulch, but keep the trunks clear of the mulch material. See page 64 for more planting tips.

Growing Tips

One great landscape virtue of all pines is how well they manage dry and droughty situations. Shore pine adds greater adaptability by handling wet soils. Don't fertilize the first season after planting; allow the roots to develop first. Fertilize lightly the second spring; after that, no fertilizer is needed. Both shore pines and lodgepole pines grow fairly fast as they establish.

Care

Some shore pines can be bothered by European pine shoot moth, which causes distorted shoots. Remove and destroy affected shoots (keep them out of compost). Pines retain their needles for at least three years; don't be surprised by the natural browning and dropping of the oldest needles in late summer, fall, and winter. Allow them to accumulate as a natural mulch.

Landscape Merit

Shore pine can be trained as a small, mounded landscape tree. It adapts to Oriental garden designs because it thrives with thinning and pruning to shape landscape specimens. Branches grow open, with more irregular character than mugo pines. Lodgepole pine contributes an upright, rigid form useful for screening.

We Recommend

Shore pine 'Frisian Gold' makes a low, mounded form (3 feet tall and 5 feet wide) with a year-round yellow tinge to the needles. Shore pine 'Spaan's Dwarf' develops into an attractive irregular plant growing very slowly to 3 feet tall and 4 feet wide.

Native to lowland parts of western North America, shore pine is named for its adaptation to seaside wind and salt spray. The species name, contorta, refers to the twisted appearance of its young shoots, but it could be said to describe the wind-wracked specimens growing along the coast. The very prickly needles grow in bundles of two. A close relative, tall lodgepole pine (Pinus contorta var. latifolia) grows at higher elevations, has yellowish green needles, and does better in colder climates. More often planted east of the Cascades, lodgepole pine stays straight-trunked through most of its life. Shore pine is particularly beautiful when pruned to emphasize its attractive branch formation. All pines, once old enough to develop mature cones, produce seeds relished by birds.

Other Common Name
Beach pine

Bloom Period and Seasonal Color
Evergreen

Mature Height × Spread
20 feet × 10 feet; lodgepole pine 50 feet × 30 feet

Zones
3 to 8

Shrub Juniper
Juniperus species and cultivars

Toughness defines the junipers, from ground huggers to large trees. Most valuable and attractive in landscapes are the smaller trees and shrubby cultivars, capable of taming hot, dry, exposed sites and enduring seaside winds. Available in an astonishing number of colors, forms, and growth habits, junipers most common in landscapes include Chinese juniper (J. chinensis), shore juniper (J. conferta), and creeping juniper (J. horizontalis). Foliage on junipers varies with the cultivar and the age of the plant; younger foliage often resembles a very small pine needle, and older foliage looks lacy and scalelike, as on western red cedar. Color ranges from deep blue through greens and even to yellow and gold or variegated. Sun lovers, junipers provide choices to meet many landscape design demands.

Bloom Period and Seasonal Color
Evergreen; blue, green, gold, and variegated foliage

Mature Height × Spread
1 to 10 feet × 2 to 15 feet, depending on species

Zones
2 to 9

When, Where, and How to Plant
Choose a full-sun site with good drainage. There's no compromising; junipers can succumb to root rot in soggy soils. Plant in spring or fall from container plants; it's unusual to find junipers balled and burlapped. Prepare a raised bed or berm at least 18 inches high if planting over clay or hardpan soil. The soil can be either acidic or neutral as long as it drains well. Choose a juniper whose mature size will suit your landscape need. They're annoyingly prickly to work on and don't respond well to the heavy pruning required to keep them small. Turn to page 64 for more planting advice.

Growing Tips
Once established, junipers need no summer water except in the hottest areas. Irrigation puddling can cause root rot; run soaker hoses for the first two to three years. Avoid overhead irrigation. Fertilize lightly with a slow-release nitrogen product 6-2-2 after the first season. Overfertilization and overwatering lead to disease.

Care
Prune carefully; deep chops into the interior wood leave ugly brown stubs and makes a sad landscape sight. Junipers won't regrow foliage from old wood. The tam juniper (*J. sabina* 'Tamariscifolia') suffers from insect problems; do not choose it for our region.

Landscape Merit
Overplanted Pfitzer juniper can grow to 6 feet tall and 12 feet wide. A better choice for a small spot is *J. squamata* 'Blue Star', which gets 2 feet tall and 3 feet wide. Mulch lightly, with 2-3 inches of compost, allowing air circulation under and around it. Try junipers as exclamation points: *J. scopulorum* 'Skyrocket' grows narrow and tall, 2 feet wide by 15 feet tall. Several narrow upright junipers can make a screen. Ground covering by *J. procumbens* 'Nana' results in a foot-tall plant. Beautiful accompaniments to herbs, they set off artemisia, rosemary, and lavender in hot dry spots.

We Recommend
J. scopulorum and its cultivars settle well into the toughest sites. A particularly beautiful shrub, 'Table Top Blue' grows to 5 feet tall and 6 feet wide as a background plant.

Western Hemlock

Tsuga heterophylla

When, Where, and How to Plant

Set out balled-and-burlapped or container-grown plants in spring or fall in most areas, but only in spring in cold-weather areas. Long lived and cold hardy, hemlocks don't tolerate hot dry winds; they need ample water. (Native trees grow more densely in high-rainfall areas.) Soils can be acidic or alkaline, but western hemlock requires moisture-retentive soil amended with compost and providing good drainage. See page 64 for more on soils and planting. Full sun, partial sun, or partial shade suits them, with extra summer irrigation required in sunny areas. Apply mulch 3 inches deep after planting.

Growing Tips

Don't allow these plants to desiccate during summer. Water to root depth every two weeks. Apply a slow-release fertilizer.

Care

Pruning lightly after growth opens can reduce the plant's size. Allow one central leader to form if the tree is being grown as a specimen. Hemlock woolly adelgids can attack, especially affecting hemlock stressed by being grown in hedge form. Needles drop prematurely, weakening the tree. Adelgids can kill the trees, so prune out and destroy heavily infested branches. Call an arborist for help with large trees; small trees and shrubby forms can be sprayed with a stream of water to remove adelgids, which are tucked under protective white woolly tufts. Western hemlock and mountain hemlock (*T. mertensiana*) resist infestations better than eastern hemlock cultivars. There are no diseases to note.

Landscape Merit

Western hemlock planted in groves about 15 feet apart will create an attractive, screening woodland. It's often planted in lines, 4 feet apart, and sheared to make an attractive textured hedge.

We Recommend

Two small cultivars of native western hemlock, 'Conica' and 'Iron Springs', grow well as shrubs. Western native mountain hemlock (*T. mertensiana*), frequently a specimen in a rockery, slowly reaches 20 feet. It demands less water but must have perfect drainage and full sun. A variegated eastern hemlock, *T. canadensis* 'Gentsch White', lights a shady area with frosted-white branch tips.

Graceful and common in landscapes west of the Cascades, western hemlock thrives in cool moist conditions. Its familiar tree form, with the top leader drooping into a recognizable downward curve, joins Douglas fir and western red cedar in native forests. Soft needles on small twiggy branches seem to clothe the tree in large ferns, giving it beautiful textural presence. Useful for single accent plants, screening, or hedges, western hemlock also bears small pendant brown cones that add winter interest and attract birds and native squirrels. T. heterophylla has few cultivars, but the related Canadian hemlock (T. canadensis) produces many, often dwarf, forms that suit rockeries and foundation plantings. With summer watering provided for best growth, hemlock makes a stunning garden shrub or tree.

Bloom Period and Seasonal Color
Evergreen; new growth light-green

Mature Height × Spread
60 feet × 30 feet

Zones
5 to 8

Western Larch
Larix occidentalis

Like the eastern larch (Larix laricina), *also called tama-rack, western larch adorns the garden year-round by changing its foliage with the seasons, as if it were a deciduous tree. Truly conifers, but needle-dropping, larches progress from brilliant soft-green needles in spring to dark-green in summer, and on to stunning yellow-gold in fall. The pegged buds of next spring's growth stud the branches, and cones often hang on through winter. Western larch tolerates the cold and endures winds; as a specimen tree, it suits any location throughout the region. Larch makes an eye-catching center for a shrub border where space allows. Narrower than most conifers, this tree seems especially open in winter. Plant it where you'll enjoy the delicacy and progress of its seasonal changes.*

Other Common Name
Tamarack

Bloom Period and Seasonal Color
Spring; green foliage; gold in fall

Mature Height × Spread
50 feet × 25 feet

Zones
3 to 8

When, Where, and How to Plant
Plant western larch in spring or fall in mild areas, but in areas where the soil freezes, plant only in spring. All larches tolerate acidic or alkaline soils but require moisture to grow well, doing poorly in exposed or hot locations. They accept planting in boggy spots. If planting these trees as a small grove, allow at least 25 feet between them. Plants you find in nurseries will more likely be European larch (*L. decidua* and its cultivars); conservation and native restoration agencies may have seed-propagated western larch. See page 256 for nursery contacts. All larches are easily grown from seed, and nursery stock may be either grafted, in the case of cultivars, or seed grown. More planting tips are on page 64.

Growing Tips
Larch needs water during the driest times of summer. Water to root depth weekly during the first two summers, up until fall rains return. In subsequent years, extra irrigation only twice a month will help the trees thrive. Fertilize in spring with a slow-release low nitrogen formula, and keep plants mulched.

Care
Larches can be pruned to reduce height, but you'll lose some of the single leader's grace because the tree will revert to a bushy form. Fallen needles in autumn can be raked into an effective mulch, an appropriate use since larch has no disease problems. No insect problems bother this tree.

Landscape Merit
One of the loveliest fall foliage trees, bright-yellow larch complements red native maples (*Acer circinatum*) and Japanese maples (*Acer palmatum*). In spring, as the center of a bulb garden, the emerging chartreuse foliage behind daffodils and tulips creates a memorable scene. Weeping Japanese larch (*L. kaempferi* 'Pendula') makes an attractive small tree whose landscape presence resembles a small willow.

We Recommend
If the species grows too tall for landscape use, consider some of the smaller cultivars, such as *L. decidua* 'Corley', which remains under 6 feet tall at maturity. Adventurous gardeners may wish to make bonsai of larch, fascinating in all seasons.

Western Red Cedar
Thuja plicata

When, Where, and How to Plant

Most common in western areas, western red cedar can grow well east of the Cascades if watered. It prefers moist, acidic soil and will survive damp boggy spots that retain water both summer and winter, though it doesn't grow in standing water. See page 64 for planting techniques. Full or partial sun suits it, but avoid hot windy spots. Plant in either spring or fall in milder areas, but in spring where winters regularly freeze the soil. If planting as a hedge, set seedlings 5 feet apart. When planting in colder areas, look for the hardiest cold-enduring trees—choose plants grown from seeds originating in the mountains or east of the Cascades. Mulch with composted bark.

Growing Tips

Western red cedar requires little fertilizer; apply a slow release low nitrogen product as growth starts in the second year. Set soaker hoses or other irrigation to water deeply to the roots each week during summer. In the open landscape, late in summer, mature cedars that haven't been watered will "flag"—whole sections of leaves turn brown and drop off. Cedars ordinarily lose their fourth-year foliage; water more if recent foliage browns on newly set plants. Winter rains generally allow normal spring foliage to recover.

Care

This tree has few pest problems.

Landscape Merit

Where space allows, western red cedar grows into an incomparable single specimen. For a narrow, tall shape, choose 'Hogan'. With good contrasting gold foliage tinge, 'Stoneham Gold' lights up partial shade and stays below 20 feet. Landscapes often feature western red cedar as hedging, its intricate lacy foliage dense after trimming. *Thuja plicata* 'Atrovirens' grows to 15 feet by 4 feet wide without pruning. Unless using the trees for hedging, allow enough space to keep the lower limbs; you want to emphasize the sweeping character of the plant's form. The drooping branches accentuate the foliage's beauty.

We Recommend

T. plicata 'Zebrina' alternates stripes of green and gold; it reaches 60 to 70 feet in gardens and retains its brilliant gold edging in either sun or shade.

Both culturally and economically vital to the Pacific Northwest, western red cedar shaped life for the natives here and drew settlers, who harvested fortunes from cutting its straight, 200-foot-tall trunks. Beautiful from all angles, the branches sweep to the ground and form a broad conical shape where it has room to spread. Western red cedar grows tallest in high-rainfall areas. In drier sections of the coastal region, it colonizes ravine bottoms and spots where water is plentiful. Dark-green, lacy, flattened foliage holds tiny 1/2-inch cones, plentiful on mature trees. Ancient durable specimens grow in older landscapes where people can step inside under the low branches to stand next to the trunk. Ornamental cultivars give contemporary gardeners choices for smaller gardens.

Other Common Names
Canoe cedar, giant cedar

Bloom Period and Seasonal Color
Evergreen

Mature Height × Spread
75 feet × 25 to 30 feet

Zones
5 to 7

White Pine

Pinus strobus species and cultivars

Native to both eastern and western regions in America, white pines share these traits: They have five needles in a bundle and definite blue tones to the needles, and are quite soft to the touch. Many more cultivated landscape plants have developed from eastern white pine (P. strobus) than from western white pine (P. monticola). Western white pine is seldom planted though fairly common throughout our area. Beautiful landscape texture characterizes all white pines—the graceful motion of their needles in wind and the sturdy brown pendant cones, 6 inches long on eastern white pine and up to 10 inches on the western. Gardeners can find compact forms and dwarf forms of eastern white pine that will tuck into a landscape and add year-round interest.

Bloom Period and Seasonal Color
Evergreen; appears blue-silver from a distance

Mature Height × Spread
50 feet × 25 feet

Zones
2 to 8

When, Where, and How to Plant

Install white pines in spring from container plants or balled-and-burlapped specimens. Prepare the soil deeply to allow for the taproot (common to all young pines). White pines prefer acidic soil with a pH of 5.0 to 6.0. Good drainage in full sun suits them, but if planting east of the Cascades, avoid exposed windy spots. See page 64 for more planting advice. Mulch 3 inches deep, but don't touch the trunk.

Growing Tips

Use a slow-release fertilizer the second year, with a moderate formulation like a 6-2-2. Water weekly during summer until established and then every two weeks. Eastern white pine doesn't fully tolerate drought in Northwestern climates. Keep trees mulched.

Care

All white pines will take shearing to keep them small and symmetrical, but don't cut into bare wood. Like all pines, they won't break new growth from old wood. Pinch back the expanded candles just before the needles unfold to keep the plant smaller (a labor-intensive but effective method). White pines don't tolerate salt spray or air pollution (such as might be present on a curbside planting). They shed the third year's brown needles in late summer and autumn, often alarming their growers, but it's normal. Shake and comb out the old needles on small plants both to improve air circulation and to maintain a tidy appearance. All needle pines can get white pine blister rust.

Landscape Merit

As specimens or accent plants, white pines offer a graceful character not present in other pines. Plant several to create a small woodland, then underplant with bleeding heart, trillium, and sweet woodruff. The smaller cultivars make handsome container plants.

We Recommend

Pinus strobus 'Nana' (also sold as 'Radiata') grows very slowly, reaching 3 feet in twenty years. Both needles and cones are proportionally smaller on dwarf forms. The delightfully named 'Sea Urchin' stays quite small with a permanently rounded shape. 'Pendula' adds intriguing form with its drooping branches, but requires staking.

Taxus × media species and cultivars

When, Where, and How to Plant

Plant from containers in spring, or year-round where the soils don't freeze. Yews take all light exposures, from full sun to shade. They don't tolerate soggy soils, so provide good drainage. Prepare the soil by amending it well, digging the compost in across the entire planting area, not simply in the planting hole. See page 64 for details. Nonnative types prefer neutral to alkaline soil but can grow well in acidic soils if mulched with compost. Native *Taxus brevifolia* (which is seldom available in nurseries but may be found through native plant revegetation sales) needs acidic soil. Mulch all types after planting.

Growing Tips

Water yews weekly when first planted, soaking roots deeply. Once established, these plants need water only monthly in the cooler summer areas, but more often where heat prevails. In hot areas, planting in deeper shade helps them thrive. Yews don't need much fertilizer but benefit from a slow-release 5-10-10 or 6-2-2 in the first years.

Care

Renew the mulch in fall. Prune anytime, though if growing a formal hedge or topiary sculpture, prune just before spring growth and again in late summer. Cut back only as far as the green growth points; don't clip into brown wood. Trimmed plants fill in quickly. No insects or diseases bother yews. **Note:** The needles and seeds are toxic, though the red aril, often eaten by squirrels, is not. Surprisingly, deer chew yews avidly.

Landscape Merit

Among the most beautiful evergreens, yews form handsome screens and fences, becoming fully opaque once established. Useful as foundation plantings and additions to shrub borders, some—such as *Taxus × media* 'Densiformis'—need little shearing, growing as a low, nearly ground-covering plant no taller than 3 feet. With the right cultivar, pruning may seldom be necessary.

We Recommend

Cultivars suitable for low hedges and small landscape features include *Taxus × media* 'Green Wave', forming a low mound 2 feet tall and 8 feet wide. *T. × media* 'Hicksii' stays columnar, forming a natural hedge that grows slowly to 15 feet.

The only conifer that takes deep shade well, yew lends particularly beautiful dark-green texture to the landscape in either sun or shade. These are perfect hedge plants because they can be sheared deeply, looking appropriate in both formal and informal situations. Yews don't resemble other conifers; their very soft needles cover the branches so densely that the basic structure is invisible. Yews provide lots of early-spring pollen but no cones; instead, they produce red fleshy berries (called arils) with seeds (only the female plants produce the seeds). Western native yew (T. brevifolia), cherished as a source of tamoxifen for cancer treatment, makes a somewhat open and sprawling bush but can be effective in native landscapes as an understory shrub beneath Douglas firs and western cedar.

Bloom Period and Seasonal Color
Evergreen; spring growth lime-green

Mature Height × Spread
20 to 25 feet × 6 to 8 feet

Zones
4 to 9

Ground Covers *for Washington & Oregon*

The incredibly shrinking lawn has made way for a tapestry of ground covers—low-growing plants with interesting foliage and seasonal blooms, providing a much-desired alternative to water- and fertilizer-dependent turf.

Plants classified as ground covers range widely from horizontally spreading or dwarf forms of our favorite evergreen shrubs to glossy-leaf vines and ethereal perennials. They are generally defined as plants that provide continual coverage of the soil, growing together in a seamless or interconnected style.

We appreciate ground covers for the challenges they solve in the landscape: to blanket or stabilize otherwise unplanted soil, obscure weeds, or provide the first "layer" of a multilayered design scheme.

Mixed Heaths and Heathers Covering a Hillside

Ground covers can cloak an area quickly or take a few years to fully establish. Not every ground cover is appropriate for the "carpet" treatment. Some are more useful in small areas, such as the narrow strip between a walkway and a home's foundation. Ornamental ground covers pay homage to the more statuesque plants above them—woodland shrubs and trees are more charming when skirted with the fabulous red-tinged leaves of bishop's hat; a rose border is improved when underplanted with long-blooming hardy geranium.

Ground Cover Selection Tips

Ground covers allow you to blanket your garden with cushioned textures and interesting leaf patterns, not to mention suppress weeds! You can choose ground covers that satisfy varying points of view—ranging from purely utilitarian to sheer aesthetics. Strive for somewhere in-between these two extremes and you'll be rewarded with an area that is both well-covered in ornamental vegetation and an attractive complement to the perennials, bulbs, ornamental grasses, shrubs, and trees that grow above it.

Here are some important considerations to add to your ground cover checklist:

- Is the plant you are considering evergreen? Most of the ground covers recommended in this chapter will hold onto their foliage through winter.
- How quickly will it spread? Are you willing to wait three years for an area to "fill in" with ground covers? If you're eager to carpet a bed or planting area, choose a ground cover known for its fast-spreading habit.
- Can it withstand foot traffic? Some ground covers, especially the woody varieties, are useful to edge a walkway or path, but they will break if stepped on. If you have a high-traffic area, select one of the herbal groundcovers that withstands a moderate degree of footsteps.

Pachysandra and Vinca Lining a Walkway

Preparing the Site

How a ground cover thrives in your landscape's cultural conditions is equally important to design considerations. Because they grow closer to the ground than most of the garden's other plants, ground covers are often susceptible to how well or how poorly you have prepared your soil. If you are planting ground covers to fill a large area, evaluate the soil type and consider light exposure and drainage features. (On a slight slope or a steep bank, you'll have the added benefit of gravity helping provide good drainage.)

Northwest soils are generally found on either end of the soil continuum. That is, you'll likely have either mostly clay soil or mostly sandy soil. The former requires amendments such as organic compost in order to improve drainage; the latter requires similar amendments in order to slow drainage and help retain moisture in the soil. For guidelines on evaluating and improving your soil, see page 11.

To prepare a large planting area for ground covers, remove any vegetation (sod, weeds, old plants) and loosen the soil 6 to 8 inches deep, screening out root clumps and rocks. Add 2 to 3 inches of organic matter, such as compost or composted manure, spreading it evenly across the area. After amending the soil, add a granular nitrogen fertilizer, working it into the ground to the level of the root zone (fertilizer packages will provide the correct measurements for the square footage of your planting area). Organic matter and fertilizer will give any ground cover you plant an excellent start at getting established. Subsequent feedings are generally added before the blooming season.

Planting Ground Covers

If you are planting in a large area, check the spacing requirements given for a specific ground cover. It's tempting to place ground covers close together to "jump start" the process of individual plants growing together, but consider the plant's mature spread.

Periwinkle

Herbaceous plants generally fill in an area more quickly than woody plants. You can probably tinker with a plant's suggested spacing by 2 to 4 inches per plant, but keep in mind that crowded ground covers are often more likely to suffer from disease than well-spaced ones with adequate air circulation.

Don't place ground cover plants in even rows. Instead, like building a wall with bricks, it's more attractive to stagger each row with offset plants for a natural appearance.

Most ground covers are purchased in plastic nursery pots, and those determine the depth of your planting hole. Some smaller ground covers, such as woolly thyme and blue star creeper, are sold in flats. If you're planting with flat-grown plants, gently slide each plant out of the container, taking care to separate the roots and spread them evenly in the planting hole.

One way to help suppress weeds and prevent soil in a planting area from drying out is to spread 1 to 2 inches of organic mulch between newly planted ground covers.

Watering Issues

If you plant ground covers in fall, precipitation during the winter and spring months that follow will deliver adequate moisture to help the plants begin to establish roots before summer's dry weather. If you plant ground covers in early spring, Mother Nature will probably deliver a few months of good rainfall. Then you'll need to provide supplemental irrigation until the plants establish (usually for two to three growing seasons).

Good drainage enhances the performance of your ground covers. Overwatering often causes plants to stand in damp soil as water slowly drains, leading to crown rot. Observe ground covers for indications that you may be underwatering, such as foliage that wilts, browns completely, or yellows at the edges. Try to rejuvenate a dry area by zigzagging soaker hoses on top of the ground cover and allowing their moisture to slowly saturate the area (throughout the root zone).

Watering terms used throughout this chapter include:

Moist soil: Cool, slightly damp soil in the top 6 to 8 inches or through the root area.

Regular or moderate water: Weekly or twice weekly watering. Soil is not allowed to thoroughly dry out between waterings.

Dry periods: When a plant needs water during "excessive dry spells," this refers to a typical Northwest summer where there is no significant precipitation for two weeks or longer. When you irrigate, water deeply, to at least 8 inches or through the root area.

Maintenance

This chapter refers to some general guidelines for ground cover maintenance, using terms such as *shearing* (cutting off spent blooms) and *grooming* (edging or trimming areas of ground cover that have escaped from the desired planting area). Most ground covers are undemanding, but they can benefit from a yearly cleanup, especially when used in high-traffic areas. Don't be fooled into thinking you'll never see weeds creeping up through ground covers. Be diligent about pulling any noticeable weeds so that the ground cover remains attractive. Very few ground covers should be mown, although dwarf whitestripe bamboo is best controlled with an annual mowing.

Do your homework, and observe how other landscapes in your neighborhood are treated. If you see a hard-to-mow slope that's been planted with kinnikinnick, you'll appreciate the way it evenly covers the area with its medium-textured foliage. Likewise, there's nothing more alluring than walking through a cool, partially shaded side garden where blue star creeper cushions the steppingstones with its delicate five-pointed blue flowers and tiny lime-green foliage.

—DP

Geranium 'Johnson's Blue'

Bishop's Hat
Epimedium grandiflorum

With a distinctive peaked bloom that resembles a bishop's mitre, this glossy ground cover is cherished for its heart-shaped leaves and low-growing, spreading habit. It appears on nearly every garden designer's list of best plants for dry shade—a landscape challenge for many Northwest gardens. Bishop's hat is ideal for woodland and shade gardens. With a crimson-pink tinge on the margins of its foliage, this deciduous form of the plant grows as a beautiful carpet under dense conifers. It doesn't command much root space; perhaps that's why it thrives where other ground covers fail. By spring, graceful stems of pale-yellow, pink, or cream flowers emerge above the foliage. With the arrival of cooler temperatures, the foliage takes on a burgundy hue, enhancing the autumn garden.

Other Common Name
Barrenwort

Bloom Period and Seasonal Color
Spring; yellow, rose, cream, and bicolored blooms; reddish fall foliage

Mature Height × Spread
8 to 12 inches × 12 to 18 inches

Zones
5 to 8

When, Where, and How to Plant
Plant container-grown bishop's hat in spring or fall. This plant prefers partial shade and well-drained soils, although many forms tolerate dry shade conditions. Follow the general suggestions for planting ground covers on page 79. Plant 12 to 18 inches apart. Dig the planting holes deep enough so that the soil level in the pot is the same as the ground. Water thoroughly.

Growing Tips
Known for its low-moisture requirements, bishop's hat should be watered during extended dry spells or it will suffer. In average soils, fertilization is not required. You'll find more tips in the chapter introduction.

Care
This durable ground cover is generally free of pests and diseases. Slugs ignore bishop's hat! Groom sections of this ground cover by shearing away dried foliage in late winter, before new blooms emerge. Bishop's hat can be propagated by divisions. Lift the sections to be divided, and pull apart or cut the relatively tough roots into clumps. Replant the sections, making sure to water well; mulch to help retain moisture.

Companion Planting and Design
Use bishop's hat as a ground cover under other broadleaf evergreens, including rhododendrons, azaleas, and camellias. It also makes a nice edging for shade garden beds or walkways. It works well in Asian-inspired landscapes, as it is native to China, Korea, and Japan. It's also attractive in alpine and rock gardens, as long as the site is in partial shade or filtered sunlight. You can use the leathery foliage and waxy blooms in small floral arrangements.

We Recommend
More than 30 species of evergreen and deciduous plants fall in the genus *Epimedium*. *E. grandiflorum* (bishop's hat or longspur barrenwort) offers fresh spring foliage and delicate blooms. 'Rose Queen' has crimson flowers with white-tipped spurs. 'White Queen' features large, pure-white flowers, nearly 2 inches across. *E. × rubrum* (red barrenwort), a cross between *E. grandiflorum* and *E. alpinum*, forms spreading clumps of new green leaves tinged in pink.

Blue Star Creeper
Pratia pedunculata

When, Where, and How to Plant

Blue star creeper is generally sold in 4-inch nursery pots. A plant this size can spread to fill 12 inches in one season if given the proper conditions. Plant in early spring. Blue star creeper prefers fertile, loamy, relatively moist soil in partial sun or partial shade. East of the Cascades, where summers can be very hot, this plant prefers shade. Follow the general suggestions for planting ground covers on page 79. Plant at least 12 inches apart. Dig the planting holes deep enough so that the soil level in the pot is the same as the ground. Water thoroughly.

Growing Tips

Water this plant regularly until established. Blue star creeper appreciates relatively moist locations, but it won't suffer during an extended dry spell. Fertilization is not required.

Care

As blue star creeper spreads, you can keep its edges groomed with small floral scissors— or let its matted foliage creep up and over the edges of stepping stones. The flowers don't require deadheading; they're too tiny to notice once they've finished blooming. You can divide blue star creeper at any time of the year by digging up a sizable section of the plant, cutting it into 4- to 6-inch pieces, and replanting. Water divisions well after transplanting. Disease-free, blue star creeper is occasionally affected by slugs.

Companion Planting and Design

With the mossy green appearance of baby's tears (*Soleirolia*), this look-a-like ground cover has the added bonus of starry blue flowers. Plant it to discourage weeds and fill in bare dirt. Ideal for rockeries and walkways, it quickly blankets spaces between stones. Keep its delicacy in mind; don't pair this tiny-leafed ground cover with large, woody, or evergreen shrubs. Its proportions are better suited for perennial and rose borders, woodland paths, and lush fern gardens.

We Recommend

Pratia pedunculata 'County Park' features violet-blue flowers spring to fall.

With delicate, pale-blue, starry blooms no larger than 1/2-inch across, blue star creeper is deceptively durable. This fast-spreading perennial ground cover is suitable for planting between steppingstones or in rockeries. Blue star creeper hugs the ground, making it difficult for weeds to take root, and carpets planting nooks with an evergreen mass of tiny rounded or oval medium-green leaves. It prefers moist soils but can survive dry spells. The five-petal star-shaped flowers bloom on short, upright stems. They emerge in early summer and bloom for much of the season like a sprinkling of dainty sequins across green velvet. Some forms may spread too eagerly, which is why blue star creeper is one ground cover well suited for stone pathways, where it can be somewhat restrained.

Bloom Period and Seasonal Color
Summer; pale-blue and white blooms

Mature Height × Spread
2 to 3 inches × indefinite

Zones
5 to 7

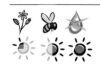

Carpet Bugle
Ajuga reptans

A landscaper once told me this was his "instant-gratification" ground cover for clients who wanted their garden looking fully planted the first season. When grown in well-drained soil, carpet bugle spreads readily, covering the ground with glossy, purple-tinged or variegated foliage 3 to 4 inches long. Two-lipped, tubular flowers in shades of violet-blue or cream emerge above the foliage in spring or early summer, borne on spikes up to 6 inches tall. Plant carpet bugle in shady borders where it fills in below other perennials, hedges, or shrubs. Carpet bugle spreads by runners, forming a textured mat of colorful foliage that's quite attractive after the blooms have faded. It can spread too eagerly, so avoid planting carpet bugle near lawns where it can take root.

Other Common Names
Ajuga, bugleweed

Bloom Period and Seasonal Color
Late spring to early summer; blue, white, and pink blooms

Mature Height × Spread
3 to 8 inches × 12 to 14 inches

Zones
3 to 9

When, Where, and How to Plant
Plant container-grown carpet bugle from spring to early fall. Carpet bugle prefers any moist soil in partial sun to shade (it will scorch in full sun). This ground cover can tolerate most types of soil if regularly irrigated. If you have heavy clay soil, amend with organic compost to improve drainage. Follow the general suggestions for planting ground covers on page 79, spacing carpet bugle 8 to 12 inches apart. Water thoroughly until the plants are established.

Growing Tips
Carpet bugle requires no special care if it's grown in well-drained soil and occasionally irrigated during dry spells. When allowed to stand in soggy soil, the crown is susceptible to rotting. Fertilizing is not necessary.

Care
Cut back or shear tall blooms after flowering to encourage new foliage growth and keep the plants tidy. Excessively soggy foliage is susceptible to fungal diseases. Remove damaged sections. If a variegated form reverts to green, cut out the green foliage to maintain a uniform appearance. Carpet bugle is easy to divide. Dig up the sections, and separate the rooted leaf rosettes to replant. Water well after transplanting, and mulch to retain moisture. Pests generally do not bother ajuga.

Companion Planting and Design
Create a colorful tapestry of blues, greens, and purples when you plant carpet bugle in the shade border. The purple blooms complement hostas, hellebores, astilbes, lungworts, and other spring and summer-blooming shade perennials. When planted in rockeries and walkways, carpet bugle rapidly carpets spaces between stones. Since it can invade lawns, plant carpet bugle where it can be controlled, such as along a sidewalk or as edging for a path.

We Recommend
The variegated form 'Burgundy Glow' (or 'Burgundy Lace') features silvery-green leaves washed in reddish burgundy. 'Bronze Beauty' has hints of bronze, with deep-blue flowers. Popular 'Catlin's Giant' features bronze-purple foliage and flowers to 8 inches tall.

Creeping Mahonia
Mahonia repens

When, Where, and How to Plant
Plant container-grown creeping mahonia in spring or fall, situating it in moderately fertile, moist, well-drained soil. Like many mahonias, the ground cover form prefers partial sun to partial shade, although it can grow in full sun if the soil is not too dry. This is an excellent ground cover solution for dry shade. Avoid planting in exposed, windy sites. Follow the general suggestions for planting ground covers on page 79. Space creeping mahonia 18 to 24 inches apart, making sure the top of the container soil is level with the ground. Water thoroughly until established. Don't plant creeping mahonia along walkways or near the front of a border, or this prickly plant will snag anyone passing by.

Growing Tips
Appreciated for its drought tolerance, creeping mahonia requires little irrigation unless you notice the plant is stressed due to sun or wind exposure (indicated by foliage with dried edges or dieback). Consult page 17 for information on fertilization.

Care
In general, prune creeping mahonia only to keep it tidy. Cut away dead or damaged stems, removing them where the branch connects with the trunk. Deadheading is unnecessary. Creeping mahonia generally resists disease, but it can be susceptible to a small looper caterpillar, which may leave telltale bites but won't damage the plant.

Companion Planting and Design
Creeping mahonia satisfies a wide array of roles in the landscape, from covering a woodland ravine to hiding a home's exposed concrete foundation. This is a great ground cover for tricky areas that don't regularly receive water, such as spots beneath dense evergreens or below an overhanging roof. Mahonia is a relative of barberry, so consider pairing this low-growing form with taller forms of burgundy barberry for a textural explosion. Echo its golden blooms by planting creeping mahonia near a brilliant-yellow forsythia for a lovely early spring display.

We Recommend
'Rotundifolia' is a taller form with rounded leaflets; it grows to 5 feet.

Mahonia is an excellent evergreen shrub, important in Northwest gardens as an attractive native plant with stunning yellow blooms. The low-growing creeping mahonia is truly a four-season plant, rewarding the gardener with its foliage, fragrant blooms, and berries throughout the year. With a shrubby habit, creeping mahonia has matte-green spiny-edged leaves that resemble holly. Each leaf has seven leaflets, giving creeping mahonia a wavy, textured appearance. It produces deep-yellow flowers in spring, formed by dense racemes about 3 inches long, which may attract hummingbirds in search of early spring nectar. The flowers are followed by blue-black berries in late summer. This form of mahonia provides excellent winter color. The foliage turns bronzy or pinkish when temperatures drop, giving the woodland garden much-needed brilliance.

Bloom Period and Seasonal Color
Mid- to late spring; dark-yellow blooms

Mature Height × Spread
12 to 18 inches × 3 feet

Zones
6 to 8

Creeping Rosemary
Romarinus officinalis 'Prostratus'

Transport yourself—and your garden—to sun-drenched Mediterranean landscapes when you grow creeping rosemary in a warm, bright spot in the garden. Like most types of the species Rosmarinus officinalis, *creeping rosemary requires heat and excellent drainage to thrive. It will suffer in wet or shady locations and during extreme cold. Creeping rosemary is very happy scrambling across the top of a rockery or spilling over a concrete retaining wall with its characteristic evergreen needlelike foliage that can spread 4 to 8 feet These plants have glossy green, linear leaves (1 to 1 1/2 inches) and two-lipped flowers that are typically pale-blue. The foliage of creeping rosemary is aromatic, infusing the air with the fragrance of the seaside as you brush against the plant.*

Bloom Period and Seasonal Color
Fall to spring; pale-lavender blooms

Mature Height × Spread
1 to 2 feet × 4 to 8 feet

Zones
7 to 10

When, Where, and How to Plant
Plant container-grown creeping rosemary in spring or fall in moderately fertile, well-drained soil. Amend heavy clay soil thoroughly with organic compost to improve drainage conditions. Rosemary prefers full sun, but will tolerate morning shade. Creeping rosemary should be planted where its branches and stems will spread along and over stones or concrete. Follow suggestions for planting ground covers on page 79, spacing creeping rosemary about 24 inches apart. Water well until the plant is established.

Growing Tips
Creeping rosemary is prone to root rot if overwatered or allowed to stand in soggy soil. This drought-tolerant ground cover requires little irrigation. It is adapted to rocky, low-fertility soils.

Care
Pinch back the tips of younger plants to encourage fuller growth. More mature plants can be sheared lightly after flowering, but cut only to the leafy wood as bare stems and branches won't releaf. Creeping rosemary should be encouraged to spread, though you can cut away unwieldy branches. If your plants become woody and bare at the center, cut back one or two of the oldest stems to the base. Unlike most upright rosemary that is hardy below freezing temperatures, creeping rosemary is relatively tender, suffering below 20 degrees Fahrenheit. It generally resists pests.

Companion Planting and Design
Excellent for sunny, dry banks, this ground cover can be used for erosion control. It looks—and smells—lovely, with tangy blue-flowered stems spilling over a brick retaining wall (brick, stone, and concrete maintain the warmth needed for this heat-loving rosemary). Plant creeping rosemary along the base of other Mediterranean plants, including silvery-leafed artemisia. It also pairs beautifully with deep-purple or streaked New Zealand flaxes.

We Recommend
Rosmarinus officinalis 'Prostratus' will trail along walls to create a fragrant green "curtain." Other trailing and spreading forms of rosemary include 'Lockwood de Forest', which mounds to 2 1/2 feet tall with bluer flowers and brighter green foliage.

Creeping Sedum
Sedum species

When, Where, and How to Plant
Plant from spring to fall, situating plants in full or partial sun. Sedums adapt to most soil conditions, if well drained. Don't plant in soggy soil. Improve drainage by incorporating sand or organic compost. In heavy or rich soil, or too much shade, sedums can splay at the center. Follow the general guidelines for planting perennials on page 79; space creeping plants about 12 inches apart.

Growing Tips
Water creeping sedums regularly until established. They require irrigation only during flowering and extended dry spells. This ground cover tolerates heat, wind, or drought. Fertilize lightly in spring to promote sturdy growth.

Care
Generally disease and pest free, creeping sedum occasionally attracts aphids, which can be washed off with a spray from the garden hose. The spreading or cascading forms require little grooming, although you can deadhead flowers after blooming. Or, leave spent blooms through autumn to provide tasty seedheads for birds. Some forms of sedum are evergreen; others die to the ground in winter.

Companion Planting and Design
Plant creeping sedum against a backdrop of larger leafed succulents to echo the texture and blue-silver or wine-tinged foliage. Creeping sedums will cheerfully fill spaces in rock gardens and retaining walls, adding unusual textures and forms to brighten a dull space. The succulent foliage also looks lovely spilling over the edges of window boxes, hanging baskets, and containers.

We Recommend
Evergreen forms abound. *Sedum spurium* 'Red Carpet' is aptly named, with flat-leafed reddish rosettes that creep on branching stems and red blossoms. 'Dragon's Blood' has reddish pink flowers and red-tinged leaves. *S. spathulifolium* features ground-hugging rosettes that spread by runners, spatula-shaped foliage that often turns bronze or red, and bright-yellow flowers. Goldmoss sedum (*S. acre*), one of the smallest creeping sedums, offers green triangular foliage (2 to 5 inches tall) and masses of yellow flowers. 'Vera Jameson' is a deciduous, low-spreading sedum hybrid with purple-gray foliage and ruby-pink flowers.

Creeping sedums spread their succulent foliage over rockeries and along the edges of sunny pathways. If you adore 'Autumn Joy', the upright classic for late-summer borders, you'll want to incorporate creeping and spreading forms of hardy sedum into the landscape. Low-spreading and mat-forming sedums contribute a carpet of geometric foliage and attractive blooms to the garden. Use creeping sedum in rock and alpine gardens, as ground and bank covers, and as accents at the front of a mixed border. This is not a ground cover that can endure foot traffic, but as an edging plant, creeping sedum is an attractive choice. Durable, low-maintenance plants, sedums thrive in well-drained, sunny sites. They bloom in late summer with bright-yellow or raspberry-tinged clusters of tiny, star-shaped flowers.

Other Common Name
Stonecrop

Bloom Period and Seasonal Color
Summer and autumn; pink, reddish, creamy-white, and yellow blooms

Mature Height × Spread
6 to 8 inches × 12 to 24 inches

Zones
4 to 9

Creeping Thyme

Thymus pseudolanuginosus

You can savor the accents of culinary thyme in a favorite stew, but when it comes to the landscape, add the soft, downy accent of creeping thyme. A fashionable cousin of common thyme (T. vulgaris), creeping thyme varieties are not savory. They are, however, delicious to see carpeting the nooks and crannies of a stone staircase or filling in blank spots in a flagstone patio. A Mediterranean plant that endures drought, creeping thyme adds a fuzzy texture as it hugs the ground. As a bonus, you'll enjoy its flush of tiny pinkish red flowers in early summer. If you want to go grass free in your garden's sunniest areas, try planting a thyme lawn. It's a low-maintenance, evergreen alternative reminiscent of a medieval herb garden.

Other Common Name
Woolly thyme

Bloom Period and Seasonal Color
Midsummer; produces a few pink flowers; grown primarily for its soft, fuzzy foliage

Mature Height × Spread
2 to 3 inches × 2 to 3 feet

Zones
5 to 9

When, Where, and How to Plant

Plant from spring to fall in full or partial sun. This carpetlike ground cover needs sun and may suffer in the shade of taller plants. Thyme is an undemanding plant if given good drainage and air circulation. Heat, drought, and cold conditions won't affect its health as much as soggy soil. Improve drainage by incorporating organic compost. For ground cover planting tips, see page 79.

Growing Tips

Water plants regularly until established. Creeping thyme requires irrigation only during flowering and extended dry spells. Continuously damp foliage may lead to rot, so give your creeping thyme good air circulation. Fertilizing is not necessary.

Care

Generally disease and pest free, creeping thyme occasionally attracts slugs, which can be hand-picked or baited with organic treatments. This thyme can withstand foot traffic, but trim away dead or dried sections where necessary. Thyme can be divided when it begins to die out at the center. Dig up a section, cut into 3- to 4-inch pieces with scissors, and replant in spring.

Companion Planting and Design

Plant along the path of an herb garden or in a classic "dry" gravel garden alongside other Mediterranean plants. Creeping thyme is a lovely ground cover through which delicate spring bulbs emerge, creating a sparkling combination of woolly silver foliage beneath clumps of small narcissus. Create an informal patchwork-quilt style by combining woolly thyme with other thymes, including dark-green elfin thyme or red thyme—the varying colors and textures are lovely together.

We Recommend

'Hall's Variety' is a profuse-blooming form; 'Longwood' grows as an attractive carpet of gray, felted leaves. Other forms of prostrate thyme are found under *T. serphyllum* ssp. or *T. praecox* ssp. *articus*. Look for cultivars that add fine texture, an aromatic scent, or delicate flowers to the pathway, including 'Pink Chintz' (1 to 1 1/2 inches) with salmon-pink flowers and 'Reiter's' (3 inches), a vigorous ground cover with lavender blooms.

Dwarf White Striped Bamboo
Pleioblastus variegatus

When, Where, and How to Plant
Bamboo is typically sold in nursery pots, although you may need to seek out good local sources through the Northwest chapters of the American Bamboo Society. Plant dwarf white striped bamboo in spring or early summer, siting it in moist, well-drained, rich soil. The variegation looks best when plants are grown in full sun, although it can grow in partial sun or partial shade. For general ground cover planting tips, see page 79.

Growing Tips
Keep the soil moist but not soggy until the second or third year, when the plant is established. During dry seasons, water deeply once or twice a week, making sure water reaches the root depth. Water regularly as new shoots appear in spring. Mature bamboo requires only periodic irrigation during dry periods. To encourage new shoot growth and provide a general feeding, in spring or fall apply a fertilizer specified for lawns.

Care
Bamboo is evergreen but tends to drop older leaves throughout the year. In fall, rake away dead leaves to discourage bamboo mites from nesting. Other pests include aphids and slugs. Deer are generally not attracted to bamboo. To maintain this bamboo as a ground cover, mow it each spring at the highest blade level (approximately 4 inches).

Companion Planting and Design
Ground cover bamboos are ideal in planter boxes and containers; for rock gardens, slopes, and parking strips; or as an understory to timber bamboos. It is excellent for erosion control or to cover a sunny bank where tidiness is not a priority. As a running form of bamboo, it spreads a few feet a year and brightens up the landscape as a highly textured edging to a walkway (it withstands some foot traffic). It pairs well with Japanese maples, heavenly bamboo, and broadleaf evergreen shrubs.

We Recommend
Other ground cover forms of bamboo include *Pleioblastus pygmaeus* (6 to 12 inches), a vigorous spreader that can be mown to maintain its dense appearance.

Dwarf white striped bamboo is native to parts of Japan and China. For the Asian-inspired garden, this variegated form is an intriguing alternative to a lawn. The striped or streaked leaves range from 2 to 6 inches long on upright stems to 18 inches or higher. To maintain dwarf white striped bamboo as a ground cover, you should mow it to the ground each spring. The new foliage takes on a paperlike texture. A gentle breeze rippling through a short stand of this attractive plant adds enjoyable sounds and sights to your garden. Dwarf white striped bamboo is a hardy, frost-resistant ground cover choice and is a delightful plant to pair with ornamental clumping bamboo. Because it is a running form of bamboo, you'll need to control it.

Bloom Period and Seasonal Color
Evergreen foliage looks best spring to fall

Mature Height × Spread
18 to 24 inches × 3 feet (if controlled)

Zones
7 to 11

Hardy Geranium
Geranium species

The presence of hardy geraniums ensures that the bare space below taller plants will be obscured by a profusion of interesting foliage and merry, long-blooming flowers. Not to be confused with zonal geraniums (Pelargonium species), which are fleshier and marginally hardy, the overall appearance of this perennial geranium is one of informality and soft texture. The modest, five-petaled blooms usually appear in soft shades of pink, blue-lavender, and white, although some dazzling hardy geranium forms have bright-magenta flowers. Foliage shapes range from lobed and deeply cut to rounded and scalloped, with a palette of bright-green, lime, gray-blue, or wine-streaked. The foliage of some forms turns red in autumn. Hardy geranium looks attractive alone and unifies mixed borders with its spreading or trailing habit.

Other Common Name
Cranesbill

Bloom Period and Seasonal Color
Late spring through summer; pink, white, blue-lavender, and magenta blooms

Mature Height × Spread
12 inches × 12 to 36 inches

Zones
4 to 9

When, Where, and How to Plant
Plant in spring and summer in moist, well-drained soil. These plants don't like to be rootbound, so transplant them soon after bringing them home. Hardy geraniums prefer rich soil, but can also grow in soil of average fertility. Locations in full morning sun to partial shade are ideal. In the hottest climates, avoid afternoon sun. Follow the general suggestions for planting ground covers on page 79, spacing hardy geraniums 12 to 24 inches apart.

Growing Tips
Easy to grow and maintain, hardy geraniums should be watered regularly until established. Irrigate during dry spells. Fertilizing is generally unnecessary.

Care
Most wide-spreading hardy geraniums take a few years to look substantial in the garden. To encourage extended blooming, lightly shear the plant after the first spring flowers fade. Cut back ragged-looking leaves in fall to help produce healthy, attractive foliage the following season. Hardy geraniums are generally pest and disease free, although they will suffer from crown rot (dieback in the plant's center) if allowed to sit in soggy soil. Hardy geranium seldom needs division, although it is an easy plant to dig and divide if you wish to distribute more sections throughout the landscape.

Companion Planting and Design
Use hardy geraniums in rock gardens, at the front of a border, or to knit together a rose garden with one plant grown between each rose shrub. Its informal habit will hide soil and disguise weeds as stems weave through nearby plants. Combine lime-foliaged forms of hardy geranium with *Hydrangea quercifolia* or *H.* 'Preziosa' for a touch of dramatic contrast.

We Recommend
Bloody cranesbill (*Geranium sanguineum*) has finely cut foliage and bright-magenta blooms that help illuminate a dull spot in the garden. 'Album' is a white selection with an open form. *G.* 'Ann Folkard' (1 foot by 5 feet) features chartreuse foliage and magenta-purple flowers. *G. cinereum* (8 to 12 inches) has soft gray-green leaves with pale-pink blooms.

Heath

Erica carnea

When, Where, and How to Plant

Plant container-grown heath in spring or fall. Choose a well-drained location with neutral to acidic soil. Some heaths tolerate alkaline soil, but this ground cover will suffer in heavy clay locations. Topdress sandy soils with plenty of organic compost when planting. Heaths prefer full sun but will grow in partial shade. Follow the suggestions for planting ground covers on page 79, spacing heaths 12 to 18 inches apart. Water thoroughly until the plant is established.

Growing Tips

Heaths need moderately moist soil. Be careful not to overwater or allow the plants to dry out entirely. Mulching each fall with organic compost is one way to improve soil health. You can also feed each spring with a fertilizer specified for acid-loving plants. Heaths grow slowly but, once established, are easy to care for.

Care

Pests and diseases rarely affect heaths. Overwatering and poor grooming may lead to powdery mildew. Once blooming has finished, shear heaths lightly to keep their uniform shape and remove spent blooms. Do not cut into bare wood.

Companion Planting and Design

Take your growing cues from heath's origins. This woody shrub is native to the Alps, northwest Italy, and Eastern Europe, where it grows in subalpine regions. Blanket a sloping hillside or accentuate a rockery with swaths of heath plants to provide lovely blooms during the winter months and attractive texture the rest of the year. A colorful addition to the conifer garden, heaths create a pink or white carpet beneath larger trees and shrubs. To enjoy multiple seasons of texture and blooms, grow heaths with summer-blooming heathers (*Calluna vulgaris*), which appreciate similar growing conditions.

We Recommend

Erica carnea 'Springwood White' and 'Springwood Pink' are two of the most popular cultivars, aptly named for their profuse white and light-pink blooms. Heaths noted for their golden or lime foliage include 'Ann Sparkes', with golden foliage and bronze tips, and 'Foxhollow', with lime-green foliage that takes on a bronze tinge in winter.

Practical and reliable, heaths have been widely used in Northwest gardens for everything from low hedging to erosion control. Their lustrous green, needlelike foliage is covered in an explosion of bell-shaped pink or white blooms during late winter and early spring. These woody plants grow in tufted mounds. When planted en masse, heaths have the uniform appearance of a ground cover. This is an excellent choice for an evergreen ground cover, as heaths provide a fine texture and flush of color at a time of year when little else blooms. They thrive in the usual acidic soils preferred by rhododendrons and azaleas, making heath a nice companion for these broadleaf evergreen shrubs. Shearing after bloom is the best way to maintain its mounded form and uniform flowers.

Other Common Names
Christmas heather, winter heather

Bloom Period and Seasonal Color
Winter to spring: pink, raspberry, and white blooms

Mature Height × Spread
6 to 10 inches × 20 inches

Zones
5 to 7

Heather

Calluna vulgaris

Where heaths are the shining stars of the winter garden, heathers take center stage in summer. Heaths are distinguished by their needles; heathers have scalelike foliage. Together, these two ground covers produce a plush, Persian carpet effect in the landscape with similar bell- or urn-shaped blooms. In the Northwest garden, heather makes an ideal small, upright branching ground cover that forms finely textured mats. It flowers profusely when grown in full sun, which means bees swarm to the nectar with vigor. Some green heather takes on a bronze tinge in winter as temperatures drop. Newer cultivars have added silver, gold, and red to the heather spectrum. A bit more challenging to grow than heaths, heathers will thrive if given plenty of sun and excellent drainage.

Other Common Name
Scotch heather

Bloom Period and Seasonal Color
Summer to fall: pink, raspberry, and white blooms

Mature Height × Spread
6 to 24 inches × 24 inches

Zones
5 to 7

When, Where, and How to Plant
Plant container-grown heathers in spring or fall, adding organic compost and fertilizer for acid-loving plants to the soil surface after planting. They prefer neutral to acidic soil with excellent drainage, grow well in sandy, low-fertility soils, but suffer in heavy clay locations. Heathers prefer full sun but can grow in partial shade (although flowering is sparse). Protect them from exposed winds. For general ground cover planting tips, see page 79.

Growing Tips
Provide regular irrigation during a plant's first year in the garden, and avoid letting the soil dry out. Once established, heather is relatively drought tolerant, requiring irrigation only during excessively dry spells. Heather will suffer if allowed to stand in soggy soil. Mulch to keep the roots from drying out. Little or no fertilizer is required.

Care
Heathers respond well to annual grooming; shear them by about 1 inch after they flower. Spent blooms fall off in late summer or autumn, leaving unsightly stems. Maintain the plant's bushy form by cutting back to the base of the spent flowers in early spring. If grown in poor conditions, heathers are susceptible to mites and scale. See page 248 for tips on pest control.

Companion Planting and Design
Heathers grow well on protected slopes, in gravel gardens, or in containers. Their soft habit calls for informally designed beds where the branches and flowers resemble a well-woven carpet. For a mass planting, grow heathers low to the ground (the lowest branches can touch the soil), grouping plants in odd-numbered clusters. A favorite texture combination pairs 'Wickwar Flame' heather with the wiry-looking 'Quicksilver' hebe. The stems intermingle, creating a silver and gold tapestry. Heathers also pair beautifully with heaths, ensuring alternating blooms throughout the year.

We Recommend
'Wickwar Flame' (to 18 inches) features gold foliage in summer and mauve flowers from late summer to fall. 'Tricolorifolia' has white-tipped, dark-green foliage in spring and lavender flowers in late summer. The foliage takes on a chocolate hue in winter.

Hebe
Hebe species

When, Where, and How to Plant
Plant this woody shrub in spring and fall, in full or partial sun not exposed to wind. Most forms will adapt to a wide variety of soils if there's moderate to good drainage. Follow the suggestions for planting ground covers on page 79, spacing hebes 18 to 24 inches apart. Water well until the plant is established.

Growing Tips
Water regularly until hebe is established and during dry spells. This plant doesn't like dry summer heat—keep the soil moderately moist, but don't allow it to become soggy. Apply low rates of a nitrogen fertilizer monthly to improve poor growth.

Care
Mildew and root rot are likely results if you overwater hebes. The presence of aphids is occasionally problematic; a shot from the garden hose or treatment with a natural pesticide spray may help. Keep hebes looking tidy and compact by trimming back stems to one-half after blooming. Hebes that die back in the center can be rejuvenated by cutting them back hard—they typically produce new foliage on leafless wood.

Companion Planting and Design
Plant smaller hebe as an evergreen element to mixed borders. The crisp foliage is a wonderful accent for rose gardens and perennials. The lovely white or lavender blooms that cover some hebes add a subtle touch of color but don't compete with the more showy flowers in your garden. Small-leafed forms are ideal in rockeries, along the edges of paths, and as a soft, green "carpet" when underplanted beneath a Japanese maple. Hebes make excellent structural additions to mixed-summer containers; the foliage can be cut for floral arrangements.

We Recommend
Hebe pinguifolia 'Pagei' (10 inches) has chubby blue-gray foliage with red margins and small, white flowers. *H. buchananii* (12 inches) has small, dark-green leaves on blackish branches. Other notable choices are 'McKeanii' (12 inches), which resembles a dwarf green conifer bearing scalelike leaves, and *H. pimeleoides* 'Quicksilver' (12 inches), with a wiry habit and dark-black stems.

Visually appealing, geometrical and orderly, the smaller species of hebes are a great choice for evergreen structure in the landscape. Where you might be tempted to plunk down a common dwarf boxwood, consider instead one of the blue-gray, silver, or red-tipped options offered by hebes. Hebes hail from southern hemisphere locales such as New Zealand, but many forms are durable enough for Northwest gardens west of the Cascades. There are small hebes suitable for rock gardens, while others serve as excellent low-hedge plants that can be lightly clipped. The squarish stems of hebes are covered with pairs of opposite leaves marching from base to tip. While many gardeners admire hebes for foliage and structure, they also enjoy the bottlebrush-like blooms that appear on several forms.

Bloom Period and Seasonal Color
Spring to early fall; white, pink, and lavender blooms

Mature Height × Spread
8 to 18 inches × 2 to 3 feet

Zones
7 to 10

Japanese Spurge

Pachysandra terminalis

A reliable evergreen ground cover for Northwest land-scapes, Japanese spurge provides an attractive blanket of glossy, notched foliage for the woodland or shade garden. This ground cover is ideal in areas where you're trying to replace an invasive English ivy, because it spreads slowly by underground runners but is not aggressive. Japanese spurge creates a uniform, tidy appearance of rich-green foliage that obscures any emerging weeds. Small spikes of white flowers appear from late winter to early spring. The roots of Japanese spurge do not compete with trees for moisture and other resources, making this an excellent plant for carpeting beneath tall conifers. When exposed to full sun, the foliage of Japanese spurge turns yellow, so be sure to plant it where shade is provided.

Other Common Name
Pachysandra

Bloom Period and Seasonal Color
Spring; white blooms

Mature Height × Spread
6 to 10 inches × 8 to 12 inches

Zones
4 to 8

When, Where, and How to Plant

Plant container-grown Japanese spurge in spring, early summer, or fall. Situate plants in full to partial shade to ensure healthy and attractive growth. Japanese spurge tolerates most soil types. Since it is somewhat slow to establish, place plants about 6 inches apart to help an area fill in sooner. Water well. Mulch new plants to retain moisture and suppress weeds until established. For general ground cover planting tips, see page 79.

Growing Tips

Provide regular irrigation during Japanese spurge's first year in the garden; don't let the soil dry out during dry spells. Use soaker hoses to water a large area of Japanese spurge. If you wish to stimulate growth, topdress beds with compost or leaf mold in late winter or early spring.

Care

Once established, Japanese spurge creates a dense mat of foliage that makes a great weed deterrent. Pinch off or trim browned foliage in late winter to improve appearance. Mature Japanese spurge can be dug and divided to increase coverage or establish new beds. In full sun, this ground cover may be susceptible to leaf scorch.

Companion Planting and Design

Japanese spurge is a lovely, undemanding ground cover choice for the woodland garden. You can use it to carpet areas below Douglas firs or western red cedars. Line a woodland pathway with Japanese spurge, trimming away any foliage that creeps onto steppingstones. Incorporate a surprise of color into a bed of Japanese spurge by tucking spring-flowering bulbs into the soil. Tiny narcissuses will shine as they emerge through the glossy green foliage. If you want a little more brilliance from Japanese spurge, grow one of the creamy variegated forms.

We Recommend

'Green Carpet' (4 inches) is dense and deep green. 'Variegata', sometimes sold as 'Silver Edge', features creamy-white margins. 'Cut Leaf' has interesting dissected foliage. Allegheny spurge (*Pachysandra procumbens*) is another species that produces grayish green, oval or round foliage. It spreads more slowly than Japanese spurge, producing fragrant white or pinkish flowers.

Kinnikinnick
Arctostaphylos uva-ursi

When, Where, and How to Plant
Container-grown kinnikinnick can be planted in spring or fall. Situate plants in full sun to partial shade in moist, well-drained average soil. Amend heavy clay soil with organic compost to improve drainage. Space plants about 18 inches apart to more quickly cover a large area of bare soil. A single kinnikinnick plant can eventually spread across a 15-foot area, creating a finely textured blanket of green. Mulch new plants thoroughly to retain moisture and suppress weeds until established. For general ground cover planting tips, see page 79.

Growing Tips
Provide regular irrigation until kinnikinnick is established. Water while the plants are flowering; otherwise, only during extreme dry spells. Kinnikinnick does not usually require fertilizer.

Care
A carpet of kinnikinnick is easy to care for, especially when grown in full sun or partial shade. Don't over-water or allow plants to stand in soggy soil; doing so leads to a variety of fungal diseases, including leaf spot. Avoid problems by growing disease-resistant varieties. Pruning is generally not required. Kinnikinnick does not transplant or divide easily.

Companion Planting and Design
Like Japanese spurge, kinnikinnick is a lovely, undemanding ground cover. Where Japanese spurge is a great choice for shady gardens, kinnikinnick prefers to hug the ground in sunny areas like banks and rock gardens. Grow kinnikinnick at the edge of high-traffic areas, at the front of a mixed woody border, or to control erosion. Emphasize its pinkish blooms by planting kinnikinnick around pink- and rosy-flowered rhododendrons, camellias, and azaleas.

We Recommend
There are numerous forms of kinnikinnick to address your own tastes or landscape needs. 'Alaska', a compact, flat-growing form, offers small, dark-green foliage; 'Emerald Carpet' (10 to 18 inches) tolerates shade better than most cultivars, producing dark-green leaves that take on a reddish bronze winter hue. 'Vancouver Jade', an introduction from the University of British Columbia Botanical Garden, is known to resist leaf spot.

The playful name of this native spreading shrub reflects its happy disposition in the landscape. An evergreen ground cover with all-season interest, kinnikinnick produces pinkish white spring flowers, autumn red berries, and small leathery leaves that take on a reddish purple hue in cold temperatures. Slow growing, kinnikinnick is a stellar ground cover once established; a single plant can spread to nearly 4 feet. Grow it to cover large banks, the parking strip, or sections of a rockery. It's a low-maintenance plant that requires little pruning and thrives with little water. Birds find the berries a tasty source of food, while bees are attracted to the flower nectar. Like many Northwest natives, kinnikinnick can handle partial shade, making it an excellent choice for woodland gardens.

Other Common Name
Bearberry

Bloom Period and Seasonal Color
Late spring: pinkish white blooms

Mature Height × Spread
4 to 6 inches × 18 to 48 inches or more

Zones
2 to 6

Point Reyes Ceanothus
Ceanothus gloriosus

Point Reyes ceanothus is a lovely, flowering alternative to the ubiquitous tam juniper seen in older Northwest landscapes. With many cultural attributes of taller ceanothus (also called wild lilac), Point Reyes is a great shrubby ground cover from California. This broadleaf evergreen prostrate shrub can handle dry, sunny banks and is a good choice for coastal gardens. Opposite leaves are 1 to 2 inches long, glossy and serrated, covering stems that spread to 12 feet wide over rockeries or retaining walls. In March and April, Point Reyes produces inch-long medium to light blue-purple flower clusters that delight humans and bees alike. Ceanothus in any form is generally short-lived, remaining in the garden for five to ten years before eventually failing, often because of root rot.

Other Common Names
Ceanothus, Point Reyes creeper, wild lilac

Bloom Period and Seasonal Color
Spring; lavender-blue blooms

Mature Height × Spread
12 to 18 inches × 12 feet

Zones
7 to 9

When, Where, and How to Plant
Transplant nursery containers in spring or fall, situating in full to partial sun in well-drained, average soil. In native conditions, most ceanothus grows on rocky slopes. In heavy clay soil, improve drainage by incorporating organic compost to the entire bed, or topdress after planting. Space these plants 2 to 3 feet apart. For general ground cover planting tips, see page 79.

Growing Tips
Water regularly until plants are established, after which ceanothus requires irrigation only during dry spells. Ceanothus is more likely to die from overwatering than from any other problem. Feeding is unnecessary.

Care
Give this prostrate form of ceanothus a surface on which to spread, such as a brick wall or rockery. These sites will also provide necessary retained warmth for this sun-loving ground cover, which often suffers in extreme cold. Prune lightly after flowering to remove spent blooms and direct branching. Pinch back branch tips to encourage fuller growth. Powdery mildew, leaf spot, and root rot are common diseases, mostly caused by overwatering. See page 248 for tips on pest control.

Companion Planting and Design
The evergreen foliage of Point Reyes ceanothus provides a consistent show of textured green, and the tiny blooms that resemble miniature vibrant-blue lilac sprays are incomparable. For high contrast, plant Point Reyes ceanothus on a rockery where you've incorporated shades of bright yellow, such as the golden form of barberry or 'Emerald 'n Gold' euonymus. For a softer touch, use Point Reyes across the front of a pastel border of pink, cream, and pale-yellow blooms.

We Recommend
'Anchor Bay' (20 inches by 6 feet) has dense growth and dark-blue flowers. *Ceanothus gloriosus* 'Emily Brown' (2 feet by 8 feet), the best choice for heavy soil, bears dark violet-blue flowers. For a dynamic alternative to Point Reyes ceanothus, try the popular new *Ceanothus griseus* var. *horizontalis* 'Diamond Heights'. Grown primarily for its foliage, 'Diamond Heights' is a creeping form of ceanothus with lime-green and emerald splotched foliage.

Prostrate Cotoneaster

Cotoneaster species

When, Where, and How to Plant

Plant in spring, early summer, or fall. Situate plants in full to partial sun in moderately fertile, well-drained soil. Cotoneaster tolerates poor soil as long as there is adequate drainage. Follow the general guidelines for planting ground covers on page 79, spacing prostrate cotoneaster 2 to 3 feet apart. Mulch to suppress weeds until adjacent plants grow together. Prostrate cotoneaster resists frost but should be protected from wind.

Growing Tips

Water regularly until plants are established, after which cotoneaster is relatively drought tolerant. You should provide supplemental water during dry spells. Fertilizing is not generally required.

Care

Prune to manage this plant's overall appearance. It's difficult to prune while the branches are bare, but once the foliage appears, you'll notice old, damaged, or dead twigs. Thin these out by cutting to the base of the branch. If you're trying to cut back a section that grows next to a sidewalk or curb, don't shear the tips of branches. Instead cut back to lower branch joints to maintain the plant's form. Prostrate cotoneaster is generally pest free. It may suffer from occasional bouts of spider mites or powdery mildew. See page 248 for tips on pest control.

Companion Planting and Design

Prostrate cotoneaster's attractive horizontal layer of branches look best when grown against a foundation, retaining wall, or rockery. While typically grown as a ground cover, it can be trained in an espaliered pattern along a sunny wall for an elegant display. Use this ground cover to carpet a collection of gold or silver foliage conifers or broadleaf evergreen shrubs. Highlight the red berries by planting prostrate cotoneaster with other winter-interest plants like witch hazel and hellebores.

We Recommend

Cotoneaster horizontalis is a flat, spreading form with a unique zigzagging branch structure. *C. atropurpureus* 'Variegatus' features white-edged leaves. Another spreading form is *C. perpusillus* (1 foot by 6 feet), with similar branch structure and red fall foliage.

Pronounced "ca-tone-ee-aster," not "cotton Easter," this fabulous berry-laden ground cover is the prostrate form of deciduous and evergreen shrubs for Northwest gardens. Prostrate or creeping cotoneaster is an ideal solution for sunny banks, rockeries, or even parking strips. A durable ground cover for every season, prostrate cotoneaster produces an abundance of tiny white or pale-pink blooms in spring and brilliant-red berries in winter. Even when bare, the branches spread in an attractive fishbone pattern. Prostrate cotoneaster withstands poor soil conditions where other ground covers suffer. In fall, as temperatures cool, the foliage turns an attractive reddish purple. The plant is a boon to hungry winter birds, which feed on the berries all season. Tackle an overgrown cotoneaster with hard pruning, and it responds vigorously.

Other Common Name
Rockspray cotoneaster

Bloom Period and Seasonal Color
Spring; pale-pink to white blooms; foliage reddish-purple in fall

Mature Height × Spread
12 to 36 inches × 5 to 6 feet

Zones
5 to 7

Saxifrage
Saxifraga species

The genus Saxifraga is favored for rock gardens. Derived from two Latin words, saxum (rock) and frango (to break), saxifrage's name explains why it thrives in crevices of boulders and along stone pathways. Saxifrage is distinguished by its dense tufts of evergreen foliage, rounded, serrated, or in rosettes, above which emerge tiny five-petaled or star-shaped flowers on upright stems (some species bloom in spring; others in summer). The overall appearance is of flowering needles sticking out of a pincushion cluster. Some forms of saxifrage have splashy, variegated foliage; other types have dark-green foliage with a reddish green underside. This ground cover prefers partial shade and thrives in cooler climates. Saxifrage can grow in morning sun, especially when protected from hot afternoon heat.

Bloom Period and Seasonal Color
Spring to summer; pink, reddish, and white blooms

Mature Height × Spread
12 inches (flower stems to 18 inches) × 12 inches

Zones
6 to 10

When, Where, and How to Plant
Plant evergreen saxifrage in spring, early summer, or fall. Grow in moist, well-drained, humus-rich soil in deep or partial shade. (There are deciduous forms of saxifrage that can grow in sunnier locations.) Follow the guidelines for planting ground covers on page 79, spacing saxifrage 12 inches apart. Water well, and mulch to retain moisture.

Growing Tips
Keep the soil evenly moist. Do not allow the soil to dry out, but do not overwater either, because saxifrage will rot in soggy conditions. This plant has a relatively shallow root system. If your garden does not have adequate drainage, create a rockery or raised planting area to help keep saxifrage from having wet feet. This plant generally does not require fertilizer.

Care
This easy-to-grow perennial deserves more use in the landscape. Strawberry geranium (*S. stolonifera*) spreads by shoots, which produce offspring at the tips. These "babies" can be dug up, roots and all, and transplanted. Divide other forms in spring, watering transplants well until they become established. Other than occasional attacks from aphids, diseases and insects do not typically bother saxifrage.

Companion Planting and Design
While the most common use for evergreen saxifrage is in a rock garden, this is an excellent plant to cover a small area in front of taller shrubs or shade perennials. Pair saxifrage with a variety of shade-loving herbaceous plants, including astilbe, hosta, some heuchera forms, fern, and bergenia. The interesting foliage and delicate blooms are a charming addition to other, more popular, perennials. And because it is evergreen, saxifrage adds lovely interest to the winter landscape.

We Recommend
Saxifraga umbrosa produces green foliage in stiff rosettes, with rose-pink flowers on upright stems. The popular cultivar *S.* × *urbium* London Pride is a cross, with *S. umbrosa* as one of its parents. Strawberry geranium (*S. stolonifera*) features serrated, kidney-shaped, green foliage that forms dense mounds. Its white flowers (often spotted red or yellow in summer) are borne on 16-inch stems.

Vinca
Vinca species

When, Where, and How to Plant

Plant in spring, early summer, or fall. Vinca adapts to most soil types but grows best in well-drained soil. It handles sunny conditions in cooler climates, but east of the Cascades, grow it in shady locations. Follow the guidelines for planting ground covers on page 79, spacing these plants 2 feet apart. Vinca is such a vigorous grower that you may need only a few pots to cover a large area.

Growing Tips

Water vinca lightly until established; after that, it may need irrigation only during dry spells. This plant continues to thrive even when neglected. Fertilizer is unnecessary.

Care

Vinca spreads by sending out long trailing and rooting stems, which ultimately sprout new plants. You can easily dig up the young plants to grow them elsewhere or share them. Control vinca's spread by cutting back hard in early spring, mowing or edging the perimeter of a planted area. Aphids, leaf spot, and dieback occasionally affect vinca. See page 248 for tips on pest control.

Companion Planting and Design

Ideal for quickly blanketing a large area, such as a sloping hillside or infertile parking strip, vinca also makes a lovely addition to the shrub border, obscuring bare soil and providing delicate starlike flowers. Its shallow roots won't compete with trees or shrubs under which it grows. Variegated golden or white-and-green forms of vinca are great additions to planted containers, the stems draping over the edge. Even while growing above the ground in a container, vinca should be kept trimmed back. Otherwise, once it touches the ground, this plant tends to scamper away.

We Recommend

Dwarf periwinkle (*V. minor*) is the best choice as a mat-forming ground cover; it's less aggressive than *V. major* (1 to 2 feet by unlimited spread, if uncontrolled). Choose from among numerous cultivars, including *V. minor* f. *alba*, which bears white flowers; 'Illumination' with variegated yellow-and-green foliage; and 'Atropurpurea', featuring dark plum-pink blooms.

An evergreen perennial that grows in both sun and shade, vinca offers an informal, evergreen ground cover solution for many landscapes, including beds, borders, and container gardens. Lance-shaped leaves arranged oppositely along wiry stems distinguish its appearance. Ranging from light to dark green, vinca's foliage is one of its best assets; several variegated cultivars add a golden or creamy glow wherever they're planted. Equally charming are vinca's five-petaled, single blooms that appear where a leaf joins the stem. From spring through fall, blooms offer a floral spectrum ranging from white to lavender and bright pink. There seems to be no limit to periwinkle's maximum spread, and it can become invasive if not managed. Plant this ground cover where you can control its habit.

Other Common Name
Periwinkle

Bloom Period and Seasonal Color
Spring through fall; white, bright-pink, lavender, and blue-purple blooms

Mature Height × Spread
8 to 18 inches × 5 to 10 feet (if controlled)

Zones
7 to 11

Lawn Grasses *for Washington & Oregon*

As gardeners plan the use of their Northwest landscapes, lawns contribute in many ways. Green sets off the home and plants, and invites a game of badminton or a romp with children and dogs. For a comfortable, informal play surface, nothing beats a lawn. Its breathing green surface invites picnics or simply allows us to stretch out and gaze at the sky. For many homes, only a lawn provides this combination of beauty and utility. But lawns take special management for best results, with attention paid to the different growing conditions in separate climate areas of our region.

Choosing a Lawn Site

Many gardeners find they've inherited lawns planted by others, already in place and requiring care. These lawns aren't always well located. Avoid asking turf to undertake mission impossible! Grasses originate on open prairies where they get good deep soil, full sun, and frequent moisture. Lack of water, dark shade,

poor drainage (soggy in winter), or steep slopes too hard to mow make life tough for turf and for the gardener. If grass dies, weeds slip into the open spot left behind. If the lawn grows poorly in shade or on a steep slope, substitute better adapted ground covers. (See the Ground Cover chapter, page 78.)

Choose a spot that's as level as possible, in full sun. Plan the size of the lawn to meet the needs of the landscape, but don't make it too large. Washington and Oregon lawns require summer watering, and it's more economical and sensible to care for a smaller spot of turf. Consider water supplies: Is water available all summer? At what cost?

What Kind of Seed?

Seed choices for the lawn contribute substantially to its healthy survival; be sure you get the right seed mix for your climate area.

Well-Defined Mowing Edge Around Annual Plantings

An Inviting Lawn

Western Region: A mixture of perennial ryegrass and fine fescue makes the best general lawn, manages some light shade, and takes foot traffic once established. Fine fescue, though it takes shade well, will not grow in soggy wet shady spots. Turf-type tall fescues (quite drought tolerant) and colonial bentgrasses, often added to mixes, do grow well.

"Combination" lawn mixes: Gardeners in western areas may wish to try a lawn mixture developed at Oregon State University by Dr. Tom Cook; containing both grasses and broadleaf perennials like yarrow and English daisies, it resembles a meadow when in bloom. This mix, sold as EcoLawn and Fleur de Lawn (and other names) suits those who don't require a pure "putting green" lawn. It tolerates drought somewhat.

Unsuitable grasses: Bermuda grass, buffalo grass, zoysia, St. Augustine, and dryland native grasses will not grow in western coastal areas. Avoid nationally packaged mixes with high percentages of Kentucky bluegrass in them (up to about 20 percent is okay), choosing mixes for western Northwest lawns instead.

Eastern Region: Gardeners east of the mountains have more choices in lawn grasses. Perennial ryegrass, fine and turf-type tall fescues, and Kentucky bluegrass suit eastern conditions.

For a wilder area, native dryland grasses such as big bluegrass, bluebunch wheatgrass, and Idaho fescue will survive without supplemental summer irrigation once established. These bunch grasses grow in clumps and aren't suitable where a smooth surface is necessary, as in playfields. Seed dryland grasses in early spring before rains stop.

Unsuitable grasses: zoysia, mondo grass, bentgrass.

When to Plant West of the Mountains

Planting from seed: Grass seed germinates and fills in best at temperatures between 60 degrees and 85 degrees Fahrenheit. West of the mountains, April and May are ideal planting times. If planting in fall, plant early before cold weather sets in during winter, with six to eight weeks of growing time allowed for the emerging seeds, allowing the seeds to be well-rooted by October's cold weather. Roll the area after seeding to ensure firm contact of seed with prepared soil (in all regions).

Planting from sod: Western Washington and Oregon can plant sod nearly year-round, the ideal times being mid-March through mid-November.

When to Plant East of the Mountains

Planting from seed: Spring establishment, in April and May, works well; keep in mind the necessity to water the turf as it grows throughout summer. The second choice for seeding is August to September in eastern areas, earlier in that period if possible so that seeds establish before cold weather. Keep seedlings watered during early fall.

Planting from sod: Sod can be installed April through October, provided the turf is irrigated with an inch of water a week. The later it's laid in summer, the harder it is to maintain.

Installing the Lawn

Don't skimp on soil preparation before planting. Correct drainage problems, especially for lawn protection during extended wet winter weather. If the lawn puddles up or people walking across it sink to their ankles, the lawn won't grow well and roots will drown for lack of oxygen.

Get a soil test to check the pH of the existing soil. Commonly used local grass types will grow well in pH levels between 5.5 and 6.5. If you determine that lime is necessary (in western areas) to raise the pH, add it when preparing the soil and mix it in well. Turf grasses need well-drained soil with at least 6 inches of good root room, but grow best over 8 to 10 inches of well-drained soil with level terrain and full sun. If possible, use the native soil, unless it's heavy clay or largely gravel. Rototill the area, then add any amendments, tilling again after adding. Well-composted organic material (at about 10 percent by volume) can improve the water-holding ability of the soil, but it breaks down over 2 to 3 years, giving only a short-term benefit. But it can help get sod and seeds off to a good start. Level and grade the area before seeding or sodding.

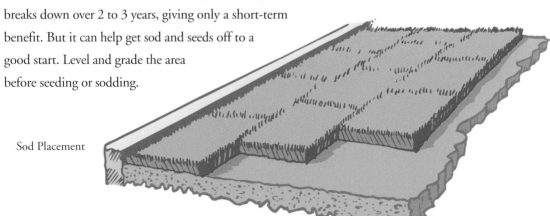

Sod Placement

Magnified View of Kentucky Bluegrass

Taking Care of the Lawn

Fertilizer

Healthy lawns require fertilizer. In all areas, consider *grasscycling*, a method of returning fine clippings to the lawn rather than removing them. This technique can supply nitrogen, often as much as 25 percent of the total yearly need for the lawn, reducing the need to apply chemical fertilizers. To grasscycle, mow often enough so that only one-third of the grass blade is being removed. (This won't work with long grass.)

Western Areas: Lawns need a 3-1-2 ratio fertilizer that supplies phosphorus and potassium, as well as nitrogen. If your lawn slopes toward water, such as a lake edge, where phosphorous is a potential water pollutant, reduce the phosphorus by selecting a formula with only nitrogen and potassium. Apply 4 pounds of actual nitrogen per year, 3 pounds if grasscycling.

Apply fertilizer four times: November 15 to December 7 (don't skip this winter fertilization), April 15, June 15, and September 1. Be sure to water after the September 1 feeding, since fall rains won't have returned. If grasscycling, you could eliminate the June 15 feeding. (Choose a slow-release form of fertilizer in late November, because it provides nutrients gradually through winter.) Some fall fertilizers also contain sulfur, which generally helps slow down lawn diseases like red thread during damp weather.

Eastern Areas: Fertilize with the 3-1-2 ratio, although lawns in eastern areas may require only nitrogen. Apply 4 pounds actual nitrogen per 1000 square feet, just as in western areas, reducing by 1 pound if grasscycling.

Apply fertilizer once between November 1 and 15, and again on May 1, June 15, and September 1 in eastern areas.

Water

Keeping the lawn green during Washington and Oregon's dry summers takes some management. Many growers allow the lawn to brown out (go dormant), returning to green with fall rains. But to show off the lawn in summer, watering is required. Proper watering soaks the roots all the way (water to 6 inches if the roots of the grass are 6 inches deep). Water in the early morning, first checking the soil moisture. Probe with a shovel or trowel; irrigate when the top 2 inches are dry and crumbly. Light, frequent sprinklings result in shallow roots. How often to water depends on air temperature and possible rainfall, because both will influence how rapidly the roots dry.

Restrictions on municipal water or the diminishment of well water sometimes reduce water supplies. If no water is available for lawns, take steps in spring to protect the turf. Dr. Gwen Stahke, Turf Agronomist at Washington State University, suggests the following:

Root Growth of Light Watering vs. Deep Watering

1. Remove any thatch to allow what water there is to penetrate.
2. Reduce fertilizer applications; once soil moisture depletes, do not fertilize. This often means skipping the June application.
3. Mow higher: 2 inches in western areas, 3 inches in eastern.
4. Control weeds by spot treating them before May 1 to keep them from using available moisture.
5. If water can be used, water the lawn to the deepest roots two or three times during the summer.
6. Keep heavy traffic off dormant lawns.
7. Reseed in fall (by October 25 in western areas). Reseeding may work best in spring in eastern areas.

Mowing

Sharpen the mower blades often, and keep them sharp. Mow often enough to cut off only one-third of the blade. In eastern areas, cut to $1^1/2$ to $2^1/2$ inches; in western areas, to 1 to 2 inches. Grasscycling allows the fine clippings to drop back onto the lawn where they break down into nitrogen and water. They don't cause thatch.

Mowing Pattern

Weed Management

Tolerating some weeds in the lawn will make chores easier. Don't think of the highly maintained golf course model, but rather a more casual and easily handled but healthy lawn.

Whatever you plant, whether sod or seed, will gradually be colonized by types of grasses that you didn't start with, and the texture of the lawn will change. Lawns over five years old contain coarser tuft grasses, as well as annual blue grasses that wave seedy stalks. While it's difficult to keep the original seed mixture established without change, overseeding will help to fill in gaps and prevent weed intrusion. (See the seeding section on page 100.)

Lawn weeds grab the opportunity to jump into spaces where grass has died; the best defense against them is maintaining a healthy, thick lawn. If you weed but don't overseed the spot, another weed will surely appear in the space. Dig out perennial weeds or spot treat them with herbicides; take weed samples to a nursery or Extension Master Gardener clinic to get them identified before choosing a specific weed-killer.

Local university specialists do not recommend using "weed and feed" type mixtures because they apply pesticides all over the lawn area, not just on the weeds. Also, stream samples from western Washington revealed the components of these products in surface water, further endangering threatened fish stocks. Lastly, they can harm nearby trees, whose roots share the same soil.

Renovation of the Existing Lawn

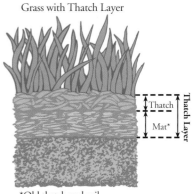

Grass with Thatch Layer

In all regions, improvements to the lawn are best done in spring, but can also be done in fall in western areas. If the lawn doesn't absorb water well or has accumulated a thick layer of thatch (dead material over the crown and roots), dethatch it. Mechanical equipment (easily rented) rakes and yanks out the thatch.

If thatch isn't a problem, but the ground is compacted, rent an aerator to pull out plugs of soil, increasing oxygen to lawn roots. Be sure to aerate after rains have left the soil moist; otherwise, the soil cores don't hold together to be pulled out. After aerating or thatching,

*Old thatch and soil

the lawn will have patchy bare spots. Reseed to allow new grass to fill in those spots and revive the lawn.

Get the Best Results

Colder eastern sections experience the end of the lawn season with ground-freezing winter temperatures. But in western Washington and Oregon, our mild winters allow the lawns to continue growing, though more slowly, and to stay green throughout winter. Gardeners expect no less, hoping that the lawn will set off winter shrubs and conifers with magazine-photo emerald color. Lawns that look best through winter in western areas have had good care during the other three seasons.

Making and following a lawn maintenance plan gets the best results in all areas. Lawns respond to sensible care; they need not be perfect, but they'll provide a frame for the garden and places to romp if given good basic attention.

— MR

Ornamental Grasses
for Washington & Oregon

Ornamental grasses, featured in many contemporary garden designs, bring texture, motion, and subtle year-round color. Many offer meadowlike freshness in spring, soft airy summer flowers, and tan seedheads holding beauty through winter. Ornamental grasses fit into nearly all landscapes, and most grow easily. From 6-inch edging plants to 10-foot traffic stoppers, there's a grass to suit your landscape need. Their popularity results in abundant new cultivar choices available for selection in nurseries.

Types of Ornamental Grasses

Grasses are classified "cool season" or "warm season" depending on their response to air and soil temperatures. Cool-season grasses such as feather reed grass, blue fescue, or blue oat grass begin their new growth early in spring and flower early. Trim them in late winter just before new growth begins. They're best for garden areas on display early in the year and make fine companions to spring bulbs.

Look to the warm-season grasses for late-summer bloom, elegant fall seedheads, and often, good fall color. They're excellent for spectacle in full-sun perennial borders or for combining with shrubs and trees for fall color interest. Warm-season grasses don't begin growth until late spring and need warmth to ripen flowers and reach their full height, often looking their best in September after a hot summer.

Tips for Successful Growth

Usually planted in spring, ornamental grasses grow slowly at first, reaching their full landscape size in their third year. Most require deep, well-prepared soils with good drainage. An organic mulch such as composted chicken manure or steer manure, applied each spring, gets them off to a good start. Fertilizer is generally not needed, but if used should be a slow-release, low-nitrogen formula applied only in spring. Too much nitrogen, especially with the larger grasses, will cause lax, floppy stems.

Ornamental grasses differ in their needs for summer water. Some, like *Carex secta* (grass look-alikes but not strictly grasses), can settle happily in bogs and along water edges. Many others tolerate dry summers. They'll cope with drought once their roots establish, but should be watered regularly for their first two garden seasons.

Early spring trimming before growth starts will take care of most maintenance for the year. Evergreen

Mixed Ornamental Grasses

grasses like blue fescue may simply need old foliage tugged loose without a full trim. But most benefit from pruning dead leaves. To trim a very large grass easily, bind it with garden twine, leaving a clear space about 6 inches above the crown for cutting. As grasses enlarge, it's necessary to enlist power tools to help with the trimming, electric hedge shears being particularly helpful.

Easily grown, ornamental grasses seldom have pest problems. Not being able to digest grass efficiently, deer won't bother them.

Choose Carefully

Choose grasses carefully. Some can become garden problems because of vigorous seeding or

Mixed Grasses of *Festuca* and *Pennisetum*

spreading by roots. Several to grow with caution or keep ontainerized are *Stipa tenuissima* (often recommended in designs), *Calamagrostis brachytricha*, and ribbon grass (*Phalaris arundinacea*). With so many rewarding choices, it's easy to skip the troublesome types.

Ornamental grasses suit the high, dry country of eastern Washington and Oregon. Once established, these take tough conditions in the coldest areas:

Big blue stem (*Andropogon gerardii*)

Quaking grass (*Briza media*)

Leather leaf sedge (*Carex buchananii*)

Blue fescue (*Festuca glauca* 'Elijah Blue')

Idaho fescue (*Festuca idahohensis*)

Blue oat grass (*Helictotrichon sempervirens*)

Chinese silver grass (*Miscanthus floridulus*)

Maiden grass (*Miscanthus sinensis* 'Gracillimus')

Red switch grass (*Panicum virgatum* 'Rehbraun')

(Source: Jan and Ray McNeilan, *The Pacific Northwest Gardener's Book of Lists*, Dallas, TX: Taylor Publishing Company, 1997.)

Getting to Know Them

Getting acquainted with ornamental grasses is like learning about perennial flowers or ground covers. Analyze what the situation needs. Think of the plant's use and contribution to the landscape: Will they be screening or focal points, using the tallest grasses such as switch grass? Or will they be woven into shrub and tree borders, or used as woodland edges? Perhaps they'll keep company with flowers in perennial borders. Many rural gardeners also use the shorter grasses on septic drain fields. For the most intimate gardens, smaller grasses such as blue oat grass or the Japanese forest grass grow happily in containers. Variations in hardiness and sun or shade needs also influence selection. Color and texture varies; grasses can provide strong foliage accents in yellow, blue green, autumnal tints, or variegated in white and green.

—*MR*

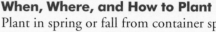

Blue Fescue
Festuca glauca

Blue fescue grows in hummocky rounded tufts up to 1 foot tall, with narrow blades of slaty blue-green covering it evenly. The growth habit gives blue fescue distinction as a ground cover when used in masses, or for accents in flower borders. One cultivar name, 'Sea Urchin', describes the visual effect, a firm half-sphere softened by foliage texture. Nearly evergreen (or everblue), blue fescue keeps its color during winter and maintains its shape year-round. A cool-season grass (see page 106) it begins fresh growth very early in spring. Easily grown, blue fescue tolerates summer dry conditions once established and requires little maintenance other than spring trimming. Summer seedheads, subtle but noticeable, repeat the blue leaf color and mature to a tan color in fall.

Bloom Period and Seasonal Color
Spring to winter; soft blue-green

Mature Height × Spread
1 to 2 feet × 1 foot

Zones
4 to 8

When, Where, and How to Plant
Plant in spring or fall from container specimens. Blue fescue needs full sun and well-drained soil for best appearance and health. It manages acidic to neutral soils but isn't good for alkaline areas where pH exceeds 8.0. Amend heavy clay soils with compost or other organic material, because blue fescue can't tolerate soggy winter conditions. Like all grasses, it develops strong roots and needs well-prepared, amended soil. Measuring from the plant centers, set these plants about 18 inches apart to allow for the best display of their rounded form without crowding.

Growing Tips
Water blue fescue weekly during its first two summer seasons, and keep it mulched. Although blue fescue is labeled "drought tolerant," it needs irrigation to its root depth at least once a month during the driest summer months even after establishment. Fertilizer isn't needed.

Care
Blue fescue grows well in summer-cool areas such as coastal Washington and Oregon. In extreme heat, it grows slowly and may appear more tan than blue by the end of summer. Ripe tan seed stalks can be trimmed off after fall or allowed to stand through winter depending on the landscape effect you prefer. In earliest spring, cut the foliage down to the crown. Do this before new growth begins. Divide when plants become crowded or the center dies out.

Companion Planting and Design
For a color echo and effective texture contrast, try blue fescue with artemisias, lavender, and rosemary, using it to edge an herb garden. In shrub borders, blue fescue contributes zest with small mugo pines and sedum 'Cape Blanco'. For a water-wise planting, blue fescue can edge Russian sage and rockroses (*Cistus* species) Its form and color benefit from sharing space with plants of contrasting texture.

We Recommend
For the best slaty blue tones, 'Elijah Blue' stands out. Hybridized in our region, 'Siskiyou Blue' makes a good accent plant, taller than most at 2 feet.

Blue Oat Grass
Helictotrichon sempervirens

When, Where, and How to Plant
Plant in spring from containers. Requiring full sun where summers stay cool, blue oat grass will take partial sun in the hottest summer regions. It needs well-drained, organically amended soil, either acidic or neutral; (see page 106 for more soil advice). Blue oat grass won't grow in soggy winter soils, so place these plants on raised beds if soil drainage can't be improved. Set them about 18 inches apart, spreading the roots and pulling them apart if matted. Good air circulation prevents disease. Mulch after planting with 2 to 3 inches of well-composted material.

Growing Tips
Water weekly during its first two summer seasons in the ground. Once established, blue oat grass will survive dry summer months with only natural rainfall. It's native to Mediterranean areas with climates resembling western Oregon and Washington. Although it doesn't require as much summer water as many other flowering perennials, it will prosper if paired with plants that do receive irrigation. Fertilizer isn't necessary. Nearly all grasses grow well without supplementary fertilizer.

Care
Trim in late winter or earliest spring, cutting old foliage off at crown level. Turn to page 106 for more grooming tips. Keep mulched to help with weed control and water retention. Blue oat grass resists pests and diseases other than rust, which can affect it in areas of high summer humidity. Blue oat grass doesn't seed itself prolifically, but if preferred, blooming stems can be trimmed away above the foliage, removing the tan developed in late summer. The seedheads don't develop as much fall drama as those of switch grass or miscanthus.

Companion Planting and Design
Blue oat grass suits windy seaside gardens and combines well with blue-flowered catmint (*Nepeta racemosa*) and artemisias, as well as other herbs. It's handsome in flower borders, setting off the pinks and blues of columbine and larkspur.

We Recommend
Blue oat grass is generally available as *Helictotrichon sempervirens*, without many cultivars. It's handsome and effective. You may see 'Saphirsprudel' (Sapphire Fountain), which has deep-blue foliage.

A handsome, graceful moderate-sized plant, blue oat grass grows in a fountain shape to about 3 feet. Cold hardy, drought tolerant, and holding its color nearly year round, it's a useful accent and helpful where much larger grasses would overwhelm available space. Flowers in early summer open pale-green and mature to soft-tan, with stems rising above the foliage. Resembling oats before harvest, flowers dangle attractively as seeds ripen. This cool-season grass starts vigorously in early spring, giving it good garden presence before warm-weather grasses commence growth. Use blue oat grass against rocks, in perennial borders, or informally on mixed-planting hillsides. It's easily grown, requiring full sun but otherwise undemanding. In the coldest winters, its blue foliage fades, but revives after spring trimming.

Bloom Period and Seasonal Color
Year-round; blue foliage; tan blooms in fall

Mature Height × Spread
2 to 3 feet × 2 feet

Zones
4 to 8

Chinese Silver Grass
Miscanthus sinensis

Chinese silver grass, a big clump-former, can soar 6 to 7 feet with some of the most beautiful foliage and flowers of any ornamental grass. A warm-weather grass, it develops reluctantly in cool spring temperatures, reaching full size in late summer, producing soft feathery flower plumes held well above the leaves. Foliage and flowers mature to silvery tan, with a presence that stays through winter to grace the dormant landscape, shining with rain and snow. Grown for centuries in Japan and China, and celebrated in Asian art, Chinese silver grass provides nearly year-round beauty. Nurseries carry many cultivars that vary in ultimate height and foliage color, but all types demand space, being best used as specimen plants in shrub borders, or as translucent screening.

Other Common Names
Maiden grass, Japanese silver grass

Bloom Period and Seasonal Color
Summer; pinkish blooms; tan-gold in fall and winter

Mature Height × Spread
5 to 8 feet × 3 to 5 feet

Zones
5 to 9

When, Where, and How to Plant
Plant in spring from container plants or rooted divisions, keeping crowns at soil surface. *Miscanthus sinensis* needs full sun in cool-summer areas and well-drained soil. Sun needs vary with different cultivars. Most require full sun to keep the clumps sturdy and compact, but maiden grass (*Miscanthus sinensis* 'Gracillimus') can manage in partial sun of four hours a day. Warm temperatures help with flower and seedhead production; in cooler shady locations, it may not flower well. Set the divisions at least 3 feet apart—visualize a 7-foot plant in the spot!

Growing Tips
Ultimate size depends on the amount of summer irrigation. Water weekly during the first few years until the plants are deeply rooted. Miscanthus doesn't tolerate our region's dry summers and needs twice-monthly irrigation even after establishment. But like many plants grown here, it's smaller and sturdier with less water and will thrive if irrigated to root depth monthly rather than more frequently. Fertilizer isn't necessary if the soil is well mulched with compost. Keep 2 to 3 inches of mulch over the roots.

Care
No pests bother Chinese silver grass. Like many ornamental grasses, miscanthus reaches its ultimate size slowly, often taking three years to display its full landscape effect. Divide in earliest spring. Grass expert Piet Oudolf suggests slicing divisions off the rootball without removing it from the ground, leaving the main plant intact and rooted.

Companion Planting and Design
Elegant as single specimen plants or as a grouping behind lower growing perennial flowers, miscanthus offers several seasons of interest. As a pond edging, not in water but adjacent, its fountainlike presence is spectacular. In a shrub grouping, it complements mugo pines, nandina, and purple-leaved smokebush.

We Recommend
More choices abound in miscanthus cultivars than in other grasses. Maiden grass (*Miscanthus sinensis* 'Gracillimus'), with its white-striped leaf stays at 4-5 feet. 'Sarabande' and 'Andante' have wider foliage blades and flower reliably. Try 'Morning Light' for its greater drought tolerance.

Feather Reed Grass

Calamagrostis × *acutiflora* 'Karl Foerster'

When, Where, and How to Plant

Plant in spring from containers in full sun. Feather reed grass doesn't adapt to shade, becoming spindly and floppy. Soil pH should be between 6.0 and 7.0, the same range necessary for most flower and vegetable gardens. Set plants about 2 feet apart at the same level they were in the containers. Mulch with compost 2 to 3 inches deep.

Growing Tips

Water weekly during the first summer season. This grass grows well in moist soils, but will adapt to drier conditions once its roots are established (see page 106 for more details). It grows taller with regular water. Like many grasses, feather reed grass doesn't require fertilizer if the soil is well amended with compost. Too much nitrogen reduces flowering and grows lax, droopy stems.

Care

Feather reed grass doesn't seed itself or become invasive, although the clumps will gradually grow larger over the years. A perennial but deciduous grass, its leaves die down over winter to be replaced with new spring growth. Divide plants, when necessary, in earliest spring before active growth starts. (Feather reed grass initiates growth earlier than most ornamental grasses, often as early as March.) Older clumps may require chopping apart with mattock or axe, because their tough matted roots resist shovels. Allow dried seedheads to remain standing over winter, then cut the plants to about 6 inches in spring—before growth commences. It suffers from no pests or diseases.

Companion Planting and Design

These make handsome small hedges for patio and walkway edges, looking best in summer and fall. Large enough to be specimen plants, a trio can anchor a late-summer flower border including rudbeckias, asters, and purple-leaved barberries.

We Recommend

Both showy and easy to grow, 'Karl Foerster' suits many garden designs. A selection from it, *Calamagrostis* × *acutiflora* 'Overdam', grows slightly shorter, with variegated leaves (to about 3 feet). Yellow spring leaf margins turn white as summer progresses, combining well with yarrow and white boltonia.

Grass with panache, feather reed grass offers vigorous deep-green summer foliage, producing tall, sculptural tan-orange seedheads through fall and into winter, when the entire plant turns gold. Feather reed grass grows upright, making it a useful partner for see-through hedges and an excellent accent in a perennial flower border. The "reed" in its name signifies the firm stems, while "feather" connotes both the summer bloom and the ripened fall seeds as they move with wind. This cool-season grass comes into strong growth in early spring rather than waiting for warm temperatures. Its summer height can reach 4 feet once established, with flower stalks rising taller, blooming in tones of soft purple-brown through mid- to late summer. Here's an all-season winner.

Bloom Period and Seasonal Color

Spring; green and purple blooms; golden seedheads in fall and winter

Mature Height × Spread

5 to 6 feet × 2 feet

Zones

5 to 9

Sedge

Carex species and cultivars

Varied and useful for many different soil types, ever-green and deciduous, sedges can adapt to situations from soggy shade to full sun. Tractable and easily grown, they shine when massed as ground cover. They appreciate cool summers, and many settle nicely into woodlands. Most sedges remain evergreen throughout winter in their zonal range, and some have permanently brown foliage. They're not grasses, botanically speak-ing, but their fine foliage and clumping form give them a grass effect in landscape design. They don't flower prominently as grasses do, but provide year-round value for fine texture and color. From 1 to 3 feet tall, they tuck into designs as fillers and edgers. Sedge thrives in container plantings and contributes contemporary freshness when used in mixed perennial groupings.

Bloom Period and Seasonal Color
Year-round foliage color; yellow, white, green, bronze, and bicolors

Mature Height × Spread
1 to 3 feet × 1 to 5 feet

Zones
4 to 9

When, Where, and How to Plant
Plant in spring from containers or divisions. Choose light exposure depending on an individual cultivar's specific needs. All thrive in partial sun, though color on golden cultivars is strongest in bright light. Prepare well-amended soil. Set plants about 1 foot apart, except for the *Carex comans* types, which can spread to 5 feet in diameter and should be planted at least 4 feet apart from center to center.

Growing Tips
Sedge doesn't require fertilizer. Keep mulched, using 2 to 3 inches of compost. Water require-ments differ depending on the species, so check with the nursery when purchasing. All types need regular watering, weekly, for their first two years.

Care
Pests don't bother sedge. Spring care for the ever-green and bronze types consists of pulling and combing out old foliage with your fingers to make room for new growth. *C. elata* 'Aurea' is deciduous and can be cut down in late winter. Though flowers aren't noticeable on sedge, many seed themselves readily.

Companion Planting and Design
Used as soft "bridge" plants, sedges fill in spaces between stiffer, more upright plants in perennial borders. Sun-loving *C. testacea*, its pale-green leaves tinged with orange, looks great in front of yarrow and daylilies. Many sedges take the partial shade of woodlands, such as bronzy *C. flagellifera*. For edging paths in partial shade, *C. morrowii* 'Variegata' features white leaf margins. Plantain-leaf sedge (*C. plantaginea*) tolerates dry shade.

We Recommend
Check labels carefully; needs vary. For winter cold and summer dryness, try *C. morrowii* 'Aureovariegata', growing 1 foot tall with green and yellow striped leaves. *C. buchananii* stays bronze year-round in zone 7 and makes a good accent plant in containers. For pond edges, Bowles' golden sedge (*Carex elata* 'Aurea') can endure con-stantly wet soils, but it can also partner with perennials if irrigated regularly. *C. comans*, ever-green and tidy, makes a neat ground cover, often spreading to more than 3 feet wide; it has a brown cultivar, *C. comans* 'Bronze Form'.

Switch Grass
Panicum virgatum

When, Where, and How to Plant

Plant in spring or fall from containers; the larger grasses like switch grass are easier to handle when they are dormant in late winter, just after trimming, but they will also survive fall planting. Switch grasses cope well with either well-drained sandy soils or those holding water in winter. (Wet, but not a permanent bog.) They need full sun, as do all prairie plants. This fine seaside grass tolerates either salt spray or direct wind. Space them 2 feet apart, mulching after planting.

Growing Tips

Switch grasses originate in areas that receive more summer rain than do Washington and Oregon. The less water the grass gets in the garden, the shorter and less lush it will be. Provide regular water through the first growing season to get it established, and then observe how the grass adapts to dry summers in following years. Water monthly if you want it taller once established. The "dry size" switch grass may suit your landscape. Fertilizing isn't necessary, though some growers use a low-nitrogen formula like a 5-10-10 in the first growing season, providing only mulch in subsequent years. Too much fertilizer tends to make switch grass lanky and encourage its tendency to flop open rather than stand tall.

Care

Cut back winter foliage in earliest spring, leaving about 6 inches above the crown. Divide in early spring after cutting back. No pests bother this grass; deer don't eat grasses.

Companion Planting and Design

Switch grasses make natural companions to spring-blooming bulb plantings because they're short during bulb flowering but shoot up to disguise the fading foliage. Hillside or slope plantings, combined with other prairie plants like rudbeckias and annual sunflowers, provide casual but fascinating late-summer beauty.

We Recommend

'Shenandoah' and 'Heavy Metal' start with blue-toned leaves, turning deep tan in fall. Both reach 5 feet with taller flowers. Red-tinged foliage in August makes 'Rotstrahlbusch' a standout, especially when sited where afternoon sun backlights it.

Switch grasses, native to the American prairies though not to the coastal West, get their "ornamental" title from the beauty of their flowers and the varied colors of their foliage. Warm-season grasses (see page 106), they grow slowly until soil and air temperatures increase. Hot days rocket them into height, with foliage to 3 to 4 feet, in tones of mid-blue or mid-green. Late-summer flowering brings a gauzy veil of soft pinkish tan blooms on 5-foot stems. Sturdy and cold adapted, switch grasses form large but well-shaped clumps, turning gold or even deep burgundy in fall. Their best garden value lies in the vividness of their late summer and autumn presence, when seedheads turn gold, persisting into late winter.

Bloom Period and Seasonal Color
Summer; tan blooms and blue-green foliage; gold and red in fall

Mature Height × Spread
5 feet × 3 feet

Zones
4 to 9

Perennials *for Washington & Oregon*

Gardeners everywhere have had a long love affair with perennials. There's an old adage that we love flowers when we're young gardeners, only to "mature" and move on to more substantial preferences such as shrubs and trees. Even if this saying is partially true, we can't live without flowers in our lives. There's a perennial to fit every design challenge, backyard condition, or garden style around. Perennials are the plants that keep on giving!

Many Choices

The true definition of a perennial encompasses trees, shrubs, and flowering plants, since they each complete their full life cycle in three or more years. In this chapter, we use the term *perennial* to refer to *herbaceous* perennials, plants that generally die to the ground with the onset of frost, only to renew their growth the following spring.

In the milder areas of the Northwest, *perennial* can also include some woody herbs, or subshrubs (such as lavender, artemisia, and germander), and evergreen perennials that do not lose their foliage in winter (such as pinks, bergenia, or bear's breeches).

Get to know and grow the 40 perennials featured in this chapter. They are some of our favorites, but represent only a small sampling of hundreds of incredible plant choices available to you.

You can explore the Northwest perennial world by joining a perennial plant society, touring any number of spectacular perennial display gardens, and shopping at plant sales where you can meet many talented growers who run their own plant trials before recommending them to home gardeners. Local organizations include:

Northwest Perennial Alliance
P.O. Box 85565, Seattle
WA 98145-1565
425-814-1481
www.northwestperennialalliance.org

Hardy Plant Society of Oregon
1930 N.W. Lovejoy St.
Portland, OR 97209-1504
503-224-5718
www.hardyplantsociety.org

Willamette Valley Hardy Plant Group
c/o Deb Parmalee, Treasurer
174 Mecca Avenue
Eugene, OR 97404
www.thehardyplantgroup.org.

Purple
Coneflower

Developing Good Planting Habits

To help you use the plant profiles, here are general recommendations defining planting, growing, and care tips.

Planting perennials in autumn is a wonderful habit to adopt, as it affords plants a few months in the ground to establish their roots before going dormant. You can often find great perennials at fall plant sales or, better yet, enjoy good discounts on perennials that have just spent the entire summer in a plastic nursery pot. Those are the ones you'll need to plant immediately in September or October to help them settle into the ground before winter.

East of the mountains, spring planting is generally preferable. You can plant in early spring (west of the Cascades) or late spring (east of the Cascades), giving perennials a chance to grow in milder conditions before summer's dry season arrives.

Hardy Geranium Border

Where to plant is determined by your garden's conditions. This chapter suggests 20 great sun perennials and 20 great shade perennials. Sun and shade perennials encompass a vast continuum; so feel free to experiment with those midrange plants that require partial sun or partial shade. You'll find that sun-loving perennials bloom less prolifically in the shade or that a partial-shade perennial can thrive in a sunny mixed container, with frequent watering.

We like to joke that all the best plants require "moist, well-drained soil." But that kind of garden utopia is hard to come by, and you will likely require amendments to improve your soil. Follow the guidelines offered in our general introduction (see pages 9 to 18) to determine the type of soil in your garden.

Aster 'Purple Dome'

Planting herbaceous perennials gives you opportunity to amend soil for each individual plant, adding organic amendments and fertilizer to the soil surface for a plant's specific need. If you are planting a border or large bed, however, plants will benefit if you prepare the entire area. Choose a location that is level or sloped, but avoid low-lying areas of the garden where water will pool or drain slowly. These tips are appropriate for both perennial plantings and mixed plantings that incorporate shrubs, bulbs, and annuals along with perennial plants.

The main goal of amending a planting area is to improve drainage, as research has shown that herbaceous plants in mild areas are more likely to die from overwatering and soggy soil conditions than from cold temperatures.

Begin by removing any unwanted plants such as turf or weeds (make sure to dig down deeply to remove the root system). Remove larger rocks and stones. To loosen soil deeply, many gardeners like to "double-dig," a technique of digging up 6- to 8-inch-deep "trenches" and tossing the dirt into the next row you've dug until an entire area is worked, with the soil from the first row being moved back to fill in the last. This method also helps incorporate oxygen into the soil.

If that sounds too ambitious, then build up your planting area by incorporating organic matter, such as composted yard waste or well-composted manure, into the planting bed. A good ratio is to add one-third by volume (or 4 inches per 12 inches of soil).

When adding a few perennials here and there, you may not be able to prepare a large planting area. In that case, dig a hole equal to the depth of the nursery pot and at least twice its width. Enrich each planting area by adding organic compost over the native soil. Be sure to situate the perennial so that the top of the soil in the nursery pot is level with your garden soil.

Watering Is An Art

Learning how to water appropriately is one of the most nuanced skills a gardener can obtain. In addition to following our advice and plant-specific suggestions later in this chapter, try cultivating the art of observation in your garden. Watch your perennials for clues as to whether they need water.

Your plant is probably not receiving adequate irrigation if the foliage is wilted or dry around the edges, or if otherwise long-blooming flowers fade quickly.

Just-planted perennials require about an inch of water per week, delivering water to developing roots. As perennials establish, even by the second season, you can switch to infrequent watering that deeply saturates the plants' root area. Typically, the frequency of spring showers on the west side of the Cascades means you may not need to provide supplemental water until Memorial Day or later. East of the mountains, watering may be needed much earlier in the spring. In spite of dry times, more perennials suffer from overwatering than from underwatering, so if you err, err on the side of restraint. It's much easier to quickly resuscitate a thirsty perennial than to try to "dry out" a waterlogged one.

Once the extended dry periods of June, July, August, and September arrive, you'll need to supplement irrigation with a soaker hose, drip irrigation, in-ground irrigation, or hand watering. And after October 1, your watering tasks will diminish greatly, with the arrival of precipitation in the form of rain or snow and the fall dormancy of plants that have stopped growing.

You'll find some general tips about watering in this book's introduction (see page 14). A key with perennials, as with most plants, is to water at the base of the plant, keeping water off the foliage. Moisture on foliage increases disease problems like powdery mildew.

As with annuals, follow these watering guidelines:

Moist soil: Cool, slightly damp soil in the top 6 to 8 inches or through the root area.

Regular or moderate water: Weekly or twice weekly watering. The top 1 to 2 inches of the soil may dry out before rewatering.

Dry periods: When a plant needs water during "excessive dry spells," this refers to a typical Northwest summer where there is no significant precipitation for two weeks or longer. When you irrigate, water deeply, to 8 to 12 inches or through the root area.

Another term used in this chapter is "evenly moist," which refers to the way in which you apply water, making sure the plant's root zone or site is watered without uneven puddles or dry spots.

Fertilizing Tips

The care and feeding of perennials includes fertilization with a light hand. Overfeeding can lead to a profusion of leafy foliage and few flowers. A general-purpose feeding at the beginning of the blooming season is a good practice. Use a general-purpose fertilizer, such as a 5-1-1 or 6-2-2, which is good for perennials. When added to the planting hole, they help stimulate healthy root growth.

If you plant perennials in well-prepared soil that's been amended as mentioned above, if you add fertilizer after planting, and if you mulch well to retain moisture, you may not need to fertilize for the first several years after you've planted a perennial in your garden. Subsequent fertilizer should be added as spring growth begins, following label instructions. Fertilize moderately.

The Best Defense Is A Healthy Plant

The perennials recommended in this chapter are generally free of pests and diseases. Yet the presence of annoying pests (slugs, aphids, leaf miners, and spider mites) is a fact of life in any Northwest garden. Gauge your desire to eradicate pests against the importance of keeping synthetic pesticides out of the earth and our region's water table. Can you address pest removal in organic, nontoxic ways, such as blasting aphids with a jolt of water from the nozzle or slathering an infestation with insecticidal soap? Can you lower your standards of perfection and accept a few bites in the hosta foliage?

Keep in mind that a pest- or disease-infested perennial may be susceptible because of cultural conditions that have put the plant under stress. Weak perennials are more susceptible to attack. Look first at the health of your garden's soil (and drainage) before you embark on a pest-control campaign. Evaluate whether plants require removal of dead or damaged foliage and whether they are being watered appropriately. For more tips on plant health care, see page 248.

Poor growing conditions can encourage fungal diseases, such as powdery mildew. Follow good grooming techniques and you'll improve air circulation around perennials. If you are stumped, or need additional tips for addressing pest and disease control in the perennial garden, check the experts at your local specialty nursery or through the plant diagnostic clinic run by local Extension Master Gardeners. And remember, if a plant is infested with disease or pests, perhaps you really don't want it in your garden after all. We should enjoy the beauty and fragrance of perennials in the landscape, rather than spending our time keeping a poor performing one alive.

As for grooming, you'll want to follow these general guidelines:

Deadheading: By removing old or spent flowers on perennials, you not only tidy up the plant's appearance, you help it continue to produce new blooms (and stop putting its energy into seed production). Cut off the plant's spent flower head using pruning shears or floral scissors (the density of the stem will determine what tool you use). If the plant is as receptive to deadheading as daylily (*Hemerocallis*), bare hands will work! You can cut off the terminal bud (the flower at the end of the stem), which will often result in new buds emerging from the leaf axil below the dead bud. Perennials such as yarrow, campanula, gaura, and helenium respond well to being deadheaded, often reblooming.

Sometimes you should cut the entire blooming stalk back to the crown of the plant, either to encourage rebloom (as with delphinium) or to tidy the plant, as with daylilies or peonies that have finished blooming. Deadheading can also help control some recurrent diseases, as with peony botrytis, especially if affected foliage is also removed. Experiment with how well deadheading improves the appearance of each perennial in the garden.

Staking: If a floppy perennial needs to be staked, select an unobtrusive method, such as encircling the plant with twigs and thin branches you've pruned from a tree. A gifted garden designer we know relies on thin, black plastic ties that are typically used by electricians. She can tie up tall perennials (she often anchors them to nearby woody plants or the branches of rose shrubs) and the black tie visually disappears. When the season is over, the inexpensive tie can be cut and thrown away.

Shearing: Shearing of certain perennials occurs after blooming and should be done with long gardening clippers or hedge shears. The goal is to remove spent blooms and gently shape the perennial, on woody plants like lavender or ground cover types like lady's mantle, so that the foliage regrows or fills in for the rest of the growing season. Cut just below the blooms or lower down on the stem, depending on the look you want.

Cutting back: There is no right or wrong place to cut back a tall perennial that's finished blooming. Sometimes it's desirable to leave the seedhead on the plant (such as with black-eyed Susan or purple coneflower) so that backyard birds can enjoy the seeds. Other times, you should cut to the base of the stem or partway down the stem to create a clean or tidy appearance. Before the start of the spring growing season, you can cut back any perennials that haven't been groomed. Notice the new basal growth and cut any old stems to just above this location.

Perennial Favorites

Whether you want a cutting garden filled with sturdy flowers that will hold up in a vase of water for a week's time or you want to plant drifts of architectural blooms that add pattern and texture to your garden, perennials are for you. They can be high maintenance, but we've recommended a selection of choice perennials that are strong on beautiful features with easy maintenance. Once you become a "perennialist," you'll appreciate the diversity and landscape value of many herbaceous flowering plants. With little attention, they return year after year with glorious flowers, fabulous foliage, and interesting forms. No wonder we enjoy the term "perennial favorites"!

—*DP & MR*

Artemisia
Artemisia species

Artemisia is a woody evergreen herb that adds appealing, soft textures to the landscape. In hot, sunny sites, it provides a restful, silvery counterpoint to bold colors and forms. A member of the daisy family, artemisia is more appreciated for its foliage than its tiny yellow or white flowers. Finely cut or feathery, billows of artemisia serve as delicate accents to the summer border. Their eye-catching foliage is even more noteworthy during winter months. Some forms of artemisia are considered aggressive, although it's possible to control eagerly spreading plants with pruning. Use the upright forms to create a halo of silver that backs dark-purple and wine-colored plants. Trailing forms are ideal for containers and rockeries. This plant is a must for the water-wise garden. —DP

Other Common Names
Wormwood, white sage

Bloom Period and Seasonal Color
Evergreen; grown for its silvery foliage

Mature Height × Spread
2 to 3 feet × 2 to 3 feet

Zones
4 to 9

When, Where, and How to Plant
Artemisia can be planted in spring or early summer and in fall, when temperatures again cool. Choose a sunny, well-drained location. Artemisia will grow in most types of soil, although it tends to spread more in overly moist, clay soil. Plant in informal groupings or use upright forms as a tidy edging to a formal border (you can clip artemisia). Follow the general guidelines for planting perennials on page 115. Space plants 2 to 3 feet apart.

Growing Tips
Water regularly until the plants are established. Do not allow artemisia to sit in soggy soil. Fertilizing is unnecessary; it will encourage aggressive spreading. See page 117 for more watering tips.

Care
Artemisia generally resists pests and diseases, especially if planted in a hot, well-drained location. It can suffer from root rot if overwatered. This is a plant that responds well to pruning. Remove dead or broken stems, and watch for aggressive spreading by underground runners. Keep artemisia in check by digging and dividing every few years. You can renovate artemisia by cutting back hard in late spring after the threat of frost has passed.

Companion Planting and Design
As an artist would gild a dark wooden frame with touches of silverleaf, the lacy forms of artemisia can embellish your garden with glowing touches of appealing foliage. Plant a border as a backdrop to dark-leafed heuchera and purple New Zealand flax. Artemisia can set off bold, sunny border plants like crocosmias, daylilies, and black-eyed Susans. It can also be paired with a palette of pastel bloomers, such as lavender and yarrow.

We Recommend
Use an upright form for borders, such as *Artemisia ludoviciana* 'Silver Queen'. *Artemisia* 'Powis Castle' is a classic addition to the formal garden, softly spreading below taller, more architectural plants. 'Silver Brocade' is a lovely, trailing form that is a good choice for containers and baskets. For a variegated surprise, try *Artemisia vulgaris* Oriental Limelight 'Janlim', with finely cut gold-and-green foliage.

Aster
Aster species

When, Where, and How to Plant
Plant in spring or early summer. Asters prefer moist, average soil in full sun. Some varieties tolerate partial sun, while other varieties tolerate extremely wet conditions, so check plant tags for additional growing information. Follow the general guidelines for planting perennials on page 115. Space plants 3 to 4 feet apart, allowing for good air circulation.

Growing Tips
Water regularly until the plants are established, then water during dry spells. Always water at the base of the plant in order to keep the foliage dry and free of mildew free. You can retain moisture with a 2-inch layer of organic mulch. Asters generally don't require fertilizer.

Care
Asters prefer a sunny, airy location where they won't be crowded. Choose mildew-resistant varieties. Pinch out the tips of young plants to encourage a compact form. To ensure maximum flowering, cut back the plant at the base of flowers after blooming. Remove dead twigs and thin branches of crowded plants. Asters benefit from frequent division. Dig and divide in fall, after blooming, or in early spring.

Companion Planting and Design
Asters add a soft pillow of color to mixed borders with dwarf conifers and flowering shrubs. They also pair well with ornamental grasses for a prairie-style design. Determine where to grow asters by evaluating your garden in late summer. Note the "bare" spots, and consider whether a punch of purple blooms could improve the appearance. Some of the heath asters have dark-purple foliage and sprays of tiny white flowers, adding a much-needed touch of drama to the border. Plant them informally to cover a sunny bank or as a mid-height addition to the perennial border.

We Recommend
Aster novae-angliae 'Purple Dome' produces heavy swaths of purple on an 18-inch mounded plant. *Aster novi-belgii* has toothed foliage and hundreds of cultivars, including 'Little Red Boy', a 24-inch plant with masses of bright-red flowers. Compact *Aster lateriflorus* 'Prince' features dark-purple foliage, with pink-centered white flower heads.

The happiest flowers of the late-summer and fall garden, asters seem always to bloom just when all the other perennials are wrapping up their performances. A group of more than 250 mostly herbaceous perennials, asters carry the last act of your garden's summer show, sharing small daisylike blooms in masses of intense color. The bushy New England aster produces sprays of 1- to 2-inch yellow-centered purple and pink flowers. The New York aster has delicate flowers on toothed foliage. The heath aster is a favorite for its tiny, billowing flowers. Asters require some maintenance, from shearing after they bloom to staking the taller forms. But the pure joy asters bring to a late-summer garden overcomes the work required to keep them looking tidy. —DP

Other Common Name
Michaelmas daisy

Bloom Period and Seasonal Color
Late summer and fall; lavender-blue, pink, purple, and white blooms

Mature Height × Spread
1¹/₂ to 5 feet × 2 to 4 feet

Zones
4 to 8

Astilbe
Astilbe hybrids and cultivars

The ferny foliage of astilbe would enliven moist shade and woodland gardens even without bloom, but with astilbe you gain summer color unsurpassed in shade. Fluffy panicles of flowers from crisp white to deep burgundy make choosing just one difficult. If you select cultivars that bloom at different times, you'll enjoy a summer-long show. Early types include many of the garden hybrids like pale-pink 'Rheinland', followed in August by A. chinensis var. taquetii, with dark-magenta spires, and A. chinensis 'Pumila', dusty pink blooming into September. Red or burgundy cultivars, such as 'Fanal' have red-tinged foliage in spring. Some stay only 1 foot tall, spreading gradually into attractive ground covers. Winter interest from bronzed leaves and dried mahogany flower stems gives nearly year-round value. —MR

Other Common Name
False spirea

Bloom Period and Seasonal Color
Summer; white, cream, pink, red, and burgundy blooms

Mature Height × Spread
1 to 4 feet × 1 to 2 feet

Zones
3 to 8

When, Where, and How to Plant
Plant in spring from containers, in soil amended with compost. Fall planting also works, but in cold areas install during September when the soil is still warm enough for good root establishment. The more light astilbes receive, the more water they require. Along pond edges, place astilbes above the immediate water edge on higher ground for drainage. It does best in rich, well-amended soil, staying evenly moist. But well-drained soil is vital. Slow to establish, astilbe comes into its full beauty in its third year and then continues as a long-lived perennial. The tallest forms stand sturdily without staking, even when flower stalks reach 4 feet. *Astilbe chinensis* 'Pumila' will stand zone 3 and takes drier soil, especially if in rich soil in shade. For general guidelines on planting perennials, see page 115.

Growing Tips
Fertilizer is necessary to support vigorous growth. Apply a high-nitrogen fertilizer (6-2-2 or 10-10-10) in early spring just as new growth begins. Composted manures, spread around plants in spring and fall, also help. Astilbe dies in dry soils, requiring careful placement of irrigation to get it through even normal summers here, when rain is always scarce. Plants lacking moisture show brown leaf edges at first, followed by the loss of whole leaves and the death of the plant's crown.

Care
Allow blooms to stand through winter for their attractive dried plumage; cut them back in earliest spring as growth starts. Pests don't bother these plants, though deer can munch them to nubbins.

Companion Planting and Design
Astilbe harmonizes with Victorian, formal, or cottage garden designs, its plumes of color striking in contrast with hostas, Solomon's seals, and ferns. Along water margins, combine them with *Iris spuria* or another Japanese iris.

We Recommend
'Sprite', a shell pink, makes a good ground cover when planted in groups. For a white garden, *Astilbe × arendsii* 'Bridal Veil' shines out at night with Casablanca lilies. 'Glow' lives up to its name with deep-red flowers.

Bear's Breeches
Acanthus mollis

When, Where, and How to Plant
Plant in spring, choosing a full- or partial-sun site with well-drained soil. Bear's breeches requires moisture-retentive soils amended with compost or other organic material. (See page 115 for tips on planting perennials.) Another species, *Acanthus spinosus*, grows well in gravelly soils in more sun than *Acanthus mollis*; it's also hardier, to zone 5. Allow ample space for the plants of either species to expand. Propagate by 2- to 3-inch root cuttings or by dividing the plants in spring (being certain to water them through the subsequent summer).

Growing Tips
Fertilize once in spring, using a moderate nitrogen formula such as a 5-1-1 when growth starts. Soaker hoses around the plants can help with establishment. Both species tolerate less than 1 inch per week water in summer once established. Mulch after growth stops in late fall.

Care
The foliage is winter hardy in zones 7 and above; remove the most tattered leaves at the end of winter as new growth emerges. This plant may not bloom until settled for two to three years. In cold-winter areas, the plants may be killed to the ground but will produce new leaves; in coldest winters, the plant won't flower the following summer. In dry soils, the plants spread less vigorously. Slugs may damage plants in earliest spring. *Acanthus spinosus* develops heavily spiny leaf edges, and spines persist on the flowers; prune when the plants go dormant before winter, since the leaves are so large that their winter decline creates a noticeable mess.

Companion Planting and Design
Acanthus mollis associates well with the perennial sword fern (*Polystichum munitum*), providing strong textural contrast. Try it fronting plants like wax myrtle (*Myrica californica*) with their very slender leaves. It's also a good formal foundation planting, ideal for Mediterranean-style gardens.

We Recommend
Where you want color contrast, use *Acanthus mollis* 'Hollard's Gold', which grows to only 2 feet and has brilliant-yellow spring foliage shading to green later in summer.

Sculptural presence comes with bear's breeches, showy in both leaf and flower. Individual leaves, often evergreen in milder areas, can spread to 12 inches across with distinctive deeply cut edges. The form is familiar from ancient architecture when the leaves were copied for the design topping Corinthian columns. Shiny, deep-green leaves with a leathery texture often reach 3 feet tall on a plant 4 feet wide. Once established, bear's breeches sends up summer bloom stalks above the leaves in subtle tones of white striped in purple for the basic bloom and deep purple-gray bracts hooded over the flower. Suited to woodland edge plantings, it thrives in partial sun and naturalizes vigorously. Slow to establish, acanthus settles in for decades once it does, forming distinctive clumps.
—MR

Bloom Period and Seasonal Color
Summer; cream and purple blooms

Mature Height × Spread
3 to 4 feet × 4 feet

Zones
5 to 10

Bellflower
Campanula species and hybrids

Fill your garden with bells of purple, blue, and white when you plant this beautiful perennial. With more than 300 species, you can readily find a bellflower to grow in a sunny border, a rockery, or a meadow. Choose from erect forms with tall stems resembling true-blue delphiniums to delicate creeping bellflowers that are at home in rock gardens. Large, open bells or tiny fluted starlike blooms offer their charm on stems emerging from leaf rosettes. Many bellflowers come from the Mediterranean region, reflecting their sun-loving nature, although there is also a species found wild in Alaska. This is an easy-to-grow perennial to incorporate into a cottage garden, where the addition of blue adds a cool comfort to pastel shades and more intense colors alike. —DP

Bloom Period and Seasonal Color
Early to midsummer; blue, purple, and white blooms

Mature Height × Spread
8 to 24 inches × 8 to 14 inches

Zones
4 to 7

When, Where, and How to Plant
While bellflowers enjoy sunny, warm locations, they don't tolerate drought and will fail in dry soil. Choose a location in moist, well-drained soil in full or partial sun (afternoon shade is ideal). Follow the general guidelines for planting perennials on page 115. Space bellflower plants about 1 feet apart.

Growing Tips
Water regularly until the plants are established, then irrigate well during dry spells. You can help roots to retain moisture with a 2-inch layer of organic mulch. In poor soil, feed bellflower with a nitrogen fertilizer in spring.

Care
Bellflowers are generally pest free, although slugs sometimes chew lower leaves. If situated properly, bellflowers should be free of disease. You can either deadhead to encourage a second flush of blooms or cut the stem back to its base. Taller forms of bellflower may require staking, although some gardeners grow them between tall companions to prevent flopping. To maintain the vigor of bellflower's bloom, dig and divide every two to three years in spring or fall. Feed lightly after dividing and replanting sections. Or pot up divisions and donate them to a friend's garden.

Companion Planting and Design
Use the inviting blue shades of campanula to complement other cool-toned perennials, including Russian sage, catmint, and Jacob's ladder. The cup-shaped blooms serve as soft, romantic companions in rose borders, helping to hide thorny stems. Choose a spreading form like Dalmatian bellflower to carpet a rockery or edge a border. Peach-leaf bellflower is a popular choice for the cutting garden.

We Recommend
Carpathian bellflower (*Campanula carpatica*), a low-growing species, forms a thick clump of foliage covered with cupped blooms in pale-blue or white. *C. latiloba* has fantastic spikes of purple-blue blooms to 3 feet in midsummer. *C. portenschlagiana* 'Resholt's Variety' is a sweet form, ideal for a rockery, with deep-blue bells. Peach-leaf bellflower (*C. persicifolia*) features narrow, wavy-edged foliage. It grows to 3 feet on sturdy stems, with voluptuous blooms up to 2 inches.

When, Where, and How to Plant

Usually available for spring planting, bergenias can also be planted or divided in fall. Plant in full or partial sun, or partial shade, in moist soil, well amended with organics. Not fussy about soil type, bergenia tolerates acidic or alkaline conditions. These plants endure summer heat well if in partial shade. The more sun it gets, the more moisture it needs during the active growing season. If your plant features good winter leaf color, the sunnier locations help to develop that color richness. Set rhizomes at least 4 inches deep. Often seen tucked into rockeries where drainage is perfect, bergenias spread by thick rhizomes that resent soggy soils. In colder areas, site in a warm microclimate—harsh winter freezes may kill flower buds. For general guidelines on planting perennials, see page 115.

Growing Tips

Bergenias prefer moderate moisture but can survive without summer irrigation. Once established, they endure summer dry spells well but grow and look better with occasional water. Bergenia needs little fertilizer, simply a 5-1-1 or 6-2-2 in spring.

Care

They're easy-care plants, but root weevils can chew the leaf margins. Damage is more noticeable on older leaves; prune it off in spring. Grooming is simple: Allow winter leaves to remain for their color and interest. Cut back older leaves when new growth begins in spring. If leaves look damaged in summer, prune selectively. Divide every three to four years in earliest spring, Keep the soil mulched; as the plants expand, rhizomes may poke above the surface and must be kept covered.

Companion Planting and Design

Large bergenia leaves cover the ground, so they need to share with other vigorous plants such as shrubby aucuba. The red-toned leaves sparkle with winter-blooming Chinese witch-hazel, especially orange-flowered 'Jelena'.

We Recommend

'Bressingham Ruby' offers lovely winter color. 'Baby Doll' stays under 1 foot, with soft-pink flowers and occasional repeat bloom in September. 'Silberlicht' has white flowers and deep-green foliage; it's handsome in spring with brunnera and snowdrops.

Bergenia can seem almost as persistent in the landscape as a shrub, with many newer cultivars that show polished evergreen leaves with winter colors of bronze, wine, and deep crimson. Substantial clumps, they're often grown for leaf interest over bloom, since leaves persist throughout seasons and pink or red flowers primarily show in spring. Bergenias, favorites in nineteenth century gardens, have emerged from a period of horticultural neglect, now cherished as favored winter and spring plants. Count on them to be weed smothering in light shade or sun once established; their 6-inch leaves form thick layers that keep light from penetrating to the ground. Bergenia cordifolia, native to Siberia, takes zone 3 happily. Solid, sturdy, with noteworthy garden presence, they expand handsomely over time. —MR

Other Common Name
Heartleaf bergenia

Bloom Period and Seasonal Color
Spring; white, pink, rose, and red blooms

Mature Height × Spread
1 to 2 feet × 1 to 3 feet

Zones
3 to 8

Black-Eyed Susan
Rudbeckia species

With dark-brown centers surrounded by a collar of golden petals, black-eyed Susan is an unforgettable perennial of summertime. A commanding presence in the garden, with cheery flowers on tall stems, black-eyed Susan belongs in the mixed border, island beds, or your cutting garden (it's a great addition to late-summer country bouquets of hydrangeas and sunflowers). Hardy and easy to grow, these colossal perennials carry masses of large, golden-yellow daisies. Dwarf, double, and varied color forms increase your choices. Grow black-eyed Susan where it complements other button-centered flowers, including purple coneflower and sneezeweed, giving your garden a casual meadow appearance. Come late summer, let black-eyed Susan go to seed. Instead of dead-heading the blooms, leave them as a tasty cool-season treat for birds. —DP

Bloom Period and Seasonal Color
Mid- to late summer; orange-yellow blooms

Mature Height × Spread
2 to 3 feet × 2 feet

Zones
4 to 9

When, Where, and How to Plant
Plant black-eyed Susan in spring or early summer. Choose a sunny, open area with average soil. These plants prefer moist, well-drained soil and tolerate heat if adequately irrigated. In partial shade, your plants may not flower as profusely as in sunnier spots. Follow the general guidelines for planting perennials on page 115. Space black-eyed Susans about 2 feet apart.

Growing Tips
Water regularly until the plants are established, then irrigate consistently. These are not drought-tolerant plants. They respond dramatically to moisture, producing prolifically when well watered. Fertilization is typically not needed. A 2-inch layer of organic mulch helps retain moisture at the root level.

Care
Pests or diseases generally don't bother black-eyed Susan. Mildew can occur late in the season; prune away damaged foliage. Pinch back plants (below developing buds) in early summer to encourage bushier growth. Deadhead spent blooms. You will need to dig and divide this perennial every three years or so. Divide in spring or fall, lifting the plant and using a garden knife or the sharp edge of a spade to slice the crown in half. Cut away any damaged or dead areas (usually at the center of the crown). When replanting, fertilize lightly and mulch well.

Companion Planting and Design
Purple is the complement to golden yellow, so plant some drama into your borders by pairing black-eyed Susan with amethyst salvias, gayfeather spires, or bellflowers. The classic country perennial, black-eyed Susan looks lovely in a drift, grown along a split-rail or white-picket fence. Incorporate black-eyed Susan into a painterly composition of ornamental grasses, yarrow, and 'Autumn Joy' sedum.

We Recommend
At 3 feet tall, *Rudbeckia fulgida* var. *sullivantii* adds a lovely height to the border, with 4-inch flower heads. *R. f.* var. *s.* 'Goldsturm', a German cultivar, offers even larger flowers. A novelty perennial that's fun to grow, *R. occidentalis* 'Green Wizard', has large black centers with bright-green sepals.

Bleeding Heart
Dicentra spectabilis

When, Where, and How to Plant

Plant from containers in spring as growth starts. Handle carefully; both stems and roots break easily. Plant at the same level they were grown in the container. Site in partial shade; these plants die out rapidly in hot, sunny, exposed spots. Well-drained moisture-holding organic soil is required. Bleeding heart performs poorly in clay soils and will not take soggy roots in winter. Garden bleeding heart isn't particular about soil, but the native *Dicentra formosa* subsp. *oregana* requires slightly acidic conditions. The stems and blooms are fragile; avoid windy spots like ocean edges. Native forms will take summer drought after going dormant. For general guidelines on planting perennials, see page 115.

Growing Tips

Fertilize in early spring as growth starts. There are no pest problems other than occasional aphids; wash plants gently with a stream of water to treat those. Provide consistently moist soil, topdressing with compost in spring to increase soil moisture. Mulch in fall for winter protection.

Care

Garden bleeding heart disappears in July or early August, perhaps earlier in hot-weather areas. Don't be surprised! The absence can be disguised by surrounding plants. Mark their location to avoiding digging into the dormant plants. Since it prefers cool weather, bleeding heart may be short lived or transient in eastern Washington and Oregon. Increase your stock of the natives by division. West of the mountains, divide in fall after dormancy; in colder areas, divide in spring before the leaves emerge. The western native has more persistent foliage and may bloom intermittently throughout summer if kept moist. No pest problems bother it.

Companion Planting and Design

A gentle companion to many late-spring perennials, bleeding heart is beautiful with May-blooming tulips such as 'White Triumphator'. In the shaded border, it complements hosta, Japanese painted fern, and sweet woodruff.

We Recommend

Dicentra spectabilis 'Alba', the white garden cultivar, looks crisp on spring evenings. Try the native western cultivar *Dicentra* 'Bountiful', with deep purple-red flowers.

A fairytale-like garden presence, bleeding heart carries long arching stems of heart-shaped flowers gracing the traditional spring and early-summer perennial garden in partial shade. Held above the fine, blue-green ferny foliage, the flowers remind us of living valentines. Once established, they can live for years, expanding slowly in moist shade. Some cultivars, such as 'King of Hearts', bloom intermittently throughout early summer. Western native bleeding heart (Dicentra formosa) grows shorter than the cultivated types, with narrow fernlike leaf segments in a distinct bluish green. Small rose flowers duplicate the shape of the garden types but rise in clumps rather than on arching stems. Native D. formosa oregana blooms yellow. The native bleeding hearts settle well into damp woods, along with Trillium ovatum. —MR

Other Common Names

Dutchman's breeches, lady's locket

Bloom Period and Seasonal Color

Spring to summer; white, pink, rose, and yellow blooms

Mature Height × Spread

6 to 36 inches × 10 to 36 inches

Zones

3 to 9

Cape Fuchsia
Phygelius species

With tubular blooms in dusky shades of mauve, deep coral, and yellow, cape fuchsia is a stellar perennial. Its common name comes from drooping, fuchsialike flowers dangling from graceful, architectural branches. This woody perennial is related to snapdragon and foxglove. Cape fuchsia reaches 3 to 4 feet, offering structural interest to mixed borders. It blooms from summer to fall, providing a reliable accent of flowers on erect stems, with soft gray-green foliage. Cape fuchsia draws its heritage from two species that have been frequently crossed to create numerous hybrids in a delightful spectrum of warm hues. Semievergreen in milder climates, cape fuchsia is treated as a perennial in most Northwest gardens. It will die back with the arrival of frost and return in early spring. —DP

Bloom Period and Seasonal Color
Midsummer to fall; yellow, coral, mauve, and red blooms

Mature Height × Spread
2 to 6 feet × 2 to 4 feet

Zones
7 to 9

When, Where, and How to Plant
Plant in spring, early summer, or fall, in full to partial sun and in fertile, moist, well-drained soil. Avoid soggy locations. While cape fuchsia thrives in heat, it requires regular moisture. Follow the general guidelines for planting perennials on page 115. Space plants 3 feet apart.

Growing Tips
Water regularly until the plants are established. This perennial dislikes dry conditions, so be sure to irrigate during extended dry periods. Fertilization is typically not needed. A 2-inch layer of organic mulch helps retain moisture at the root level.

Care
Pests or diseases generally don't bother it. Where temperatures drop below freezing, treat it as an herbaceous perennial: Cut it back to ground for winter. Add protective mulch during winter; refresh it in early spring. Protect cape fuchsia from harsh temperatures and wind by planting against a southern- or western-facing wall or in a sheltered area. Cut back old flower stalks to keep tidy. Cape fuchsia spreads by suckers; when you notice them, remove unwanted sections by cutting through underground stems.

Companion Planting and Design
Any border of hot-colored blooms will welcome cape fuchsia for its vibrant palette and delicate, tubular flowers. Combine the yellow-blooming form with red-hot poker and vivid orange-red 'Fireglow' euphorbia for a sun-loving display. The mauve- and dark-pink-flowered cape fuchsias provide a lovely counterpoint to plants with tropical or bold foliage, including the pink-striped New Zealand flax and plum-striped cannas. Cape fuchsia is an excellent container plant, pairing well with yellow-and-cream-striped carex and burgundy sweet potato vine.

We Recommend
Phygelius aequalis has staggered clusters of dusty-rose flowers. A cultivar named 'Yellow Trumpet' offers pale-yellow blooms on a dense, bushy habit. *P. capensis* produces masses of orange or red tubular blooms. Among the shrubby cultivars are some stunning offspring, such as 'Salmon Leap' (orange flowers) and 'African Queen' (pale reddish orange flowers).

When, Where, and How to Plant

Plant catmint in spring, early summer, or fall. Select a full- to partial-sun location with soil of average fertility. Catmint thrives in well-drained or sandy conditions but suffers in heavy or soggy soil. Follow the general guidelines for planting perennials on page 115. Space catmints 2 to 3 feet apart, depending on the variety. To create a "hedge" appearance, place plants slightly closer, 18 inches apart.

Growing Tips

Water catmint regularly until plants are established. This drought-tolerant plant may need only occasional irrigation during a drought. Fertilization is typically not needed.

Care

Catmint has an informal style that gives your garden a soft, billowing appearance. If planted in a sunny, well-drained spot, catmint will bloom late spring to early summer. After it flowers, cut back the stems to encourage rebloom. If the catmint in your garden is in too much shade or heavy, wet soil, you will notice it splaying out from the middle. Renovate the plant by digging up the clump and dividing. Remove any rotted or dead sections from the center, and replant divisions in sunny, dry areas. Water well until established. Pests generally are not a problem.

Companion Planting and Design

This easy-to-grow garden workhorse rewards you with romantic blooms and a tidy form. Not only does this perennial herb bloom at the same time as most roses, but it serves as a dreamy complement to the more structured rose shrubs. An informal hedge of creamy-white 'Iceberg' roses looks glorious when underplanted with the violet-blue flowers of *Nepeta racemosa* 'Walker's Low'. You can grow catmint as an informal edging plant, allowing the gray-green foliage and lavender-blue studded flower spikes to spill onto a brick walkway.

We Recommend

Nepeta 'Six Hills Giant' grows up to 3 feet tall with deep-blue flowers and tolerates moist locations slightly better than other catmints. *N.* × *faassenii* is a European species with numerous cultivars, including 'Snowflake', which produces white blooms.

If you've grown the feline-seductive variety of catmint that attracts all the neighborhood cats to your garden, Nepeta cataria, *you're probably wary about growing other forms of this aromatic herb. There are numerous species and cultivars better suited for the landscape—and the only wildlife they'll attract are pollinating bees.* Nepeta × faassenii *is a tidy species that blooms profusely, mixing well with herb gardens and rose borders. This is a great plant for sunny sites reminiscent of the Mediterranean climates so often compared to maritime Northwest gardens. Catmint is a long-blooming perennial that can be used to edge beds and pathways, offering delicate lavender, blue, and pale-pink tubular blossoms on upright stems. With continued breeding, gardeners have a wide variety of catmint choices. —DP*

Bloom Period and Seasonal Color

Late spring to midsummer; lavender-blue, pale-pink and white blooms

Mature Height × Spread

1 to 3 feet × 2 to 3 feet

Zones

4 to 8

Columbine
Aquilegia species

With pastel flowers floating above blue-toned finely dissected foliage, columbine possesses airy charm. Gardeners have many choices; depending on the hybrid or species, sizes run from 1 to 3 feet tall; some, like the McKana group, float above other summer perennials. The flower form stands out because of hanging spurs that dangle like the ribbons on a kite. Aqueligia formosa, the western native, brings brilliant red to the garden in midspring, reliably attracting hummingbirds. Use in a woodland garden, naturalize in borders, or choose a showstopping plant (Music or Songbird series) for the cutting garden. Columbine is often bicolor: red and yellow, or pinks and blues with white. Though grown for flowers, columbine adds leaf texture. Cold-hardy columbine adapts to spring gardens throughout our region. —MR

Other Common Name
Granny's bonnets

Bloom Period and Seasonal Color
Spring to early summer; white, pink, yellow, blue, and red blooms

Mature Height × Spread
12 to 36 inches × 6 to 18 inches

Zones
2 to 9

When, Where, and How to Plant
In early spring or fall, plant in clumps for best effect, setting three columbines in a triangle 1 foot apart. Partial shade, partial sun, or full sun (with extra water) suits them. Columbine takes various soil types, either acidic or alkaline, but requires good drainage. Avoid extremely windy or exposed areas if planting the larger hybrid cultivars like 'Monarch' or the McKana group. Mulch with compost after planting to protect shallow roots from heat. For general guidelines on planting perennials, see page 115.

Growing Tips
Fertilize once in spring with a 6-2-2. Water weekly until established; no water is needed in late summer when plants go dormant.

Care
After bloom, deadhead unless you want seeds to develop. Ripe seeds remain viable for about three months and often produce plants that bloom the following year, though hybrids will not come true. To preserve a population of just one type, isolate it from other columbines because they cross-pollinate readily. Divide in fall or early spring to keep the stand healthy; columbine tends to die out after about three years. Many growers trim off tattered foliage after bloom; with watering, new foliage and occasionally new bloom follows. You might not want to force this new growth on *Aquilegia formosa* or *A. canadensis*, but it's a help for perennial borders. New growth in early spring can be bothered by leafminers, which tunnel into the leaves and mark them. In some areas, the columbine sawfly defoliates plants, leaving only stalks. The best control for leafminers or sawflies is to cut the plants to the ground and water them to allow fresh growth. Native columbine seems less affected by leafminers than garden hybrids. Deer, thankfully, don't bother columbine.

Companion Planting and Design
Larger long-spurred 'McKana' hybrids pair well with spring bulbs, catmint and poppies, or with hardy geraniums. Try native species with low-growing mahonia (*Mahonia repens*).

We Recommend
The hybrids of *A. longissima* carry pale-yellow flowers 4 inches long that tolerate heat.

When, Where, and How to Plant

Plant in spring, early summer, or fall, in moist, well-drained, humus-rich soil and in partial sun or light shade. A site that receives morning sun and afternoon shade is ideal, as the foliage tends to burn in hot sun. Space plants 12 inches apart. This excellent container plant offers mounding foliage that complements taller bloomers. For general guidelines on planting perennials, see page 115.

Growing Tips

Water regularly until young plants are established. Keep the soil moist, especially during dry spells. A 2-inch layer of organic mulch helps nourish the root system and retain moisture. Coralbells in fertile soil generally don't require feeding.

Care

Many gardeners remove the flower wands, treating coralbells as a foliage plant; cutting spent flowers stimulates reblooming. You can also cut the stems to use fresh blooms in floral arrangements. In well-drained soils, coralbells are generally free of disease; don't let them sit in soggy soil, or the plants suffer from root rot. Some varieties of coralbells "heave"—lift themselves out of the soil. Mulching and periodic divisions prevent this tendency. Dig and divide every three to five years, cutting away dead or woody sections. After transplanting divisions, water regularly to establish.

Companion Planting and Design

The rainbow palette of coralbells has captured the imagination of clever designers, who rely on dynamic foliage forms and colors to highlight unique combinations. The many purple-, burgundy-, and brown-leafed forms, including *Heuchera americana* 'Ruby Veil' and 'Garnet', offer a sultry complement to gold and silver foliage plants. *H. micrantha* 'Palace Purple' is a best-selling hybrid with maple-shaped foliage. Plant it along the walkway in your shade garden, alternating with another popular introduction, *H. americana* 'Green Spice'.

We Recommend

H. americana 'Chocolate Ruffles' is an award-winning selection with burgundy-mocha foliage measuring 9 inches across. *Heuchera* 'Amber Waves', a stunning head-turner with amber-gold foliage, simply glows in the landscape.

Enthusiastic hybridizers have given a major facelift to the old-fashioned favorite, coralbells, breeding for their mammoth foliage size and a tapestry of alluring leaf colors, from golden-amber and spicy-green to cream-and-green splashes and a seemingly endless range of purples. Many gardeners have embraced the trend, calling this hot perennial by its botanical name, heuchera. But don't be so seduced by the foliage that you overlook the bell-like coral blooms for which this plant first earned its reputation as a great perennial. Spring-blooming selections showcase tall wands covered with coral-pink flowers that emerge to 24 inches above the clump of ruffled or lobed foliage. Mix several colors together for a vibrant display. Coralbells are semievergreen, ideal for four-season plantings and foliage-strong container designs. —DP

Other Common Names
Alum root, heuchera

Bloom Period and Seasonal Color
Late spring to fall; reddish-pink, magenta, and white blooms; many cultivars grown for their dynamic foliage

Mature Height × Spread
12 to 24 inches × 12 inches

Zones
4 to 8

Fleabane
Erigeron karvinskianus

With tiny, yellow-centered pink, mauve, or white daisylike flowers, this amazing perennial packs a punch in the mixed border, blooming nearly all summer long. A native of Mexico, fleabane is one of those delicate but durable workhorse plants, surviving dry summers, average soil, and even neglect. You can grow it as a ground cover, at the front of the border, and in containers and rockeries. The 1-inch flowers bloom at the tips of slender stems, which softly intertwine with neighboring plants or spill onto a nearby path. The toothed, medium-green foliage remains tidy and compact, forming a low-growing mat that fills in spaces between larger perennials. Fleabane naturalizes and can be removed easily if it appears in an unwanted spot in your garden. —DP

Other Common Name
Santa Barbara daisy

Bloom Period and Seasonal Color
Spring to fall; white, pink, mauve, and lavender blooms

Mature Height × Spread
12 to 24 inches × 24 inches

Zones
5 to 7

When, Where, and How to Plant
Plant in spring, early summer, or fall, in full sun to partial shade and in average to rich soil. Well-drained or sandy locations are ideal. If you have heavy clay soil, create planting pockets, placing landscaping rocks or small boulders in the garden and filling the space between them with high-quality planting soil where you can grow fleabane. Follow the general guidelines for planting perennials on page 115. Space fleabanes $1^{1}/_{2}$ to 2 feet apart.

Growing Tips
Water regularly until young plants are established. Fleabane flowers more profusely if watered moderately through dry spells. Feeding is generally unnecessary.

Care
This is a low-maintenance plant, but you can keep fleabane tidy by cutting back spent blooms (this also helps encourage rebloom). If the center of your plant splays or dies back, it's time to dig and divide. Do so every two to three years, discarding any dead sections and replanting. Water transplants until established. Fleabane is generally free of pests. It can suffer from powdery mildew if the plant isn't pruned or regularly divided.

Companion Planting and Design
The first time fleabane caught my attention, it was planted in a lovely grouping with *Sedum* 'Autumn Joy' and 'Stella d'Oro' daylilies along the outside of a latticework fence. Fleabane's yellow centers and pinkish white blooms provided a carefree complement to the mauve sedum and bright-yellow daylilies. When planted in the nooks and crannies of a rock wall or along the edges of a stone staircase, fleabane's misty form brings a soft charm to the architecture. This is an ideal plant to tuck into bare spaces in the mixed-sunny border; as it matures, fleabane helps knit together other plants.

We Recommend
Erigeron karvinskianus, the Santa Barbara daisy, is a long-blooming species that works well as an informal ground cover. *E. glaucus*, also called beach aster, has large-centered blooms, growing to 12 inches tall with a 24-inch spread. *Erigeron* 'Quakeress' offers light mauve-pink blooms.

When, Where, and How to Plant

Plant in spring when purchased as containers from nurseries, or in fall from seed. Foxgloves grow easily from seed. The common foxglove (*D. purpurea*) doesn't need rich soil but does best in good drainage. Hybrid garden types and species, such as yellow foxglove (*D. grandiflora*), need more compost and nutrients. Mulch with 2 to 3 inches of compost after planting. For general guidelines on planting perennials, see page 115.

Growing Tips

Fertilize when spring growth starts, using a 5-1-1 or a low-nitrogen product only. Water needs vary depending on the species or cultivar. Most need spring moisture before bloom. *D. purpurea* requires water during spring but can manage dry times in later summer when it slides into dormancy. Rusty foxglove (*D. ferruginea*), reliably perennial and native to Turkey, handles dry soil well.

Care

Because bloomed-out plants won't perform again the next year, prune off the old foliage to tidy the area. Old plants may show powdery mildew as they die back; removing the foliage removes the problem. Squirrels, voles, mice, and deer leave foxglove alone because of the plant's significant toxicity. Protect all young seedlings from slugs and snails. Though biennial, *D. purpurea* seeds so prolifically it seems perennial as plants replace themselves readily. Allow foxglove to seed itself, or remove the blooming stalk just after flowering if you don't want thousands of volunteer plants. Foxglove forms new rosettes around the mature plant; these can be separated and replanted after flowering to bloom the following year. Discard the central, bloomed-out stalk and leaves. *D. grandiflora* perennializes; plants can last three or more years rather than dying out in the second. When plants decline, divide them.

Companion Planting and Design

Foxgloves of all types mix well with daylilies, bulbous alliums, and small landscape roses such as 'Carefree Beauty', which can take morning sun and afternoon shade.

We Recommend

Watching hummingbirds visit common foxglove and other rosy cultivars like *Digitalis purpurea* Foxy group livens up any summer morning.

Foxgloves, both species and cultivars, grow as flower spires, lifting bloom stalks above low leaves forming ground-clinging clumps. The common garden foxglove, Digitalis purpurea, *escaped from early gardens throughout the Pacific Northwest. Seeing it in the wild, many people consider it a native plant, which it isn't. Generally a biennial, foxglove produces seedlings one year that bloom the next.* Digitalis, *like* digit, *is Latin for finger, suggesting the fingertip-sized tubular flowers. Early summer brings many different species into our perennial gardens, including yellow-flowering rusty foxglove (D. ferruginea) and deep-raspberry D. × mertonensis. Foxglove's design possibilities lead growers to hybridize more types yearly. All parts of* Digitalis *species contain poison, from roots to blooms, but it's formerly had medicinal uses and produces the medicine digitalis. —MR*

Bloom Period and Seasonal Color
Summer; white, pink, rose, raspberry, and yellow blooms

Mature Height × Spread
1 to 4 feet × 1 to 2 feet

Zones
4 to 9

Germander

Teucrium chamaedrys

The first time I really noticed how well germander works in the landscape, I was wowed by its compact form, glossy green foliage, and bee-swarmed purple flowers. That the landscape designer had planted germander to create an elegant border around formal rose beds captured my imagination—here was a lovely, evergreen alternative to common boxwood or casual lavender. Germander is a Mediterranean native that can endure most types of soil if well drained (it is fairly drought tolerant). Its dark-green leaves are delightfully serrated or toothed. Like boxwood, germander responds well to clipping for knot gardens or hedging. But far better, it produces masses of red-purple or white flowers that add to its charm in a perennial garden or as edging along a pathway. —DP

Other Common Name
Wall germander

Bloom Period and Seasonal Color
Summer; pink to purple blooms

Mature Height × Spread
1 to 2 feet × 3 to 6 feet

Zones
5 to 9

When, Where, and How to Plant
Plant container-grown germander in spring or early summer. This is a woody perennial that should have warmth to help roots establish. Select a well-drained site in full sun. Germander adapts to most soils except those that are soggy. Follow the general guidelines for planting perennials on page 115. Space these plants 18 to 24 inches apart.

Growing Tips
Water regularly until germander is established. Irrigate during extended dry periods. Germander generally does not require fertilization. To improve drainage, mulch with a fine layer of crushed rock, which helps wick moisture away from the crown.

Care
This durable evergreen plant is a hardworking addition to the garden. If sited appropriately, germander requires little care. It may be cut low (to 2 to 3 inches above the base of plant) in spring to encourage a more compact habit. If you like a more informal plant, lightly prune the ends of the branches after flowering to stimulate lateral growth. Some forms of germander can be trained into topiary designs. This plant is generally free of pests and diseases.

Companion Planting and Design
Edge walkways with germander, spaced about 18 inches apart so that the plants grow together as a hedge within a few seasons. Plant at least 12 inches from the pathway to allow germander to spill onto concrete, brick, or pavers, but not obstruct foot traffic. A formal garden looks lovely when outlined in tidy rows of clipped germander. It provides a glossy, textured element to knot gardens, contrasting well with the pewter shades of santolina and lavender. Heavy clipping is not required, of course. Casual mounds of this charming plant are also useful in the perennial garden, providing pale-pink to intense-purple blooms throughout summer.

We Recommend
'Prostratum' grows to 6 inches and spreads to 3 feet or more, serving as an excellent evergreen ground cover. Bush germander (*Teucrium fruticans*) has gray-green foliage and reaches 4 to 8 feet, with lavender-blue flower spikes.

Hellebore
Helleborus species and cultivars

When, Where, and How to Plant
Plant in spring or in fall from containers. Growing in most light conditions, hellebores bloom best in partial shade or partial sun. Set three or more in clumps 18 inches apart. Well-drained, humus soil well amended with compost suits them. Hellebores prefer a slightly alkaline pH and grow better in acidic soil when lime is worked lightly into the soil in fall every third year (5 pounds per every 100 square feet of plantings) or with a mulch of limestone chips that slowly leach into the soil. For general planting guidelines, see page 115.

Growing Tips
Fertilize in spring with a 5-1-1 as new growth starts. Hellebores handle summer dry spells well but only when established; they need water weekly the first two summers and occasionally once established. If you find hellebore collapsed from a dry spell, with leaves lying flat on the ground, just water it. Keep plants mulched with 2 inches of compost.

Care
Prune out old leaves at winter's end, being careful not to nick the emerging fresh leaf growth. Flower stalks may be left until the seeds drop (late spring and early summer). *H. foetidus* forms a thick stem topped with green pendant flowers; prune the entire stalk after bloom. Long lived and tough, hellebores seldom need dividing and may recover slowly from transplanting or division. But if necessary, divide them immediately after bloom finishes. Hellebores bloom better after two to three years. Seedlings often appear beneath the leaves; lift them gently and replant after they have at least one set of true leaves. Hellebores cross-pollinate; you may discover delightful surprises when the seedlings bloom in three or four years. They're pest resistant.

Companion Planting and Design
Try them with fragrant sarcococca or as an evergreen background to low spring bulbs such as anemones. Site hellebores along a stairway—where you can look up into them.

We Recommend
Helleborus foeditus Wester Flisk group has distinctive reddish stems contrasting with long-lasting green flowers.

Opening the garden season by blooming in late winter and earliest spring, hellebores engage gardeners by their intriguing flower shapes, colors, and leaf forms. Hybridizers happily produce new cultivars from the many species, most beautifully from Lenten rose (Helleborus × orientalis). Hellebores remain favorites of perennial garden designers. Flowers can remain attractive for two to three months, gradually fading to pale green. Plants stay evergreen throughout winter in most of the region. Stiff, leathery leaves help endurance for summer water use. Flower colors go to extremes, from pale cream to darkest burgundy-black, many freckled with contrasting spots and marked with bicolors. Cold hardy and tough, hellebore will spread in shade or light shade, doing better with protection from hot sun exposure and occasionally summer watering. —MR

Other Common Names
Christmas rose, Lenten rose

Bloom Period and Seasonal Color
Late winter to early spring; white, cream, green, yellow, pink, rose, red, and purple-black blooms

Mature Height × Spread
1 to 3 feet × 1 to 3 feet

Zones
3 to 8

Hosta

Hosta species and cultivars

Classically elegant, hosta holds court as a great "basic" perennial, with clumps of layered leaves unfolding from a center. Bold and sculptural, they're cherished for their leaf form and the many color variations on green, blue tones, cream, and yellow accents. Tolerant of both winter cold and summer heat, if given shade conditions, hostas suppress weeds well. So many cultivars exist that gardeners often think of color first. Your woodland could be lit by the yellow of specimen plants like 'August Moon'. Size deserves consideration also, since hostas grow from small 6 inchers to large vigorous plants like 'Sum and Substance' that can occupy over 5 feet in height and width. Shade-lovers, they thrive in woodland soil. Look for their summer flower spikes, often fragrant. —MR

Other Common Names
Plantain lily, funkia

Bloom Period and Seasonal Color
Summer; white, cream, and light-purple blooms

Mature Height × Spread
$^1/_2$ to 5 feet × 1 to 5 feet

Zones
3 to 9

When, Where, and How to Plant
Hostas are available from containers spring, summer, or fall. Some nurseries ship bare-root plants in spring. Plant in well-prepared, moisture-retentive soil, in full or partial shade. As you might do when planting peonies, prepare for a plant with a long life span in the garden by being thorough about soil amendment. If the soil is adequately mulched with composted manure, little fertilizer is needed. For general guidelines on planting perennials, see page 115.

Growing Tips
Watered regularly, these plants stay fresh throughout summer. Without additional water, established plants go dormant in August. Fertilize in spring with a slow-release nitrogen formula.

Care
Mark their locations; hostas emerge slowly in spring, often waiting until after tulips bloom. It's all too easy to conclude that they've disappeared. For all their virtues, hostas experience serious pest attacks. Slugs chew them unmercifully and can reduce the thinner-leaved types to lacy remnants. Thicker, crinkled leaves resist damage; cultivars like rumple-leaved 'Frances Williams' survive slugs better but aren't immune. Slug management is vital with hostas, so use the newer iron phosphate baits like Sluggo™ and pick them off by hand. Deer consider hostas salad and can be deterred by commercial repellent, but the only real protection for hostas is an effective deer fence. Divide them by digging out a chunk from the side of the plant, taking part of the center and then filling in the gap with rich soil. If done in fall, both the division and the mature plant will grow well the following spring. Plants increase slowly but steadily once rooted.

Companion Planting and Design
Hosta leaves hide spring bulb foliage as the bulb goes dormant. Effective ground covers under Japanese maples and other choice deciduous trees, hostas are wonderful with summer-blooming lilies and astilbes. Container growing also suits hostas; a large pot with a specimen like blue-leaved 'Krossa Regal' will accent shade.

We Recommend
Handsome *Hosta sieboldiana* var. *elegans*, with deeply crinkled leaves, resists slugs.

Inside-Out Flower
Vancouveria species

When, Where, and How to Plant

All three species, native only to the Northwest, should be planted in spring from containers. Division of existing plants is also best done in early spring before new leaf growth begins. Prepare the soil as for all native landscapes, with ample compost dug in and 2-3 inches of mulch over the plants once installed. *Vancouveria* species grow well in acidic soils so are particularly suited to western Washington and Oregon. Shade or partial sun, particularly with protection from scorching afternoon light, will suit these best. For general guidelines on planting perennials, see page 115.

Growing Tips

After the first two years, once established, *Vancouveria hexandra* will thrive with absolutely no care. Soaker hoses around the planting for the first two years helps with establishment. No pests bother it, and it's able to stay alive without supplementary irrigation. But for faster growth and fresher foliage, water every three weeks during summer. Fertilize once with a 5-1-1 in earliest spring.

Care

Trim off winter-damaged leaves in early spring, cutting plants to the crowns. Once new foliage appears, it's impossible to avoid snipping off the emerging leaves. Mulch with compost after the winter trim. Established plants will grow from pieces of root, which explains their occasional rambunctious behavior—they can grow insistently. It's a good idea to keep them away from tender woodlings like trillium and anemones. Inside-out flower resists pests.

Companion Planting and Design

Used as a filler for native plant gardens, *V. hexandra* adds a lacy ground cover under pink-flowering native currant and native rhododendron. It's useful for the driest shady spots in any garden, backing up hellebores and all shade-loving spring bulbs or carpeting under vigorous shade shrubs like aucuba. *V. chrysantha*, with yellow flowers, shares partial-sun spots well with epimedium.

We Recommend

V. planipelata stays reliably evergreen west of the Cascades, but it's easier to find *V. hexandra* in nurseries. During mild winters, *V. hexandra* often retains its leaves and becomes evergreen.

Native to western North America, inside-out flower settles into gardens as a great ground-covering perennial. A member of the barberry family, related to epimedium but airier in form, its dark-green leaves resemble maidenhair fern but are far tougher. The leaves move in wind with a fine textured presence. In late spring, creamy-white flowers, on stalks with 30 or more flowers per stem, float above the leaves. Brief in bloom, the plants are most valued for their shiny, persistent, often evergreen foliage. The genus name honors Captain George Vancouver, who explored the coastal Northwest in the 1790s. This native will cover dry ground under conifers, a tough situation indeed. Hiding its rigorous sturdiness beneath an air of delicacy, inside-out flower is at home in all woodland gardens. —MR

Bloom Period and Seasonal Color
Spring; creamy-white blooms

Mature Height × Spread
18 inches × 12 inches

Zones
5 to 8

Italian Arum
Arum italicum

Three seasons of interest arrive with this intriguing plant—but summer is left out! Handsome leaves, arrow-shaped, deep green marked with white, emerge in autumn and persist, looking fresh and attractive, until late spring when creamy spathes of flowers bloom. Plants then go dormant, disappearing throughout summer. The summer vanishing act makes these ideal for water-wise gardens, where they suit dry, dark, shade conditions. In late August, tall leafless spikes of knobby green berries come up, turning bright orange-red just in time to harmonize with fall leaf color. Spreading both by seeds and tuberous roots, Italian arum could be classified as a bulb-type plant. Covering the ground in a green and white pattern, winter leaves maintain their presence and grace no matter the weather. —MR

Other Common Names
Lords and ladies, painted arum

Bloom Period and Seasonal Color
Fall and winter; red berries and deep-green leaves

Mature Height × Spread
6 to 16 inches × 6 inches

Zones
6 to 9

When, Where, and How to Plant
Italian arum grows well when planted in either spring or fall, though spring nursery availability is most common when plants are in leaf. It requires shade and well-drained soil, amended with compost or other organic material. Set the heavy tubers 4 inches below the soil surface, and water well when planting. Fertilize with a 5-1-1 after planting, and then mulch, using at least 2 inches of compost.

Growing Tips
To help maintain soil fertility, renew mulch yearly in fall as fresh leaves emerge. Fertilizer isn't needed on established clumps. Some growers find this plant settles all too well in moist shade; restricting water by not irrigating in late spring and early fall will keep patches from spreading.

Care
Allow the leaves to become completely shriveled in early summer; then tug them out of the ground. Don't take off the standing bloom spike, or you'll lose the fall show of red berries. If you don't mind the brown foliage, or if it's covered by other summer plants, leaving it on the plants won't harm them. Start these plants from either seeds or tuberous roots. The seedheads, held firmly upright early in fall, bend to the ground as seeds ripen, dropping them on the soil surface. New leaves hide the fallen stems. With mulch present, they often germinate and form small new plants in spring. No pest problems bother this sturdy plant. Winter mulch in zone 5 can help the plant perennialize.

Companion Planting and Design
Red-berried stalks pick up the orange and red of crocosmia and gleam with the fall brilliance of Japanese maple. Glossy winter leaves tucked under or in front of daphne, aucuba, and wax myrtle bring extra vividness to those dry-shade shrubs.

We Recommend
Arum italicum 'Pictum' carries the strongest white leaf marbling. As a background for early snowdrops and small daffodils like 'February Gold', it provides leaf shine and contrast. *A. maculatum* sends up purple-spotted leaves in spring, followed by yellow flower spathes.

Jacob's Ladder
Polemonium species

When, Where, and How to Plant

Plant Jacob's ladder in spring or early summer. This native perennial is well adapted to moist, fertile soil conditions west of the Cascades, especially when given good drainage. The lower-growing forms are ideal for rock gardens with sandy or gritty soil. The upright form of Jacob's ladder prefers filtered sunlight, making it a good candidate to grow beneath deciduous trees. The foliage will scorch in direct afternoon sun, which is one reason to grow Jacob's ladder where it will receive morning sun or dappled afternoon sun. Follow the general guidelines for planting perennials on page 115. Space these plants approximately 18 inches apart.

Growing Tips

Water regularly until established. Jacob's ladder prefers moderately moist soil. Don't let it stand in soggy soil. Fertilize once in spring, before blooming.

Care

Jacob's ladder looks best when spent blooms are deadheaded, which also prevents reseeding. Powdery mildew can be a problem if you overwater. To propagate more plants, divide Jacob's ladder in late summer or early fall. Pests generally don't bother this perennial.

Companion Planting and Design

Grow Jacob's ladder with woodland perennials, ferns, and hostas. The pale bell-shaped flowers bloom just as spring tulips fill the garden; as the bulbs die back, Jacob's ladder's interesting stair-stepped foliage hides them. The height and texture of this perennial provide interest to the mixed border, especially when paired with plants that have enormous rounded foliage, such as bergenia and brunnera. Grow lower forms with saxifrage and sea pink (*Armeria maritima*) for a lovely floral display in the rock garden. Jacob's ladder has a light, sugary fragrance that will add more enjoyment to the garden.

We Recommend

Polemonium caeruleum is the tallest upright species, with stems bearing 1-in lavender-blue flowers. Reaching to 3 feet, 'Brise d'Anjou' doesn't bloom as profusely, but its green foliage outlined in white is a stunning accent to the garden. *P. pulcherriumum* is a western native form ideal for rock gardens.

When I first studied herbaceous perennials, it was easy to remember the botanical name of Jacob's ladder, making the connection between the Biblical hero Jacob who dreamed of a ladder to heaven and the idea of returning to earth by sliding down a "pole" (Polemonium). This is a statuesque perennial with fernlike foliage, reminiscent of rungs on a ladder. Jacob's ladder is a joy to grow in the mixed-perennial border, both for its pillowy pale-purple flowers and for its unusual foliage that looks good all year long. There are forms native to Northwest meadows and low-growing varieties that can be grown as mounding ground cover. One of the most popular recent introductions, Polemonium caeruleum 'Brise d'Anjou', brightens up the landscape with striking variegated foliage. —DP

Bloom Period and Seasonal Color
Spring to early summer; lavender, pale-blue, white, and peachy-pink blooms

Mature Height × Spread
1 to 2 feet × 1 to 1^1/$_2$ feet

Zones
4 to 8

139

Japanese Anemone
Anemone × hybrida and cultivars

A late-season bloomer, flowering when most perennials have finished their show, Japanese anemone rises from its basal leaves with a 3- to 4-foot flower stalk in early autumn. It lights shady corners with creamy-white or rose flowers centered by yellow stamens in neat circles. The flower form resembles its spring-blooming relatives, the DeCaen anemones and Grecian windflowers. Japanese anemone's dark-green leaves look attractive throughout summer, adding to its garden value, as do the round chartreuse button buds appearing in August. Individual blooms last only a day or two and do not survive when picked for bouquets. But the buds continue to open throughout fall. The value of Japanese anemone lies in its superb ability to provide interest as perennial gardens decline. —MR

Bloom Period and Seasonal Color
Fall; white, pink, and rose blooms

Mature Height × Spread
3 to 4 feet × 2 feet

Zones
4 to 9

When, Where, and How to Plant
Plant Japanese anemone from containers in spring or fall, and divide in early spring, setting plants about 18 inches apart. Plant at the same level as in the container; if planting from divisions, place the ropelike roots 4 inches underground. Protect from afternoon heat and sun exposure, but morning sun suits them. Japanese anemones need well-drained compost-enriched soil. In colder areas, mulch for winter. For general guidelines on planting perennials, see page 115.

Growing Tips
Japanese anemone needs a few seasons to establish and bloom freely. Despite its many virtues, it can become invasive in moist soils. Dig around the clumps in early spring to remove wandering roots. (This plant propagates by root cuttings and will regrow from bits left in the soil.) It spreads less in drier soil and almost tolerates summer drought in shady spots, surviving with only monthly deep watering. An extremely long-lived perennial (which may contribute to its tendency to spread), it's best without dividing for up to ten years.

Care
Cut back bloomed-out bare stems in late fall, but allow leaves to remain near the ground in milder areas where they may show evergreen for much of the winter. East of the Cascades, freezes blacken the foliage, and it can either be removed or left until spring. Soggy winter soil can kill these anemones (as all anemones). No insect or disease pests bother these significantly. These plants can sometimes show a bit of powdery mildew disease late in the blooming season, but it's not harmful. Prune out affected areas.

Companion Planting and Design
Japanese painted fern (*Athyrium nipponicum* var. *pictum*) and hosta complement the silvery-pink *Anemone × hybrida* 'September Charm'.

We Recommend
'Whirlwind', with double white flowers, and white 'Honorine Jobert' give a summer boost to moon gardens, especially when flowering after late-blooming aurelian lilies. A valuable relative is *Anemone nemerosa*, a low woodland bloomer with small white, pink, or blue flowers in midspring, spreading well in moist shade.

Knotweed
Persicaria virginiana

When, Where, and How to Plant

Plant knotweed in spring, early summer, or fall. Most forms of this perennial can take average soil conditions, although it is best to situate in moist, well-drained soil. Plant in full sun to partial shade. If you are concerned about it spreading, situate knotweed where it is partially confined, such as next to a sidewalk or in a container. Follow the general guidelines for planting perennials on page 115. Space plants 18 to 24 inches apart.

Growing Tips

Water regularly until plants are established. Knotweed prefers moist soil, so you may need to provide supplemental irrigation during dry spells. A 2-inch layer of mulch helps retain moisture and keep roots cool. These plants generally don't require fertilizer.

Care

Once you plant knotweed, it generally requires little care other than irrigation. It may be attractive to slugs; chewed or damaged foliage can be cut away. Most flowering forms produce spikes in late summer; remove after blooming. Many forms of knotweed are deciduous and will die back with first frost. Cut back damaged or dead foliage, and lightly mulch the crown to protect during winter.

Companion Planting and Design

Knotweed is a great foliage accent in the border. Highlight interesting variegation with contrasting companions. For example, purple heuchera or New Zealand flax will intensify the drama of *Persicaria virginiana* 'Painter's Palette', which has cream-streaked foliage banded in deep pink. Wine-and-pewter-streaked *Persicaria microcephala* 'Red Dragon' deserves pairing with silver-leafed licorice plant. Emulate the romantic meadows of American designers James van Sweden and Wolfgang Oehme and plant long-blooming drifts of *Persicaria milletii*—countless rose-crimson spikes will gently sway in the breeze, seeming to float above clumping mounds of deep-green foliage.

We Recommend

We admire the dynamic *P. microcephala* 'Red Dragon' noted above for its intense black-purple foliage, highlighted with silver chevrons. *P. bisorta* 'Superba' has large, dense spikes of light-pink flowers.

The many forms of knotweed are rapidly catching the imagination of Northwest garden designers, both for the bottlebrush floral spikes that bloom on tall stems and for variegated and patterned foliage in shades of gold, green, silver, and wine. Knotweed is an upright perennial with unusual jointed stems stretched out in a zigzag. You can enjoy the dynamic oval and arrow-shaped foliage—with multicolored chevrons and streaks—in spring and summer. Later in the summer, the pink and crimson flowers emerge on upright spikes, blooming above the foliage. Knotweed is an undemanding perennial for the mixed border, mass plantings, and container designs. Some forms may spread too eagerly, but this can be easily managed by digging up and potting "volunteer" plants and giving them away. —DP

Bloom Period and Seasonal Color
Spring to summer; variegated foliage; pink, crimson, and white foliage late summer to early fall

Mature Height × Spread
$1^{1}/_{2}$ to 4 feet × 2 to 4 feet

Zones
5 to 9

Lady's Mantle
Alchemilla mollis

Lady's mantle provides good late-spring and early-summer clumping form and fresh green color to the perennial garden. It's a must-have garden edger, joining and weaving other plants together. The leaves open by spreading pleats, almost like a fan, and their soft texture makes them touchable (just asking to be tucked in May baskets!). Scalloped leaf margins are rimmed with tiny notches nearly like fringe. Look early in the morning to find dew held on the leaf margins, each notch carrying one shining drop. Leaves contribute the most garden value, but the flowers, bunched on stems held above the leaves, glow lime-yellow. Their fine texture moves in breezes like a yellow haze. Evergreen in milder areas, lady's mantle may go dormant during frigid weather. —MR

Bloom Period and Seasonal Color
Spring and early summer; lime-yellow blooms

Mature Height × Spread
1 to 2 feet × 2 feet

Zones
3 to 9

When, Where, and How to Plant
Spring or fall planting from containers or division will work well. If summer temperatures get very hot in your area, choose a shadier location; lady's mantle can manage partial sun where summers stay cool. Prepare the soil by amending with organic material; provide excellent drainage. Space between 12 and 18 inches apart depending on the size of your plants, from 4-inch to 1-gallon containers. Miniature *Alchemilla alpina*, only 3 inches tall and 6 inches across, with silvery-edged leaves, is less long lived and needs to be sited where more vigorous plants don't obscure it. For general guidelines on planting perennials, see page 115.

Growing Tips
If the plant declines during summer hot spells, cut off all foliage and keep it well watered to encourage new growth. Mulch with 2 to 3 inches of organic material, taking care not to bury the crown. Fertilize in spring once growth starts with a 5-10-10 formula or a balanced organic fertilizer. (For more details, see page 117.)

Care
Trim off dead leaves at the end of winter to allow fresh foliage to develop. Even in midsummer you can transplant seedlings or small plants, because it's not fussy about root disturbance. Water consistently after summer transplanting. Lady's mantle will seed itself over a wide area. Trim off the fluffy yellow flowers just as bloom fades if you don't want seedlings. Slugs will chew it, but it produces fresh leaves so quickly when growing well that the damage won't be noticeable. Otherwise, lady's mantle thrives easily without problems.

Companion Planting and Design
Both leaf and flower colors harmonize with blues and purples, like catmint. It's lovely under roses because its roots don't compete. Or try it with violets or in front of tulips or daffodils in the heritage garden.

We Recommend
Alchemilla mollis may be common, but it's far from ordinary. Miniature *A. alpina* is a silvery gem but requires careful placement so larger plants don't obscure it.

Lavender
Lavandula species

When, Where, and How to Plant
Plant container-grown lavender in spring. Lavender thrives in hot, sunny conditions, although it can also handle partial sun if given good drainage. Though it prefers sandy soil, it can succeed in average soil with adequate drainage. But lavender suffers greatly in soggy conditions. You can also plant this cherished herb in raised beds or rock gardens designed to create good drainage. Follow the general guidelines for planting perennials on page 115; space plants 18 to 24 inches apart.

Growing Tips
Water regularly until the plants are established, after which lavender is relatively drought tolerant. Use crushed rock rather than organic compost as a mulch and to promote fast drainage. Little or no fertilizer is required.

Care
Maintain lavender by keeping it well groomed. Follow the methods of Northwest lavender farms; trim back or shear plants by one-half to one-third after blooming. This will keep plants compact and uniform. If stems become thick and woody, trim out the oldest branches or replace the plant. Lavender is generally not bothered by pests.

Companion Planting and Design
Grow lavender as a lovely hedge in a formal garden, incorporating other herbs and perennials that lend themselves to clipping or knot designs, such as boxwood, santolina, catmint, and germander. Drifts of lavender can create a dreamy atmosphere along a bank or terraced garden where good drainage is ensured. Plant French lavender (*Lavandula dentata*) for its velvety silver-toothed foliage and dark-purple flowers. English lavender (*L. angustifolia*) is a sweet-smelling, hardy species native to southern Europe. Spanish lavender (*L. stoechas*) is grown for its dark-purple flowers topped with distinctive "wings" or bracts.

We Recommend
Lavandula 'Goodwin Creek Grey' is an Oregon hybrid with year-round silver foliage and long-blooming, deep-violet flowers. *L. angustifolia* 'Hidcote' is a superb dark-purple English lavender that keeps its color when dried. *L. stoechas* 'Wings of Night' is a choice dwarf Spanish lavender.

The romance of lavender is one of the joys of gardening in the sunshine. Bees flock to the aromatic purple blooms, and when you brush against a row of lavender, it rewards you with the fragrance of southern France. There are so many excellent forms of lavender for the landscape, from English and French lavender to the spring-blooming Spanish lavender. Grow this evergreen perennial herb for its silvery-gray foliage and long-blooming purple spikes. Edge a border, plant a field, or fill a cutting garden with versatile lavender. Harvest dark-purple 'Hidcote' lavender, weaving the stems with satin ribbon for scented gifts. All this plant needs is well-drained soil and plenty of sunshine. If you're not blessed with Mediterranean-like conditions, create a lavender container garden. —DP

Bloom Period and Seasonal Color
Early to midsummer; lavender and purple blooms

Mature Height × Spread
18 to 30 inches × 2 to 5 feet

Zones
5 to 9

New Zealand Flax
Phormium species and cultivars

New Zealand flax delivers high design to the containers and borders of Northwest landscapes. We love the spiky, architectural form of this tropical-looking plant. As long as New Zealand flax has excellent drainage, it can handle most garden conditions. This exotic perennial provides height, structure, and dynamic color to the mixed border. From deep-purple to gray-green and variegated striped forms, with blades more than 1 inch wide and as narrow as ¹/₂ inch, New Zealand flax is incomparable for the presence it adds to the garden. You can indicate the entrance to your garden by planting a pair of New Zealand flaxes on either side of a gate. Create a focal point by elevating a decorative container planted with New Zealand flax on a pedestal. —DP

Bloom Period and Seasonal Color
Evergreen; grown for year-round foliage interest; tall floral stalks late spring to early summer

Mature Height × Spread
3 to 5 feet × 1 to 3 feet

Zones
8 to 10

When, Where, and How to Plant
Plant in spring or autumn. Like many plants from Mediterranean-like climates, New Zealand flax is durable but prefers moist, well-drained soil in full to partial sun. Don't allow the crown or roots to sit in soggy soil or the plant will rot. This is a deceptively small plant when purchased in a 1-gallon nursery pot, so be sure to allow space for it to enlarge in the garden, or consider repotting container-planted New Zealand flax every two to three years. For general guidelines on planting perennials, see page 115.

Growing Tips
Water regularly until the plants are established, after which they are relatively drought tolerant. Little or no fertilizer is required.

Care
Maintain this plant by cutting away dried or damaged leaves at the base. Groom it each spring by removing exterior blades that suffer from sun or windburn. Protect from frost by mulching in late autumn. West of the Cascades, when extended freeze is uncommon, New Zealand flax should winter over. If freeze occurs, cut your New Zealand flax to the ground and it may regrow in spring. If given appropriate soil and light conditions, this is a disease- and pest-free plant.

Companion Planting and Design
With swordlike blades fanning out in an elegant symmetrical pattern, New Zealand flax is a commanding presence in the perennial garden. Use it in masses to fill an island bed. Its slender or chubby blades measure more than 3 feet long, an eye-catching backdrop for the mixed border. New Zealand flax is a singular choice for an urn or large container, pairing nicely with other Mediterranean-style perennials.

We Recommend
Phormium tenax and *P. cookianum* are the two species in this genus. Eye-catching cultivars include *P. tenax* 'Purpureum', a bronzy-purple form that grows 6 feet or taller, and *P. tenax* 'Jack Spratt', a dwarf purple form that grows to 1¹/₂ feet tall. Colorful hybrids, selected for distinctive foliage, include *P.* 'Maori Sunrise', with pinkish orange striped foliage.

Peony

Paeonia lacitiflora and cultivars

When, Where, and How to Plant

Bare-root peonies are ideally planted in fall, while container-grown peonies are frequently sold for spring planting. Situate peonies in full to partial sun. This herbaceous perennial prefers moist, rich, well-drained soil. Amend areas with heavy clay soil with organic compost before planting. Dig a large hole, twice the width of the container or bare-root crown. Place the crown on an elevated mound at the base of the hole, spreading sections equally and making sure the eyes of the crown face upward (the crown should be 1 to 2 inches beneath the soil's surface). After planting, pack the soil firmly and water thoroughly. Place peonies 3 feet apart.

Growing Tips

Water container-grown plants regularly until established. Fall and winter rains typically provide enough irrigation for the bare-root plants. In spring, water regularly during dry spells, especially before blooming. Feed peonies in spring with a balanced organic fertilizer—but too much nitrogen will encourage foliage growth over bloom growth. Protect crowns in winter, raking away excess mulch (anything that's left) in spring.

Care

Insects, except for ants, rarely bother peonies. If you see ants crawling around the buds and blooms, gently spray them off with a hose. When cutting flowers for indoor arrangements, make sure to leave the ants outside. Remove any blackened leaves caused by botrytis blight. Overwatering can cause crown rot. Use guards, stakes, or supports to keep the blooms upright. Deadhead the spent blooms, and cut back foliage in late fall.

Companion Planting and Design

A border of peonies is a breathtaking sight in springtime. Incorporate single, double, and fluffier forms of this lovely flower into mixed-perennial beds or rose borders. Peonies bloom at the same time as Siberian irises, making for a doubly attractive combination.

We Recommend

Paeonia lacitiflora 'Bowl of Beauty' has gorgeous lavender-pink outer petals (the "bowl"), filled with fringed white centers. 'Gay Paree' features cerise-pink outer petals and a blush-of-pink center.

From ball-shaped bud to attractive glossy-green foliage, peonies have brought delight to generations of gardeners. During the four weeks when they bloom each spring, there's nothing more alluring than the 6- to 10-inch blooms of a charming peony. Nostalgic plants that thrive for decades, peonies have enjoyed a renaissance among floral designers and brides alike. Perhaps it's because of the alluring contrast between the tight bud and the voluptuous petal-packed bloom, but we can't have enough of these flowers. An important part of a cutting garden, peonies offer many hues and forms. As a landscape plant, this is a foolproof perennial that is lovely in bloom, offering romantic foliage that can hide dying spring bulbs or mask the bare stems of taller plants. —DP

Bloom Period and Seasonal Color
Late spring to early summer; white, pink, crimson, cream, and bicolored blooms

Mature Height × Spread
2 to 3 feet × 3 feet

Zones
4 to 8

Pinks

Dianthus species and cultivars

Commonly called "pinks" for the fringed edges of their flowers (tailor's scissors that cut zigzag edges are called pinking shears), the genus Dianthus is characterized by hardy forms of the florist's carnation. Pinks offer an intense color palette—from deep maroon and vibrant red to cotton-candy pink and bicolored forms. You'll appreciate this tiny bloomer for its delicious fragrance, tidy habit, and long-lasting performance as a cut flower. Pinks require good drainage and lots of sunshine. Plant these minicarnations in a rock garden or along the edge of a border or pathway. They will reward you with profuse, spicy blooms emerging from a low mat of blue-green foliage. Pinks combine beautifully with other rock garden plants, such as sea thrift (Armeria maritima) and creeping thymes. —DP

Bloom Period and Seasonal Color
Late spring to midsummer; white, pink, cherry-red, and maroon blooms

Mature Height × Spread
9 to 18 inches × 12 to 18 inches

Zones
5 to 9

When, Where, and How to Plant
Pinks appreciate a site combining excellent drainage with full sun. Select a sandy or loamy location with good drainage. If you have heavy or clay soil, amend with organic compost before planting pinks. Some gardeners incorporate a 20 percent ratio of finely crushed rock into the planting soil to improve drainage. Follow the general planting guidelines for perennials on page 115, spacing pinks 18 inches apart.

Growing Tips
Water pinks regularly until established; after that, they are relatively drought tolerant. Irrigate during extended dry spells. Do not allow pinks to sit in soggy soil, or the roots will rot. Mulching can also contribute to rotting. Pinks do not require fertilization. You can add lime to the soil if it's highly acidic.

Care
Slugs occasionally nibble at pinks in the garden. Some forms of pinks are susceptible to rust, which can be avoided by keeping the area around plants free of wet mulch or excessive watering. Deadhead pinks at the flower base after blooming, and you may enjoy a secondary bloom. Pinks benefit from division every two to three years. Divide in early spring or autumn by digging up a carpet of dense foliage, separating it into sections with a garden knife, and replanting those into a rock garden or well-drained soil. Make sure divided sections have adequate root material; water until established.

Companion Planting and Design
Because they're shorter than average, move pinks to the front of a perennial border, tucking them between other sun-loving plants like lavender or fleabane. Rock gardens are ideal for pinks. Create your own rock garden environment for pinks by piling three rocks together, filling the openings with sandy soil and planting pinks in the center.

We Recommend
Dianthus gratianopolitanus 'Tiny Rubies' is a dwarf cheddar pink selection with double ruby-red flowers on 4-inch stems. Cottage pink (*D. plumaris*) is the famous European species with matted gray-green foliage and spicy-fragrant blooms on 12- to 18-inch stems.

Primrose
Primula species and hybrids

When, Where, and How to Plant

Plant in earliest spring, in shade in moist soil containing ample organic amendments. Clay soils and sandy, gravelly soils won't grow primrose. Set plants about 6 inches apart, farther if they are among the widest spreading. Mulch with 2-3 inches of compost after planting. Avoid all hot, windy, exposed locations. For general guidelines on planting perennials, see page 115.

Growing Tips

Mulching and a constant supply of water benefit primroses. Light fertilization, using a 5-1-1 in early spring, also helps their health. Once rains cease after May, they require regular deep watering. With some plants, water needs can be flexible once the plants establish, but not with primroses. No matter the age of the plant, water's a necessity. Many, such as yellow English cowslip (*Primula florindae*), thrive along pond and stream edges. With sufficient water supplies, primroses can handle partial sun. Mulch, soaker hoses, and the shade of deciduous trees such as flowering crabapple or cherry will agree with them.

Care

Slugs love these. You'll have to use all possible management methods: hand-picking, vigilance, and beer traps or iron phosphate slug bait to protect the leaves and bloom. Powdery mildew can bother them late in the season; removing affected foliage usually helps. Primroses may be divided after flowering, but they increase slowly and can prosper for years without division.

Companion Planting and Design

In a protected, moist woodland, primroses will cover the ground, sharing spring space with pulmonarias and the emerging foliage of astilbes. To provide primroses with conditions they need, plant them in large containers, several to a 14-inch pot. They're safe from deer, easy to water, and delightful to observe.

We Recommend

Deep-copper and yellow *Primula veris* 'Sunset Shades', each with a lime calyx, the flowers carried above the leaves, make a vivid garden presence. Along a pond or water edge, drumstick primrose (*P. denticulata*), in lilac or white, can produce blooms nearly a foot tall, with a long period of flowering.

Primroses fascinate gardeners, appearing for centuries in poems and stories. In nurseries and even grocery stores during earliest spring, you'll find the rather squat plants of hybrid primroses, with their brilliant primary colors— and fragrance. Often treated as annuals, these only hint at the possibilities of the floriferous and prolific primrose family. If your garden has ample water and shade, you can tuck in many different types. Primula veris, great for shady waterside edges, has clear-yellow flowers 12 inches above the leaves. Flower shapes standing tall mark the candelabra primroses, sometimes reaching 2 feet and defying ideas of primroses as dumpy ground-hugging plants. Color, scent, and form combine in spring and summer primrose blooms to lead gardeners into appreciating moist, shady spots. —MR

Other Common Name
Cowslip

Bloom Period and Seasonal Color
Spring and summer; yellow, pink, rose, red, blue, purple, and bicolored blooms

Mature Height × Spread
4 to 24 inches × 4 to 12 inches

Zones
4 to 8

Pulmonaria
Pulmonaria species and cultivars

Spring perennial season often opens with pulmonaria, invaluable on the shady woodland edge following hellebore's bloom. Leaves and flowers combine to brighten shade, with stems of dangling flowers held above the leaves, often showing clear blues and bright pinks on the same stem. Leaves brightly speckled with white help them stand out. Flowers open when foliage does, sometimes preceding the full leaf expansion. Pulmonaria spreads slowly into ground-covering masses, but doesn't become invasive. Though dozens of cultivars exist, you'll likely find only a few in spring nursery offerings. All pulmonaria satisfy in shade and, with enough moisture, can stay nearly evergreen through winter in milder areas. Pulmonaria even manages the darker north edges of gardens, blooming cheerfully in daunting spots. —MR

Other Common Names
Soldiers and sailors, blue cowslip

Bloom Period and Seasonal Color
Spring; white, pink, blue, purple, red, and salmon blooms

Mature Height × Spread
6 to 18 inches × 12 to 24 inches

Zones
2 to 8

When, Where, and How to Plant
Woodsy soil, well amended with compost, will help pulmonaria cover well if set 6 to 10 inches apart in shade. Moisture-retentive soil and a consistent supply of water are vital for best growth. Plant in spring or fall. In light shade, plant bulbs like grape hyacinth (*Muscari* species) and cover the top of the planting with pulmonaria. It's seldom planted from seed but will seed itself if established. For general guidelines on planting perennials, see page 115.

Growing Tips
Fertilize lightly in early spring, using a slow-release 5-1-1. Pulmonaria requires irrigation to keep its foliage healthy in summer.

Care
Clear old foliage in late winter for a fresh look in spring, just before new leaves unfold. Many will retain leaves through winter, though this doesn't always occur. Avoid nicking the growing tips when trimming. Remove dead leaves when they brown out. Pulmonaria can develop severe powdery mildew on old leaves in midsummer; trim them off. If the plant goes into winter with leaves pruned off because of disease, cover it with a protective mulch. 'Excalibur', with blue flowers, resists mildew. If the planting area is poorly drained, with persistent soggy spots, the plant's crown may suffer from rot. If so, lift the plants, discard the affected sections, and replant. Some pulmonaria are self-fertile and will replicate themselves by seeds. Others do not, or result in varied plants. If you don't want seedlings, remove the spent flower. Divide immediately after bloom or in fall, taking large sections to allow for quickest recovery. Water after dividing if fall rains haven't arrived. In the coldest areas, confine division to spring.

Companion Planting and Design
Dark-flowered 'Blue Ensign' makes a fine companion for the small white daffodil 'Thalia' in midspring. Planted in front of fall-blooming anemone, the growing anemone leaves cover pulmonaria's summer decline.

We Recommend
Pulmonaria rubra 'Redstart' blooms with clear coral; 'Benediction' presents the deepest blue flowers—like lake depths.

Purple Coneflower

Echinacea purpurea

When, Where, and How to Plant

Purple coneflower can be planted in spring or summer. While this perennial tolerates most soil types, including dry or heavy conditions, it prefers moist, well-drained average soil. Purple coneflower will perform best in full sun, although it can also be planted in partly sunny locations. For general guidelines on planting perennials, see page 115.

Growing Tips

Water purple coneflower regularly until established, after which time they are relatively drought tolerant. Do not overwater or allow purple coneflower to sit in soggy soil. This is an undemanding perennial that does not require fertilization.

Care

When planted in a well-drained site, purple coneflowers are disease free. But if the plants are too close or become crowded, you may notice foliar mildew or fungus. Remove the diseased leaves, and thin the crowded stems (you can divide purple coneflower every four years). Fungal diseases, such as powdery mildew, are typically caused by overwatering. See the plant health care section on page 248 for tips on avoiding the onset of powdery mildew. Deadhead to encourage prolonged blooms. At the end of the summer, leave the flowers on the plant to dry; they provide the delicious seedheads that feed winter birds.

Companion Planting and Design

Stiff and bold, purple coneflowers belong in large beds or islands rather than in tiny cottage gardens. Their rugged looks reflect their prairie heritage, which makes purple coneflower a good companion for ornamental grasses, Joe-pye weed, black-eyed Susan, 'Autumn Joy' sedum, and other tough, long-blooming perennials. Purple coneflower is a great choice for cutting gardens, as it will hold its color and form in a vase of water for as long as a week.

We Recommend

Echinacea purpurea 'Magnus' has massive purple-pink blooms that measure up to 7 inches across. 'White Lustre' has white rays and reaches to $2^{1}/_{2}$ feet tall. The newer red-orange form is a vibrant cultivar called 'Art's Pride'.

If you love seeing acres of lavender, wait until you catch a glimpse of a field planted with purple coneflowers. Emulate commercial Echinacea purpurea growers, and plant this dark-pink-petaled perennial in masses. For height (pink and white blooms to tower on stems 3 to 4 feet tall) and graphic impact (the center is a textured orange cone), you can't beat purple coneflower. This is a sun-loving North American native perennial that shines in late summer, when other flowers are losing steam. Purple coneflower pairs nicely with ornamental grasses and other tall perennials and is a long-lasting cut flower for garden-fresh arrangements. Keep an eye out for the newest twist on purple coneflower, as breeders are busy rolling out melon, orange, and peach cultivars.
—DP

Bloom Period and Seasonal Color
Mid- to late summer; rose-pink and white blooms

Mature Height × Spread
2 to 4 feet × 2 feet

Zones
3 to 9

Red-Hot Poker

Kniphofia uvaria and hybrids

This stiff, towering perennial is the favorite of my two boys—its red-hot scepters have captured their imaginations with storybook ideas of valiant knights. On its own, red-hot poker looks a little rigid, so integrate it with other architectural perennials and grasses, where it serves as an exciting exclamation point of sizzling color. These tropical-looking, sun-loving flowers are typically found blooming red and orange from midsummer to fall. If you want a softer statement, plant the lemon-yellow and apricot forms, which look great with silver-foliage plants like cardoon or ornamental artichoke. Red-hot poker has robust blades of foliage that are attractive even after the flowers have bloomed. Relatively drought-tolerant, it's easy to grow and always prompts the question "What's that?" when seen by young garden visitors. —DP

Other Common Name
Torch lily

Bloom Period and Seasonal Color
Midsummer to fall; coral-red, orange, yellow, white, and pale-green blooms

Mature Height × Spread
2 to 6 feet × 2 to 6 feet

Zones
6 to 9

When, Where, and How to Plant
Plant red-hot poker in spring or early summer, in moist, well-drained soil. This South African native prefers sunny locations, but will bloom in partial sun. It must have moisture in order to produce the elongated flowers formed by many tiny tubular blooms. Follow the general planting guidelines for perennials on page 115, spacing red-hot poker 18 to 24 inches apart.

Growing Tips
Water plants regularly until established, keeping the soil moist until the pokerlike flowers have bloomed. Red-hot pokers can handle boggy summer conditions if the area in which they grow tends to dry out in winter. They generally do not require fertilization.

Care
Depending upon the variety, red-hot poker can bloom throughout summer into fall. Encourage reblooming by removing spent flowers at the base of the stem. Leave the foliage in place over winter to protect the growing crown; tie the grassy blades into a bundle to lift them off the wet ground. In spring, cut back any tattered or dead leaves to keep the plant looking tidy until new growth emerges. Protect from slugs and snails. Plants bloom more prolifically after a few seasons. Divide every three to four years after blooming.

Companion Planting and Design
Red-hot poker is a distinctive plant that commands attention. Grow stands of this perennial at the back of a border, allowing the torchlike blooms to peek up over other sun-loving perennials, such as euphorbias and daylilies. Pair with exotic-looking plants, such as hardy bananas and hardy palms, to create a sultry garden oasis. Cut the long stalks to use flowers in dramatic floral arrangements.

We Recommend
Kniphofia uvaria produces the classic coral-red "hot poker" blooms on stems 3 feet tall. Many hybrids have been bred from this parent, including *K.* 'Little Maid', a dwarf form with creamy-white blooms to 2 feet tall. *K.* 'Shining Scepter' has 3-foot-tall tangerine blooms. *K.* 'Malibu Yellow' features 5- to 6-foot stems with lime-green buds opening to 8-inch-long yellow flowers.

Russian Sage

Perovskia atriplicifolia

When, Where, and How to Plant

Plant in spring or early summer, in most types of soil, as long as the drainage is good. This perennial thrives in full sun. If grown in partial sun, its appearance suffers, as the stems will flop over while reaching for heat and light. Follow the general planting guidelines for perennials on page 115, spacing Russian sage 24 to 30 inches apart.

Growing Tips

Water plants regularly until established, after which time Russian sage tolerates drought. Do not allow the soil to get soggy. This low-maintenance plant doesn't require ongoing irrigation or feeding.

Care

Generally disease and pest free, Russian sage will thrive in full sun and good drainage. This woody subshrub doesn't fully die back in winter. Cut back old stems in early spring when there are signs of new foliage emerging. Trim back tangled branches to about 6 inches, thinning at the center. Cut spent blooms to encourage extended flowering. Because it is a woody perennial, Russian sage does not respond well to divisions. Propagate by softwood cuttings.

Companion Planting and Design

Russian sage provides a cool antidote to the hot sunny border, or when planted where its textured form spills onto the walkway. It is especially attractive when grown in masses of three or five, creating an airy haze of soft, lilac-purple blooms. For high contrast, plant with cheery-yellow companions, such as black-eyed Susan or 'Stella d'Oro' daylilies. Its presence in cut arrangements provides height and a delicate touch of purple. For a perfectly romantic bouquet, insert sprigs of Russian sage between the massive purple or pink heads of cut hydrangea blooms. Russian sage can also be dried for everlasting arrangements.

We Recommend

Nurseries typically carry improved hybrids of *Perovskia atriplicifolia* and *P. abrotanoides*. One of the most widely available is 'Blue Spire', which has deep-violet blooms. 'Blue Mist' is a lighter purple form. 'Filigren' has finely cut silvery foliage that glistens in sunshine and is topped with steely-blue flower spikes.

Its open, informal style and velvety lavender flowers make Russian sage an irresistible perennial for the summer garden. It is an ideal plant for softening and blending with more rigid-looking flowers, thanks to its silvery-gray branches and toothed foliage. When given the right conditions of full sun and good drainage, Russian sage grows to 4 feet tall and spreads to nearly 3 feet. As a flower for the cutting garden, it is a floral designer's delight, adding a dreamy quality to arrangements. Russian sage pairs equally well with vibrant hot-colored perennials like purple coneflower and intense-orange daylilies, and with romantic, silvery herbs and pastel bellflowers. Or plant masses of Russian sage on a dry, sunny bank for a delicate haze of soft purple. —DP

Bloom Period and Seasonal Color
Early summer through fall; lavender-blue blooms

Mature Height × Spread
3 to 4 feet × 3 feet

Zones
6 to 9

Sea Holly
Eryngium species

Just when the garden is getting too predicable, the curious sea holly adds a jolt. An otherworldly perennial, sea holly offers wild texture and amethyst hues to the mixed border. Just don't plant this thorny perennial near a walkway, or it may catch on your expensive sweater! Cherished for its unusual barbed bracts, cone-shaped flower, and steely-purple color, sea holly is an astonishing sight in the border, interrupting soft billows of old-fashioned perennials with its deadly spikes. Sea holly is ideal for the hot border, as it can thrive in poor, dry soil. With heights to 5 feet and varieties in blue, purple, or silvery white, sea holly is an unforgettable plant. It can be added to fresh floral arrangements or dried as an everlasting. —DP

Bloom Period and Seasonal Color
Summer through fall; purple, blue, and white blooms

Mature Height × Spread
1 to 5 feet × 1 to 2 feet

Zones
5 to 9

When, Where, and How to Plant
Plant sea holly in spring or early summer, situating plants in areas receiving full sun. This perennial can handle many soil conditions, as long as it receives good drainage. Follow the general planting guidelines for perennials on page 115, spacing sea holly about 24 to 30 inches apart.

Growing Tips
Water the plants regularly until established, after which time sea holly requires irrigation only during dry spells. Some forms tolerate drought. Do not allow the soil to get soggy, or the crown will rot. This is a low-maintenance plant that doesn't require feeding.

Care
Generally disease and pest free, sea holly may suffer from powdery mildew if its foliage is wet or crowded. Slugs and snails can also be a problem. Flowers are often left on this long-blooming plant to add late-summer texture and interest. Trim back stems and foliage in early spring, before new growth emerges. Some species reseed vigorously, in which case, you should deadhead before they go to seed.

Companion Planting and Design
The thistlelike flowers and barbed foliage of sea holly are sharp enough to discourage you from growing it near high-traffic areas of the garden. Instead, plant sea holly near the back of a border or surround it with softer plants to avoid injury to you and your guests. Create an eerie drama by pairing purple sea holly with purple globe thistle, incorporating black-plum New Zealand flax for contrast. The stems, foliage, and bracts of sea holly are typically frosted in silver or shades of blue-amethyst, making it a good companion for drought-tolerant gray-green companions like lamb's ears, Russian sage, and artemisia.

We Recommend
Eryngium giganteum 'Miss Willmott's Ghost' is a biennial or perennial that typically reseeds in the garden, producing blue-silver cones surrounded by silvery bracts, to 5 feet. *E.* 'Sapphire Blue' has coarsely toothed leaves and numerous stems topped with vibrant-blue flowers in late summer, growing to 3 feet.

Sedum

Sedum species and cultivars

When, Where, and How to Plant

Plant from spring to fall, situating plants in areas receiving full sun. Sedums adapt to many soil conditions, as long as the drainage is good. In heavy or rich soil, upright sedums are prone to splaying at the center. Follow the general guidelines for planting perennials on page 115, spacing plants according to selection.

Growing Tips

Water the plants regularly until established, after which time sedum requires irrigation only during flowering and extended dry spells. Sedums generally tolerate heat and drought. You do not need to fertilize them.

Care

For the most part disease and pest free, sedums occasionally attract aphids, which can be washed off with a spray from the garden hose. To improve the performance of 'Autumn Joy' and other upright sedums, cut back the entire plant by one-half around July 4. It will grow sturdier stems and produce lovely, late-summer blooms (you can try rooting cut sections in sandy soil to produce more sedum). Spreading or cascading forms require little grooming, although you can deadhead flowers after blooming. Or leave spent blooms through autumn to provide tasty seedheads for birds. The plant dies to the ground in winter.

Companion Planting and Design

Drifts of 'Autumn Joy' give perennial borders a lavish, bold feeling. You can edge plantings of taller perennials with a row of upright sedums, which serve as a tidy frame for other sun-loving perennials like ornamental grasses, daylilies, and knotweeds. Sedum is a good cut flower for bouquets, adding appeal with succulent foliage and rosy, tufted blooms. Soften the edge of a rock garden with the draping forms, or plant mat forms between steppingstones. (See the Ground Covers chapter on page 78 for more suggestions.)

We Recommend

Sedum telephium 'Atropurpureum' is a sturdy upright form with fleshy burgundy stems and foliage, and showy purple-red blooms to 24 inches. 'Autumn Joy', a classic cultivar, produces dark-pink blooms that take on a bronze tinge in late summer; it grows to 24 inches.

Hardy sedums are ideal plants for Northwest gardens because they require little maintenance, can handle sudden drops in temperature, and tolerate both wet and dry conditions, especially if the drainage is good. 'Autumn Joy', the all-time late-summer favorite, offers everything a good perennial should: great foliage, long-blooming performance, and attractive seedheads. Every sun-loving border should include the mauve and plum crests of 'Autumn Joy', upright and uniform in bloom. Hardy sedums include some that cascade nicely over a rock wall and others that look happy wedged between steppingstones. With succulent stems and foliage in hues of silvery-gray, blue-green, and maroon, sedums look great even when not in bloom. Because they thrive in heat but require good drainage, sedums make great container plants. —DP

Other Common Name
Stonecrop

Bloom Period and Seasonal Color
Summer through fall; pink, plum, creamy-white, and yellow blooms

Mature Height × Spread
2 to 24 inches × 12 to 24 inches

Zones
3 to 10

Siberian Bugloss
Brunnera macrophylla

Less common than other garden colors, blue is most welcome in spring when it contrasts with the emerging chartreuse of new leaves and the pastels of spring bulbs. Siberian bugloss carries bright-blue flowers in panicles, with dozens of flowers to a stalk, showing distinctly above the heart-shaped leaves in early spring. The flower shape resembles annual forget-me-nots, without the weedy tendencies. Neatness and sturdiness mark this plant, a long-lasting perennial once established. Brunnera prospers from midspring to early summer, when the shapely leaves show their best. It gradually develops clumps with some tolerance for late-summer dryness. Less used than it should be in our gardens, brunnera thrives on both sides of the mountains—a good plant for nearly all zones in Washington and Oregon. —MR

Bloom Period and Seasonal Color
Spring; blue blooms

Mature Height × Spread
12 to 18 inches × 12 inches

Zones
3 to 7

When, Where, and How to Plant
Plant in early spring or fall. This plant manages most soil types but requires excellent drainage, as do many shade plants. Settle it in partial sun or shady woodland edges, or plant it over hardy spring-blooming bulbs. If the soil lacks organic components, work in well-composted materials before planting. Spreading 3 inches of compost on the soil surface and digging it into the 12-inch level will provide excellent conditions for this and other woodlanders.

Growing Tips
Fertilize in early spring with a balanced, moderate nitrogen level fertilizer such as a 5-1-1. Siberian bugloss requires more moisture in spring than in summer; if spring rains slacken, give it at least an inch of water a week. Some cultivars don't tolerate dry conditions, especially those with white leaf edges, such as *Brunnera macrophylla* 'Variegata'.

Care
Brunnera requires relatively little attention. If you prefer to allow it to go dormant later in summer, watering less will accelerate the disappearance of leaves as fall approaches. To refresh the plant for fall, it's possible to cut the leaves away in summer, but you must then water sufficiently to support new growth. Or you can let the dead leaves remain until earliest spring to protect the growing crown, and then clip them off just as new growth starts. The white-edged forms require shadier spots to prevent leaves browning out. Ripe seeds often drop under leaves where new seedlings can start unobserved; check for them in spring. If you want to propagate it, taking root cuttings in spring results in new plants ready for installation by fall. No pests bother Siberian bugloss.

Companion Planting and Design
This plant adds to the charm of ferns, hostas, and shade-loving spring bulbs in a moist, protected corner and is a useful edger for plantings of *Narcissus* 'February Gold'.

We Recommend
Brunnera macrophylla 'Jack Frost', with distinct white leaf markings, and 'Langtrees', featuring silver-white spots on dark-green leaves, tolerate more late-summer dryness than other cultivars.

When, Where, and How to Plant

Plant in early spring from containers, in rich, thoroughly amended, and well-drained acidic soil with shade from afternoon sun and heat. Settle plants at the same level as they were when potted. Rhizomes should be 1 to 2 inches beneath the surface, no deeper. Mulch over the roots to a depth of about 1 inch.

Growing Tips

Fertilize in spring with a low-nitrogen organic fertilizer such as fish emulsion. These plants require moisture weekly through the bloom period and definitely until established, after two years. During summer, as growth slows they can handle drier conditions and may need watering only every three weeks.

Care

In fall, as the stems and leaves yellow, allow them to die down or trim them off. Avoid yanking on the stems since the rhizome is close to the surface. Renew the mulch yearly, using shredded leaves if possible. Few pests bother Solomon's seal, though deer do. Slugs can nibble in early spring but not as stems grow tougher. To move plants by division, dig up part of the heavy, dense roots and reset them in earliest spring or fall after the plants have gone dormant (replant in spring cold-winter spots). Look for upward pointing tips on roots, each of which will form a new stem and flowers. Set the roots 2 inches underground, with growth tips pointing in the direction you wish growing stems to face. Water well when first planted. They can be slow at first but once comfortable will be great garden residents, growing large each year. Mulch is vital to keep rhizomes from climbing out into the light; they are close to the surface and can be damaged.

Companion Planting and Design

Epimediums, ferns, hosta, and columbines combine with Solomon's seal, making woven tapestries in woodland or shade gardens. A natural for heritage gardens, it's been grown for hundreds of years.

We Recommend

Try *Polygonatum odoratum* 'Variegatum', lightly fragrant with a painted edge of white around each leaf.

Solomon's seal, with several different species, provides one of the most valuable plants for shade, even dark shade. It's known for its graceful arches of leaves and its small flowers rising above the ground. Handsome in spring, summer, and fall, the arched stems hold firm, glaucous-green leaves, touched with a hint of teal blue underneath in spring. Where the leaf meets its stem, dangling bell-shaped flowers bloom in late spring. Small blue ball-shaped fruit may appear later; they don't seem to feed any particular wildlife. Brilliant-yellow leaf color greets fall. Resistant to cold winters and hot summers, Solomon's seal establishes wide colonies of rhizomes, gradually expanding. This long-lived plant returns year after year, growing vigorously but avoiding invasiveness, being easily managed. —MR

Bloom Period and Seasonal Color
Spring; cream and green blooms

Mature Height × Spread
2 to 5 feet × 2 to 5 feet

Zones
3 to 8

Spurge
Euphorbia species and cultivars

I can't forget the botanical name Euphorbia *because it reminds me of "euphoric," which is the mood portrayed by the many exuberant forms of spurge. Who needs flower color when you can have acid-green, burgundy, and bright-yellow bracts (called cyathium), modified leaves that create the fascinating blooms of hardy spurge? There are more than 2,000 species in the spurge family, including December's favorite red flower, poinsettia, a tender form. Northwest gardeners have fallen in love with hardy forms of spurge large and small, including enormous, chartreuse* Euphorbia characias, *vivid* E. griffithii *'Fireglow', and mounded forms like cushion spurge. Where you have full to partial sun and excellent drainage, euphorbia is a great evergreen choice with interesting bottlebrush foliage and long-blooming, bright floral bracts.* —DP

Bloom Period and Seasonal Color
Midspring to early summer; yellow, orange, chartreuse, and lime blooms

Mature Height × Spread
6 to 36 inches × 12 to 24 inches

Zones
4 to 9

When, Where, and How to Plant
Plant in spring or early summer. Choose a site with average well-drained soil in full sun or part shade. Plants perform best in full sun, although you can grow spurge in part shade if soil is well drained. Spurges typically tolerate poor, sandy soil. For general guidelines on planting perennials, see page 115.

Growing Tips
Water spurge until well established. When grown in well-drained soil, spurge requires little additional irrigation. They will suffer in soggy or poorly drained soil. Spurges usually perform well without regular fertilization.

Care
Pests or diseases do generally not bother spurge varieties. Their worst enemy is lack of drainage and sunlight. If a plant splits open to reveal the center, it may be an indication it's in too much shade or soggy soil. While you can cut back sprawling stems to partially renovate the spurge, it may be better to relocate it to a sunnier area. The broken or cut stems and leaves produce a milky white sap that can irritate the skin.

Companion Planting and Design
Spurge could be elected "friendliest plant in the garden" for its ability to blend well with almost any other plant preferring the same culture. Dwarf conifers, ornamental grasses, flowering perennials and spring bulbs are great companions for spurge. Because of its unique bottlebrush-like whorled foliage and vibrant chrome, maroon, and lime-colored bracts, spurge provides bright texture and carefree form to the border. The evergreen foliage is a bonus where winter interest is preferred. Some types of spurge happily self-sow in the garden, but "babies" are easily handpicked to discourage spreading.

We Recommend
Cushion spurge (*E. polychroma*) features mounded foliage with fluorescent green-yellow spring flowers (to 2 feet). Popular with floral designers because of its white-green variegation, snow-on-the-mountain (*E. marginata*) is usually grown as an annual. *E. griffithii* 'Fireglow' has vivid orange-red bracts that turn copper in autumn. Donkey-tail spurge (*E. myrsinites*) features stems of blue-green pointed foliage that sprawl to 20 inches.

Sword Fern
Polysticum munitum

When, Where, and How to Plant

Prepare well-drained, compost-amended soil to a depth of at least 12 inches. Plant in full sun, partial shade, or shade. Plant at the same level sword fern grew in the container, setting plants 2 feet apart. Work the soil carefully around the dark, stringlike roots, firming it to avoid air pockets. Fern roots don't have the fresh white look of many herbaceous plants; healthy roots are brown-black. Water well.

Growing Tips

Fertilize in early spring. Composted manure is acceptable, a boost the plants seldom receive in the wild. Use organic fertilizers such as fish emulsion since native fern roots don't respond well to processed chemical fertilizers. Sword fern can grow without summer water—it is completely xeric once established. However, the more water it receives, the more quickly it will grow. Mulch with 2 to 3 inches of compost, or shredded leaves if available.

Care

By late summer sword fern may go dormant; even though the roots welcome winter rains, the new growth won't return until spring. Trim off last year's leaves just before leaf growth begins. Otherwise the clump becomes a mass of dead leaves that obscure the fresh fronds. Sword fern has no pests or diseases. You'll see circular orange-brown bumps beneath mature fronds—these are spore casings called *sori*. Many rarer ferns can be propagated from spores, but sword fern seldom is because it's easy to divide. An excellent way to divide it is to leave the mother plant in place and slice off a chunk from the sides containing as many fronds and roots as desired. This allows the established plant to avoid the stress of being dug. All ferns establish slowly the first year.

Companion Planting and Design

Ferns convey an air of settled completion to the garden, either as accents or as edging for walkways. Combine with tall *Mahonia aquifolium* and narcissus 'Quail' for a deer-proof spring scene.

We Recommend

Sword fern can hardly be improved, thriving without care and adding garden dignity.

Durable, reliable, and tough indeed, the native western sword fern can take the heat, the cold, and the dry times. Fronds open with tender green softness in spring, rapidly firming up to dark evergreen sturdiness when weather warms. Douglas fir forest edges may be paved with sword ferns, which can also colonize road cuts and spread into clumps 4 feet tall in suburban landscapes after land clearing. Fronds arch from the center, providing a graceful vase form. Established plants defy wind and can take shady seaside planting. The most common native fern in the Pacific Northwest, sword fern is an invaluable evergreen garden plant. These extremely long-lived plants settle in for decades once established. Whether your garden is casual or formal, sword ferns complement any design. —MR

Other Common Name
Holly fern

Bloom Period and Seasonal Color
Evergreen

Mature Height × Spread
3 to 5 feet × 3 to 4 feet

Zones
4 to 8

Tickseed
Coreopsis species and cultivars

A floriferous bloomer, tickseed is a cheery presence in country gardens and cottage borders alike. This undemanding perennial is a member of the sunflower family. With pale to bold shades in yellow, pink, and maroon, tickseed combines well with most other sun-loving choices in the garden and adds a lovely texture of fine, threaded foliage. Fill a dry bank or meadow with masses of tickseed for a wildflower-style appearance. When planted in full sun with adequate drainage, this is an undemanding perennial that generously blooms all summer long. The daisylike heads of tickseed have tiny centers that resemble "ticks" when dried, although it's wise to deadhead spent blooms to encourage reblooming. You can also leave late-summer seedheads to feed birds in winter. —DP

Bloom Period and Seasonal Color
Early summer to fall; yellow, pink, and maroon blooms

Mature Height × Spread
1¹/₂ to 3 feet × 2 to 3 feet

Zones
4 to 9

When, Where, and How to Plant
Plant nursery-grown tickseed in spring or early summer. This is one perennial that can be sown directly from seed in spring (cover with ¹/₈ inch of soil and pack firmly). Tickseed requires a location with full sun and moist, but well-drained, average soil (it will languish in damp, cool locations). Follow the general guidelines for planting perennials on page 115, spacing container-grown plants 2 to 3 feet apart, depending on selection.

Growing Tips
Water tickseed until well established, after which time it is drought tolerant. Additional watering and fertilizing are rarely required.

Care
Tickseed generally resists pests and diseases, although if overwatered the foliage can be susceptible to powdery mildew. This is a plant that responds well to continual deadheading. While this sounds time consuming, you can quickly shear away spent flowers every week or so—and you'll be rewarded with continual blooms. After the first several years in your garden, tickseed will begin to die out in the center and splay apart. The plants can be dug and divided in springtime. Water replanted divisions until established. Tickseed will self-sow.

Companion Planting and Design
This rugged plant adds sunny hues, textured foliage, and charming 2-inch daisylike flower heads to cutting gardens, cottage borders, and naturalistic meadows. Use masses of tickseed to blanket a dry bank. Plant the shorter form as an edging along the front of a perennial bed or a ground-cover-style planting paired with the creamy-white and soft-pink shades of yarrow. Combine taller varieties with prairie perennials including ornamental grasses and black-eyed Susan. Pack a punch of contrast by combining yellow tickseed with purple sea holly.

We Recommend
Coreopsis verticillata 'Moonbeam' (12 to 18 inches) features pastel-yellow blooms above mounded dark-green foliage. The large-flowered form, *C. grandiflora* 'Early Sunrise', blooms early summer with semidouble yellow flowers (12 to 24 inches). *C.* 'Limerock Ruby', a hybrid, has true ruby-red flowers that need little or no deadheading (24 inches).

Yarrow
Achillea species and cultivars

When, Where, and How to Plant
With its fluffy foliage, yarrow is an interesting ingredient of EcoTurf, the Northwest-developed seed mix created for low-water-use gardens (mixes may also include perennial ryegrass, English daisies, and alyssum). While yarrow typically grows to 12 inches or taller, the low-growing forms can be mown as part of this fabulous lawn mix. Not many flowers will bloom in your lawn, but you'll enjoy the green, textured foliage. Plant in spring or early summer, in well-drained, average soil in full sun—avoid shade. Yarrow tolerates sandy soils and dry locations. It doesn't perform well in shady or wet conditions. Space yarrow about 2 feet apart.

Growing Tips
Water regularly until yarrow is established. Unless there is an extended dry period, you won't need to provide additional irrigation. Yarrow generally doesn't require fertilization. Avoid mulching, which may keep the soil around the plant's base too moist.

Care
If you're growing yarrow for its height, textured foliage, and colorful blooms, you should routinely cut back spent blooms to encourage continual blooms. Divide every four years or when clumps appear crowded. Aphids and powdery mildew may appear. See page 248 for tips on addressing these common garden challenges.

Companion Planting and Design
Clusters of yarrow are ideal companions for other heat-loving perennials in equally vibrant shades, such as Russian sage, lavender, tickseed, and catmint. It pairs well with ornamental grasses in meadow-style plantings, especially as an alternative to water-hungry turf. Golden flat-topped yarrow blooms look dramatic when paired with the vertical spires of purple lavender or salvia. Drought-tolerant gardens with silvery and woolly-leaved plants (such as lamb's ears and santolina) complement stands of yarrow, with feathery, gray-green foliage.

We Recommend
Achillea millefolium 'Roseum' has bright rose-pink flowers with purple-black centers and grows to 3 feet. 'Paprika' is a zesty red form with yellow centers. *A.* 'Coronation Gold' is a cultivar favored for radiant gold flowers that fade to a softer tint; it grows to 3 feet.

Yarrow's flat-topped blooms are actually clusters of tiny florets, radiating warmth in the garden. Upward-facing blooms stand erect on strong stems of aromatic gray-green foliage. The fernlike leaves serve as a great backdrop to the pastel and bold flower heads, especially noticeable when yarrow is mass planted. As the umbel-shaped flower heads develop to 2 to 4 inches across, numerous small flowers open, showing off brightly contrasting pin-dot centers. Yarrow has a wildflower appearance, although more compact forms can be grown in rock gardens and as ground covers. Some taller forms require staking, although most yarrows are low-maintenance plants that thrive in drought-tolerant gardens. Plant yarrow in your cutting garden for use in summer bouquets. It can also be dried for everlasting arrangements. —DP

Other Common Name
Milfoil

Bloom Period and Seasonal Color
Early to late summer; yellow, pink, cream, coral, gold, and crimson blooms

Mature Height × Spread
$1/2$ to 5 feet × $1^1/2$ to 3 feet

Zones
3 to 8

Roses *for Washington & Oregon*

Roses intrigue gardeners, from beginners to the most advanced, bringing voluptuous flowers, fragrance, and often long-season interest to the landscape. Growers and breeders now concentrate on offering easily grown roses for the small garden or for their use as features, such as ground covers. Gardeners have never had more choices in rose types; it's possible to plant a rose with centuries of history or choose one newly released in the current season. Whatever the rose, providing basic needs will result in bountiful bloom and handsome leaves.

Selecting Roses

Climate variations in the Washington and Oregon region demand differences in rose selection and details of care, depending on how low winter temperatures go, from zone 8 on the western side to zones 4 or 5 on the eastern edge. Roses that do well in maritime areas without winter protection will need mulching, or wrapping, if grown in colder sections. Check the individual zone before choosing and caring for roses.

Look for disease-resistant roses. We've listed those recommended by local rose societies as growing well in this region, though individual garden conditions may vary. Resistance isn't immunity, but rather an ability to withstand disease pressure and succumb more lightly if affected.

Most roses require a minimum of six hours of sun daily during the growing season. Summer heat also affects rose success, with cool summers in the western area causing poor growth on familiar roses like 'Chrysler Imperial' that do well in other parts of the United States. Check local lists and nurseries to find those best adapted to your individual garden.

Soil Preparation and Planting

For the best blooms, roses require loose, amended, well-drained soil with a pH of 6.0 to 6.5. They need oxygen around the roots, so they don't do well in tight clay soils. Don't walk over rose roots, which compacts the soil, or site them where foot traffic crosses them. Native soils in western areas may be acidic, and it's advisable to get a pH test if planting roses in a new garden (obviously, if they are already thriving, this isn't as important). If the pH is low, amend the soil in fall with 5 pounds of dolomitic lime per 100 square feet of planting area, allowing three to four months for the lime to affect the soil.

Roses come bare root, bagged in plastic, or even boxed, as well as in plastic pots. Remove all packing material when planting; "boxed roses" will sometimes indicate

Hybrid Tea Rose
'Double Delight'

Roses 'Constance Spry' and 'Johann Strauss' with Delphinium and Clematis

on their labels that the box can be buried, but this doesn't get good results in our region because the box may dry out and keep the roots from growing.

With grafted plants, the union is a visible "bump" often about 3 inches in diameter just above the roots. How deeply to plant this depends on the zone.

Western areas, zones 7 to 9: Plant so that the graft union is visible above the soil surface.

Eastern areas, zones 4 to 6: Plant with the graft union below the soil surface, about 2 inches. If no winter protection will be provided (mulching over the plant), install the graft at 3 to 4 inches below surface. Miniature roses, which aren't grafted, should be planted slightly deeper in containers for the coldest zones.

Care

Pruning. Prune in early spring when temperatures stay above freezing, removing mulch before pruning. Don't do significant pruning in fall, unless you are shortening canes for winter coverage in the coldest zones. In spring, remove all diseased or damaged wood, thinning if necessary to allow better air circulation.

Winter Protection

In all zones, stop feeding roses by July 30 to allow growth to ripen and harden off before freezing temperatures. Stop deadheading in late August, and allow roses to form hips (seeds), which are often decorative and bright red. Remove all leaves, if feasible, to force dormancy after freezing weather arrives and before mulching for winter. (This is easiest with smaller roses and not possible on large climbers or other big roses.)

Western zones, 7 to 9: Rake fallen leaves and petals to remove disease organisms. Apply 8 inches of loose mulch, compost, or soil back over the roots and graft union after the first heavy frost.

Eastern zones, 4 to 6: Hybrid tea and floribunda roses need cover for winter protection. Cut back canes to about 30 inches, and heel over with soil to a depth of 10 inches; follow that with a deep covering of loose material like pine needles, held in place with a wire cylinder. Hardy shrub roses such as the Parkland series don't need this much protection; 3 inches of mulch will do. Miniature roses resent being covered by soil and should get a light covering of pine needles instead.

Roses grown in containers in zones 4 to 6 should be removed from containers in fall and planted in the ground, with soil mounded over them for winter protection.

Climbing Rose 'Weller Bourbon'

In all zones, remove winter mulch when nighttime temperatures moderate to above 30 degrees Fahrenheit. Work carefully to avoid breaking new emerging canes.

Irrigation

Roses need about an inch of water a week throughout the growing season whether by rain or irrigation. One deep watering once or twice a week is best. It allows necessary moisture to reach the roots so they develop into larger and deeper roots.

Insects

The main insect pests here are aphids, caterpillars, thrips, spider mites, leafminers, spittlebugs, leafhoppers, raspberry horntail wasps, rose slugs, and cane borers. If few chemicals are used in your neighborhood, you may have many beneficial insects that will keep the undesirables under control. If spotted early, insects such as aphids, spittlebugs, and caterpillars, can be pinched between the fingers to control. If infestations get out of hand, try insecticidal soaps. Aphids and spittlebugs can be washed off with a hard stream from the hose if the foliage will dry in less than two hours. Cane borers can be controlled by sealing the ends of canes with white glue (such as Elmer's®) after pruning.

Diseases

The major problem in rose growing in the Puget Sound area is disease. The key is *prevention*. Plant resistant varieties; allow good air circulation; and clean up and destroy all old leaves, prunings, and other organic material from the bush before new growth begins in spring.

Blackspot: This disease starts on the most susceptible plant parts—new, expanding leaves and new first-year canes. The fungus starts as raised, purple-red, irregular blotches, which later turn to black feathery-edged spots. As the number of spots grows on a leaf, the leaf turns yellow and falls from the bush. The fungus overwinters on canes and leaves, both on and off the bush. This fungus does not live in the soil, only in organic material. Prune the infected canes and clean up all rose leaves to reduce the supply of spores. Fungus transmits to other areas mainly by tools, insects with sticky body parts, and people. The primary infection period is spring when rain splashing on leaves and organic material on the ground moves spores onto lower leaves and canes. Seven to eight hours of foliage moisture—typical of our spring rains—will induce blackspot spores to multiply and infect leaves. This is why it is important to water plants in the morning in summer; that way, the leaves can dry in fewer than seven to eight hours. This is also why prevention sprays are important in spring but are not needed during dry summer weather. Chemical sprays are effective during the infection stages but not after the black spots are seen on the leaves or canes. You can prune out any infected canes or leaves if less than a third of the bush is infected.

Powdery mildew: The most common fungus on roses, powdery mildew starts on new shoot tips and is seen as twisted, distorted growth before becoming covered with white powdery growth. The first white powder usually appears on the bud; spraying at this stage often stops further damage. The fungus attacks and sticks to the leaf surface of new growth. The spores overwinter on fallen leaves and the bud scales of the canes where the leaf was attached. They travel on air currents. Good air circulation allows the spores to keep moving. To germinate, the fungus requires two to four hours of high humidity at 65 to 75 degrees Fahrenheit in the daytime and 40 to 60 degrees Fahrenheit at night. So the fungus becomes a major problem late in August and into September after a dry, disease-free summer. The accumulation of white powder reduces the plant's photosynthesis.

Fungicide sprays applied at the first sign of the disease and repeated twice, once each week, will frequently hold the disease at bay for the remainder of the season as the new growth slows in fall. Lighter feeding, just the May and June schedule, will limit new growth in late summer and can reduce the incidence of powdery mildew.

Rust: Like powdery mildew, rust is transmitted on air currents; it attacks the leaves through openings and then overwinters on bud scales of canes and fallen leaves. To germinate, the spores require two to four hours of continuous moisture at 60 to 70 degrees Fahrenheit. Late spring during rainy weather and in August or September after the first rainy day will bring out the bright-orange pustules on the underside of leaves. Later, orange or brown blotches develop on the upper leaf surfaces. In fall, the orange pustules are replaced with black sooty-looking growth, which is the overwintering form. Picking leaves off and destroying them as soon as you notice them is the best response.

Fungicide sprays only prevent infection; they cannot cure an infection in the leaf. Sprays should be applied when spore germination conditions first appear. Rust can defoliate the plant and severely hinder photosynthesis.

Read and follow the labels carefully when using any garden chemicals. Alternate spray material from the broad-spectrum and the narrow-spectrum list each time you spray to prevent fungus from building resistance to the spray material. Choose disease-resistant plants to help reduce the need for chemical sprays.

— MR

Climbing Rose
Rosa species and cultivars

Both small and large gardens come alive with climbing roses, adding the dimension of height and the pleasure of being able to look up into blossoms. When well established, climbers and ramblers (a type included with climbers) provide lengthy one-time blooms or bloom all season, depending on the variety. Climbing roses need encouragement; since they don't grow natural attachments to arbors or fences, they must be tied and pinned securely where you want them. Climbers vary in their flowering type because they're often hybridized from other roses, so they can have an "English rose" look, as with 'Constance Spry', or resemble billowing floribundas like 'Climbing Iceberg'. Allow time for the full garden effect, since each rose must develop framework canes, but many persist for decades.

Other Common Name
Rambler

Bloom Period and Seasonal Color
Summer; blooms in all colors

Mature Height x Spread
8 to 50 feet x 3 to 30 feet, as allowed by training

Zones
3 to 9

When, Where, and How to Plant
Plant in spring from containers. *Before* planting, choose a support that matches the ultimate height and growth type, which will vary. Some examples include 'Dortmund', red with a white eye, which can be pruned to a short trellis or allowed to scramble 24 feet across an arbor. White rambler 'Bobbie James' can charge 40 feet. The soil needs for climbing roses are the same for other rose types; see page 160 for soil and planting tips. Wind protection is particularly necessary. Some climbers thrive in partial sun or partial shade, with protection from the hottest late-day sun.

Growing Tips
Watering and fertilizing needs resemble those of other rose types; see page 162 for more details. However, a long-established climbing rose with deep roots will better tolerate summer drought than a hybrid tea will. If rose roots run under roof overhangs, be sure to irrigate the areas where the rain does not reach.

Care
Correct pruning is essential to the beauty of climbing roses. "Framework" canes, generally five to six per plant, persist from year to year, secured to the support. They generate the new wood that produces flowers. You must maintain the basic framework year after year, cutting out weak canes and deadwood, and shaping in spring. Every two years, remove a few of the oldest canes. One advantage of tying roses horizontally to supports is increased flowering; the more horizontal the cane, the more bountiful the blooming. Choose disease-resistant cultivars because managing diseases on a large sprawling climber or even deadheading is often impractical.

Companion Planting and Design
Climbers add excitement to fences and clothe overhead summer shade spots. They serve as architectural elements for framing views and define the "country garden" theme.

We Recommend
'Altissimo', an open, single, bright-crimson with golden stamens in its center, performs brilliantly. Or try penetratingly fragrant white 'Sombreuil', one of the most poetic of roses. Soft pink 'Handel' blooms continuously and resists blackspot.

English Rose
Rosa species and cultivars

When, Where, and How to Plant
Early spring planting results in best establishment, and the English roses may be found bare root or in containers. Bare-root planting is terrific, often more economical, and gets good results; soak bare-root roses in plain water eight to twelve hours before planting. (B-1 vitamins added to the soaking water do not improve any rose's survival.) Choose sun-filled locations. Some growers supply English roses ungrafted, on their own roots; though initially small, these catch up well within two years. (See page 160 for more tips.)

Growing Tips
Water as you would hybrid teas (see page 168). Fertilize moderately once a month, until the end of July.

Care
Prune in spring, but do not reduce canes on English roses as much as on hybrid teas. Remove only about one-third of each established cane. Remove crossing or winter-damaged branches, and always cut to an out-facing bud. When cutting flowers, trim back to a five-leaf growth point. New buds will form and bloom in about six weeks. Deadheading spent roses will force new blooms. In colder weather areas, mulch heavily after the first frost. Many bloom well in cool summers west of the Cascades, but can also succumb to rose diseases, so select the most disease-resistant and provide some disease protection. (See pages 160 to 163 for more on rose care.)

Companion Planting and Design
English roses chime well with herbaceous perennials, adding height and interest to mixed flower gardens. Pink 'Mary Rose' grows well as a 6-foot hedge. The old-fashioned form and fragrance of these roses lends character to cottage-garden designs, and some, like 'Gertrude Jeykll', grow well in containers.

We Recommend
English roses offer such a winning combination of appearance, fragrance, and long bloom that it's hard to choose just one. Apricot 'Abraham Darby' blooms in peach, with deep-green crisp foliage to set off the flowers. 'Graham Thomas,' flowering in deep yellow, grows strongly enough to be trained up a trellis or serve as a standout accent.

Among the best adapted and versatile of roses for the Northwest, English roses, many hybridized by grower David Austin in England since the early 1960s (and by others including Harkness Rose Nursery in England), deliver punch in their multibranched flowering, with many blooms on each stem like floribundas. They bloom throughout summer, continuing until late frosts. Their forms echo the densely petaled antique roses, and they often emit a nostalgic fragrance. The bushes generally stay compact, 3 to 6 feet, though some, such as yellow 'Graham Thomas', can get tall enough to be tied on trellises. These roses represent a genuinely new type, manageable in small gardens yet reminiscent in form and scent of centuries past. Though sometimes classed as shrub roses, their garden value merits their own category.

Other Common Name
David Austin rose

Bloom Period and Seasonal Color
Recurs throughout summer; all colors except blue

Mature Height x Spread
3 to 9 feet x 3 to 6 feet

Zones
4 to 9

Floribunda Rose
Rosa species and cultivars

Think of the floribunda as the "abundant rose," with blossoms covering the plant, each cane carrying dozens of buds and flowers. Their clustered blooms can be classic hybrid tea shape, or open and charming as wild roses. Flowers cover the plants almost continually throughout the season for dependable garden interest. Public display gardens sometimes plant them in groups, eight to ten at a time, creating memorable color splashes. They're terrific cut flowers, because one stem fills a vase. Floribundas tend to be shorter than hybrid teas, making them easier to use. The smaller floribundas are sometimes designated "patio roses" and breeders have been busy developing adaptable, vigorous plants to suit compact garden designs. Versatile, often fragrant, floribundas give generously in return for their care.

Bloom Period and Seasonal Color
Summer; white, cream, yellow, orange, pink, and red blooms

Mature Height x Spread
2 to 5 feet x 2 to 3 feet

Zones
4 to 9

When, Where, and How to Plant
Floribundas, either bare root or in containers, grow best when planted in spring, in full sun with well-drained soil. Like hybrid teas, they do not tolerate shady spots but demand the best light your garden can provide. Shade results in fewer blooms and longer spindly canes. (See page 160 for more planting tips.)

Growing Tips
Follow regular watering and fertilizing regimes found on page 162.

Care
Pruning doesn't have to be as drastic as that of hybrid teas; you can encourage a floribunda to grow taller by leaving longer canes when doing spring tidying. You'll gradually learn how much of last year's growth you want to leave for the spot your rose occupies. Taking off one-third to one-half of the growth may suit the garden situation. Deadheading and tidying canes will result in a heavier second flowering, desirable because the summer-long show is one of the best features of floribunda roses. Deadhead the trusses when most of the flowers have dropped petals. Some floribundas suffer from blackspot and mildew. Mulch with 2 to 3 inches of compost after planting, and avoid walking over the roots.

Companion Planting and Design
Consider patio roses such as 'Rosy Future' for containers, pairing them with pots of annual petunias and fragrant lavender. Allow at least 5 gallons of root room for patio roses to reach best growth. Rather than spotting them around the garden, plant floribundas three at a time for color density and impact. 'Sunsprite' combines clean, glossy foliage with brilliant clear-yellow flowers and is lovely beside outdoor patios. 'Iceberg', a frilly clear white, one of the greatest of modern roses, lines walkways in formal gardens. Some of the larger floribundas like 'Eye Paint' (red and white) can even be trained up short pillars.

We Recommend
'French Lace', a fragrant ivory and peach combination, blooms well in partial shade. 'Angel Face' bears intensely fragrant, lavender, disease-resistant flowers. 'Intrigue' offers deep plum color and memorable fragrance.

Ground Cover Rose

Rosa cultivars

When, Where, and How to Plant

Plant in spring in full sun. If planting on slopes, form water-holding wells around the plants. Eliminate all perennial weeds from the area before planting. Taller landscape roses can be set as tidy, controllable hedges. Many of the ground cover roses grow lax canes that suit hanging baskets, so choose a strong but light plastic container and well-set hooks for installing them. One rose per 16-inch basket will make a great show by midsummer. Use a well-drained potting soil mix, and fertilize monthly. (See page 160 for more soil and planting tips.) Ground cover roses may stretch to more than 6 feet across; plant them 3 feet apart to allow them to fill in. Pin down long canes to encourage surface rooting.

Growing Tips

Water weekly until established. Ground cover roses don't need monthly fertilizing; if the soil is fertile, an early spring fertilizing plus 2-3 inches of mulch across the area, followed by one midsummer fertilizing, is sufficient. Always water before the summer fertilizing to avoid root burn. Setting soaker hoses around the planting can help. Landscape roses carry few thorns and are easy to work among.

Care

Using clippers, shear ground cover roses being grown in masses in late winter instead of pruning conventionally. Look for the first emerging new growth points, then shear. Take off one-third to one-half of the plant, and don't worry about exact placement of the cuts. Ground cover roses are seldom bothered by rose pests or diseases.

Companion Planting and Design

Ground cover roses blend easily with other plant choices; their bloom abounds. These roses work naturally as small hedges, herb bed edgings, or perennial flower borders. They're superb for covering sunny slopes with good soil.

We Recommend

Try these easy-success types: pink 'Baby Blanket' offers gentle color; for more vividness, choose bright 'Electric Blanket'. The coral 'Flower Carpet' suits containers. 'Carefree Beauty' has sweetly scented 5-inch single blooms.

Your grandparents wouldn't recognize this category: ground cover and landscape roses represent a contemporary effort by hybridizers to meet the needs of smaller gardens and busier gardeners. These are compact, free-flowering, and often quite disease free—roses that work well in low-maintenance situations. The ground cover types, growing wider than tall, can cover slopes. They bloom throughout summer. Flower form is often single, with clusters of flowers resembling wild roses. Landscape roses, many patented by their developers, include 'Carefree Wonder'™ and 'Flower Carpet'™ with a range of colors in each type, including pinks, reds, coral, and whites. Check out the new 'Dream'™ series for a strong, vigorous yellow that grows 3 feet tall by 3 feet wide and suits mixed-flower border plantings.

Other Common Names
Patio rose, landscape rose

Bloom Period and Seasonal Color
Summer; all colors

Mature Height x Spread
2 to 5 feet x 3 to 5 feet

Zones
4 to 9

Hybrid Tea Rose
Rosa species and cultivars

Familiar and widely loved, hybrid tea roses often define what "rose" means to the casual observer since they're commonly grown for cutting and presentation bouquets. One elegant flower tips each cane end. On most hybrid teas, buds and blooms show a characteristic pointed shape, with opened petals circling a tight center. The plant shape tends to be upright, with firm strong canes, giving the plants a formal aspect and providing long stems for cutting. They flower nonstop right up to frost. Descendants of delicate tea roses (named for their scent) brought from China in the nineteenth century, hybrid teas demand careful selection to be satisfactory in Northwest gardens; choose for disease resistance and winter hardiness. Their classic beauty attracts both amateur gardeners and show rose specialists.

Bloom Period and Seasonal Color
Summer; white, cream, yellow, orange, pink, red, and bicolored blooms

Mature Height x Spread
3 to 8 feet x 3 to 4 feet

Zones
3 to 9

When, Where, and How to Plant
Plant in early spring, when the soil is no longer frozen, in a well-drained spot amended with organic compost. Choose a site with maximum sun. Avoid low-lying frost pockets where cold air drains. Provide shelter from direct hard winds, but avoid jamming hybrid teas against walls or where air circulation is restricted. (See page 160 for planting instructions.) If planting from packaged boxes, remove the rose from its box and treat it as a bare-root rose, because dry summer conditions in Washington and Oregon often lead to boxes wicking moisture from roots. Prepare a raised bed if the soil stays soggy in winter. If planting is delayed on bare-root roses, heel in the roots to prevent drying before planting. Dig a shallow trench, lean the rose against it, and cover the spread roots. Water thoroughly, and plant before leaf growth advances. Mulch about 2 inches with an open, nonpacking material.

Growing Tips
Hybrid teas need growing room and ample nutrients. A balanced fertilizer formula with trace elements, applied monthly from early March through the end of July, is vital. Water 1 inch a week, applying once deeply rather than frequently and shallowly. Hybrid teas require regular water since they're in such active growth all summer. To help prevent diseases, arrange soaker hoses or irrigation systems to keep water off summer foliage.

Care
Prune in spring after heavy frost danger passes (new growth is sensitive to frost kill). Rose diseases, particularly blackspot, can damage plants (see more on page 162).

Companion Planting and Design
Colors and forms of hybrid teas demand attention but also associate nicely with shallow-rooted flowers such as annual violas or annual alyssum. Lavender and rosemary look good with roses but require less summer water and should not be placed on top of rose roots.

We Recommend
Roses with fragrance attract gardeners. Look for 'Fragrant Cloud' and yellow 'King's Ransom'. Apricot 'Just Joey' draws raves from growers west of the Cascades but requires Zone 6.

Miniature Rose

Rosa cultivars

When, Where, and How to Plant

Miniature roses usually grow on their own roots. They adapt well to pots and are easy to find throughout summer in containers. But they do best when treated just as larger roses, planted in early spring in their permanent positions. Full or partial sun suits them, and they need well-prepared, well-drained soil just as for all roses. Miniature roses can be quite cold hardy, often more than many hybrid teas, but require protection from wind. When planted in containers, allow sufficient root room; a container at least 12 inches in diameter suits the larger miniatures.

Growing Tips

Water and fertilizer needs resemble those of larger roses (see page 161). But since their root systems are smaller, miniatures can dry out quickly in pots. When growing in pots, fertilize twice a month at half strength.

Care

Miniature roses are tougher than they look. They require pruning in early spring to reduce cane length and remove winter dead material. Keep all old flowers pruned off to prolong the show until frost. They require maximum sunlight if brought indoors and do best when their houseplant life is brief and they can return to outdoor conditions. Monitor for disease problems, especially powdery mildew and blackspot; see page 162 for disease management advice. When growing in containers, apply liquid rather than granular fertilizer (to better reach the roots). Plunge outdoor pots into soil at the end of summer to shelter the roots over winter, and mulch over the pot edges. Roots exposed in pots freeze more readily than those in garden beds.

Companion Planting and Design

A small raised bed with several plants of one type, such as medium-pink 'Baby Grand', stands out with an edging of petunias for summer. A good hanging-basket type is deep-lavender 'Sweet Chariot', featuring trailing stems and the capacity to take afternoon shade.

We Recommend

'Snow Bride' grows vigorously with open white flowers and frilly yellow prominent stamens. 'Rise 'n Shine', a strong yellow, has double flowers.

With the proliferation of miniatures that combine smaller flowers with short plant stature, roses can grow in every garden, even those confined to balconies. Imagine the perfect shape of the hybrid tea rose but only 1 inch long, or a fragrant floribunda style with a 3-inch spray of bloom. They bloom constantly and settle nicely in containers or in raised beds edging a patio. Many descend from nineteenth century roses, and their popularity increases yearly as growers introduce new cultivars and people discover their garden usefulness. 'Starina', a brilliant-red with perfect buttonhole flowers, exemplifies their beauty. You'll even find climbers and trailing types that suit hanging baskets. Like hybrid tea roses, miniatures appreciate sun and careful attention, rewarding the gardener with distinct charm.

Other Common Names
Mini rose, mini-flora rose

Bloom Period and Seasonal Color
Summer; all colors and bicolored blooms

Mature Height x Spread
1$^1/_2$ to 3 feet x 1 to 3 feet

Zones
3 to 10

Old Garden Rose
Rosa species and cultivars

Definitions vary, but old or antique roses usually mean those in cultivation before the development of the first hybrid tea in 1867. Many growers also include in this category those introduced up to the early twentieth century. They've been cherished for their scent and garden presence for hundreds of years. Old roses bloom once in summer, with dense multipetaled bloom shape and often intense fragrance. Cold hardiness, some drought tolerance, and disease resistance help them fit into many different climate zones. Their drawbacks include thorniness and a sprawling growth habit that demands garden space. The old garden roses include many different types: alba, damask, gallica, moss, tea, hybrid perpetual bourbon, china, and noisette. There's an old rose for nearly every landscape and gardener's taste.

Other Common Names
Antique rose, heritage rose

Bloom Period and Seasonal Color
Early summer, with some rebloom depending on variety; all colors, many in deep-purples

Mature Height x Spread
5 to 15 feet x 5 to 12 feet

Zones
3 to 10

When, Where, and How to Plant
Site according to the ultimate size of your selected rose type, from 3 feet to the sprawling albas that may reach 12 feet tall with equivalent spread. Select a sunny spot and plant in spring, either bare-root or from containers. The later in the season that container roses are planted, the more sparse the current year's blooms will be. Antique roses may require more than one growing season to come into their full beauty. (See pages 160 to 163 for more planting tips.)

Growing Tips
These roses need water weekly through the first season. Once they've become established, antique roses, like species roses, can manage with less water than hybrid teas. Set soaker hoses and time irrigation to keep roots deeply watered twice a month. Fertilize less often than other roses. As spring growth begins, once a month suits them.

Care
Removal of spent flowers isn't as necessary as with hybrid teas or floribundas, because many antique roses form beautiful seedpods, or hips, in fall, giving another season of interest. Also, because they flower once, you aren't protecting a second flush of bloom. For protection from winter windstorms, trim back the longest canes by a third in fall to prevent breakage. Otherwise, prune lightly in spring. Too much pruning reduces bloom. Many types resist blackspot but need good air circulation to prevent powdery mildew. Allow them space.

Companion Planting and Design
Try *Rosa* × *alba* 'Könignin von Dänemark', also called 'Queen of Denmark', soft pink, deliciously fragrant, and set off by foxgloves, hostas, and sages. All old roses naturally suit heritage plantings. After bloom, the old roses recede in garden importance, but many come back to prominence in fall with strong yellow foliage color and attractive seed hips. 'Rose de Rescht' stays 4 feet tall and 3 feet wide with bright-pink flowers and repeat bloom.

We Recommend
Moss rose 'William Lobb', deep purple with pink reverse on the petals, gets to 8 feet and can take partial shade; 'Gruss an Aachen', a pale pink, also manages blooming in shade.

When, Where, and How to Plant

Select a spot to allow for the rose's eventual size. Plant in spring either from bare-root or container plants, in full or partial sun. If the soil drains poorly, create a raised bed at least 18 inches high before planting. See page 160 for more planting tips. Mulch with 2 to 3 inches of compost after planting.

Growing Tips

Fertilize in spring; water 1 inch a week until established. Refer to page 162 for more about watering and fertilizing.

Care

Remove one-third of the branches each spring, and take out the oldest canes yearly once the shrub becomes established. Cane removal will keep new blooms coming. Allow air circulation between a shrub rose and other plants. Prune once-flowering roses after they flower; they will set buds for the next season on wood that grows after pruning. Avoid siting suckering roses like rugosas on septic drain fields where their roots may invade the system. Deadhead roses that bloom more than once a season. Tie or trim exposed canes in late fall to prevent winter storm breakage. In cold weather areas, pile mulch at least 6 inches deep over the roots and crowns of roses, waiting until after the first light freeze when the rose is dormant.

Companion Planting and Design

Plant shrub roses as barriers and fences. *Rosa rugosa* and its hybrids, such as 'Hansa', form fragrant, prickly, and attractive hedges for sunny spots. Many rugosas also manage dry summers well and can thrive where more tender roses would suffer. Try white 'Blanc Double de Coubert' with herbs and artemisia in an exposed spot such as a seaside edge. (Rugosas cope with salty wind.) Some shrub roses such as white 'Sally Holmes' can be trained up small arbors, though they aren't usually classified as climbers.

We Recommend

Arctic weather? Beautiful 'Morden Blush' takes zone 3 temperatures and blooms light-pink in hot summers. Another terrific cold-hardy option is the deep-pink 'William Baffin'. An easy-care and fragrant rugosa is 'Rosaraie de l'Hay', deep-red with a potpourri scent.

Shrub roses signify variety. One grower says that shrub roses could be everything that isn't a hybrid tea or a floribunda. Tolerance for cold weather enhances their garden usefulness, for many shrub roses are bred to take chill. The Canadian Explorer series and the Parkland Morden types manage ferocious zone 2 to 3 temperatures. Shrub roses share an arching, open growth habit ranging from the petite 2-foot polyantha 'The Fairy' to plants like 'Gloire de Dijon', which can gallop 15 feet. Superb disease resistance in the Rosa rugosa hybrids adds to the value of this group; rugosas stay clean west of the Cascades where diseases can be severe. Look for great fall leaf color, reds and yellows, and long-lasting seedpods (hips) on many of these.

Bloom Period and Seasonal Color
Summer to fall; blooms in all colors, plus red hips in fall

Mature Height × Spread
2 to 15 feet × 2, as allowed by pruning

Zones
2 to 9

Shrubs *for Washington & Oregon*

Discovering the variety and landscape value of shrubs presents gardeners with a great adventure. Shrubs form permanent woody branches like trees but are generally multistemmed (lacking a single trunk) and at maturity reach less than 12 feet tall.

Like planting trees, choosing woody shrubs means selecting permanent parts of the landscape. They'll gradually grow into their ultimate size and form. It's vital to allow space for the plant to expand into its ideal dimensions. The most common landscape error with shrubs involves placing them where they will grow crowded or, worse, obscure windows and impede pathways. Under the best soil and water conditions, most achieve about three-fourths of their size within five years of planting, then grow to their full height in ten years.

Selecting the Right Shrub

Get acquainted with the seasonal contributions of shrubs: the spring-flowering forsythia, azalea, camellia, and rhododendron; the summer viburnum, ceanothus, and mock orange; the fall color of barberries and nandina; and the winter interest from many broadleaf evergreens, such as mahonia and the smaller conifers (see the Conifers chapter). Certain desirable shrubs, such as *Viburnum plicatum* f. *tomentosum* 'Mariesii', offer spring leaf, summer flower, and autumn brilliance, as well as branch structure for winter. Exploring nurseries and observing shrubs in landscapes helps in selection, and in discovering those with proper light and water needs for the intended location.

Like tree selection, shrub choices may suit the garden best if they're made at the nursery during the main season of interest—if choosing for flowers, look during flowering; if for fall color, find those with

Barberry 'Nana', Juniper, and Birch 'Whitespire'

Lacecap Hydrangea 'Bluebird'

the most brilliant leaves. Plants differ even within the same genus and species, and finding the most pleasing plant helps the garden design.

Soil Preparation and Planting

Since shrubs will live for years, they benefit from proper soil preparation before planting. (See the General Introduction for more information.) Smaller shrub specimens, such as those in 1-gallon pots, will quickly catch up with larger, more expensive ones. But remember not to work amendments only into the planting hole, but rather to amend the entire planting area to keep the planting hole from holding water in winter and causing potential root rot. If it's not possible to amend the entire area, dig a hole three times as wide as the rootball and exactly as deep and then set the shrub in, being sure that the top of the rootball is at the same level as it was in the container, or even an inch higher. Then fill in with native soil. After planting, mulch with 2 to 4 inches of coarse composted organic material, making a shallow raised edge around the plant to hold water. Keep mulch away from the trunk, which can suffer disease problems from mulch piled against it.

Care

Fertilize once in early spring before growth starts, using a slow-release nitrogen fertilizer with a 5-1-1 ratio of nutrients. Keep shrubs watered weekly during dry spells for the first two to three summer seasons and into fall until the rains return. After two or three years, those adapted to drought will be able to cope with far less water and some, such as native mahonia, will need no water at all, nor will they need fertilizer.

Prune shrubs to shape and enhance them, not to keep them small enough to fit an inappropriate site. Selecting the right plant reduces pruning chores. Remove any dead or diseased wood, or any crossing branches, during dormancy. Spring-flowering shrubs such as forsythia and rhododendron must be pruned during and immediately after bloom to allow time for the development of the next spring's buds.

Pruning also helps rejuvenate old crowded shrubs. Remove three to five of the oldest stems each year, and allow new, vigorous growth to fill in. Unless the shrub is being grown as a hedge, avoid shearing, which can cause unsightly tip growth to obscure the form of the plant while the inside branches lose leaves.

For flowering, fragrance, attractive foliage, and intriguing structure and shape, there's a useful shrub for every garden need. Invaluable for screening, enhancing buildings, and providing year-round green, shrubs can also act "treelike" in limited garden spaces.

— MR

Aucuba

Aucuba japonica and cultivars

Deepest shade suits the evergreen shrubby aucuba, with glossy light-capturing leaves that bring shine to dark spots. Long-lived, water-wise, and adaptable to almost any soil, aucuba earns its garden space. Aucuba, like holly, has both male and female plants; both are necessary for the female plant to produce the deep-red or shiny yellow berries that often stay on through winter. The dark-maroon spring flowers may go unnoticed because they are tucked along stems. Aucuba's attractive leaves, often patterned with splashes of yellow, will scorch in sun. A favorite plant for heritage landscapes, aucuba was a stalwart in long-ago gardens; it's been rediscovered for its valuable ability to thrive in the driest shade. Against a north wall or complementing yew in shade, aucuba looks good year-round.

Bloom Period and Seasonal Color
Year-round; red or yellow berries in fall

Mature Height × Spread
5 to 12 feet × 3 to 10 feet

Zones
5 to 8

When, Where, and How to Plant
Aucuba grows best in soils amended with moisture-holding compost. Plant in spring or fall from containers, in full shade. Aucuba isn't particular about the soil pH, growing well in acidic or alkaline conditions. It can live in dry shade under tree roots where most shrubs expire. Aucuba also adapts to windy spots and seaside salt spray. It proves extremely tough, but a good start helps. See page 173 for planting tips.

Growing Tips
Once established, aucuba does not require additional summer irrigation, but it will do fine if planted with other shade lovers that do require water, such as ferns or hostas. This plant's greatest value lies in its ability to cope without summer watering, once established. See the chapter introduction for fertilizing guidelines.

Care
Prune to reduce size, if necessary, by removing whole branches down to the ground, keeping the plant somewhat open, unless a completely opaque screen is desired. Leaf scorch from sun disfigures aucuba; the plant will form new leaves and improve if moved. Aucuba is pest free, but deer will eat it. The berries are quite showy in fall and winter, but to ensure berry production, plant both types: One male plant pollinates several females. Birds ignore the berries.

Companion Planting and Design
Native sword ferns, sarcococcas, Zabel's laurels, and hellebores can tuck into the partial shade edges in front of aucuba, making an attractive winter display. For an excellent screen, plant three aucubas 5 feet apart in a triangle. Japanese aucuba thrives as a containerized houseplant, a strange aspect of its toughness. First grown as Victorian-era houseplants, aucubas provide lively foliage color on a shady porch. In a large container that protects the roots, aucuba may even survive in warmer areas without winter protection.

We Recommend
Since their foliage is glossy, green-leaved forms also reflect light, as with 'Grandis'. Variegated cultivars of aucuba glow in darker areas. Try the female 'Crotonifolia', with small, even, gold splashes on the leaves, or 'Mr. Goldstrike', a male version.

Azalea
Rhododendron species and hybrids

When, Where, and How to Plant

Azaleas have fine roots close to the surface. They require acidic soil with good drainage and moisture-holding amendments. Poor soil conditions, especially soggy or dried out soil, will kill them, so it is vital to prepare the soil properly. Plant from containers in spring or fall, setting plants just slightly higher than they were in the container to allow for settling without placing roots too deep. If the soil cannot be amended to create good drainage, plant azaleas in a raised bed or berm. Arrange soaker hoses or other irrigation methods around them. See page 173 for planting techniques. Avoid areas with exposed afternoon sun. Keep mulch light over the surface roots, 1 to 2 inches, keeping mulch away from the trunk. Avoid walking on the roots or cultivating heavily around them; the roots damage easily.

Growing Tips

Fertilize plants just as growth begins; use a slow-release formula designed for rhododendrons. Water deeply after fertilizing, especially if weather conditions become dry, as they often do in May and June after azaleas bloom. Provide a steady supply of moisture throughout summer, watering thoroughly each week. Azaleas do not adjust to dry conditions no matter how long they remain in the landscape.

Care

Prune in early summer immediately after bloom. The worst problems are root rot from inadequate drainage, lack of air circulation from crowded plantings, and suffocation of roots from deep mulches or planting too deeply. Some deciduous azaleas flower on bare wood, before leaves emerge; others flower simultaneously with leaves. Contact your local nursery for details about pest problems.

Companion Planting and Design

Taller deciduous azaleas combine with native lilies and evergreen rhododendrons in partial-sun woodland plantings. Smaller low-clumping evergreen azaleas make charming foundation plantings with the small hemlocks 'Gentsch White' and 'Bennett'.

We Recommend

Deciduous azaleas, such as Mollis hybrids and Knap Hill-Exbury hybrids, with creamy-yellow, salmon, or rose flowers, mix beautifully with ferns in partial shade, scenting the garden in late spring.

Among the most colorful of spring-blooming shrubs, azaleas inhabit the Rhododendron *genus, botanically part of the larger rhododendron group. Available in many sizes, they can grow comfortably in containers or become treelike, edging a woodland. Evergreen as well as deciduous, some azaleas flower so densely that from a distance, shrubs look like one big blossom without visible green leaves. Though relatively few rhododendrons lose their leaves, many azaleas do, and their leaves are generally smaller than those of rhododendrons. Certain cultivars like the Exbury azaleas offer memorable sweet fragrance, as does the native western azalea (Rhododendron occidentale). Morning sun and afternoon shade suit them. Use evergreen azaleas as foundation plantings or as small hedges. Deciduous varieties turn yellow and red for a good fall show.*

Bloom Period and Seasonal Color
Spring through early summer; white, cream, yellow, orange, red, rose, and purple

Mature Height × Spread
2 to 15 feet × 2 to 8 feet

Zones
4 to 7

Barberry
Berberis species and cultivars

Rays of sun with yellow flowers in spring and brilliant leaf accents in fall, barberries come in many different forms, both deciduous and evergreen. Some deciduous barberries have purplish red leaves that glow brighter in fall, dropping off to reveal attractive brown branch patterns in winter. Whether you prefer an evergreen or deciduous barberry depends on the landscape use. Evergreen barberries have small leaves resembling tiny holly leaves, often flushed red in fall when deep-blue berries appear. Deciduous barberries, such as the Japanese barberry (Berberis thunbergii), may turn vivid red or orange-red before leaves drop. All barberries wear spines, sometimes small and slightly soft, sometimes fiercely prickly. Cold-hardy, long-lived, and impervious to pests, barberries add both tactile and visual interest to the landscape.

Bloom Period and Seasonal Color
Spring to fall; yellow and gold blooms; green, yellow, and red-purple foliage

Mature Height × Spread
2 to 8 feet × 2 to 8 feet

Zones
4 to 8

When, Where, and How to Plant
Plant from containers in spring or fall; see page 173 for guidelines. Site in sun in a well-drained soil. Bright light brings out good leaf color in both summer and fall. Barberries prefer neutral soil and don't adapt well to alkalinity. They handle exposure, either summer heat or cold winds, even when large. Space them 5 to 6 feet apart for a massed screening area. Mulch after planting.

Growing Tips
If planting where rain doesn't reach, check the moisture supply every two weeks in winter and water if the roots are dry. Rock hardy once established, barberries need water their first two to three years. Apply a slow release 5-1-1 fertilizer in spring until the plant is established. Renew mulch yearly.

Care
Choose plants based on their mature size. Many resist pruning, their thorniness an obvious disadvantage. Shaping and thinning regularly and lightly immediately after flowering suits them best. Poorly drained soil causes root problems. No pests bother barberries; deer don't eat them.

Companion Planting and Design
Whether an impenetrable hedge, a graceful accent plant, or a source of fall color as foundation planting, barberries complement the sunny landscape. Choose small, softer-leaved varieties for areas where people will brush by; 'Crimson Pygmy' stays short at 2 feet with soft red-purple deciduous leaves. For a traffic-thwarting hedge, try *Berberis × gladwynensis* 'William Penn', with large thorns to repel trespassers; it grows to 6 feet tall and 4 feet wide. Pair the evergreen barberry with bright chrome-yellow narcissus 'Quail'.

We Recommend
Chilean natives, Darwin barberries originate in growing conditions similar to the maritime Pacific Northwest. The evergreen rosemary barberry (*Berberis × stenophylla*) makes a fine hedging plant, and can reach 8 feet by 8 feet with arching branches covered with soft-yellow flowers. For limited space, rosemary barberry 'Corallina Compacti' remains 1 foot in all dimensions but keeps the intriguing leaf shape and flower tone of its parent, creating a handsome ground cover when massed. Birds love the seeds on Darwin barberry.

Camellia
Camellia species and cultivars

When, Where, and How to Plant
Plant from containers in spring, fall, or winter. Many gardeners select camellias in bloom. Camellias need protection from wind and direct, hot, late-afternoon sun. Plant in shelter such as under trees or against a wall, in partial sun, choosing well-drained, acidic soil. Soggy winter soils contribute to root rot. Amend the entire planting area well with compost. Loamy soils help improve camellias' eventual tolerance for summer drought. Set plants slightly above the soil level to allow for settling. Planting too deep damages the roots. Mulch after planting but don't pile the mulch against the trunk; keep it several inches away.

Growing Tips
Feed lightly with an acidic formula fertilizer, at half the recommended strength, before bloom and once again just after bloom. Large plants over five years old need no fertilization and little extra moisture in summer, but newly planted specimens require weekly summer irrigation. Keep the roots mulched.

Care
To renovate a large overgrown camellia, remove individual branches all the way to the ground, opening and thinning. Shearing camellias into formal shapes, circles or rectangles, reduces their beauty by chopping their leaves into pieces. The plants do fill in again, but camellias look better when allowed their full leaf extension. Scale insects may infest; use a registered low-toxicity pesticide. If single branches develop variegated yellow patterns caused by virus, prune them out. Deer eat camellias, and squirrels can chew the opening buds. Frosts may damage some buds, but buds that develop later will open.

Companion Planting and Design
Camellias work best as single landscape accent plants or when planted for screening in groups of three chosen to flower at different times.

We Recommend
Camellia sasanqua 'Yuletide' offers brilliant-red flowers early in the season. In zone 6, grow hybrids of *Camellia oleifera*, such as rosy 'Winter's Peony'. Cultivars based on *C.* × *williamsii* drop spent flowers, keeping the shrub tidy; one of the best is the renowned soft-pink 'Donation'.

Camellias bloom with waxlike perfection but also grace the mild-climate garden with glossy evergreen leaves year-round. The shapely leaves seem perfectly designed to showcase flowers. And camellia's flowers, both singles and doubles, open successively over many weeks rather than all at once, as do rhododendrons and azaleas. By selecting different species and hybrids, from the early sasanquas to the latest japonicas, gardeners can enjoy several months of flowering from late winter through spring. Established plants can be long-lived and durable, managing dry summers well with little extra water and providing handsome shrubs for screening and accents. Though most valuable as permanent landscape features, in the coldest areas camellias grow well in containers brought into winter shelter. My mother cherished camellia 'Debutante' in an Ohio greenhouse.

Bloom Period and Seasonal Color
Evergreen fall through spring; white, cream, yellow, red, rose, pink, and bicolors

Mature Height × Spread
6 to 20 feet × 4 to 8 feet

Zones
6 to 9

Cotoneaster

Cotoneaster species and cultivars

Cotoneaster lacks a memorable common name; what about "Indispensable Cotoneaster"? Available in ground-hugging or treelike forms, both deciduous and evergreen, this useful shrub produces attractive leaves and brilliant fall berries, with a form for nearly every full-sun need. The evergreen types require warmer winters, while the deciduous ones, such as cranberry cotoneaster (Cotoneaster apiculatus), can handle zone 4 cold. A vigorous plant for difficult spots, cotoneaster thrives on dry slopes and in exposed, hot spots. It endures salty seaside winds. Birds like the berries, though they often wait until late in winter to take them, allowing the garden a long season of bright interest. Also valuable as attractive, durable ground covers, they're truly garden worthy. Drought tolerant once established, cotoneasters complement water-wise plantings and low-maintenance landscapes.

Bloom Period and Seasonal Color
Spring through fall; white blooms, red berries

Mature Height × Spread
1 to 12 feet × 3 to 12 feet

Zones
4 to 8

When, Where, and How to Plant
Plant in spring or fall from containers, in spring in the coldest areas; see page 173 for details. Full sun, with well-drained soil, suits them. If planted in shade, the evergreen types such as *Cotoneaster lacteus* will not produce as many flowers or berries. Cotoneasters don't need richly amended soil; they thrive in sandy or gravelly spots. Set ground cover types 2 feet apart; control weeds until the plants fill in. Smaller cotoneasters look best in groups of three to five.

Growing Tips
Fertilize with a 5-1-1 slow-release formula in spring; keep up the mulch annually with coarse organic materials. After establishment, cotoneasters seldom require fertilizer and tolerate summer drought well. They do need supplemental water during establishment.

Care
Overgrown cotoneasters endure being cut to the ground just as spring starts, but require two to three years to fill in again. Select plants based on mature size to avoid that, but older landscapes may have shaggy or shabby cotoneasters that require radical pruning. When pruning, make thinning cuts to keep the plant graceful. If grown as a hedge, allow cotoneasters to keep an informal shape rather than shearing them. Avoid *Cotoneaster horizontalis*, which is prone to rust, fire blight, and webworms. Substitute another low-growing type, such as creeping cotoneaster (*Cotoneaster adpressus*). Deer avoid cotoneasters, though they may sample now and then.

Companion Planting and Design
Pines make particularly attractive backgrounds for cotoneaster. As screening and specimen plants, the red and green cotoneaster carries fall beauty on into winter. Grow the low-growing ones in groups, massing them as weed-resisting ground covers.

We Recommend
Cotoneaster lacteus, with leaves about 2 inches long, can reach 12 feet with arching graceful branches and bright-red berries often persisting through light snow, an effect as elegant as holly but with far fewer pest problems. Hardy throughout our region, *C. dammeri* 'Coral Beauty', at only 6 inches, provides a terrific colorful ground cover.

Evergreen Huckleberry
Vaccinium ovatum

When, Where, and How to Plant
Plant in spring from containers or bare root; page 173 provides planting guidelines. Plants dug from the wild rarely transplant well; it's much better to acquire huckleberries from nurseries. Evergreen huckleberry needs moist shade or partial sun, with protection from harsh direct afternoon sun, especially when plants aren't established. The more sun exposure, the shorter the plant. Acidic soil well mulched with composted bark or other organic material will suit it. Unlike its edible-blueberry relatives, evergreen huckleberry needs good drainage. It grows best in moister forest areas. Plants grow slowly for the first two or three years, then fill out more quickly.

Growing Tips
Water regularly for the first two or three years, depending on the local rainfall and the plant's age. Because evergreen huckleberries are native to wooded areas, they can endure summer dryness, though watering improves their berry crop and the appearance of the foliage. This plant benefits from moderate amounts of a rhododendron fertilizer in early spring, until it is established.

Care
No pests bother evergreen huckleberry. In native ranges, it returns from the roots after forest fires. Plants exposed to too much sun or lacking in water will die back to the ground but often recover the following season. This plant needs no pruning.

Companion Planting and Design
As an informal partner in woodland gardens, evergreen huckleberry can be an airy screen or an accent plant. Branches gathered from native woodlands are valued by florists, letting gardeners know what a good background plant it can be. It associates well with other natives, such as sword fern and *Mahonia repens* under conifers, especially limbed-up Douglas firs. Evergreen huckleberry reaches 12 feet in moist woods, especially on Washington's Olympic Peninsula, but tops out at about 5 feet in managed landscapes. In more formal areas, the tidy evergreen leaves complement rhododendron, sweet box, and hellebore.

We Recommend
Any native planting benefits from evergreen huckleberry. There are no hybrids or cultivars.

Valuable in native and informal landscapes, evergreen huckleberry provides year-round interest. Native to the west coast from California to British Columbia, it resists drought or winter cold once settled in the landscape. New spring growth is distinctly tan or reddish, changing in early summer to firm, small, dark-green leaves that completely cover the stems. Creamy-white late-spring flowers resemble those on madrona tree and strawberry tree, which are also in the Erica family. Though related to edible blueberries and cranberries, evergreen huckleberries handle much drier landscape conditions. Fall berries, prized for pies and jam, feed birds and bears, so humans have to be alert to harvest them. Responsive to pruning, evergreen huckleberries can be trained as small tidy hedges, though shearing removes the berry-producing flowers.

Bloom Period and Seasonal Color
Spring through fall; white blooms, red foliage

Mature Height × Spread
3 to 12 feet × 2 to 4 feet

Zones
6 to 9

Fothergilla

Fothergilla species and cultivars

Less familiar to gardeners in the Pacific Northwest than in other regions, fothergilla is native to the eastern United States, a clue that it requires summer moisture. Named for John Fothergill, who financed early plant-hunting expeditions in America, this valuable spring bloomer with excellent fall color has been cherished in England since the eighteenth century. Deciduous, fothergilla can be kept tidy by winter pruning to control its suckering habits, which recall its relative the witch hazel. Lightly fragrant spring flowers shaped like bottlebrushes perch on the branch ends, contrasting with the just-opening green foliage as they bloom. The highlight season is fall; fothergilla's strongest landscape value are the brilliant reds, yellows, and oranges, an entire autumn's beauty tucked onto the branches of a single plant.

Other Common Name
Dwarf witch alder

Bloom Period and Seasonal Color
Spring to fall; white blooms, orange and red foliage

Mature Height × Spread
2 to 8 feet × 2 to 10 feet

Zones
5 to 8

When, Where, and How to Plant
Plant fothergilla in spring from containers in a sunny site with well-drained, moisture-retentive soil. Amend the soil with compost or other organic material when planting; see page 173 for more about planting. Set soaker hoses or other irrigation producers around the plants before mulching if preparing an entire planting area.

Growing Tips
To maintain fertile soil, mulch with 2 to 3 inches of coarse organic compost annually. Preferring a fertile, acidic soil, fothergilla requires sulfur to lower the pH if planted in alkaline soils. It's easier to grow west of the Cascades where soils are naturally acidic, although it's perfectly hardy in many Northwest areas and manages winter freezes well. The major problem in growing fothergilla is keeping its roots deeply watered.

Care
Pests don't attack, but deer eat it. Fothergilla responds well to being mulched with shredded leaves or leaf mold. Pack disease-free fallen leaves into a plastic bag, wet them thoroughly unless they are already damp from rain, and top the bag off with a scoop of compost or garden soil; the result after six months to a year in the closed bag will be crumbly weed-free mulch, especially good for use around woodland natives like fothergilla and rhododendrons. Apply it 3 to 4 inches deep.

Companion Planting and Design
Because it needs damp soils and can take partial sun, fothergilla makes a natural companion for rhododendrons, providing flower contrast and fragrance in spring, and standing out against rhododendron's dark leaves when in fall color; add a hardy fuchsia in milder regions and the combination will shine. Fothergilla is also a good shrub for mixed perennial borders with moisture lovers like Siberian iris and bleeding heart. If the landscape has space for a small tree, the native *Fothergilla major* grows to 10 to 12 feet.

We Recommend
The small dwarf fothergilla (*Fothergilla gardenii*) stays bushy and tops out at 3 to 4 feet; cultivars aren't easily found, but *Fothergilla* 'Mount Airy' has blue-green summer foliage with fine fall color.

Hardy Fuchsia
Fuchsia species and cultivars

When, Where, and How to Plant
Plant in spring from containers into well-drained, compost-amended soil. (See page 173 for more on soils.) These plants need shade or partial shade, though they bloom best with some sun; they can take morning sun or afternoon sun with some protection. Fuchsias cannot endure hot, dry, exposed conditions; where summer temperatures are high, shelter them under arbors or trees and provide extra water.

Growing Tips
Hardy fuchsias don't require heavy fertilizer applications. Once established, the straight species, *Fuchsia magellanica*, native to Chile, tolerates late-summer drought. Others, including many of the cultivars and hybrids, need regular watering.

Care
Don't divide established shrubs in fall; root disturbance affects their ability to survive cold. Allow all the branches to remain during winter. They aren't attractive once their leaves fall, but keeping branches in place protects the roots. Mulch deeply, covering the crown with 4 to 5 inches of compost or leaf mold once frost kills the leaves and flowers. Generally, no pests bother them. Hardy fuchsias root easily from tip cuttings taken in early summer, overwintered in shelter, such as on a cold frame, and planted in spring. Prune in late spring after removing the protective mulch; shrubs that appear dead will often sprout from the crown, often as late as May. After mild winters, existing branches may leaf out to their tips, allowing earlier flowering.

Companion Planting and Design
Sharing space with ferns, hostas, and hellebores in the light shade garden, fuchsias are perfectly at home. Add one or two next to rhododendrons to bring color when they're out of flower. *Fuchsia magellanica* blooms strongly from late July until frost, lighting the garden, especially if placed so afternoon light falls behind the slender crimson and purple flowers.

We Recommend
Try 'Versicolor', with early, copper-pink leaves and dark-purple flowers. 'Joan Leach' grows to 3 feet with large lavender and light-pink flowers.

Hardy fuchsias surprise gardeners by living throughout winter and returning, rather than simply being transient annuals planted in spring. They are native to South America and New Zealand. Though resilient, hardy fuchsias confine survival to zones 7 to 9. Summer weather west of the Cascades suits these perfectly, with cool days and nights that prolong their beauty. Resident hummingbirds seek them, providing a perfect garden picture as the birds hover for nectar. Their edible purple berries can be added to a morning bowl of yogurt. As accent plants in the autumn border, the taller forms glow in afternoon light. Smaller types like the 1-foot 'Mrs. Popple' will edge the shady perennial border. Gardeners can experiment by setting out basket fuchsias; many, like 'Double Otto' and 'Swingtime', are hardy.

Bloom Period and Seasonal Color
Summer; white, pink, red, purple, and leaf variegation

Mature Height × Spread
1 to 6 feet × 1 to 4 feet

Zones
7 to 9

Heavenly Bamboo
Nandina domestica and cultivars

Not a bamboo but certainly heavenly, this Japanese native is a rugged landscape shrub related to barberries; heavenly bamboo manages to look delicate despite its sturdiness. Its bamboolike stalks are usually hidden by fine compound leaves that give heavenly bamboo a light texture in the landscape. Late-spring flowers in creamy white stand at the ends of the stems, adding to the delicacy. Red fall berries complement the leaf color, often brilliant oranges and reds in autumn. Generally evergreen, nandinas make fine accent shrubs, foundation plantings, and ground covers when the smallest, such as 'Harbor Dwarf', are planted en masse. Japanese myth says that a heavenly bamboo plant at the doorstep will listen to the householder's troubles, but perhaps its beauty simply lifts the spirits.

Bloom Period and Seasonal Color
Spring through fall; white blooms; tan, red, and gold foliage

Mature Height × Spread
1 to 8 feet × 3 to 6 feet

Zones
7 to 9

When, Where, and How to Plant
Plant in spring or fall from containers; transplant in late winter or early spring. Nandina can take shade, partial sun, or full sun, but in full sun, it needs more water and protection from the coldest winter winds. It prefers well-drained soil, acidic to neutral. See page 173 for planting tips.

Growing Tips
Once established, heavenly bamboo will endure considerable summer drought, requiring watering deeply once a month in the driest times. Fertilize once in early spring with a 5-1-1 formula. Mulch 2 to 3 inches deep, keeping the mulch away from the canes.

Care
Older plants gradually form clumps, with new canes spreading slowly. Regular pruning keeps the plants graceful and small; remove older canes at ground level in fall. If temperatures drop sharply, nandina defoliates, but well-established plants come back from the roots and eventually reach their original size. Never shear this plant, or it will become a mass of graceless twigs. No pests bother it. Deer refuse it, just as they do most members of the barberry family.

Companion Planting and Design
As a landscape accent, heavenly bamboo is lovely year-round with mugo pines and low-growing rosemary in full sun. One or two at the doorstep make fine foundation plantings. When planted in partial shade, the smaller cultivars look at home with perennial epimedium and native *Mahonia repens* for a tough, handsome informal area under conifers. Underplanted with clumps of small narcissus like 'February Gold', the ground cover types beautifully echo the yellow and then mask the narcissus as it goes dormant. 'Fire Power' grows well in containers, even throughout winter, with distinct maroon foliage during cold weather.

We Recommend
Nandina domestica grows taller than most of its cultivars, eventually forming an open hedge, 6 to 8 feet, or an accent specimen. 'Gulf Stream' reaches 3 to 4 feet with attractive blue-green summer foliage and strong autumnal and winter red, becoming tawny in spring when new growth emerges.

Hydrangea
Hydrangea species and hybrids

When, Where, and How to Plant
Plant in spring or fall from containers. (See page 173 for planting tips.) Prepare well-drained, organically amended soil. Hydrangeas don't grow well where soils are distinctly alkaline, with a pH over 8. In general, they won't tolerate dry soils. They can endure full sun in cooler summer areas, but where summers get hot, hydrangeas need the shade protection of structures or trees.

Growing Tips
Hydrangeas benefit from two applications of a 10-10-10, or fertilizers with higher nitrogen levels, one in early spring and one as buds open. Well-known grower Dan Hinkley suggests using a nitrate-based fertilizer for the best blue color. All hydrangeas require deep root watering; they don't tolerate drought anywhere in Washington or Oregon.

Care
Many hydrangeas respond to soil pH by changing the colors of their flowers. The lower the soil pH, the bluer the flowers. West of the Cascades, where soils stay somewhat acidic, it's generally not necessary to amend soil for blues. To alter acidic soil for pinker or redder flowers, add garden lime in fall, allowing four months for it to alter the soil acidity before planting. To make the soil more acidic where it's alkaline, in order to create blues instead of pinks, add aluminum sulfate according to package directions, again allowing time before planting. Many newer cultivars of hydrangeas aren't as affected by soil acidity as the old familiar mopheads, *Hydrangea macrophylla*. Few pests bother them, but deer munch them avidly. Pruning technique varies with type; consult a nursery for precise directions.

Companion Planting and Design
Often combined with perennial flower beds in partial shade, hydrangeas suit both formal and cottage garden designs and can be fine accent plants. They're at home as foundation plants accenting traditional architecture.

We Recommend
The new cultivar 'Endless Summer' blooms continuously with vivid bright-blue flowers. For tough shade conditions, try oakleaf hydrangea (*Hydrangea quercifolia* 'Snow Queen'), which has yellow and red fall foliage. It takes drier spots once established.

Hydrangeas appeal to the fanciful and romantic style of gardening, with stunning large clusters of blue, pink, or white flowers floating at the ends of branches in early summer. All hydrangeas are deciduous. They make fine accent shrubs in partial shade, with deep-green leaves that often turn yellow or reddish before falling. Shrubs, though of different species, resemble each other in outline and garden usefulness, but the types of flowers differ in effect. Perhaps most familiar is the hortensia type, more casually called mophead, *which carries ball-shaped flower heads with fully open blooms. Lacecaps show tight colored centers, the fertile flowers, surrounded by a frill of petals. Several are vines—see page 237 for a profile of climbing hydrangea. Hydrangeas thrive in seaside conditions if provided with moisture.*

Bloom Period and Seasonal Color
Summer to fall; white, pink, and blue

Mature Height × Spread
3 to 8 feet × 3 to 6 feet

Zones
4 to 9

Japanese Holly
Ilex crenata and cultivars

A vigorous, useful landscape contributor, Japanese holly is related to the more familiar prickly holly with red berries. But it's valued for its firm, glossy attractive evergreen foliage rather than its quite inconspicuous fruit. The foliage is oval, but not thorny. Available in hundreds of cultivars, Ilex crenata grows in many forms: columnar, globe-shaped, ground cover, or even treelike if you plant the straight species, which can grow to 15 feet. Pest resistant and somewhat drought tolerant, Japanese holly resembles both boxwood (for which it's often mistaken) and holly, with fewer disease or insect difficulties. As accent plants or ground covers, it provides tidy, rather formal shapes suited to nearly any landscape design. Generally carefree, the newer cultivars maintain their handsome forms without much pruning.

Bloom Period and Seasonal Color
Evergreen; white blooms, black berries

Mature Height × Spread
Varies with cultivar

Zones
5 to 9

When, Where, and How to Plant
Plant from containers in spring or fall. Full or partial sun works well, as long as the soil drains well. It grows in acidic or slightly alkaline soils. Seaside winds don't bother it. Amend the soil with organic material, digging it in thoroughly over the entire planting area (see page 173 for soil preparation tips).

Growing Tips
Keep plants mulched with 2 to 3 inches of composted bark or other organic material. *I. crenata* won't grow in soggy soils. It's easy to grow and tolerates drought once established.

Care
Prune or clip just after spring growth if maintaining a formal hedge. *I. crenata* grows back well from pruning, filling in where branches are shortened. Don't prune in fall in the coldest areas, where new soft growth is more susceptible to spring freezes. Plants are either male or female, but the flowers are insignificant and the black-berried fruit is seldom seen. 'Sky Pencil' is female, as are many of the common Japanese holly cultivars, all with few pest problems.

Companion Planting and Design
Japanese holly is so versatile that the landscape use depends on the selected cultivar. Formal hedges composed of *I. crenata* 'Convexa', a cultivar familiar in nurseries for decades, look good even after zone 5 winters. Japanese holly can be shaped as topiary forms; one of the simplest is to trim the rounded globe forms into perfectly shaped balls.

We Recommend
I. crenata 'Helleri' grows 18 inches tall and 3 feet wide, with a gently mounded shape that works as both foundation plantings and tucked on the edge of shrub borders. 'Golden Gem' reaches 2 feet, with distinctly yellow leaves and a spreading tendency. It needs full sun to keep the best leaf tones. Where a columnar accent is needed, 'Mariesii' grows slowly to 3 feet tall; 'Sky Pencil' reaches 6 feet but stays narrower, to only 10 inches.

Lilac
Syringa species

When, Where, and How to Plant

Plant in spring or fall, in full sun; lilacs need at least six hours of sun daily. They prefer neutral to slightly alkaline soil and must have lime when planted in acidic soil. Air circulation is vital to keep them healthy, as is good drainage. Lilacs bloom less vigorously in zone 8 than in colder areas. They are easily transplanted from suckering shoots that spring from the roots. See page 173 for planting tips.

Growing Tips

Drought tolerant once established, lilacs need regular irrigation for the first few years. Be patient; they may not bloom for several seasons after planting. Apply a balanced 5-1-1 fertilizer yearly before buds begin to swell. Mulch with compost.

Care

Flowers form on old wood from the previous year, developing just below the current year's flowers. It's not necessary to remove spent flowers. Lilacs begin to form new buds for the following year soon after bloom; stems that bloom one year generally bloom the next. Allow the plant to grow without much pruning until it begins to bloom, which may be several years. Regular pruning and tidying keeps plants healthy by improving air circulation. For major renovation, prune in midwinter when the plant's form is visible, removing a few of the oldest canes at the root level. To keep the plant open, pull or break off suckers as they come up. Powdery mildew and lilac leaf blight can affect the leaves, especially in the warmer, milder areas, causing defoliation. Rake and dispose of fallen leaves, keeping them out of compost.

Companion Planting and Design

Deep-purple lilacs backing a perennial garden complement early euphorbias, late tulips, and peonies. Smaller cultivars can grow along a walkway or as foundation plantings when combined with evergreens such as mugo pines.

We Recommend

Perfumed deep-purples like 'Ludwig' define the best of lilacs, as does white 'Vestale'. For smaller spaces, try *Syringa patula* 'Miss Späth Kim', which grows to 4 feet.

Lilacs bring cherished associations to many gardeners; the perfume and color of these long-lived spring-flowering shrubs carry us back to remembered gardens. Their powerful beauty caused some pioneers to tuck their roots into wagons headed west. With trusses of fragrant blooms about 8 inches long, some doubles, sturdy lilacs can live for decades and grow stronger by the year. Deciduous plants, lilacs carry attractive heart-shaped leaves of midgreen. They look best as big hedges or background shrubs, reaching 20 feet or more when old and settled, although newer hybrids keep much shorter growth habits for smaller gardens. Lilacs grow and bloom better in the coldest climates; they require freezing winter temperatures. Spokane, Washington, City of Lilacs, celebrates May by honoring their fragrance and color.

Bloom Period and Seasonal Color
Spring; white, yellow, lavender, blue, purple, and bicolors

Mature Height × Spread
4 to 20 feet × 4 to 20 feet

Zones
2 to 8

Mahonia
Mahonia species and hybrids

Mahonias, with their striking evergreen foliage and yellow flowers in midwinter and earliest spring, provide a landscape boost early in the gardening year. Like their relatives the barberries, mahonias have yellow sap and prickles, though their armor grows on leaves rather than stems. The leaves are compound and pinnate-shaped; they look like large feathers held stiffly away from the branches, giving mahonia a distinct sculptural form. Needing little summer water, mahonias suit the dry shady garden. Types with winter flowers help supply nectar for overwintering hummingbirds in the lowlands west of the Cascades. An invaluable, handsome evergreen, mahonia also adds interest as the emerging spring foliage changes color from its initial soft-tan through butterscotch and gradually to summer green. Dark-blue midsummer berries feed the birds.

Other Common Name
Oregon grape

Bloom Period and Seasonal Color
Late winter to spring; yellow blooms, with red foliage tints in fall

Mature Height × Spread
2 to 8 feet × 3 to 6 feet

Zones
4 to 8

When, Where, and How to Plant
Plant in spring or fall from containers. In spring, you'll find bare-root native forms, *M. aquifolium* or *M. nervosa*, at conservation and reforestation sales. Soak bare-root plants four to eight hours before installing; water native plantings the first two summers. Acidic soil and well-composted mulch suit mahonia. Avoid hot sun areas and cold winds; mahonia needs the shelter of taller plants or trees. Page 173 has more planting tips.

Growing Tips
When neglected, as in a native landscape where they receive no fertilizer, mahonias will survive. In a cultivated area, they benefit from a slow-release fertilizer applied in early spring until they establish and monthly watering during summer. Keep plants mulched with 2 to 3 inches of compost.

Care
Plants may not bloom the first two or three years, but once established, they'll bloom consistently. Mahonia responds well to pruning; new branches form readily. Cut blooming stems off young plants after bloom; the plants will develop more bushiness and more flowers for the next year. Once mahonia reaches about 6 feet, only light pruning is needed. When settled in the landscape, this plant reacts to transplanting by growing very slowly. In full sun, it may suffer from leaf marking and spotting, which disappears when the plant is moved to a more sheltered spot. Mahonias occasionally get powdery mildew in late summer but outgrow it with the next season's growth. These plants are generally pest free, and deer avoid them.

Companion Planting and Design
In a shaded planting with native ferns, epimedium, *Camellia sasanqua*, and sweet box (*Sarcococca ruscifolia*), mahonia helps banish winter in milder areas.

We Recommend
Shrubby tall mahonia hybrids 'Charity' and 'Arthur Menzies' adorn winter landscapes. 'Winter Sun', an Irish hybrid, blooms a bit earlier with erect, soft-yellow flowers. Native *Mahonia aquifolium*, growing to 5 feet, produces edible fruit that's somewhat more a curiosity than a food source. *M. repens* forms an excellent dry shade woodland ground cover at 1 to 2 feet.

Osmanthus
Osmanthus species and cultivars

When, Where, and How to Plant

Plant from containers in spring, fall, or even winter; see page 173 for planting tips. This plant grows in just about any type of soil—acidic, neutral, or alkaline, but choose well-drained soil; osmanthus gets root rot from winter-soggy soils. If drainage can't be provided, plant on a raised bed or berm. Remarkably, osmanthus grows well in full sun, partial shade, or full shade. When planted in full shade, all osmanthus will grow more open, with leaves farther apart, stems more limber, and fewer flowers. It does, however, flower well in partial sun, particularly under deciduous trees. While it does manage full sun, some shelter from the hottest late-afternoon light helps leaves resist leaf spot in midsummer.

Growing Tips

Once settled, after two or three years , osmanthus tolerates summer drought. Fertilize in early spring with a slow release 5-1-1. Keep 2 to 3 inches mulch renewed yearly.

Care

Osmanthus sometimes suffers from being chopped into a formal hedge shape; while it will allow this, the bloom usually disappears and the form of the leaves suffers. Plant where it can be allowed to grow into a natural shape. Trim spring-blooming types informally after bloom. Fall-blooming *O. heterophyllus* should be pruned, if necessary, in midwinter when it's dormant, after bloom. This plant has few pest problems, though deer eat it.

Companion Planting and Design

Osmanthus makes an attractive foundation planting in full sun or shade, especially if sited beside a walkway or doorway to bring the fragrance close. *O. delavayi* grows into a arching shape, about 6 feet tall; if used as a hedge, keep it graceful and informal, resisting any temptation to shear it. Osmanthus can join rhododendron in the shrub border or accompany Japanese anemones, larger hostas, and ferns.

We Recommend

Long-lived *O. delavayi*, featuring handsome leaves for spring bloom, produces rather showy creamy-white flowers. *O. heterophyllus*, its leaves slightly prickly, is more hollylike than other species; it blooms white in midfall.

Versatility and reliability come with osmanthus, with several different species reliable in zones 7 to 9. Graham Stuart Thomas described this plant as "one of the choicest of evergreen shrubs," a serious accolade, given his encyclopedic plant knowledge. Osmanthus has small, glossy green leaves, smooth-edged or prickly, which can thrive in either full sun or shade. This plant isn't particular about soil type, either. Superficially it resembles Japanese holly (see page 184) but adds the benefit of fragrance. Creamy-white flowers, somewhat tubular and quite small, scent the garden in spring, growing as an arching shrub or trained into a tree. The flowers of Osmanthus fragrans make a jasminelike scented Chinese tea. Slow growing but long lived, osmanthus holds its beauty for decades.

Bloom Period and Seasonal Color
Spring to fall; evergreen, with white blooms

Mature Height × Spread
6 to 20 feet × 6 to 8 feet

Zones
7 to 9

Pacific Wax Myrtle
Myrica californica

Pacific wax myrtle provides screening and green background while being almost carefree. Easily grown and tough, it's one of the most useful of west coast natives for gardens in milder areas. Midgreen foliage covers long graceful branches completely, making the plant helpfully opaque when used as screening. Because it grows to 12 to 15 feet, it can settle on a boundary line and help hide unwanted views. Dark and almost invisible, spring flowers disappear into the foliage. Fall berries, dark blackish purple, persist on the plants and do not seem to be taken by birds. Though related to eastern bayberry (Myrica pensylvanica), these berries lack a harvestable waxy coating. Pacific wax myrtle is used effectively at the Woodland Park Zoo in Seattle for both hedging and screening.

Other Common Name
California bayberry

Bloom Period and Seasonal Color
Evergreen

Mature Height × Spread
10 to 15 feet × 5 to 15 feet

Zones
7 to 9

When, Where, and How to Plant
Plant in spring or fall from containers. Choose full or partial sun sites with well-drained acidic soil. If planting for a screen, set the plants about 5 feet apart, in a slightly irregular line. They grow fast but are long-lived and fill in quickly. See page 173 for planting tips.

Growing Tips
Apply 2 to 4 inches of coarse organic mulch annually. Once the plants settle in, they don't require regular mulches or fertilization. Water for the first two years; after that, they manage without supplementary irrigation in summer.

Care
Pacific wax myrtle responds well to trimming to shorten the plants, but isn't suitable for shearing; if it's growing too tall, cut it back to a growth point (bud) where new growth will soon fill in. Mature shrubs may become nearly as wide as they are tall, and can be used as specimen plants with some pruning. Keep plants mulched with 2 to 3 inches of compost. Deer won't eat it, but my plants have been savaged by mountain beaver, an ancient rodent common to the Cascades, which have denuded it of branches. They're thoroughly annoying but less common than deer, with no real remedy. Wax myrtle will fill in again from growth buds down on the remaining branches.

Companion Planting and Design
The native range of *Myrica californica* is dune country, making this an obvious choice for a seaside landscape. It adapts to being planted in woodland areas but looks most at home along the shore. Where conditions are windy, the shrub grows lower and flatter. Useful as an informal hedge or screen, Pacific wax myrtle fills space beautifully. Leaves stay deeply green year-round, providing a striking background for the native maple (*Acer circinatum*) or for Japanese maple (*Acer palmatum*) when they turn to autumn color. For an intriguing texture, pair with yew as a mixed hedge.

We Recommend
Plant the species; there are no hybrids or cultivars.

Pieris
Pieris japonica and cultivars

When, Where, and How to Plant
Plant in spring from containers, choosing a sheltered position with partial shade. You'll find planting tips on page 173. Pieris will survive in dark shade but blooms better with light; morning light and protection from late-afternoon heat and sun will suit it. The soil should be acidic and well amended to hold moisture. Good drainage is also essential. See basic soil management instructions on page 11.

Growing Tips
Keep the plants watered through the driest parts of summer. Pieris needs regular moisture to keep the foliage attractive. It survives summer drought once established but isn't as lushly beautiful and may suffer twig die back. A slow-release fertilizer for acid-loving plants (such as a rhododendron fertilizer) is helpful if growth is lacking. Mulch to 2 to 4 inches annually, using composted yard waste or composted leaves, if available.

Care
Prune out winter-damaged branches or dead interior twigs before bloom. The shrub's form, with branches drooping and sweeping down, their flowers held along the branch, needs little pruning. The tallest types, like Chinese pieris (*Pieris formosa* var. *forestii*) may be limbed up to form small attractive trees. Prune off the old flowers after bloom. New bud clumps will dangle throughout fall and winter. Pieris has few pest problems.

Companion Planting and Design
Combine pieris with rhododendrons, azaleas, and Pacific wax myrtles in a shady border. Choose companions carefully to complement the brilliant rosy-red spring foliage. Pieris looks good with white or certain pink rhododendrons. It thrives in containers, adding drama to gathered pots of spring bulbs. Elegance and grace make it an effective accent plant.

We Recommend
Red-flowered *Pieris japonica* 'Valley Valentine' grows to 7 feet. 'Purity', 4 feet high, features white flowers. For leaf color, 'Flaming Silver' lives up to its name, its new growth red with pink margins, maturing to green with white margins. Familiar and worthwhile, *Pieris* 'Forest Flame' reaches 6 to 8 feet with white flowers and brilliant-red leaves that turn green.

Pieris adds dimension to the landscape by bursting into color in spring, partly from the striking dangling flowers but primarily from the new leaf color. During other seasons, the shrub remains quietly evergreen with glossy 2-inch, narrow, pointed leaves. Some forms have white leaf edges, lovely with the white flowers, which are borne thickly in dangling clumps resembling bunches of tiny grapes 3 to 6 inches long. Spring leaf color can be cerise, deep-rose, bright-peach, or shocking pink, especially vivid in newer cultivars. Related to rhododendron, pieris requires the same moist, protected conditions, with shade particularly necessary in hot-summer areas. A valuable evergreen with an old-fashioned feeling, pieris settles comfortably into mixed floral and shrub plantings and looks at home in heritage landscapes.

Other Common Names
Lily of the valley shrub, Japanese andromeda

Bloom Period and Seasonal Color
Spring; white, pink, and red blooms, brightly colored new leaf growth

Mature Height × Spread
3 to 7 feet × 3 to 5 feet

Zones
6 to 9

Potentilla
Potentilla fruticosa

Useful in the water-wise garden, potentilla covers itself in small bright flowers throughout summer. Resembling buttercups, though in the rose family, the flowers are commonly yellow, but garden cultivars in soft orange and white add to its color range. Fine-textured foliage, usually deciduous, can be deep-green, light-green, or silvery-green on small plants, usually 2 to 3 feet high. In full bloom, it reminds me of a pioneer's calico dress. Potentilla's casual charm is suited to a mixed-flower border. Drought tolerant and native to mountains throughout the West, potentilla manages cold, heat, and stress. Older plants can grow out of their original mounding form, developing longer woody branches and becoming more open. The native Potentilla fruticosa suits open, exposed spots and full-sun rocky areas.

Other Common Name
Shrubby cinquefoil

Bloom Period and Seasonal Color
Summer; yellow, orange, and white

Mature Height × Spread
2 to 4 feet × 3 to 5 feet

Zones
3 to 7

When, Where, and How to Plant
Plant from containers in spring or fall (see page 173 for planting tips), but you can select this plant in bloom. Since colors vary, it's helpful to see the plants in flower before installing them. Plant in summer from containers as long as they get water in the first year. Cultivars with orange, red, or pink flowers may show fading colors in the brightest sun; 'Red Ace', pink 'Royal Flush', and 'Tangerine' may benefit from protection from the hottest afternoon sun, though they still need light to set buds. Choose a full-sun site, with well-drained soil of any type—acidic, neutral, or even alkaline. Plenty of air circulation is vital. Potentillas do not grow well in stagnant air.

Growing Tips
Water for the first two years, soaking the plants deeply about every two weeks during dry spells. After that they need no water although if planted where irrigation occurs they won't suffer as long as the soil drains well. Apply a coarse organic mulch annually to maintain fertility.

Care
Potentillas present few problems, being almost carefree once they have settled roots in the landscape. Prune to open the plants. Powdery mildew can affect them in late summer, especially where plantings are crowded. Deer eat them avidly, just as they do roses.

Companion Planting and Design
Although native to different parts of the world, rockrose (*Cistus*) and potentilla like exactly the same growing conditions—hot, dry, and challenging. Since most rockroses have yellow flower centers, they chime well with potentillas on slopes, along with other sun lovers like herbs, or even as low mixed hedges along a flower garden border.

We Recommend
For the summer flower garden, try 'Tangerine', with soft-orange flowers, in front of daylilies and erysimum. 'Royal Flush' blooms bright-pink. Lighter yellows stand out on 'Katherine Dykes' and 'Primrose Beauty'.

Red-Flowering Currant
Ribes sanguineum

When, Where, and How to Plant
Choose well-drained soil in full or partial sun; see page 173 for planting tips. This plant doesn't require any particular soil type, nor much fertility. It grows naturally on dry, exposed, logged-over spots and other disturbed areas. Plant from containers or bundled bare roots available from conservation district spring sales. Soak bare-root plants four to eight hours in plain water before installing. Never allow bare roots to be exposed to drying air and sun. Mulch after planting, peferably with 2 to 3 inches of composted bark.

Growing Tips
Completely drought tolerant once established, red-flowering currant handles summer weather perfectly. It will coexist with border plants that require more water, but if watered too heavily in shade, it develops weak, lank branches. Fertilize lightly in the first season. Once established in the garden, native currants need little care, thriving without extra water or nutrients. Keep plants well mulched with 2 to 3 inches of organic material.

Care
Pruning is seldom required but can be done during winter to remove crossing or damaged branches. This plant resists pests. Deer nibble the branches, which quickly fill in again.

Companion Planting and Design
Use for spring color in the native woodland edge or wildlife garden. Or plant it as an accent, where it can anchor the edge of a perennial flower border with small white daffodils like 'Thalia'. Red-flowering currant can also be an effective specimen plant for spring and summer screening. For bird-watching, site one near a window or outdoor seating area to observe hummingbirds. Red-flowering currant combines well with the native maple (*Acer circinatum*) for both spring and fall interest.

We Recommend
'White Icicle' has crisp white blooms that hang in good contrast to the early green leaves, making it a fine choice for a formal urban garden. Several cultivars that were developed in England include 'King Edward VII', a deep rose, and a pink, 'Claremont'. But the species glorifies gardens without any further embellishment by hybridizing.

A handsome, pest-resistant, and easily grown native shrub, the deciduous red-flowering currant lights up woodland edges in milder areas. Its flowers, intensely pink rather than red, attract the earliest hummingbirds returning from Mexico, flying north seeking the nectar of this currant as it blooms with warming temperatures from California to British Columbia. Flowers form just before this shrub's light-green, maple-shaped leaves emerge. Inland gardeners can plant the golden currant (Ribes aureum) also spring flowering, with fragrant yellow blooms in full or partial sun. All currants produce edible fruit although birds rather than humans generally eat these. Appropriate for both formal and informal landscapes, the red-flowering currant is one of the most decorative of native plants, a good choice for gardeners experimenting with natives.

Bloom Period and Seasonal Color
Spring; white, rose, and red

Mature Height × Spread
3 to 10 feet × 3 to 6 feet

Zones
4 to 8

Redtwig Dogwood
Cornus stolonifera

One of the most valuable plants for native landscapes and stream buffer replanting, this deciduous shrub is found from northern California north to Alaska. Tough and resilient, redtwig dogwood thrives in deepest winter cold and summer heat if given consistently moist growing conditions. Though related to flowering dogwood trees, redtwig dogwood is cherished not for its rather small spring flowers, but for the brilliance of its bare red branches in winter. Some cultivars have yellow stems, adding gold to the winter brilliance. These plants also have handsome summer leaves. It spreads by roots (stolons, accounting for one species name), gradually forming large thickets. Birds eat the dark blue-black berries formed after bloom. This plant is sometimes found under an alternate botanical name, Cornus sericea.

Other Common Name
Red-osier dogwood

Bloom Period and Seasonal Color
Spring to winter; white blooms, with red twigs

Mature Height × Spread
1 to 8 feet × 8 to 10 feet

Zones
2 to 8

When, Where, and How to Plant
Plant in spring from containers or bare root. See page 173 for planting tips. It's often available bundled and bare root from spring native plant sales by conservation districts. Soak bare-root plants four to eight hours before planting, never exposing them to dry air. Though adapted to moist soil conditions along stream banks, they also thrive in well-drained garden soil amended with compost. Set soaker hoses or other irrigation features around the plants for summer watering if installed away from a naturally occurring water source.

Growing Tips
If planted in well-amended soil, redtwig dogwood requires little or no fertilizer. To help it establish, apply a 5-10-10 slow-release formula for the first year. But don't use fertilizer on slopes near streams or nitrogen may leach into the water. Mulch with composted bark or other organic material. To provide water available to root depth, place soaker hoses before adding mulch.

Care
Cut to ground level in late winter every three years, just as the dormant season ends, to force new twig growth. Color is more pronounced on first-year branches. Plants will resprout in one season from radical pruning. Redtwig dogwood fills in rapidly as a multistemmed shrub; if necessary, remove its expanding shoots to keep it small enough for the cultivated landscape. It's generally pest free.

Companion Planting and Design
These plants provide screening where water is present; use them to stabilize stream banks on restoration projects. As an edging for ponds or small water features, redtwig dogwood offers winter color and sets off Japanese iris and Siberian iris when they bloom in summer. For vivid color effect, combine gold-twigged 'Elegantissima' with the red-twigged species.

We Recommend
'Silver and Gold' has yellow-gold stems in winter and green leaves edged with cream; it also requires moist conditions. The cultivar 'Kelseyi' stays 1 foot and spreads gradually to form an intriguing ground cover for damp banks. 'Sunshine' features yellow tones to the summer leaves and red winter twigs.

Rhododendron
Rhododendron species and cultivars

When, Where, and How to Plant
Plant in spring from containers; see page 173 for planting tips. Select them when in bloom; they transplant well while flowering. See the azalea profile (page 175) for specific soil requirements. Rhododendrons require acidic soil that holds water well and drains perfectly; none are adapted to soggy sites, which can cause root rot. Plant on raised beds or berms if necessary. Partial sun or partial shade suits them.

Growing Tips
Fertilize in early spring with a slow-release rhododendron (acidic type) material. Renew mulches, keeping it off the trunks. Keep plants watered in summer; moisture is vital, with regular soaking to root depth.

Care
Prune during or after bloom. Many gardeners deadhead the flowers before they go to seed. This certainly improves the aesthetic appearance of the plants, especially those that produce huge trusses. But they bloom well the following year even if not cleared of old flowers. Look carefully before breaking off the flower because it rests on top of emerging foliage buds. Rhododendrons suffer from marginal leaf chewing by root weevils. But many cultivars resist root weevil chewing, including 'PJM' and 'Crest'. Deer don't eat rhododendrons. An increasingly troublesome disease, rhododendron powdery mildew, affects many prominent older cultivars like 'Unique' and 'Virginia Richards'. Defoliation can result.

Companion Planting and Design
From rock gardens to woodland walks, rhododendrons fit naturally into Oregon and Washington landscapes. Where summer moisture is present, they combine well with ferns, hellebore, and Japanese anemone. Deciduous *Rhododendron augustinii*, a vivid soft blue, grows to 8 feet, providing a treelike presence in front of yews. The smallest types will grow in containers, if given winter protection.

We Recommend
With their attractive felted leaves, pest and disease resistance, and hardiness, the "yaks" (*R. yakusimanum* and their cultivars) suit gardens throughout our region, to about 3 feet. Yak cultivars 'Ken Janeck' and pink-flowering 'Yaku Princess', as well as 'Yaku Angel', bloom in midspring.

A classic Northwest garden plant, rhododendron's year-round evergreen presence commands attention in spring when formerly leafy plants burst into bloom. Color, flower form, and size differ by type, but all have grace and elegance. Flowers form on branch tips in trusses that can reach nearly 10 inches across, many with faint or pronounced fragrance. Suitable specimen accents or screening hedges, mature rhododendrons vary in size from 3 feet tall to over 20 feet and are frequently seen as trees in older gardens. Tree-sized specimens in Seattle survive summer with infrequent waterings. Smaller leaved forms tend to greater hardiness; in the coldest regions, choose types like 'PJM', which reliably survive freeze. Rhododendrons also prefer cool summer air; plant in partial shade where summer temperatures get hot.

Bloom Period and Seasonal Color
Spring to summer; evergreen, with white, pink, red, yellow, purple, and bicolors

Mature Height × Spread
1 to 25 feet × 3 to 12 feet

Zones
4 to 9

Rockrose
Cistus species and cultivars

Easy to grow, appreciating dry summers and sun, shrubby rockroses originate in the Mediterranean. They manage heat, positively thrive on drought, and fill in difficult spots like slopes with poor soil, growing quickly once established. With resinous, soft evergreen foliage in subtle grays, silver tones, and light gray-green, they harmonize well with herb gardens. Even without flowering, rockrose would be valuable in hot sunny spots, but they bloom, often densely, glowing with open white, pink, and purplish flowers resembling wild roses. Terrific for weed control, established plants shade the ground and outgrow even perennial weeds. Their only deficiency is lack of hardiness; they grow well to 15 degrees Fahrenheit but cannot survive well in lower temperatures, making them useful plants for milder areas.

Bloom Period and Seasonal Color
Summer; white, red, purple, and rose

Mature Height × Spread
2 to 6 feet × 3 to 8 feet

Zones
7 to 10

When, Where, and How to Plant
Plant from containers in spring, summer, or fall; see page 173 for planting tips. Choose a full-sun spot with excellent drainage. Rockrose isn't fussy about soil if it's well drained; heavy clay or standing water in winter may allow root rot. Sand and gravelly soils are ideal, though rockroses also prosper in soils amended with organic material. They can grow in partial sun if they receive morning shade and the strongest afternoon heat and light.

Growing Tips
Avoid fertilizer; you don't want to encourage floppy soft growth. Mulch new plantings with a coarse organic material. Water deeply in the first two years to allow good root development. Subsequently, they are completely drought adapted, requiring no irrigation.

Care
Though generally pest resistant, rockroses can be short lived, and may grow thin and woody after four to six years or die out after a hard freeze. Replace them as needed. Once established, they handle winter cold well within their zones, but can be assisted in survival by a light mulch of straw or evergreen boughs over the roots after dormancy. Shear lightly after bloom to keep the plants compact. For a more shapely plant, remove errant taller branches as they appear.

Companion Planting and Design
Naturally effective with rosemary, lavender, Russian sage, and artemisias, rockroses anchor a sunny water-wise garden. Beautiful with tulips, which also appreciate dry hot summer conditions, rockroses can be interplanted with other hardy bulbs. The flowers open briefly, lasting less than one day but covering the plants with prolific buds. They're valuable where wildfire prevention is a landscape necessity.

We Recommend
White rockrose (*Cistus × hybridus*), 3 feet tall and 7 feet wide, features white flowers centered by yellow, showy against dark foliage. 'Victor Reiter' stays compact, 3 feet by 3 feet, covered with sharp pink flowers. For covering exposed, poor soil banks, sageleaf rockrose (*C. salviifolius*) stays low but spreads to 6 feet.

Smokebush
Cotinus coggygria

When, Where, and How to Plant
Plant in spring or fall from containers; see page 173 for planting tips. Choose a full-sun spot to ensure the best coloration. Smokebush will grow in nearly any soil type, but grows best when kept mulched with an organic product. Choose well-drained soil. Too much moisture—or shady conditions—causes floppy growth and less vivid color.

Growing Tips
Cotinus species don't need water or fertilizer once established. Place soaker hoses to water new plants for the first two summers, then allow water from rainfall only, which may be less than an inch a month.

Care
Young plants require time and size to show off the hazy flowering to best effect. If coppiced—cut to the ground—regularly, they'll reach 3 to 8 feet with long limber summer shoots. If desired as a treelike form, allow one main trunk to develop rather than cutting it down yearly. The shrub's eventual size depends on how it's pruned, which should be done in midwinter when dormant. A very easy plant, smokebush has no pests or diseases. But deer stand in line to chew it.

Companion Planting and Design
Used behind herbs, smokebush, with its striking perfectly round leaf form, picks up the purple in sage and lavender, and contrasts well with artemisia in the perennial garden. Any of the rockroses (*Cistus*, see page 194), especially those with pink flowers like 'Doris Hibberson', also grow well fronting it. Red hot poker, blooming late in summer, adds upright punctuation in red and yellow as the leaves turn.

We Recommend
The popularity of smokebush has led to several fine cultivars, including 'Royal Purple', whose distinctly purple-blue leaves turn deep red in fall. 'Grace' offers strong color contrasts, with green and purple foliage changing in fall to orange.

If you haven't space to plant sumac (see page 198), the fall color from smokebush can light the whole yard without sumac's tendency to gallop over entire hillsides Though it can grow to 25 feet and certainly qualify as a tree, it's most generally pruned into the 8- to 10-foot range and used as a shrubby accent. Deciduous, coming into its beauty once the leaves open, smokebush is appreciated as a splendid background shrub to perennial borders or a foreground colorful eye catcher on its own. Small, nearly invisible early summer flowers precede the "smoke," clouds of tan or pinkish hairs that cover the developing seeds as flowers fade. The tree appears to be floating in haze. It's easily grown, good for the water-wise garden.

Other Common Name
Smoketree

Bloom Period and Seasonal Color
Late summer to fall; purple, orange, and red foliage, with soft tan smoky floral effect

Mature Height × Spread
5 to 15 feet × 5 to 15 feet

Zones
4 to 8

Spirea

Spiraea species and cultivars

A landscape stalwart, spirea forms mounded shrubs noted for late-spring or summer bloom, often with arching stems fully covered with tiny blossoms. It can be large, 8 to 9 feet tall and wide, or as short as 1 foot. Many different species of this deciduous plant are available; one of the most common is white-flowered bridal wreath spirea (Spirea × vanhouttei). For more limited spaces, smaller new cultivars not only stay petite, but many also have brilliant gold, yellow, or rose-tinted foliage, adding to their landscape interest when out of bloom. Hardy to zone 3, expect spireas to survive frigid temperatures. These easy-to-grow plants handle dry summers, a good quality for water-wise gardens. Long-lasting blooms complement mixed shrub borders, providing flowering interest after rhododendrons finish.

Bloom Period and Seasonal Color
Spring to summer; white, pink, and rose blooms, with gold foliage

Mature Height × Spread
1 to 8 feet × 2 to 10 feet

Zones
3 to 9

When, Where, and How to Plant
Plant from containers in either spring or fall (see page 173 for planting tips). Spireas need full or partial sun and well-drained soil. They can't tolerate alkaline soil or soggy conditions in either winter or summer. Amend the entire planting bed with compost or other organic materials. (See page 11 on soil amendments.) Set the plant slightly above grade level, and mulch with 2 to 3 inches of compost after planting; keep mulch away from the trunk.

Growing Tips
Choose spirea by its mature size. Spirea's value resides in its beautiful arching-branch form and the poise of the blooms, which disappear if the plant is chopped back to keep it small. Spireas improve with age when properly trained. They bloom on old wood produced in the previous year, so they lose their bloom potential when improperly pruned or pruned too late. Prune just during or after flowering, and avoid shearing the plant, which will cause it to produce lots of random shoots, reducing the plant's graceful arching shape. Spireas may produce random shoots that don't contribute to the line of the plant; if so, remove entire branches, cutting them back to a growth point. Spireas resist pests.

Care
Apply a balanced slow-release 5-1-1 or 6-2-2 fertilizer in spring. Keep plants watered through the first two summers; after establishment, they manage dry summers well, requiring only monthly watering.

Companion Planting and Design
Shorter spireas add color to the front of foundation plantings and can be used over spring bulbs to nicely disguise their browning foliage. Plant 'Little Princess' (to 2 feet), three in a triangle about 3 feet apart, with tall daffodils like creamy 'Ice Follies'.

We Recommend
Newer cultivars, such as 'Goldflame' (*S. japonica*), produce rainbows of color, turning in fall from bronze to yellow to green to red, with pink flowers. The most cold-tolerant, *S. japonica* offers a nearly miniature cultivar, 'Alpina' (also called 'Nana'), 1 foot tall with pink flowers.

Strawberry Tree
Arbutus unedo

When, Where, and How to Plant
Plant strawberry tree in spring or fall from container-grown plants. Choose full sun in cool summer areas, but partial shade where summers get hot. This plant grows in acidic or neutral soil but needs good drainage or it will succumb to root rot. Don't plant in the middle of a lawn in Washington or Oregon, where it may get too much summer water from turf irrigation (also true of the native madrona). See pages 173 for more planting tips.

Growing Tips
Annual mulching with compost and a light fertilizer in early spring using a rhododendron formulation will help (like rhododendron and azalea, strawberry tree belongs to the Erica family). It tolerates drought once established.

Care
Strawberry tree comes close to being a completely carefree plant once it begins growth. It tolerates seaside salt and moderate wind, but should be protected from the harshest exposures. Growing quite slowly, reaching 20 feet in 20 years, it can be pruned into a single-trunked tree by removing twiggy branches or left as an attractive multi-branched shrub. When settled, it blooms freely, though late autumn and early winter hard freezes can nip the flowers, eliminating the following season of berries and sometimes killing back branch tips. Shrubs recover well but may need extra spring pruning to tidy the damage. No pest problems bother it, though aphids can occasionally affect the emerging spring foliage. Deer love it and will completely defoliate the plants.

Companion Planting and Design
Although this plant can reach tree size, it is more often featured as a landscape shrub. It combines well with natives ferns and mahonia in a woodland or can be used quite formally as a foundation planting, particularly the shorter form 'Compacta'. The firm tidy leaves suit "controlled" landscapes.

We Recommend
If the garden has space, strawberry tree grows into an imposing presence. There's a shorter cultivar (12 feet), with deep-pink flowers, called 'Oktoberfest' (the name reflecting its time of bloom), though its blooms seem less plentiful.

A mid-sized to large evergreen shrub with soft, glossy foliage, strawberry tree grows quite slowly into an excellent and long-lived landscape feature. Native to Ireland and southern Europe, it gave the name to our own native madrona, *Arbutus menziesii*, because the early European explorers noticed the Northwest tree's resemblance to their familiar European one. They share rust-red peeling bark that reveal a smooth trunk, white flowers, and berries. Providing interest in every season, strawberry tree reaches its height of beauty in late fall when white dangling flowers complement perfectly ball-shaped bright-red berries from the previous season's flowers. While edible, the berries have no strawberry flavor, though birds like them. With the glossy evergreen foliage, the red and white combination appears created for holiday celebrating.

Other Common Name
Killarney strawberry tree

Bloom Period and Seasonal Color
Fall to winter; white blooms, bright-red berries in fall

Mature Height × Spread
6 to 25 feet × 5 to 12 feet

Zones
4 to 7

Sumac

Rhus species

To develop a garden rich in fall color in the Northwest, where the landscape isn't as thoroughly blessed with autumnal reds and oranges as other American spots, adding sumac to the garden can enliven the whole season. A somewhat sprawling shrub, sumac opens long pinnate leaves from fuzzy buds. The branches and twigs, covered with felted velvety softness, resemble young deer antlers before they mature, leading to its common name, "staghorn sumac." Choose a spot where sumac has room to ramble, because it can spread from root suckers into an entire sun-loving hillside of reddish orange. Completely drought tolerant, pest free, and winter hardy, sumac brings fernlike green leaves and fall brilliance to the neglected landscape areas, helping reclaim spots previously colonized by weeds.

Bloom Period and Seasonal Color
Fall; orange and red

Mature Height × Spread
6 to 20 feet × 5 to 15 feet

Zones
3 to 8

When, Where, and How to Plant
Plant in fall or spring from containers (see page 173 for planting tips). Though it needs well-drained soil, sumac isn't particular about soil type, growing very well in poor gravelly areas, whether acidic or alkaline. Full sun is necessary. Shade or permanently moist soils kill sumac. An excellent seaside plant, it also tolerates wind.

Growing Tips
Tree specialist Michael Dirr calls sumac culture "abysmally easy." Sumac thrives without fertilizer and requires water for only two years until fully established.

Care
Sumacs leaf out after other shrubs, often in late spring, and may look dead until then. Watch for small nubbins of emerging reddish new growth. Sumac can be trained into a treelike form if reduced to one main trunk early in its life, though this is probably the most difficult way to grow it. It wants to ramble and fill space; to limit its expanse, chop out suckers around the roots in early spring. Prune to remove dead branches and shape the plant. Pest free, sumac also resists deer.

Companion Planting and Design
Not for formal or controlled garden designs, sumac fills space casually—it's good at holding slopes in full sun. You can keep it as a specimen accent, but allowing it to roam and become a thicket is easier. Plants are male and female, with the females producing red berries that stay on all winter, only occasionally appreciated by birds. Summer and fall shelter provided by sumac clumps make it excellent in a wildlife-friendly landscape. Try it with a background of smaller conifers like noble fir.

We Recommend
Chinese sumac (*R. chinensis*) adds white panicles of flowers to its garden interest, blooming in August and September. Flameleaf sumac (*R. copallina*) forms a large shrub 10 to 15 feet or taller, with superb fall color. Staghorn sumac (*R. typhina*), the most common in nurseries, offers an excellent cultivar, 'Laciniata', featuring deeply cut fernlike leaves. Avoid smooth sumac (*R. glabra*), which has the worst invasive characteristics.

Sweet Box
Sarcococca species

When, Where, and How to Plant

Plant in well-drained soil. Sweet box tolerates summer dryness, requiring water infrequently once established (a deep soaking monthly during summer will keep it healthy). Keep this plant in full shade. The leaves scorch in too much light, losing their glossy evergreen beauty and becoming yellowed and stunted. A lovely shrub in shade, sweet box becomes unattractive in sun. It likes neutral to alkaline soil and, in acidic soil, benefits from a lime application every three years. Mulch with composted bark or other organic material.

Growing Tips

Sweet box rewards you with simple care. Fertilize only once in early spring with a low-nitrogen formula such as a 5-1-1 or 6-2-2. It tolerates dry shade once it's been settled into the garden for 2 or 3 years. If given deep soil and watered weekly while becoming established, sweet box will grow even under the edge of overhanging roofs and under evergreen trees.

Care

No specific insects or diseases bother it. Slow-growing and maintaining its form well, sweet box seldom needs pruning. Fragrant branches in bloom do not last long when cut for flower arrangements, but shrubs maintain their scent outdoors for several weeks.

Companion Planting and Design

In partial shade, sweet box sets off plantings of winter-blooming snowdrops (*Galanthus nivalis*) and perennial hellebores whose complex flowers shine against its deep-green background. It accompanies shrubby aucuba well in deep shade and looks effective with ferns, such as the evergreen sword fern (*Polysticum munitum*). Plant it near shaded walkways where the scent can be most appreciated in midwinter. The shorter plant, *Sarcococca hookeriana* var. *humilis*, a zone 5 plant, tolerates more winter cold than does *S. ruscifolia*, zone 6.

We Recommend

S. ruscifolia forms an extraordinarily handsome shrub, and it's hard to imagine winter landscapes in the milder areas of our region without it. There are no available cultivars. Nurseries sell the straight species. Shiny dark-black berries appear in fall but are ignored by birds.

Its name a reference both to its perfume and its resemblance to boxwood, sweet box lends elegance to the darkest shady spots with glistening evergreen foliage. Stems bear dark-green leaves from top to bottom, giving the plant density and allowing its use as an opaque hedge 2 to 4 feet tall. Sweet box fills unpromising dark and dreary areas such as sunless north exposures. This slow-growing shade lover would be agreeable for its sturdy constitution, but look for a delicious bonus: early winter fragrance. Tiny, unobtrusive cream flowers, resembling small silk fringe, fill the cold air with a scent like honey. S. ruscifolia becomes a tall shrub with arching branches to 4 feet; S. hookeriana var. humilis stays at 2 feet and spreads like a ground cover.

Other Common Name

Himalayan sweet box

Mature Height × Spread

2 to 4 feet × 1 to 4 feet

Zones

5 to 8

Viburnum
Viburnum species and cultivars

With viburnums, gardeners can choose from a huge, versatile, and tough plant family of shrubs, with different profiles from small globes growing to only 3 feet to spreading branched treelike forms at 15 feet. Both deciduous and evergreen types thrive throughout Washington and Oregon, providing fragrance and colorful blooms from winter through early summer. Korean spice viburnum (V. carlesii) blooms in late spring with ball-shaped intensely fragrant flowers (to zone 5). In the coldest areas (zone 3), cranberry bush viburnums prosper in sunny spots, with spring white flowers and red fall leaves and berries. Mild sections west of the Cascades can grow the perfumed winter-flowering V. × bodnantense. By selecting different types, gardeners can add spring bloom, summer leaf interest, and fall color with berries.

Bloom Period and Seasonal Color
Year-round; white, pink, and rose blooms, autumn leaf color

Mature Height × Spread
4 to 18 feet × 4 to 9 feet

Zones
3 to 10

When, Where, and How to Plant
Plant from containers in spring, in a well-drained, moisture-retentive soil amended with compost. See page 173 for planting tips. Most require acidic to neutral soil, at pH 6.5, though they will cope with variations. But Korean spice viburnum requires lime in acidic soil conditions. Full sun suits most, though the doublefile viburnums (*V. plicatum* f. *tomentosum*), which suit the woodland edges, prefer partial sun. Mulch after planting. Check planting and soil requirements for the particular type you're installing.

Growing Tips
Generally drought tolerant once established, especially the deciduous types, viburnums require regular moisture for the first one to three years. Korean spice viburnum likes an evenly moist soil and needs summer water throughout its life. Fertilize in earliest spring with a 5-1-1 or 6-2-2 slow-release formula. Don't overfertilize. Maintain the mulch at 2 to 3 inches year-round, keeping it away from the trunk.

Care
Viburnums seldom need pruning, but if shaping is necessary, prune the evergreens in earliest spring and the deciduous types during and just after bloom. For flower arrangements, cut back to a branch fork rather than shear or behead them. Occasional root weevil leaf chewing affects them, as do spring aphid infestations, though they usually outgrow any slight damage. Deer avoid them, nibbling only now and then.

Companion Planting and Design
Viburnums are perfect "trees" for small landscapes, particularly the doublefile types and *V. opulus*. The evergreens do well as informal screens, one of the best being *V. × rhytidophyllum*, with 6-inch leaves distinctly felted and gray, growing to 15 feet in zone 5 and managing drought well. As accent plants, Korean spice viburnums blend into flower borders.

We Recommend
A treelike deciduous spreading shrub, doublefile viburnum 'Shasta' stays at 6 feet, its parallel branch structure anchoring a late-spring planting of bleeding heart and Siberian iris. Burkwood viburnum 'Mohawk' (*V. × burkwoodii*) offers fragrant spring bloom.

Witch Hazel
Hamamelis species and cultivars

When, Where, and How to Plant
Plant fall or mid-winter in well-drained soil. Large specimens may be available balled and burlapped. They can be set out when in bloom or even in leaf, but they adapt best if planted in late fall while dormant. Full or partial sun suits their needs. Too much shade reduces their blooming. Well-amended, moisture-retentive soil is best, acidic or neutral. Set plants at the same level they were in the nursery, or slightly higher to allow for settling. Don't plant too deep (see page 173 for general planting instructions).

Growing Tips
Apply a slow-release 5-1-1 or 6-2-2 fertilizer in winter just as growth begins. Keep plants mulched, and water through the first two to three summers until their roots establish.

Care
Prune during bloom to use branches in flower arrangements, after bloom or in earliest winter to remove crossing or interfering branches that reduce their graceful winter silhouette. No pests bother witch hazel, though deer will munch the leaves and can alter the branch pattern. Named cultivars of *Hamamelis* may be grafted onto native U.S. rootstock; if suckers appear from the roots, pull them out to keep the plant true to its hybrid form.

Companion Planting and Design
On the sunny outer edges of woodlands or as specimen plants, witch hazels benefit from a background that displays their winter flowers. 'Jelena' and 'Diane' train well and can be effectively espaliered against a wall. Underplanted with early daffodils like 'February Gold', witch hazel starts the spring season early.

We Recommend
None are native to the Northwest. The witch hazels native to the Midwest and Eastern United States are the hardiest ones; they flower well but less brilliantly than the Asian hybrids developed by crossing *H. mollis* and *H. japonica*. Some of the best of these *H. × intermedia* cultivars are 'Pallida', an old pale-yellow cultivar; 'Diane', with brilliant red flowers and fall color; 'Jelena', a vivid orange in flower; and 'Arnold Promise', a clear yellow.

Slow to start but long lived once settled, witch hazel needs a more beautiful name. Its vigor, toughness, and hardiness alone make it invaluable, but witch hazel tops these qualities by producing fragrant flowers resembling tiny ragged bundles of ribbon blooming in mid- to late winter and early spring. Deciduous, the flowers are followed by large, fuzzy, appealing leaves, 3 to 4 inches across and nearly heart shaped. Flowers, unaffected by freezing weather, smell sweetest on sunny days. Landscape value perks up again in fall with vivid red, gold, and yellow leaves. Over time, it becomes a wide-spreading shrub with intriguing branch form that can be enhanced by pruning to emphasize mature trunks. A useful inclusion in water-wise landscapes, it remains trouble free all year.

Bloom Period and Seasonal Color
Fall to winter; yellow and red

Mature Height × Spread
10 to 20 feet × 8 to 12 feet

Zones
4 to 8

Trees *for Washington & Oregon*

Planting a tree is one gesture that changes both the garden and the gardener. It's not uncommon for beginning gardeners to be drawn to the extroverted color palette and dazzling blooms of annuals, those fleeting flowers that delight us for one growing season. As we mature as gardeners, we discover the ongoing satisfaction of perennials, which offer repeat blooms each year. But then the bare months of fall and winter arrive, when we have fewer flowering plant choices. We learn about design techniques of adding "bones" to the garden, which leads us to evergreen shrubs, plants that deliver structure to mixed borders and serve as a great backdrop to perennials.

And finally, we discover trees, stately beauties both deciduous and evergreen that bring continual joy in every season. Ironically, we should have started our gardens by planting trees!

Patience Is Key

Give your garden the vertical presence of trees, create a leafy canopy where you yearn for shade, enjoy a winter-blooming scene with early flowering cherry trees, or screen the entrance to your home with a row of trees that can be trained into a hedge.

Magnolia 'Nigra' and Peony

The trees featured here, as well as many of the conifers on pages 66 to 77, are excellent choices for Northwest gardens. As you consider which trees are right for your landscape, take note of their anticipated mature sizes and think about how they'll affect the garden's useful space. You may find that a small tree, such as a Japanese maple reaching only 15 feet at maturity, suits an intimate urban garden spot, seeming as majestic in its place as does a full-grown maple in a garden of several acres. Growing trees takes patience—resist the temptation to place them close together while young, otherwise in ten years' time, you'll have trees that are too crowded. Also be sure to leave them enough space when planted adjacent to your home. Most trees, even those requiring decades to reach full size,

Japanese Maple in Courtyard Garden

will gain handsome garden presence after ten years.

Getting Off to a Good Start

It's important to plant your tree relatively soon after purchasing it, so that it doesn't languish balled and burlapped or in a nursery container. Bare-root trees should also be planted immediately. Consider the timing— buy a tree at the ideal time for planting. Trees purchased and planted in July will take extra effort to establish, with greater stress to the tree during the heat of summer. Gardeners west of the Cascades can also plant trees in fall and winter.

Follow the general planting guidelines, as well as tips on evaluating your garden's soil and drainage, discussed in the general introduction on page 11. When planting trees, it is important to position the trunk flare where the roots spread out at the base of the tree. Make sure the root flare is not buried by soil or mulch. Also, shake away soil from container plants to check for—and remove—any circling roots. As you select an appropriate site in the landscape, follow the sun and soil suggestions listed for each tree featured in this chapter. Your tree's health depends greatly on giving it adequate drainage and proper root care when planted.

Watering and Feeding Tips

A newly planted tree will need special attention for the first two or three growing seasons, after which time it is considered "established." Mulch newly planted trees with a 4-foot-diameter ring of wood chips or coarse compost. Your priority is to help your tree's roots develop well during this time period, which is why we focus on providing "adequate irrigation" during the first few years. Follow the watering guidelines discussed in the general introduction on page 14. Many trees, especially conifers such as pines, will eventually survive summer without extra irrigation. But others, especially deciduous trees, will benefit from a twice-monthly deep watering during the Northwest's hot, dry spells July to September, at least until they're ten years old.

You should mulch a newly planted tree, but it is not essential to fertilize just-planted trees until the first year. A low rate of nitrogen fertilizer applied early in the dormant season will boost the following year's growth. Once a tree is established, it will receive nourishment from a variety of natural sources, such as grass clippings or fallen leaves that decompose at the base of deciduous trees.

If your tree shows symptoms such as pale-green or yellow leaves, reduced leaf size and retention, premature fall coloration and leaf drop, yellowing along the leaf veins, and overall reduced plant growth and vigor, it may have nutrient deficiencies or root difficulties. *It is critical to determine the actual cause before adding water or fertilizer to such trees.* The easiest and most effective method of supplying nutrients to the entire root system of the tree is broadcasting—spreading granular fertilizer evenly over the entire root zone. A slow-release fertilizer delivers nitrogen to a plant as it can use it, which helps reduce the

amount of excess fertilizer leeching into the ground.

Be sure to keep fertilizer away from driveways and other paved surfaces, where it can be washed away when it doesn't reach roots and where it may run off to cause water pollution.

Trees grown in urban or suburban landscapes may require nourishment, especially if construction or development has removed good topsoil or compacted fertile soil, reducing aeration and drainage. These trees and ones crowded by streets and sidewalks benefit from amendments such as an annual application of organic matter. Organic mulch should be spread around the base of trees (about 2 inches thick, taking care not to place mulch next to the trunk); as it decomposes, it improves the overall quality of the soil.

Refer to the tree and shrub care tips outlined in the general introduction on

A Shady Backyard Retreat

Japanese Stewartia

page 12. You'll learn that many woody plants benefit from a moderate fertilizer application in their second growing season. Once established, most trees will *not* require additional fertilizer. You can, however, nourish an established tree (and other woody plants) by applying 2 to 4 inches of fertile mulch each spring or fall. Select a coarse, lightweight but fertile material such as composted bark, wood chips, or manure. Some suppliers offer great mulch blends worthy of experimentation, such as a composted mix of yard water and steer manure.

Tree Care

General pruning tips are recommended for each tree entry. But don't overlook help from the experts, such as local organizations that teach tree-pruning techniques. For very large or mature trees, you may wish to consult a tree expert. The International Society of Arboriculture has a Pacific Northwest Chapter that can help you locate a certified arborist in your area. This professional organization also publishes guides to tree care and on hiring an arborist who can help you with a variety of tree care issues. Contact the Pacific Northwest Chapter ISA at P.O. Box 811, Silverton, Oregon 97381, (503) 874-8263, or at www.pawisa.org.

Celebrate Past, Present, and Future

When you plant one tree or many trees, you're giving your garden a sense of history. Whether you select a heritage tree that recalls childhood memories or plant a young sapling to celebrate a just-purchased home, the very act of digging a hole, spreading the roots, and tamping down the soil is one that celebrates the beauty of trees and celebrates the future.

—DP

Apple
Malus cultivars

Adding edibles to the ornamental garden is one way to diversify your landscape. When it comes to Northwest gardens, apples are fitting, as our regional heritage is entwined with the orchards east of the Cascades. Thanks to the region's excellent fruit tree trials, we've learned which apple trees resist diseases and adapt to climates on either side of the mountains. If you have room for an apple tree, enjoy its lovely spring flowers and delicious autumn fruit. If space is a premium, select a tree with a dwarf rootstock or grow an espaliered apple tree along a sunny wall. Apple trees look lovely in cottage and perennial gardens, and they are a bountiful focal point of the kitchen garden, growing amidst herbs and vegetables alike.

Bloom Period and Seasonal Color
Spring; white and pale-pink blooms, followed by edible apples late summer to fall

Mature Height × Spread
5 to 15 feet × 5 to 15 feet (if tree has dwarf rootstock)

Zones
3 to 9

Where, When, and How to Plant
Nurseries sell apple trees balled and burlapped or in plastic tubs. Transplant the tree immediately in spring or fall, locating it in sun (south or east locations are best). Apples tolerate average soil, as long as there is good drainage. Shallow hardpan soils or sites that have standing water in winter are deadly. Water well until established. Like most fruit trees, apples require cross-pollination to set fruit, so plant at least two varieties of apple trees to ensure pollination. See the general tree planting tips on page 12.

Growing Tips
Water regularly (deep soakings once or twice a week) for the first three years. As your tree matures, water once weekly during fruit development; otherwise, there should be enough rain to irrigate the tree. Excess fertilizer can delay or lessen fruit development.

Care
Typical diseases include scab and mildew, which affect leaves and fruit, and anthracnose, a wood-rotting fungus. Apple trees have a much higher rate of good health if given full sun. Shade reduces fruit quality and leads to disease. Prune late in the dormant season, removing dead, diseased, or damaged branches. Use selective pruning to keep the tree open in the center with good spacing between branches. Cooperative Extension offices and local fruit tree societies are often the best sources for answering disease and pest problems in your area.

Companion Planting and Design
Turn your garden into an edible landscape with two or more apple trees. You'll enjoy an old-fashioned charm and the reward each fall of harvesting your own fruit. Many nurseries sell young espaliered apple trees, which provide architectural form and fruit alike. Deck and patio gardens are ideal places for container-grown columnar apple trees.

We Recommend
'Akane' bears small, crisp, red fruit (scab and mildew resistant). 'Chehalis' resists scab and self-fruits, with large, yellow-green fruit. 'Liberty', a good dessert apple, is immune to scab, rust, and fireblight (but can get mildew west of the Cascades).

Cornelian Cherry Dogwood

Cornus mas

Where, When, and How to Plant

Plant in spring, situating it in full to partial sun for best growth and flower production. This easy-to-grow, durable tree adapts to most Northwest soil types (but prefers good drainage). Follow the general instructions for planting trees on page 12. If you are planting a group, space trees 15 to 20 feet apart to allow for spread. After planting, add a 3- to 4-inch layer of coarse organic mulch to help retain moisture, making sure not to apply mulch close to the trunk.

Growing Tips

Keep the root zone of a newly planted tree moist until established in the second or third year. Once established, this tree requires irrigation only during dry spells. Consult page 203 for information on fertilizing trees.

Care

Of all the dogwood species, the cornelian cherry dogwood is probably the most free of pests and diseases. It tends to grow as a large shrub with branches to the ground. Pruning up lower limbs will help transform it into an attractive canopy tree in the landscape. Prune for general appearance by removing crowded or dead branches. This is a moderate grower with an overall oval-to-round appearance.

Companion Planting and Design

Cornelian cherry dogwood brings yellow flowers into your garden well before forsythia traditionally blooms. Highlight the brilliant floral clusters by growing this tree in front of dark conifers or an evergreen hedge. Incorporate it into a mixed hedge, and allow it to keep its shrub form in a privacy screen. Or prune it into a single- or multitrunked tree. A grouping of cornelian cherry dogwoods makes a spectacular late-winter floral display, equally notable in fall when the foliage color warms and the reddish fruit contributes to its unique charm.

We Recommend

There are numerous cultivars of *Cornus mas*, including 'Spring Glow', which has bright-yellow flowers and leathery, dark-green foliage. 'Flava' is a yellow-fruited form, 'Aurea' is a striking golden-foliage form, and 'Variegata' has irregular, creamy-white margins on the foliage.

Gorgeous on the outside, tough on the inside, cornelian cherry dogwood is a great all-season tree that grows in many types of soil. This multistemmed tree with a somewhat shrubby habit brings late-winter delight with a profusion of yellow, puffy blooms covering its bare branches. Oval, shiny-green foliage takes on a golden or red-purple hue in autumn, offset by cherry-sized, brilliant-red fruits in clusters. The fruits provide a winter meal for backyard birds, and humans can also eat them (some cooks preserve the fruit). Cornelian cherry dogwood grows to 15 to 20 feet, making it a suitable tree for smaller yards. In a parklike setting where you could plant a row of cornelian cherry dogwood, yellow blossoms emerging en masse creates an unforgettable sight.

Bloom Period and Seasonal Color

Late winter to early spring; yellow blooms; golden or reddish fall color; red fall fruit; flaky tan and gray winter bark

Mature Height × Spread

15 to 20 feet × 15 to 20 feet

Zones

5 to 8

Crabapple
Malus species

If you have room for only one ornamental tree in your garden, a flowering crabapple should be your top choice. There are hundreds of crabapples available to gardeners, but many are prone to problems. Guarantee success with the ones you grow by selecting crabapples developed for excellent flower, fruit, habit, and disease resistance. Outstanding as a tree for the smaller landscape, crabapples have varying habits, from a low mounding tree to one with pendulous or narrow and upright shapes. The trees flower in late spring or early summer, with blooms ranging from white to deep-raspberry shades. Foliage ranges from light or dark green to purple-tinged. In autumn, crabapples produce small fruit (smaller than 2 inches in diameter) in red, yellow, or green.

Bloom Period and Seasonal Color
Late spring to early summer; white, pink, rose, and carmine-red blooms; tiny red, yellow, and green fruit in fall

Mature Height × Spread
15 to 25 feet × 15 to 20 feet

Zones
5 to 8

Where, When, and How to Plant
Crabapples are easy to transplant in spring or fall. Site them in full sun to receive good light and air circulation (not against a wall or fence). Crabapples tolerate most soil conditions except for poor drainage. Follow the general instructions for planting trees on page 12. Space them 20 feet apart to allow for spread and to avoid overcrowding. After planting, add a 3- to 4-inch layer of organic mulch to help retain moisture, making sure not to apply mulch close to the trunk.

Growing Tips
Keep the root zone of a newly planted tree moist until established in the second or third year. Crabapples generally don't require regular fertilizer.

Care
Success with flowering crabapples lies in the cultivar selection. To prevent the spread of diseases, groom your tree with clean pruning tools. When the tree is dormant in late winter, prune to improve form; thin crowded branches; or remove dead, diseased, or damaged twigs. Summer is a good time to remove any suckers that emerge from grafts at the base of the trunk. As with the edible apple tree, keep the center branches pruned in an open, vase shape. This promotes overall health and helps prevent diseases such as fireblight, apple scab, leaf spot, or powdery mildew. Pests such as Japanese beetle or aphids tend to attack disease-prone trees, so be sure to choose one of the excellent disease-resistant crabapples.

Companion Planting and Design
These nostalgic trees are a fitting complement to traditional architectural home styles. Their small sizes and four-season focus make them suitable for front yard, sidewalk, or street placement. The unique branching is attractive during the winter and early spring. Enhance this display by planting primroses or early-spring bulbs beneath them.

We Recommend
Choose a highly disease-resistant crabapple such as *Malus* 'Adirondack', a columnar tree (12 feet × 6 feet) that produces red-tinged white blooms, followed by orange-red fruit. 'Strawberry Parfait' is a profuse-blooming, open, vase-shaped tree (20 feet by 25 feet).

Eastern Redbud

Cercis canadensis

Where, When, and How to Plant

Plant in spring or fall, in full to partial sun to promote vigor and better flower production. Eastern redbud prefers moist, well-drained, deeply worked soils. It can tolerate most types of soil except soggy areas. Space them 15 to 20 feet apart. After planting, add a 2- to 3-inch layer of organic mulch to help retain moisture, making sure not to apply mulch close to the trunk.

Growing Tips

Water regularly throughout the life of this tree. If you have slowly draining soil, it's best to irrigate with a soaker hose or suspend watering after 15 to 20 minutes to allow any standing water to settle into the ground. Check the soil's moisture depth to determine whether the roots are wet before resuming watering. Eastern redbud benefits from annual fertilizing.

Care

This somewhat fragile tree suffers from excessive stress (lack of water, excessive moisture, or injury from tools or a lawnmower). Keep your trees healthy by regulating irrigation, fertilizing, and treating them with tender loving care. Prune dead, diseased, or damaged twigs in late winter. Watch for canker (lesions on bark caused by bacteria or fungi) or verticillium wilt (wilting of leaves or dieback of branches caused by fungi); remove any diseased branches. Pests generally don't bother a healthy eastern redbud tree.

Companion Planting and Design

Grow eastern redbud as a specimen tree or plant it in groupings of three or more. Its delicate appearance makes this a good tree for the mixed border. The rosy-pink flowers and deep-purple foliage provide a romantic character that fits well with perennials and roses. Extend the palette by growing other dark-pink blooming plants beneath the redbud. Bergenias, astilbes, hardy geraniums, and cape fuchsias are good companions for eastern redbud.

We Recommend

A perennial favorite for Northwest gardeners is *Cercis canadensis* 'Forest Pansy', a purple-leafed redbud, which needs some shade in hot climates. Other cultivars to try include 'Alba' (white flowers) and 'Silver Cloud', a variegated form.

The dark red-plum, heart-shaped leaves of eastern redbud bring appealing warmth to the residential garden. A unique tree for the smaller landscape, eastern redbud has multiseason appeal. Its rosy-pink spring flowers create a delicate display on bare branches—lasting several weeks. Emerging green and changing to scarlet-purple as each leaf opens up, the foliage is perhaps the most compelling reason for gardeners to grow eastern redbud. This is a tree that benefits from the presence of full or partial sun. It's a treat each evening to sit on the back porch and watch eastern redbud's heart-shaped red leaves glow, illuminated by the setting sun behind them. The autumn foliage turns yellow. Good health and excellent drainage are critical to this tree's success in the landscape.

Bloom Period and Seasonal Color

March to April; rosy-pink blooms; red-purple spring and summer foliage, followed by yellow fall foliage

Mature Height × Spread

20 to 30 feet × 25 to 35 feet

Zones

5 to 9

European Beech

Fagus sylvatica

Beeches contribute a stately splendor to the landscape, calling to mind tree-lined strolling gardens or richly textured hedges of the English countryside. European beech is a graceful, pastoral tree, perhaps in part because its ruffle-edged leaves make a wonderful rustling sound when caught by a breeze. Foliage color varies by cultivar, including lustrous green that turns russet or gold in autumn. Numerous purple-black forms are also available. The leaves hang from silky branches extending from a smooth, gray trunk. European beech trees are slow growing with an overall habit that ranges from pyramidal to oval or rounded. Also popular are weeping forms, which drape their branches to the ground (children and adults alike are enchanted by the secret hideaway created by this canopy).

Bloom Period and Seasonal Color
Fall; russet and yellow foliage; some forms have purple foliage

Mature Height × Spread
50 to 60 feet × 35 to 45 feet (9 to 12 feet in 10 years)

Zones
5 to 7

Where, When, and How to Plant
Many nurseries carry balled-and-burlapped or container-grown European beeches. Plant in spring or fall in moist, well-drained soil. European beech tolerates many types of soil, but suffers in soggy locations. It thrives in full sun, but can withstand partly shady locations. Follow the general instructions for planting trees on page 12, spacing multiple trees about 20 feet apart.

Growing Tips
Water regularly throughout the life of this tree. If your soil drains slowly, irrigate with a soaker hose or suspend watering after 15 to 20 minutes to allow any standing water to settle into the ground. Check the soil's moisture depth to determine whether the roots are wet before resuming watering. Consult page 203 for information on tree fertilization.

Care
European beech responds well to pruning, although most of your pruning will be cosmetic. You can prune beeches into a dense hedge (best achieved by selecting a cultivar with a columnar habit). Weeping forms may require grooming to keep branches from dragging on the ground. European beech has a dense root system that makes it difficult for lawn to survive at its base. It may also attract woolly beech aphids, which are more messy than harmful to the tree. Avoid powdery mildew by thinning crowded branches and ensuring good air circulation.

Companion Planting and Design
Grow European beech as a glorious specimen tree that provides beauty and shade alike. Group a trio of these trees to create a secret grove in a larger garden. Choose cultivars with columnar or dwarf forms for smaller gardens. The purple-leafed European beeches are dramatic when grown with golden or silver-blue conifers or broadleaf evergreen shrubs.

We Recommend
European beech fans list dozens of favorite cultivars, including *Fagus sylvatica* 'Dawyck', a narrow, upright tree that reaches 35 feet by 8 feet. 'Purple Fountain' has narrow, upright growth, with branches hanging down in a loose cascade of glossy-purple foliage. It reaches 10 feet by 3 feet in a decade.

European Hornbeam

Carpinus betulus

Where, When, and How to Plant

Many nurseries carry balled-and-burlapped or container-grown European hornbeam. Plant in spring or fall in moist, well-drained soil. European hornbeam tolerates many types of soil, but will suffer in soggy locations. It thrives in full sun, but can withstand partly shady locations. Follow the general instructions for planting trees on page 12, spacing multiple trees about 25 feet apart. You can grow trees much closer (6 to 8 feet) if planting a hornbeam hedge.

Growing Tips

Water regularly throughout the life of this tree. If you have slowly draining soil, it's best to irrigate with a soaker hose or suspend watering after 15 to 20 minutes to allow any standing water to settle into the ground. Check the soil's moisture depth to determine whether the roots are wet before resuming watering. Consult page 203 for information on tree fertilization.

Care

European hornbeam is an excellent tree for shearing into a hedge or privacy screen. Plan to prune back the side branches annually while the tree is dormant, shaping it to desired form. European hornbeam is generally pest and disease free.

Companion Planting and Design

Praised for its easy care and attractive, serrated foliage, European hornbeam is a great choice even for smaller gardens, especially because it's so easy to control with regular pruning. A single hornbeam can define a home's vertical element, such as a tall brick chimney. You can also grow European hornbeams around the perimeter of a courtyard garden, creating a leafy privacy hedge that invites dappled light through its branches. The slate-gray bark of its trunk adds a silvery contrast to the green foliage.

We Recommend

There is some confusion about the naming accuracy of *Carpinus betulus* 'Fastigiata', which may differ between European and American nurseries. Check that the tree you buy is accurately named. 'Fastigiata' has upright branching and a pyramidal-oval form. 'Globosa' is a compact, somewhat egg-shaped form. 'Columnaris' is a good hedging choice, due to its spirelike habit.

A deciduous tree that responds well to clipping and hedging cuts, European hornbeam is fitting for formal landscapes. Whether you're training a row of European hornbeams into an inviting allée or using two of them to flank an entrance to the garden, this elegant tree contributes a calming presence with its upright form and tidy, green foliage. European hornbeam is a slow to medium grower, reaching about 10 feet over a decade. Its pyramidal form takes on a rounded habit as it matures. While this highly tailored hornbeam adds a crisp appearance to the landscape while in leaf, its winter appearance gains equal appreciation. When bare, this tree has an attractive, geometric style, with slender, closely spaced branches symmetrically arranged around a central trunk.

Bloom Period and Seasonal Color
Spring and summer; dark-green foliage, turning yellow in fall; some cultivars with variegated or purple foliage

Mature Height × Spread
30 to 60 feet × 20 to 60 feet

Zones
4 to 8

Flowering Cherry
Prunus serrulata

Prunus serrulata *is one of the loveliest flowering cherries. It is from this species that nearly all the profuse-blooming Japanese flowering cherries are derived. Dating to the early nineteenth century, this tree is native to eastern Asia, including Japan, Korea, and central China. In springtime, flowering cherry is unsurpassed for its beauty, producing pendulous pink double-blooms. This tree heralds the end of winter and the arrival of a temperate, garden-friendly season. Wide, horizontal-branching forms distinguish numerous flowering cherries, although some cultivars are vase-shaped when young. Emerging foliage is bronze-crimson when young, turning dark green when fully leafed-out. By autumn, the foliage takes on an orange-red hue. These are excellent ornamental and specimen trees, useful in both formal and informal landscapes.*

Bloom Period and Seasonal Color
Late spring; long-stalked white and pink blooms with coppery-red new foliage; orange-crimson fall foliage

Mature Height × Spread
25 to 30 feet × 30 to 40 feet

Zones
6 to 8

Where, When, and How to Plant
Prunus serrulata cultivars are more appropriate for residential gardens than the species, which grows to 50 feet. Plant flowering cherry in spring or fall in well-drained soil, and in full to partial sun for optimum flower production and foliage health. Flowering cherries tolerate alkaline soil, as long as there's good drainage. If your soil is infertile, plant flowering cherry in a raised bed, 18 to 24 inches deep. Follow the general instructions for planting trees on page 12.

Growing Tips
Water regularly until the tree is established in its second or third year. Avoid excessive irrigation once established, but keep the soil moist. Flowering cherries are fully hardy and can withstand temperatures to 5 degrees Fahrenheit. Consult page 203 for information on tree fertilization.

Care
Some flowering cherries are susceptible to aphids, borers, scales, and virus diseases, so be sure to choose a disease-resistant form for your garden. Even so, this is a relatively short-lived tree that may succumb to disease or stress after 25 or 30 years. Cultivars require occasional pruning to remove damaged and crossing branches.

Companion Planting and Design
Whether you need a floriferous street tree or an elegant choice for a formal allée, flowering cherries are ideal for the residential garden. In winter, the bare branches show off an elegant, horizontal habit. The budding branches can be cut and brought indoors for Asian-inspired arrangements. Enhance the explosion of spring blooms by underplanting flowering cherries with narcissus, tulips, and other spring bulbs.

We Recommend
White goddess flowering cherry (*Prunus* 'Shirofugen') has double blooms that emerge in concert with copper-red new foliage. Kwanzan flowering cherry (*Prunus serrulata* 'Kwanzan') is known for its hardiness and uniformity. It has a vase-shaped habit when young, with deep-pink double flowers. Its mature habit becomes rounded. 'Shirotae', the Mt. Fuji flowering cherry, is pink in bud, opening to 2-inch fragrant white flowers.

Flowering Pear
Pyrus calleryana cultivars

Where, When, and How to Plant
Carefully select a healthy and reputable flowering pear cultivar for your garden. Widely overused, the first cultivar 'Bradford' is known to be short-lived, suffering from deep branch crotching that leads to splitting. See the cultivars suggested below. Transplant balled-and-burlapped or container-grown flowering pear in late winter or early spring. If planted in full to partial sun, flowering pears can tolerate many types of soils, including heavy clay. Space these trees 15 feet apart.

Growing Tips
Water regularly until the tree is established by its second or third year. You generally don't need to provide supplemental water to an established flowering pear, except during extended dry periods. Flowering pears somewhat tolerate drought and are extremely cold hardy. Consult page 203 for information on tree fertilization.

Care
The cultivars are generally pest free and have been bred to resist fireblight. Prune while the tree is dormant, in winter or early spring (before blooming), keeping flowering pear's overall pyramidal or slender form.

Companion Planting and Design
The profusion of white blooms nearly cover flowering pear in early spring, making this a lovely showcase tree that should be planted where you'll see it daily. Line a walkway or driveway with an attractive row of flowering pears, alternating the trees with a white-flowering ornamental shrub such as spirea or dwarf viburnum. Plant in each corner of a formal courtyard or on either side of an entry gate to welcome visitors. In autumn, the blaze of coppery-red or wine-purple foliage is another reason to cherish these trees.

We Recommend
Pyrus calleryana 'Aristocrat' (36 feet by 16 feet) is a top choice, as it maintains good pyramidal form without splitting. The foliage has a distinctive wavy edge, with yellow to red fall color. 'Chanticleer' (40 feet by 15 feet) is narrowly pyramidal and reddish purple in fall. 'Autumn Blaze' was selected at Oregon State University in the late 1960s. It's known for excellent reddish purple fall color and a pyramidal-rounded form.

Flowering pears add a romantic character and elegance to any landscape. The species hails from Korea and China. Since the 1960s, when the 'Bradford' cultivar was introduced, the North American nursery trade has relied on a wide selection of popular cultivars, most of which are disease free and resist fireblight. Pyramidal in form, especially while young, this tree is ideal for urban and suburban gardens—a beautiful choice for front yards, formal gardens, and even parking strips. It contributes multiseason interest with a white cloud of delicate spring blossoms, followed by excellent fall color (dark-green foliage generally turns a glossy scarlet or purple when temperatures drop). As the bark of a flowering pear matures, it takes on a grayish brown appearance with distinctive horizontal patterns.

Other Common Name
Callery pear

Bloom Period and Seasonal Color
Early to midspring; snow-white blooms; purple-red fall foliage

Mature Height × Spread
30 to 50 feet × 15 to 30 feet

Zones
5 to 8

Ginkgo

Ginkgo biloba

The ginkgo is an ancient tree for today's landscape. Because scientists date its existence to 150 to 200 million years on earth, I love telling my sons that ginkgos are older than some dinosaurs! The graceful and elegant fan-shaped foliage is thought to bring good luck, prompting children young and old to collect ginkgo leaves in autumn, once they turn golden and fall to the ground. The ginkgo is a tree to plant now for future enjoyment. It grows slowly for the first decade, but can eventually reach heights of 50 feet or more. Its habit is varied, ranging from pyramidal to wide spreading with an overall fernlike appearance. Long-lived, pest- and disease-resistant ginkgo is a durable tree for public spaces and larger residential gardens.

Other Common Name
Maidenhair tree

Bloom Period and Seasonal Color
Spring and summer; insignificant blooms; excellent bright-green fan-shaped leaves, with brilliant-golden fall foliage

Mature Height × Spread
50 to 80 feet × 30 to 40 feet

Zones
5 to 9

Where, When, and How to Plant
It's difficult to determine the sex of trees grown from seeds until maturity (females bear smelly, messy fruit). Instead, select a named ginkgo cultivar grown from cuttings (usually a male clone). Plant the ginkgo in fall or spring, in full sun. These trees prefer fertile, sandy, well-drained soil, but tolerate heavy (but not soggy) clay locations. Follow the guidelines for planting trees on page 12, spacing these 20 to 25 feet apart.

Growing Tips
Ginkgos establish without difficulty. Keep the root zone of newly planted trees moist until established (usually after two years). Adding a 2- to 3-inch layer of mulch will help retain moisture (take care not to apply mulch next to the trunk). Ginkgos generally don't require fertilizer.

Care
Ginkgos are known to be pest and disease free, having "outlived" their enemies for millennia. Pruning is not required until the tree begins to age (usually after ten years). If your garden has a mature ginkgo, prune lightly in spring to improve circulation between horizontal branches.

Companion Planting and Design
Because of the ultimate size of this large tree, most Northwest landscapes can handle only one ginkgo, planted as a glorious specimen to catch the sunlight and create attractive shade patterns below. The golden fall foliage illuminates any distant view, especially when showcased against a backdrop of evergreens. Ginkgos often appear as street trees. While they may not be the best choice for a narrow strip of land, their tolerance of pollution and drought justifies the choice. My neighbors celebrated the birth of their daughter by planting four ginkgos along two sides of their corner lot. By the time she's an adult, the trees will command attention with their splendid autumn color.

We Recommend
Ginkgo biloba 'Autumn Gold' (12 to 15 feet in ten years) is a stellar cultivar with beautiful fan-shaped leaves marked with parallel veins. 'Fastigiata' has an upright columnar form that's a good choice for smaller landscapes and street plantings.

Himalayan Birch
Betula jacquemontii

Where, When, and How to Plant

You'll find balled-and-burlapped or container trees at most well-stocked nurseries. Transplant Himalayan birch immediately, in spring or autumn. Situate this tree in full to partial sun for best performance and to highlight the attractive foliage. Birches prefer moist, fertile, well-drained soils, but will tolerate water-saturated soils during wet winters. Follow the general instructions for planting trees on page 12.

Growing Tips

Water regularly (once or twice a week deep soakings) until established. As your tree matures, water only during dry spells; otherwise, there should be enough rain to irrigate the tree. Add a 3- to 4-inch layer of coarse organic mulch to help retain moisture, making sure not to apply the mulch close to the trunk. Consult page 203 for information on fertilizing trees.

Care

Himalayan birches have some resistance to birch borer and do resist aphids. Maintain good tree health by removing any weak, damaged, or dead twigs and branches, pruning in summer or late winter before spring growth. Enhance the appearance of the white trunks by limbing up lower branches. This is moderate grower will reach 15 feet by 15 feet in ten years.

Companion Planting and Design

Plant a Himalayan birch as an eye-catching focal point of a gate or courtyard entrance. It takes on an especially dramatic appearance at nighttime if illuminated with an upward-facing landscape light. Simple planting schemes that give the starring role to Himalayan birch are ideal. Groves of white-barked birch are a romantic way to create a hidden shade garden. Plant single- or multistemmed trees about 15 feet apart in an odd-numbered stand. As they mature, the upper branches intermingle to create a bower where you can add a bench and plant ferns, hostas, and other shade plants.

We Recommend

Betula jacquemontii (also named *Betula utilis* var. *jacquemontii*) is the pyramidal, pure-white barked tree. Another stunning birch to consider is Chinese red birch (*B. albosinensis* var. *septentrionalis*), which has pink-beige peeling bark.

Himalayan birch's stark white trunk with thin layers of peeling bark is unsurpassed in the winter landscape when nearly everything else is dull or brown. In spring, when the small, serrated foliage leafs out, birches play another important role in the landscape, offering an attractive form and dappled shade. Throughout the year, birches invite rustling sounds into your garden, as breezes catch catkins and leaves alike. The foliage turns a warm gold in autumn. This is a graceful, tall, narrow tree that adds a feminine presence to the landscape, complementing perennials and mixed borders with its textural bark. Himalayan birches look especially striking in a "stand," a grouping of trees that create stunning silhouettes when planted in front of dark-green conifers.

Bloom Period and Seasonal Color
Showy exfoliating white bark

Mature Height × Spread
30 to 70 feet × 20 to 60 feet

Zones
5 to 7

Holly Oak
Quercus ilex

Although holly oaks are Mediterranean natives, Anglo-philes will recall seeing them growing at the famed Kew Gardens in London. One of numerous majestic live oaks, holly oak is a slow-growing evergreen tree that's distinguished by the prickly edges and pointed tips of its tapered, 1- to 3-inch-long leaves. The foliage is exquisite: dark green on top; silvery gray-green underneath (easy to appreciate by anyone who stands beneath it). Holly oaks can ultimately reach heights of 60 feet or taller. The bark is smooth on young trees, but as holly oak matures, attractive dark-gray flaky patches emerge. Once established, these trees are relatively drought tolerant. Holly oak's habit is dense, and broadly rounded. It produces pointed acorns held in cups.

Other Common Name
Holm oak

Bloom Period and Seasonal Color
Evergreen; textured foliage with silver-gray undersides; brownish catkins in spring; elongated greenish yellow acorns

Mature Height × Spread
30 to 60 feet × 30 to 60 feet

Zones
7 to 9

Where, When, and How to Plant
Plant in spring or fall in moist, well-drained soil. This is an ideal tree for Northwest residential gardens; other species of live oaks are better adapted for Southwest landscape conditions. Situate holly oak in full to partial sun. It can grow in just about any type of soil, as long as there is good drainage. Follow the general instructions for planting trees on page 12.

Growing Tips
Water regularly until the tree is established in its second or third year. Holly oaks generally tolerate drought and should not be given supplemental water once established. Keep irrigation away from the trunk, or root rot can set in. This tree will adapt to less-than-ideal settings, such as along streets. It stands up well when exposed to strong winds and is excellent for shelter and shade. Consult page 203 for information on tree fertilization.

Care
Holly oaks can be strongly pruned for shape or to maintain their health by removing dead, diseased, or damaged branches. If left unpruned, the tree can develop multiple leaders and take on a large shrub form. Plant a row of holly oaks along the perimeter of a garden to train them into a tall, elegant hedge. Holly oak is generally pest and disease free.

Companion Planting and Design
Slow-growing holly oak is a fitting choice for residential settings. It is suitable for coastal windbreaks, as long as it's grown in well-drained soil. Holly oak forms a picturesque rounded head, with pendulous low-hanging branches. Its size and solid evergreen character give it a imposing architectural presence.

We Recommend
Quercus ilex is named in part for its holly-looking foliage. Other interesting live oaks for Northwest landscapes include canyon live oak (*Q. chrysolepis*), a drought-tolerant tree with spiny foliage when young. It is native to foothills of southwest Oregon. Cork oak (*Q. suber*), a Mediterranean native, is indeed the source of commercial corks. The trunk and limbs have a distinctive, corky bark.

Japanese Maple
Acer palmatum

Where, When, and How to Plant

Plant balled-and-burlapped or container-grown trees in early spring or fall, out of full sun and protected from harsh winds. Japanese maples can grow in a wide range of soils with average moisture. Some experts recommend planting with the root crown slightly elevated above the soil level to prevent root rot. Spacing varies, depending on the cultivar's mature size. Follow the guidelines for planting trees on page 12, generally spacing these 10 to 15 feet apart.

Growing Tips

Provide adequate but not soggy moisture and nitrogen fertilizer annually to young trees, and they'll establish quickly. Your maturing tree requires only light feeding. Species of Japanese maples tolerate drought better than the named cultivars.

Care

Japanese maples resist disease relatively well. Heavy frost can damage younger trees; prune dead or broken branches once the foliage begins to emerge. Prune to retain the tree's true habit, avoiding end cuts or aggressive shaping. Verticillium wilt is a common problem, particularly in wet soils.

Companion Planting and Design

Courtyard and entry gardens are ideal locations to highlight the artistic beauty of a Japanese maple, where its canopy casts patterns of dappled light. Plant shade-loving hostas, ferns, and astilbes at the base of these trees. Most cultivars are slow growing and well suited to container planting. Select a container twice the size of the nursery pot or rootball. Plant the tree in a 50-50 mixture of organic potting soil and compost. Be sure to water regularly during dry spells and lightly fertilize when in leaf.

We Recommend

The species Japanese maple is larger than its cultivars, but a graceful addition to any landscape. 'Bloodgood' is an upright form with deep-crimson foliage spring to fall. 'Sango Kaku', the popular coral bark maple, has bright-green spring foliage that turns golden in fall. Its twigs and branches are a brilliant coral-red in winter. 'Seiryu', an upright vase-shaped form, is in the *A. palmatum* var. *dissectum* group, with finely cut green foliage that turns orange-red in fall.

Japanese maples are cherished by many Northwest gardeners for their delicate foliage and attractive branch structure. Moreover, this is a tree perfectly suited for the residential garden, from a dwarf form planted in a glazed urn to the grand species tree that produces a bright-green canopy of lacy foliage. Many forms of Japanese maple are cold hardy; others are prized for their attractive bark, deeply cut leaves, or eye-catching spring or fall foliage color. Some forms even have leaves with subtle variegation. Japanese maples have varied habits, from weeping to upright, bushy to spreading. The ideal tree occupies a singular spot in the landscape garden, accented by shade perennials or spring bulbs. Once established, these undemanding trees offer long-lasting interest to the garden.

Bloom Period and Seasonal Color

Spring; pale to dark-green and pink-tinged new foliage; yellow, gold, maroon, orange, and scarlet fall foliage

Mature Height × Spread

20 to 30 feet × 15 to 30 feet (species)
8 to 15 feet × 5 to 10 feet (cultivars)

Zones

6 to 8

Japanese Snowbell

Styrax japonicus

Japanese snowbell is a terrific tree for any city or suburban garden, greeting the arrival of spring with a delightful display of white, bell-shaped blossoms that dangle below upturned green foliage. Its moderate size makes this a great patio or courtyard tree, with a low-branched habit and rounded form. As Japanese snowbells mature, the branches become more horizontal, further highlighting the effect of its hanging blooms. By late summer, Japanese snowbell produces interesting oval blue-gray fruits that also hang from the branches. In winter, the bark is an attractive gray-brown. Its roots are not aggressive, which allows you to incorporate perennials, bulbs, or small shrubs at the base of the tree. Plant Japanese snowbells where you can look upward toward the charming blooms.

Other Common Names
Japanese snowdrop, styrax

Bloom Period and Seasonal Color
Spring; white bell-shaped blooms, with oval blue-gray fruits in late summer; yellow fall foliage

Mature Height × Spread
20 to 30 feet × 20 to 30 feet

Zones
6 to 8

Where, When, and How to Plant
Plant balled-and-burlapped or container-grown trees in early spring or fall, in a moist, well-drained location in full sun to partial shade. Japanese snowbells thrive in rich soil. Topdress with organic compost. Raised beds with excellent drainage offer an ideal location for Japanese snowbells. Follow the general guidelines for tree planting on page 12, spacing trees 15 to 20 feet apart.

Growing Tips
Provide adequate moisture, and annually apply a nitrogen fertilizer to young Japanese snowbells until established. This tree requires moderate moisture throughout its lifetime. Windy sites can lead to desiccated foliage. Don't let the soil completely dry out through the root zone. See page 203 for guidelines on fertilizing trees.

Care
Japanese snowbells often need pruning to maintain their treelike form, especially if lower branches interfere with pathways or adjacent perennials or shrubs. Gradually remove lower side branches to the trunk as the tree matures. Prune in late winter or early spring, before the foliage emerges. Japanese snowbells are generally pest and disease free.

Companion Planting and Design
Incorporate these trees into a white-flowering garden of peonies, roses, lilies, Japanese anemones, and white spring bulbs. This graceful specimen is best appreciated against a dark evergreen backdrop. Incorporated into a mixed border, it adds multiseason interest. Plant a trio in an entry garden to delight visitors with a spring display of blossoms. Or plant Japanese snowbell in a raised bed next to a patio or deck where you'll look up at the tiny bells during an alfresco meal.

We Recommend
Styrax japonicus 'Emerald Pagoda' offers leaves and blooms larger than the species. Its mature size reaches 45 feet, and it tolerates heat better than other cultivars. 'Pink Chimes' produces pink blooms. 'Pendula' is a small, weeping form (to 12 feet) that can be grown as a tree or shrub. Fragrant snowbell (*S. obassia*), a sweet-scented relative with cultural requirements similar to Japanese snowbell, reaches 40 feet.

Japanese Stewartia
Stewartia pseudocamellia

Where, When, and How to Plant
Japanese stewartias perform best in sunny locations with some shade protection during the hottest times of day (east-facing garden locations are ideal). Larger trees are more difficult to transplant, so select a small specimen, 4 to 5 feet tall. Transplant balled-and-burlapped or potted trees in spring or fall into rich, moist, well-drained soil. Slightly acidic soil is preferred. Follow the general guidelines for tree planting on page 12, spacing Japanese stewartia 20 to 25 feet apart.

Growing Tips
Keep the soil evenly moist throughout the root zone. Japanese stewartia requires moderate moisture throughout its lifetime. See page 203 for guidelines on fertilizing trees.

Care
You will need to lightly prune Japanese stewartia only to maintain a healthy appearance, removing dead, diseased, or damaged branches. Otherwise, this tree will retain its attractive pyramidal-oval habit over time. Japanese stewartia is generally free of pests and diseases.

Companion Planting and Design
Appreciated for its exfoliating bark, which has been likened to a patchwork quilt or puzzle pieces, Japanese stewartia is ideal for the winter garden or as the horticultural diva in a courtyard or formal garden. The bark will improve its patterned texture over time, though sometimes not until the tree is older (when branch diameters reach 2 inches or more). Pair with evergreen perennials and shrubs to provide contrast and interest when its branches are bare. Good choices include hebes, euphorbias, or heucheras.

We Recommend
Japanese stewartia produces a midsummer display of lovely cupped white blooms with showy yellow stamens. It grows 6 to 12 inches a year in its first decade. Tall stewartia (*Stewartia monadelpha*) has upward-angled branches, small flowers, and patterned cinnamon-colored bark when older, growing to 25 feet by 20 feet. Korean stewartia (*Stewartia koreana*) has many attributes similar to Japanese stewartia. It is thought to be a good choice for locations requiring heat tolerance and grows 20 to 30 feet tall.

Japanese stewartia is renowned for its incomparable bark patterning, a highly mottled display of pink, gray, and red-brown that you can't help but admire, especially in winter. A lovely small tree for residential gardens in midsummer, Japanese stewartia produces white, saucer-shaped flowers reminiscent of camellia blooms. In autumn, its serrated green leaves take on an intense orange-red hue. As a single-stemmed tree with a layered branching habit, this is a top choice for a showpiece setting, such as an entry garden or focal point. Japanese stewartia's features are best appreciated when seen against a dark-green backdrop, such as a hedge, wall, or stand of evergreen trees. This terrific tree delivers multiseason interest, ultimately reaching 20 to 40 feet when mature.

Bloom Period and Seasonal Color
Midsummer; white blooms; brilliant bronze-red fall foliage

Mature Height × Spread
20 to 40 feet × 20 to 35 feet

Zones
5 to 8

Katsura
Cercidiphyllum japonicum

Katsura is a lovely tree that contributes a feminine beauty to the year-round landscape. Pyramidal while young, katsura takes on a wide-spreading habit as it matures. Its foliage is stunning, emerging reddish purple in spring and gradually taking on a bluish green cast in summer. Slightly heart-shaped, the leaves are reminiscent of a smaller version of redbud (Cercis canadensis). The $^3/_4$- to $1^1/_2$-inch leaves overlap like flat sequins on an evening gown, shimmering in the breeze to make a pleasant rustling sound. As a shade tree, it creates lovely dappled patterning on the ground below. Autumn foliage turns apricot-orange, followed by attractive bark and multistemmed branches in winter. Katsuras can reach a stature of 40 feet up to 100 feet when mature.

Other Common Name
Katsuratree

Bloom Period and Seasonal Color
Small flowers; reddish purple spring foliage, turning blue-green in summer; yellow and orange fall foliage

Mature Height × Spread
40 to 60 feet × 20 to 50 feet

Zones
4 to 8

Where, When, and How to Plant
Katsura transplants best if purchased as a balled-and-burlapped or container-grown plant. Plant in early spring in full sun to partial shade. This tree prefers rich, moist, well-drained soil. Follow the guidelines for planting trees on page 12, spacing these 20 to 25 feet apart. Protect from exposed or windy sites.

Growing Tips
Keep the root zone of a newly planted katsura moist but not soggy. Mulch with 2 to 3 inches of organic matter to retain moisture (avoid placing mulch in contact with trunk). Provide supplemental water during dry spells, even after the tree is established. Follow the general guidelines for tree fertilization on page 203.

Care
No serious pest or disease problems affect the health of katsura trees. Your tree will thrive if you provide adequate moisture and well-drained soil. As katsuras age, they can suffer from bark splitting, for which no treatment is necessary, and some breakage of branches. Prune only to remove damaged or broken branches and stems.

Companion Planting and Design
Native to parts of Japan and China, katsura blends beautifully with Asian gardens and serves as a lovely bright blue-green contrast to burgundy-leaved Japanese maple trees. A trio of katsuras planted in a stand or grove provides an inviting "hidden" shade garden where you can place a stone bench and underplant with ferns and hostas. One of the best ways to showcase katsura is to plant it against a wall or fence and install at its base an "uplight" low-voltage landscape light. When the light shines through the overlapping leaves, the resulting shadow play is irresistible. Katsura is a fragrant tree, emitting a cinnamon or cotton-candylike aroma when the leaves drop in fall.

We Recommend
Cercidiphyllum japonicum 'Pendula' is a weeping form (to 25 feet). 'Morioka Weeping' is another cascading form that improves as it matures. 'Heronswood Globe', a cultivar selected by Washington's Heronswood Nursery, is a dwarf, globe-shaped form (15 to 20 feet).

Kousa Dogwood

Cornus kousa

Where, When, and How to Plant

Plant balled-and-burlapped or container-grown kousa dogwoods in early spring. This tree flowers best in full sun to partial shade and prefers a slightly acidic soil. Follow guidelines for planting trees on page 12, spacing trees 15 feet apart.

Growing Tips

Keep the root zone of a newly planted kousa dogwood moist but not soggy. Mulch with 2 to 3 inches of organic matter to retain moisture (avoid placing mulch in contact with the trunk). Once established, kousa dogwood is relatively drought tolerant, although you may want to provide extra irrigation during extended dry spells. Follow the general guidelines for tree fertilization on page 203.

Care

Kousa dogwoods are an excellent disease- and pest-resistant alternative to the eastern flowering dogwood (*Cornus florida*). Little pruning is necessary if the tree is given adequate room for its branches to spread. You can prune lightly in spring to remove dead or damaged branches.

Companion Planting and Design

Kousa dogwood is the last dogwood to bloom, extending into early summer with its four-pointed bracts that seem to "float" above the tree's horizontal branches. This distinct feature allows kousa dogwoods to stand alone as specimen trees, although a row of them creates a lovely display along the edge of a patio or the wall of a sunny courtyard. This is a popular tree for parking strips or along the sidewalk, as it won't take up too much space. Kousa dogwoods are also well proportioned to add vertical structure and year-round interest to the mixed perennial and shrub border.

We Recommend

The nursery trade offers dozens of excellent cultivars of *Cornus kousa*. Some good choices include 'Autumn Rose' (to 20 feet by 25 feet), which bears light-green bracts that mature to soft white; *C. kousa* var. *chinensis* 'Milky Way', a form that has better flower production than the species; and 'Satomi', which bears broad, rosy-red bracts.

Kousa dogwoods are the stars of springtime, when each branch is blanketed with four-pointed starlike bracts. A perky "button" at the center of each bloom, the kousa's rather insignificant true flower, distinguishes this profuse display of creamy-white, pink, or rose bracts. From Japan and Korea, kousa dogwoods are ideal for the smaller landscape. These relatively slow-growing trees reach mature heights of 25 feet with vase-shaped or horizontal forms. The foliage is glossy and wavy-edged, changing to reddish purple in fall. The tree bears pink or red-tinged fruits on long stalks, August to October. As kousa dogwoods age, their bark begins to exfoliate, resulting in an interesting mosaic pattern of tan, brown, and gray.

Other Common Names

Chinese dogwood, Japanese flowering dogwood

Bloom Period and Seasonal Color

Late spring to early summer; creamy-white, pink, and rose blooms; reddish purple fall foliage and red fruit

Mature Height × Spread

20 to 30 feet × 15 to 30 feet

Zones

5 to 8

Lavalle Hawthorne

Crataegus × *lavallei*

Decades-old English hawthornes (Crataegus laevigata) line the streets in many of Seattle and Portland's historic neighborhoods, cherished for their exuberant display of double raspberry-pink spring blooms and lobed foliage. Unfortunately, this old-fashioned tree is prone to disease and has fallen out of favor. An excellent alternative for today's garden is lavalle hawthorne, which is more resistant to leaf rust and provides attractive four-season interest. Semievergreen with glossy-green foliage and snowy-white flower clusters in spring, lavalle hawthorne has an erect, open form reaching heights of 15 to 30 feet. It can handle a diverse range of soils. With coppery-red foliage in autumn, lavalle hawthorne's best surprise comes in winter, when its large orange-red fruit appears to the delight of humans and birds alike.

Other Common Name
Carriere hawthorne

Bloom Period and Seasonal Color
Spring; delicate white blooms; lobed green foliage turning bronze-red in fall; bright-red fruit clusters in winter

Mature Height × Spread
15 to 30 feet × 15 to 20 feet

Zones
5 to 7

Where, When, and How to Plant
Transplant balled-and-burlapped or container-grown lavalle hawthorne in spring or autumn. It's best to plant a small tree that will adapt more readily to new soil. Lavalle hawthorne can grow in most types of soil if there is adequate drainage. Topdress with organic compost. Follow the general planting guidelines on page 12, spacing lavalle hawthornes 15 feet apart. It is possible to plant a dense hedgerow using this tree, in which case plant them 8 to 12 feet apart.

Growing Tips
Keep the soil evenly moist throughout the root zone until the tree is established. Don't let it stand in soggy soil. Lavalle hawthorne requires moderate moisture throughout its lifetime. See page 203 for guidelines on fertilizing trees.

Care
Landscaping maintenance crews dread pruning English hawthorne, which has layers of nasty 2-inch-long thorns, but lavalle hawthorne is almost free of thorns, making it less painful to prune. This tree is not typically uniform in habit, so it may require some gentle spring pruning for shape. It's generally free of pests and diseases.

Companion Planting and Design
Plant lavalle hawthorne as a single specimen, in groupings, or as a hedge or screening tree. This durable tree tolerates urban pollution, but because its fruit is messy, it's best not to plant lavalle hawthorne next to a sidewalk or patio. The delicate, lobed foliage and charming white flowers make for an overall, romantic appearance that can soften harsh architectural lines of buildings and mask unsightly structures. Pair lavalle hawthorne with sun-loving perennials for a cottage garden effect.

We Recommend
Crataegus × *lavallei* is of French garden origin, a hybrid between *C. crusgalli* (cockspur hawthorne) and another species, perhaps *C. pubescens*. It is a dense, oval to rounded tree with lustrous, dark-green foliage that turns coppery red in fall. Spring flowers are white with red stamens.

Where, When, and How to Plant

Transplant balled-and-burlapped or container-grown trees in spring or autumn, in full sun to partial shade with well-drained, loamy soil. Most species don't adapt well to alkaline or heavy clay soil, nor do they tolerate pollution. Follow the guidelines for planting trees on page 12, spacing these 15 to 20 feet apart.

Growing Tips

Keep the soil evenly moist throughout the root zone until the tree is established. Don't let it stand in soggy soil. Mountain ashes require some winter chill to flower and fruit. The tree should receive moderate moisture throughout its lifetime. See page 203 for guidelines on fertilizing trees.

Care

A relatively short-lived tree when grown in areas with high pollution (such as along a street), mountain ash enjoys a healthier lifespan in well-drained soil, protected from harsh settings or exposure. The healthier the tree, the less likely it will succumb to pests and diseases. Select a disease-resistant form. Pruning is generally required only to maintain general health.

Companion Planting and Design

Mountain ash has an appealing informality that complements many types of Northwest architecture, especially craftsman homes, bungalows, and cottages. They offer the excellent, multiseason interest of spring flowers, late-summer berries, and good fall color. Plant them along a property line to serve as a soft screen when combined with rhododendrons and azaleas. An ideal habitat for backyard wildlife, they are best suited for lawns; the fruit creates a mess in pedestrian areas.

We Recommend

Korean mountain ash (*Sorbus alnifolia*) produces a dense thicket of growth, 40 to 50 feet by 20 to 30 feet. Its undivided foliage resembles alder. Whitebeam ash (*S. aria*), from Europe, better tolerates maritime and urban conditions, growing 35 to 45 feet. From China, *S. hupehensis* 'Coral Cascade' and 'Pink Pagoda', to 25 feet tall and wide, are excellent forms with bluish green leaves and fireblight resistance. The Northwest native, *S. scopulina*, is a shrublike tree (to 15 feet) with deeply toothed leaflets and reddish bark.

Mountain ash is a great Northwest tree offering multiseason interest for the residential garden, not to mention habitat and food for backyard wildlife. A few native species have adapted well to our region's cultural conditions, although many nurseries carry species from Asian and European mountain regions. Look for a cultivar known to resist fireblight, a typical mountain ash disease. The tree is distinguished by finely cut green or bluish foliage displaying a fernlike appearance. Flat-topped creamy-white flowers bloom in spring, followed by hanging clusters of small red-orange berries in late summer or early autumn. Some mountain ashes have good fall color, turning yellow to orange when temperatures drop. The overall form is upright and pyramidal, although mountain ashes become more rounded with age.

Bloom Period and Seasonal Color

Spring; creamy-white blooms, followed by orange-red berry clusters in late summer; golden fernlike fall foliage

Mature Height × Spread

15 to 40 feet × 15 to 20 feet (varies widely by species)

Zones

5 to 8

Paperbark Maple

Acer griseum

Paperbark maple's three-part, toothed green leaflets make for a pleasant display when their silvery backs shimmer in the sunlight, but its stunning mahogany-red bark is the primary reason to acquire this tree. Especially noticeable when its winter branches are bare, this tree's bark peels away from the trunk and branches like thin, curling sheets of paper. The bark texture and appearance deliver an eye-catching display at a time when we need it most. The peeling effect generally appears by the tree's second year. From China, paperbark maple is relatively slow growing, to 25 feet, making it a great residential specimen tree. The leaves emerge late in spring, accompanied by small red flowers that develop into showy "winged" seeds. Paperbark maple's autumn foliage turns brilliant russet-red.

Bloom Period and Seasonal Color
Fall; russet-red foliage; mahogany-red peeling bark in winter

Mature Height × Spread
20 to 30 feet × 10 to 15 feet

Zones
4 to 8

Where, When, and How to Plant
Paperbark maples are hard to start from seed, so the nursery trade propagates from cuttings. This makes it hard and often expensive to find larger specimens. Plant trees in early spring or fall in full or partial sun. Paperbark maple is a welcome choice for Northwest gardeners with clay soil, as it adapts to varied soils, preferring them well drained, but tolerating clay. Follow the general tree planting guidelines on page 12, spacing paperbark maples 15 feet apart.

Growing Tips
After planting, mulch well (2 to 3 inches of organic mulch), keeping material away from the trunk. Irrigate regularly, maintaining moist soil until the tree is established in the second or third year. Once established, paperbark maples can generally thrive on rainfall in all but the driest seasons. See page 203 for guidelines on fertilizing trees.

Care
Have patience; this slow-growing tree adds 6 to 12 inches a year over a 10- to 15-year period. Prune to remove any crossing or rubbing branches. Clip away messy twigs to ensure a clean appearance. Paperbark maple has no notable pest or disease problems.

Companion Planting and Design
This is a unique specimen tree that should be sited where anyone coming to or going from your home will enjoy seeing it. Plant paperbark maple at the juncture of a walkway or path, completing the composition with a display of spring bulbs or attractive ground cover. Three trees planted in a triangle will create an attractive winter display, especially when accented below with creamy-white and pale-green hellebores. I'm particularly thrilled with a designer's suggestion to train a creamy-white clematis vine through the paperbark maple's cinnamon-brown branches—the contrast between the velvety flowers and texture bark is unforgettable.

We Recommend
Acer griseum is one of several closely related three-leaf maples. *A. maximowiczianum*, the Nikko or maximowicz maple, has a vase-shaped form to 20 to 30 feet. *A. triflorum,* the three-flowered maple, has cinnamon-red bark and outstanding orange-crimson fall foliage.

Persian Parrotia
Parrotia persica

Where, When, and How to Plant
Persian parrotia prefers the cooler climates of the north, which makes it a good candidate for our region. Plant container-grown or balled-and-burlapped trees in full to partial sun. The soil should be slightly acidic, moist and well drained. Follow the general tree planting guidelines on page 12, spacing Persian parrotias 15 to 20 feet apart.

Growing Tips
After planting, mulch well (with 2 to 3 inches of organic mulch), keeping the material away from the trunk. Irrigate regularly, maintaining moist soil until the tree is established in the second or third year. Once established, Persian parrotia trees can generally thrive on rainfall in all but the driest seasons. See page 203 for guidelines on fertilizing trees.

Care
Persian parrotia is a durable tree once established, demonstrating tolerance to heat, wind, drought, and cold. It is generally free of pests and diseases. Prune in spring, either to encourage a single leader trunk or to remove dead, damaged, or diseased branches.

Companion Planting and Design
Persian parrotia is a stunning tree that deserves more use in residential landscapes. Its out-of-the-ordinary appearance in every season never fails to prompt a "what kind of tree is it?" question from visitors. Give Persian parrotia a place of honor in a front yard, where it will have room to stretch its branches. These trees generally mature with a rounded habit, slightly wider than they are tall. Because it is slow growing (10 feet over six to eight years), you can also grow Persian parrotia at the back of a mixed border, using it to add structure and interest among perennials and shrubs.

We Recommend
With flowering and foliage similarities to its witch hazel relative, *Parrotia persica* is a star of the winter garden. This is a tree with an irregular habit, varying widely from one specimen to the next. There are a few cultivars available through mail-order sources, including 'Pendula', which tends to branch more horizontally than truly weep.

One of the most graceful specimens to grow in a small garden or to emphasize a favored spot in a larger landscape, Persian parrotia is brilliant in all seasons. It blooms in late winter or early spring on bare branches, producing clusters of tiny maroon flowers with crimson stamens. New leaves are tinged reddish purple, opening to a 3- to 6-inch dark-green oval with wavy margins. In autumn, Persian parrotia puts on an unparalleled color display, with foliage that changes along a continuum of golden yellow to orange-pink to deep scarlet. Winter highlights the smooth gray-brown bark, sections of which often flake off to reveal creamy-gray patches on mature trees. Slow growing, this multistemmed tree can be trained to have a single trunk.

Other Common Name
Persian ironwood

Bloom Period and Seasonal Color
Late winter to early spring; maroon blooms; golden-yellow, rosy-orange, and scarlet fall foliage; interesting winter bark

Mature Height × Spread
15 to 40 feet × 15 to 30 feet

Zones
4 to 7

Red Maple
Acer rubrum

If you love leaves that turn red in autumn, here's a tree that delivers excellent scarlet foliage. Like most maples, the red maple has distinctive three- to five-lobed toothed foliage. In spring, it provides a hint of its fall attire, producing deep-red flowers with crimson stems. Emerging leaves are reddish-tinged, gradually changing to medium or dark green (with the underside of leaves having a silvery-gray cast). Red maples are also distinguished by their wine-red winged seed sets, called the "samara." The bark is gray-brown on a tree that displays a pyramidal form when young. As red maples mature, their branches ascend to give the tree an irregular or rounded crown. Because of an explosion of red maple cultivars, there are numerous forms available.

Other Common Names
Scarlet maple, swamp maple

Bloom Period and Seasonal Color
Spring; deep-red blooms; vibrant-red fall foliage

Mature Height × Spread
40 to 60 feet × 30 to 50 feet

Zones
3 to 9

Where, When, and How to Plant
Red maples are easy to plant as small, bare-root trees or as larger balled-and-burlapped or container-grown trees. Select one from a reputable nursery that sells trees grown true to the cultivar name. Transplant in spring or fall, selecting a moist location in full sun to partial shade, protected from wind. Red maples adapt to many types of soil, including low, wet areas. Space red maples 20 to 30 feet apart.

Growing Tips
Irrigate regularly, maintaining moist soil throughout the root zone until the tree is established in the second or third year. After that, red maples generally thrive on rainfall during all but the driest seasons (during which time you'll need to provide supplemental irrigation as recommended on page 14).

Care
While red maples are known to suffer from aphids and can be susceptible to verticillium wilt, they are increasingly popular in urban settings due to their tolerance of low oxygen levels. Occasionally, red maples demonstrate weak branches. If breakage occurs, prune away damaged or broken stems or branches. Prune during the dormant season, in late winter.

Companion Planting and Design
Red maple adds a glorious autumn glow to the landscape, especially when planted as a singular specimen. Provide adequate room so it can assume a mature form as a superb shade tree. Red maples grow 10 to 12 inches a year if grown in full sun and moist soil. To highlight its beauty, pair it with silver- or blue-needled conifers, such as eastern white pine (*Pinus strobus*).

We Recommend
Countless cultivars are available through the nursery trade, offering varying forms and habits. Some of the best for Northwest gardens include *Acer rubrum* 'Red Sunset' (45 to 50 feet by 35 to 40 feet), with excellent orange to red fall foliage, and 'October Glory' (40 to 50 feet with a rounded form), offering long-lasting red fall color. Two excellent columnar forms are *Acer* × *fremanii* 'Armstrong' and 'Bowhall'. Both have mature sizes of approximately 50 feet by 15 feet.

Saucer Magnolia
Magnolia × soulangeana

Where, When, and How to Plant

Magnolias are somewhat challenging to move due to fleshy root systems. It's best to transplant balled-and-burlapped or container-grown trees in spring. Site them in full to partial sun, such as along the edge of a wooded area; avoid southern exposure, which can prompt premature flowering. The soil should be moist and well drained. If soil amendment is required, amend the entire bed or topdress with coarse compost. Take care not to plant the tree deeper than the original soil level. Space magnolias at least 15 feet apart.

Growing Tips

Give newly planted magnolia regular irrigation until the tree is established in the second or third year; after that, provide supplemental irrigation only during prolonged dry spells. Mulch to the outer dripline to help retain moisture in the root zone. Feed magnolias before blooming if new growth seems weak or limited. Use a nitrogen fertilizer or an organic slow-release product.

Care

Prune in late spring or early summer after flowering (but before buds set for the following year). Do not remove lower branches; they help define this tree's overall appearance. Prune any vigorous shoots growing straight up from lower limbs. Magnolias can be susceptible to mildew, blight, leaf spots, or scale, although healthy trees rarely succumb to disease.

Companion Planting and Design

This early-flowering tree makes an ideal entry garden or patio showpiece. Highlight its low-branching form and dazzling blooms against a backdrop of dark evergreens. While it's generally not wise to plant perennials beneath a magnolia, tiny spring bulbs like *Puschkinia*, *Chionodoxa* or grape hyacinth can happily exist at its feet, complementing the tree's blooms.

We Recommend

Space doesn't allow us to highlight the many excellent magnolias, including *M. grandiflora*, the classic evergreen. Of the deciduous choices, *M. × soulangeana* is a rewarding tree for multiseason beauty. Good cultivars include 'Alexandrina', which produces flowers with pink outer and white inner petals, and 'Forest Pink', a deep-pink frost-tolerant selection.

Magnolias define early springtime in the Northwest, sharing their oversized white, pale-pink, or plum blooms just when we need them most. Even before the ordinary green leaves emerge, the fuzzy buds of this French hybrid magnolia pop open, producing saucer-shaped flowers 5 to 10 inches in diameter. This magnolia's habit is multistemmed, forming a large shrub or low-branched tree with horizontal stems taking on rounded or upright habits. The blooms "float" above the branches, resembling water lilies on the water's surface. A moderate-grower (10 to 15 feet in a decade), saucer magnolia is attractive as a single specimen or when grouped together for a massed flowering display. The arrival of late frost is the biggest challenge to keeping magnolias from losing their unseasonably beautiful blooms.

Other Common Name
Tulip tree

Bloom Period and Seasonal Color
Late winter to early spring; white, pale-pink, and red-plum blooms

Mature Height × Spread
20 to 30 feet × 20 to 30 feet

Zones
5 to 9

Scarlet Oak
Quercus coccinea

Scarlet oaks contribute a grand appearance to the landscape, bringing a sense of permanence to even the newest garden setting. The familiar, lustrous, green foliage has seven C-shaped lobes that create a comforting rustling sound when caught by a breeze. In fall, as night temperatures drop, the dark-green leaves take on an unforgettable crimson-red appearance, which explains this tree's common name. When young, scarlet oak's habit is relatively upright, growing up to 2 feet annually over a 10- to 20-year period. As it matures to heights of 70 feet or higher (100 feet is not uncommon in wild settings), scarlet oak takes on a rounded, open form. The $^3/_4$- to 1-inch acorns are rounded, half-covered with a spherical cap.

Bloom Period and Seasonal Color
Fall; bright-scarlet foliage

Mature Height × Spread
70 to 75 feet × 40 to 50 feet

Zones
4 to 9

Where, When, and How to Plant
Scarlet oak is deeply rooted, so take care to dig an ample planting hole, at least $1^1/2$ times the width of the rootball. The best time to transplant a young tree is fall, though you can plant in early spring. Site in full or partial sun and in well-drained soil. Slightly acidic soil is preferred. Follow the general tree planting guidelines on page 12, allowing enough room for these majestic trees to establish without crowding.

Growing Tips
Rather than watering frequently for short periods, it's best to water a young oak less often (perhaps once a week), saturating the soil deeply to encourage root growth. Once established, scarlet oak requires only supplemental irrigation during extended dry periods. See page 203 for guidelines on fertilizing trees.

Care
These stunning trees are worth your care; ensure a healthy lifespan by keeping an eye out for pests or diseases. Prune away damaged or diseased branches during dormant periods. Oaks may host a wide array of insects, including caterpillars, which usually don't cause severe damage. Oak wilt, a fungal disease noted by wilting leaves that turn brown, may be a problem. Consult a certified arborist should your tree exhibit symptoms.

Companion Planting and Design
Larger landscapes are ideal settings for an oak that will become a favorite shade tree as it matures. Allow plenty of room when you plant an oak, ensuring that it doesn't grow too close to your home or garage. The glorious autumn foliage of a scarlet oak looks terrific backlit by the afternoon and evening sun. Oaks perform best in lawns that are not overwatered. Don't attempt to change the grade between the oak tree's trunk and drip line.

We Recommend
Scarlet oak is a moderate grower native to the Eastern U.S. Its gray-brown bark displays scalelike plates. Pin oak (*Quercus palustris*), widely planted along streets and sidewalks, features an pyramidal, upright form. It tolerates wet soils better than the scarlet oak.

Sourwood
Oxydendrum arboreum

Where, When, and How to Plant
Plant young sourwood trees in spring or fall, selecting container-grown or balled-and-burlapped specimens (it is difficult to find older trees). While sourwood can grow in most light conditions, it will exhibit the best fall color if planted in full to partial sun. Select a location with moist, well-drained soil. Sourwood prefers slightly acidic soil, although it can also tolerate drier and infertile soils. Follow the general tree planting guidelines on page 12, spacing sourwood 15 feet apart.

Growing Tips
Irrigate newly planted sourwood regularly until the tree is established in the second or third year. After that, these trees generally thrive on rainfall during all but the driest seasons. See page 203 for guidelines on fertilizing trees.

Care
No serious disease or insect problems affect sourwood. This is an elegant tree that should be pruned to enhance its natural draped or pendulous form, rather than be forced into an overt treelike shape with an exposed trunk. Prune only lightly to remove damaged or broken stems. If your sourwood is planted on a lawn, remove sod within its drip line, mulching well to retain moisture.

Companion Planting and Design
Sourwood is a superior ornamental tree that delivers four-season appeal to the residential landscape. Because it is slow-growing (to 15 feet over 12 to 15 years), this is a good tree for smaller gardens and can also be grown as the focal point in a container when young. Highlight sourwood's excellent autumn interest by pairing it with shrubs having good fall color, such as oakleaf hydrangea or fothergilla. Highlight its spring blooms with white and green foliage shrubs, such as the variegated redtwig dogwood (*Cornus alba* 'Spaethii' or 'Argenteo-marginata').

We Recommend
Sourwood is a stellar choice for any Northwest garden. Cultivars are hard to find, but offer even more variety, including 'Albomarginatum', with white leaf margins and some marbling on the foliage, and 'Mt. Charm', a sourwood appreciated for its symmetrical habit.

Sourwood tree is a breed apart from any other deciduous tree that you could choose for your garden. With its fragrant fringed creamy-white bell-shaped blooms that resemble plumed feathers and its multicolored autumn palette accompanied by panicles of seeds, sourwood is a beautiful year-round tree. A slow-growing, pyramidal habit makes it suitable for residential gardens, especially to punctuate the corner of a property where passersby will admire all its features. With a slender trunk and slightly drooping branches, sourwood has good winter interest, even after cool weather arrives and the leaves fall. The relatively narrow and slightly twisted leaves, 5 to 8 inches long, are tinted copper in spring, turn brilliant green in summer, and have varied hues of orange, scarlet, and dark-purple in autumn.

Other Common Name
Sorrel tree

Bloom Period and Seasonal Color
Summer; creamy-white blooms; multicolored fall foliage

Mature Height × Spread
15 to 30 feet × 10 to 15 feet

Zones
5 to 9

Vine Maple

Acer circinatum

If you want an easy-to-care-for tree that harmonizes with the environmental character of the Northwest, choose vine maple. Better yet, choose several, as this native maple looks beautiful in a small grove or clustered as informal screening. Vine maple's trunk size and foliage shape are somewhat similar to Japanese maple, and they can be incorporated into the garden in similar ways. Reaching heights and widths of 10 to 20 feet, vine maples tend to have multistemmed trunks and are adaptable to many regional growing conditions, including full sun or dappled shade and soil types from wet to rocky. They provide attractive autumn displays ranging from gold to burgundy and when bare, their branches serve as cool-season sculpture in the landscape.

Bloom Period and Seasonal Color
Fall; golden foliage (in shady locations) and bright-red foliage (in sunnier locations)

Mature Height × Spread
5 to 35 feet × variable

Zones
6 to 9

Where, When, and How to Plant
In the wild, vine maples grow in a haphazard manner, often "vining" along the ground before stretching upward toward the light. Cultivated vine maples have a more symmetrical habit, adding an informal beauty to the landscape. Purchase vine maples (container grown or balled and burlapped) from most retail nurseries or from local conservation districts and native plant societies. Plant in early spring or fall. Vine maples adapt to most conditions from dry to wet soil, sun to shade. But planted in shade, the trees become leggier and have less dramatic fall color. Follow the general tree planting guidelines on page 12, spacing vine maples 5 to 15 feet apart.

Growing Tips
If vine maple is growing in moist soil, you may need to water only occasionally; otherwise provide regular water until established. After that, these relatively drought-tolerant trees can exist on water provided by precipitation. As with most natives, little to no fertilizer is required.

Care
Don't prune young vine maples until they are established and you can observe the form their branches will take. If several trees are planted in a "grove," watch for trunks growing too close together. You may need to remove any branches or stems that are rubbing to prevent damage or weakening. You can dig up seedlings and plant them in containers until they reach 12 inches or so before transplanting into the landscape. This great Northwest native is generally not bothered by diseases or pests.

Companion Planting and Design
Vine maples provide excellent screening around otherwise exposed decks or patios. They combine well with woodland plantings such as native shrubs and evergreen ferns. You can plant vine maples on a hillside or slope to help bind the soil.

We Recommend
Cultivars include the cut leaf vine maple (*Acer circinatum* 'Monroe'), generally a single-stemmed tree with lacy bright-green leaves. *A. c.* 'Little Gem' is a dwarf mounded form discovered in British Columbia (4 feet by 4 feet).

Where, When, and How to Plant

Plant in spring or fall, in full to partial sun and in most soil types. The fibrous, suckering root system reaches for moisture, helping willows thrive near water or in wet soil (avoid planting near water or sewer lines, or drain fields). They can be messy, shedding foliage and broken branches, so consider planting a single weeping willow in a somewhat isolated spot in the landscape.

Growing Tips

Irrigate regularly until established. Willows suffer in dry soil, preferring evenly moist soil at all times. In fall, winter, and early spring, precipitation generally provides enough moisture to the roots. If your willow is not planted near a natural source of water, such as a spring or pond, irrigate weekly to saturate the root zone during dry spells. Fertilization is generally not necessary.

Care

Babylon weeping willow is somewhat less susceptible to disease than white willow (*S. alba*). In general, willows are short-lived and can suffer from blight, cankers, scabs, powdery mildew, and leaf spot. One of the first deciduous trees to leaf out in early spring, willow is also one of the last to retain its foliage in fall. Prune while dormant to remove damaged or diseased branches. Broken branches can easily be rooted in moist soil to produce new trees. The shrub form can be coppiced, or cut to the ground in late winter to maintain its size.

Companion Planting and Design

Plant a single weeping willow adjacent to a pond or stream where its long, graceful stems will dip into the water's surface. Plant shrub forms to help stabilize a bank or as a screen against an unattractive garage or fence. Some can be pruned as an informal hedge.

We Recommend

A Chinese native, Babylon weeping willow does well in damp Northwest gardens. 'Crispa', or ringleaf willow, is a cultivar with curled foliage. Purple osier willow (*S. purpurea*), a fine-textured blue-gray shrub (5 to 15 feet), somewhat tolerates drought in average, loamy garden soil.

There's a romantic, fluid character to willow trees that enhances gardens large or small. If your landscape has room, there's nothing more compelling than a weeping willow as its central element. Entire gatherings of small children can have lovely tea parties beneath the slender, draping stems that touch the ground to create a canopy. Smaller gardens are suitable for other Salix species and cultivars that assume shrublike habits. There's even a beautiful creeping willow ideal for rockeries. Babylon weeping willow (Salix babylonica), shown here, reaches heights of 30 to 40 feet with similar spread. Willows prefer moist soil, ideal for properties with streams or underground springs. Fast growing, willows have suckering root systems that often compete with anything nearby (making them excellent lawn trees).

Bloom Period and Seasonal Color
Fall; golden foliage; attractive bare stems in winter

Mature Height × Spread
30 to 40 feet × 30 to 40 feet

Zones
6 to 9

Vines *for Washington & Oregon*

Climbers and vines bring an incredible diversity to Northwest gardens, providing an array of design solutions to numerous landscape challenges. Vines provide much-needed privacy screening, can help shade an exposed area, and deliver beauty and fragrance to small spots in your garden.

The Cast of Characters

Vines can be woody or herbaceous, evergreen or deciduous. Some are appreciated for their lovely foliage, while several are noteworthy for their exotic appearance or profuse blooms. Others provide edible fruit. As they ascend and crawl through our gardens, vines attach themselves to supporting structures in a variety of ways:

Twiners: As the shoots and stems extend, they twist around a support. In their native setting, twiners climb around tree trunks, but in the garden, they rely on poles, posts, wires, or string. Wisterias and honeysuckles are twiners. They can be vigorous and require sturdy structures.

Tendrils: Some climbing plants have modified leaves or stems that form attractive and useful tendrils, which wrap themselves tightly around twigs or thinner supports (such as a 1-inch by 1-inch piece of wood lattice). Vines with tendrils reach out and grab hold of a "host" plant or a supporting structure. Grape vines and passion vines have tendrils.

Scramblers: Many climbing plants, such as roses and some clematis varieties, simply scramble where they want to go. Host branches and stems may hold climbers in place.

Self-clinging: Ivy, climbing hydrangea, and vines in the Virginia creeper family climb using aerial roots or suckers to cling to their support. It's best to use self-clinging vines on walls or fences, as they have a tendency to smother weaker structures.

Choose the Right Vine

If you keep in mind the cultural needs of a climber, you'll have an easier time selecting the right vine for your location. Many a vigorous climbing rose or wisteria has yanked a flimsy trellis away from a wall because of insignificant latticework. If you want to grow a vine of stature, consider building a sturdy arbor, pergola, or archway with posts at least 4 inches by 4 inches in diameter

Clematis
'Nelly Moser'

(many landscape designers recommend 6-inch by 6-inch posts for wisteria, evergreen clematis, and climbing roses).

For a small-scale use, such as growing a flowering climber for a small obelisk or ornamental structure, select a deciduous clematis or annual vine that won't demand as much support.

Many woody vines are excellent for brick or concrete walls, or trained over rockeries. These climbers can typically withstand exposed locations and less-than-ideal soil conditions, such as climbing cotoneaster and wintercreeper euonymus.

Site Selection and Planting

Individual entries for the vines featured in this chapter will guide you as to the soil and sun needs as you choose a site. The type of support you plan to use will determine the appropriate vine. Vines are

Honeysuckle on Support Underplanted with Rudbeckia

typically sold in 1-gallon nursery pots or larger containers attached with bamboo stakes to support a flowering vine (such as a clematis). Retain these stakes as you plant the vine, at least until the stems reach the permanent support.

If you plant vines in fall or early spring, they'll benefit from several months of normal rainfall before Northwest's dry summer arrives. Regular precipitation will generally provide enough moisture to the new root zone until summer's dry spells. But once summer arrives, you'll need to saturate the root zone once or twice weekly until the plant is established (generally by the second or third year). For definitions of various watering terms, see page 14.

Plant a vine as you would any tree or shrub. Unless noted differently in the plant entry, dig the hole twice the width of the rootball, keeping the depth of the hole equal to the depth of the nursery pot. To improve soil where the drainage is too sharp (sandy) or too poor (clay soil), a general rule is to plant into the native soil and topdress with organic compost.

Design Tips

Vines are incredibly versatile plants for well-designed gardens. Here are some ways to incorporate climbers and twiners into your landscape:

- **Screening:** If you can't remove a less-than-attractive structure, consider using a vine as "camouflage." Even an old tree stump can benefit from a climber planted at its base, such as a climbing hydrangea that will anchor itself to the bark, eventually covering the unsightly remnant. Perhaps your garden faces the back of a neighbor's garage—this is a perfect spot for erecting a latticework fence and training a fast-growing vine, such as honeysuckle or evergreen clematis.

- **Enhancing the view:** Use a vine to "frame" the perspective, softening a cedar arbor or an opening in a fence. Trellises, pergolas, and other vertical structures are well suited for twining vines. Variegated kiwi, passion vine, and purpleleaf grapevine provide an attractive finishing touch to architectural elements in the landscape.

- **Shade:** Use overhead vines to protect and shade a patio or courtyard. Some flowering vines are best appreciated when viewed from below—such as the Japanese wisteria. Keep the area cool and verdant by using a vine's foliage for protection. Enjoy the dappled light that shines through the canopy provided by an overhead vine.

Annual Vines in Patio Planters

234

Wisteria Arbor

General Care and Maintenance

Follow the pruning tips noted for each specific climber. Vines are relatively carefree additions to the garden and typically don't require pruning for overall tidiness, training, or grooming. As you train the stems and shoots of a climbing plant, you will probably need to attach them to supports. Use loosely secured organic ties (such as sisal or twine), which will degrade over time. Synthetic ties or anything secured tightly will choke the stems and possibly kill your plant.

If your vine attracts pests or diseases, address the problem organically. Plants under stress are more susceptible to "invaders," whether bugs or diseases. Look at the culture of your plant. Is the area at its base clean and free of debris? Are the branches tangled or the stems matted together? Before trying a pesticide or fungicide, take the time to remove any dead, diseased, or aging vines. Remove diseased material (such as fallen rose leaves) from the base. Mulch with an organic compost to help the plant's root zone retain moisture and the roots stay cool. You may discover that these practical steps go further toward plant health than over-the-counter remedies. Refer to our section on plant health care, page 248, for other organic-care tips.

Colorful Threads

Vines give vertical impact to the garden, sharing fabulous foliage and stunning flowers—easy to appreciate when viewed at eye level or overhead. If you're lucky enough to have a pergola or arbor, encourage a climber or vine to twine up the post and over the beams, creating a lovely floral canopy above. The addition of a delicate vine can add visual interest, encircling the trunk and branches like colorful threads of embroidery.

—DP

Clematis
Clematis species and cultivars

The genus Clematis provides over 200 species, with countless new cultivars available. Most are deciduous, with a few evergreens and woody varieties rounding out the list (see evergreen clematis on page 238). Clematis flowers are composed of sepals, which most people think of as petals; seek out unusual bell-shaped, doubles, or bicolored choices. Once you discover how many graceful blooms are packed onto a single vine, you'll start finding places to grow as many clematis as possible. Like adding a string of pearls to a basic black dress, clematis always enhances its backdrop. Look for places in the garden where the surprising addition of magnificent, and often fragrant, flowers is sure to please. Clematis vines pair beautifully with roses and won't harm their stems.

Bloom Period and Seasonal Color
Spring to early fall; purple, pink, white, and blue blooms

Mature Length
6 to 25 feet or more

Zones
4 to 9

Where, When, and How to Plant
Plant in spring and fall; clematis appreciates cooler soil. Site where the roots are shaded and the blooms can enjoy full or partial sun, perhaps behind a larger perennial or shrub. Dig a good-sized hole, at least half again the pot size. Topdress planted clematis with mulch to retain moisture. Provide a structure or support (such as a 1-inch stake) until the vine takes hold on a trellis or trunk. For general information on planting vines, see page 233.

Growing Tips
Water newly planted clematis regularly, but don't allow the plant to sit in standing water. Once clematis is established, water weekly during dry weather. Feed in spring with a nitrogren fertilizer, and use a liquid feed monthly during blooming season. Newly planted clematis may not bloom until the second season or after.

Care
Clematis is pruned according to a complicated schedule determined by when it blooms. The good news is you can't kill it by pruning at the wrong time. Prune deadwood or crowded vines each spring after the plant has begun to leaf out. Clematis falls into the general categories of spring, summer/fall, or twice blooming. For specific times to prune these types, check the nursery tag or consult a pruning reference book. Clematis are generally pest free.

Companion Planting and Design
Plant two clematis varieties at the base of either side of an arbor, encouraging them to twine together at the top. Or dress up a plain shrub, such as a lilac that's finished blooming, by training a vine through its branches. Go for high contrast and grow creamy-white clematis through the dark-brown branches of a paperbark maple.

We Recommend
Clematis montana is a vigorous climber with toothed, three-part green leaflets. Cultivars include 'Marjorie', with semidouble creamy-white flowers and a coppery-pink tinge, and 'Elizabeth', with vanilla-scented pale-pink flowers. *C. × jackmanii* is a profuse bloomer with rich purple blossoms that flowers summer through fall.

Climbing Hydrangea
Hydrangea anomala ssp. *petiolaris*

Where, When, and How to Plant
Plant in spring or fall. Choose a location with good drainage, or the roots will suffer. Place about 12 inches away from the base of a sturdy support, such as a porch railing or the trunk of a mature evergreen tree. Topdress with mulch to retain moisture. Site in full sun or shade. Provide a structure or support (such as a 1-inch stake) until the vine takes hold. For information on planting woody vines, see page 233.

Growing Tips
Water the root zone of new plants regularly, but don't let them sit in standing water. Once established, water the root zone deeply twice a month during extended dry periods. In spring, apply a nitrogen fertilizer. Your plant may not bloom until the third season or later.

Care
Climbing hydrangeas are generally pest and disease free. Young plants may be susceptible to root weevil damage, but older plants outgrow this problem. Remove these nighttime pests by hand using a flashlight to spot them. Along the underside of its stems, the vine produces tiny aerial roots that anchor the plant to a support, such as brick, tree bark, or stone (not slick surfaces like plastic or aluminum). Pruning isn't required, but clip off spent blooms in early spring to tidy up the vine's appearance.

Companion Planting and Design
A great vine for woodland gardens or as a backdrop to a perennial border, this vine tolerates shade. Its creamy-white blooms help illuminate a darker area of the garden, glowing in dappled light, but climbing hydrangea is equally happy in bright locations. Once established, it blankets its support with green foliage, above which the blooms seem to float. You can train it to cover a stone wall, tree trunk, or other sturdy structure.

We Recommend
You may also want to try the Japanese hydrangea vine (*Schizophragma hydrangeoides*), a close relative. 'Moonlight' is a lovely cultivar with graceful, white-lace-cap hydrangea flowers.

If you are already enchanted by hydrangeas and the way their blooms bring enduring romance to the garden, you will want to add a climbing hydrangea to your repertoire. Plant climbing hydrangea as soon as possible, though, because it may take three years to begin producing buds and flowers. The wait is worth it. This woody deciduous vine clings to its support, and can become heavy with age, so make sure you provide it with a good structure. As with many hydrangea shrubs, the graceful blooms appear in early summer and look particularly stunning against the plant's bright-green foliage. The leaves turn a warm gold in the fall, adding to seasonal interest. Even when the vine is bare, you'll appreciate its architectural structure during winter.

Bloom Period and Seasonal Color
Early to late summer; creamy-white blooms; warm-gold fall foliage

Mature Length
25 to 30 feet in 10 years

Zones
4 to 9

Evergreen Clematis
Clematis armandii

Seeing the profuse, creamy buds and blooms of ever-green clematis against almost bluish green foliage is one of the true signals that a Northwest spring has arrived. Before they open, the buds resemble an endless string of large pearls. Once you get close, the fragrance can't help but evoke a happy response. Evergreen clematis is what one landscape designer calls an "instant gratification" vine. If you want to quickly cover an arbor or screen out an unattractive garage on a neighboring property, this is the vine for you. It's tough and tender alike. The vig-orous vine requires sturdy support but readily clambers up and over most structures; delicate as porcelain, the starlike blooms seem to float above dark, shiny, straplike 3- to 6-inch long leaves.

Bloom Period and Seasonal Color
Mid- to late spring; white, fragrant blooms; evergreen foliage

Mature Length
15 to 25 feet

Zones
7 to 9

Where, When, and How to Plant
Plant in spring or fall in locations that receive at least some daytime sun. Quite easy to grow, this vine won't tolerate winter temperatures below 20 degrees Fahrenheit. It prefers cool roots, so place it in the shade of a shrub, encouraging it to grow up into the sun. Avoid windy sites. Plant in average to rich well-drained soil. Lightly mulch to keep the roots cool until established. Follow the planting tips for woody plants noted on page 233.

Growing Tips
Water regularly until established. During drought, water deeply once a month; established plants tol-erate dry conditions surprisingly well. To produce more flowers, feed monthly during the blooming season with a liquid fertilizer.

Care
You may need to tie up young stems to start it climbing, but once the vine takes hold, remove the ties so they don't choke the vine as it grows. Evergreen clematis blooms on old wood. You won't need to prune it for the first few years, but once it's established, groom away dead or damaged stems after flowering. Tidy up errant stems, or prune so there is a main stem. This vine can take aggressive pruning, especially if you need to reno-vate a tangled mass of stems. Pests and diseases do not generally bother it.

Companion Planting and Design
This rewarding vine provides quick solutions to unsightly areas of the garden. Plant it where its long, strapped foliage serves as a canopy overhead on your arbor or pergola or creates a green wall against a windowless garage. The flowers arrive as a bonus each spring, with some continued blooming through midsummer. You can train brightly col-ored deciduous clematis to grow up and through the lower stems of the evergreen clematis.

We Recommend
'Apple Blossom' produces pink buds that open to creamy-white, vanilla-scented flowers. 'Snowdrift' has pure-white, very fragrant blooms. Cut the side stems and bring them indoors so you can incorpo-rate sprays of blooms and fabulous dark foliage into floral arrangements.

Fiveleaf Akebia

Akebia quinata

Where, When, and How to Plant

Plant in spring or fall. This vine tolerates most garden soil and light conditions, so it's a good choice for difficult spots. While fiveleaf akebia can be used as a ground cover, most people treat it as a vine that twines up and around an arbor or along latticework. Ground cover plants can be spaced about 6 feet apart. For climbing vines, situate the hole 6 to 12 inches away from the supporting post to allow ample space for the roots. For fruit production, grow two plants from the same species so they'll cross-pollinate. For general information on planting vines, see page 233.

Growing Tips

Water newly planted fiveleaf akebia regularly until established. Give it a deep watering twice a month during extended dry periods. Feed in spring with a nitrogen fertilizer.

Care

Fiveleaf akebia can be vigorous and may require pruning every two years. Prune after flowering by thinning out one-third of the basal stems or trimming errant vines. Fiveleaf akebia should be trained on a sturdy support, such as a porch roof, arbor, or tree trunk. Twig dieback is sometimes a problem; it's best addressed by pruning the vine (or the damaged sections) to the ground in early spring. The plant recovers quickly with new growth.

Companion Planting and Design

Also known as the chocolate vine for its spicy-sweet fragrance, fiveleaf akebia is an appealing addition to the garden. It provides almost year-round interest in foliage, flower, and fruit. Encourage the vine to blanket a wall with its lacy foliage or to create an aromatic canopy over an arbor. Use its relatively unusual flower color as a backdrop to an all-white or pastel garden scheme.

We Recommend

Akebia quinata is a popular vine for the informal or woodland garden. Look for 'Variegata', an attractive selection with cream-splashed foliage. You can also find a three-leaf variety, called *A. trifoliata*, and occasionally a seven-leaf variety.

Native to East Asia and well-adapted to Northwest gardens, versatile fiveleaf akebia tolerates cold, grows in sun or shade, and accepts a variety of soils. In milder areas, this deciduous vine is semievergreen. Each leaf sports five dark-green, oval leaflets, 2 to 3 inches long; the leaflets are distinguished by a tiny notch on each tip. Fiveleaf akebia is a monoecious plant, with both male and female parts on the same plant. In midspring, this plant produces delicate, cup-shaped blooms that emit a light vanilla scent. Edible, sausage-shaped purple fruits follow the flowers. A carefree performer, this vine grows quickly in mild regions and more slowly where winters are cold. Fiveleaf akebia requires good support, and it can be aggressive if not pruned occasionally.

Other Common Name
Chocolate vine

Bloom Period and Seasonal Color
Midspring; soft-purple and mauve blooms; semievergreen foliage

Mature Length
15 to 30 feet

Zones
5 to 9

Honeysuckle Vine
Lonicera × heckrottii

My first encounter with an exuberant honeysuckle vine was as a community garden volunteer. I was given the task of "freeing" from a flimsy latticework trellis stuck in a large container a glorious, but vigorous vine with clusters of lemon and deep-pink trumpetlike blooms. The honeysuckle vine clearly needed room to soar; relocated, it now happily covers a cedar fence and sprawls across the roof of a tool shed. That example illustrates how to treat honeysuckle vine, a fragrant twining deciduous or semievergreen climber with several shrub relatives. Provide support, staking, and space for it to grow. While lovely, it requires annual pruning for maintenance. Hummingbirds favor honeysuckle vine's long-blooming flowers as a source of nectar; after it blooms, red berries feed other winged creatures.

Bloom Period and Seasonal Color
Spring to fall; deep-pink or lemon colored blooms

Mature Length
15 feet

Zones
6 to 9

Where, When, and How to Plant
Plant in spring or fall in full or partial sun or partial shade. This climber requires a well-drained site, so prepare the soil as needed. Situate the plant where it can be trained along a sturdy and substantial structure, such as a wall, shed roof, or massive arbor. But don't grow it over a patio or eating area; birds will make a mess, spreading seeds from the berries. For general information on planting vines, see page 233.

Growing Tips
Easy to grow and gratifying for its extended flowering, honeysuckle vine typically adapts to most growing conditions if there's adequate drainage. Water new plants regularly until established, followed by monthly irrigation during extended dry periods. This plant generally does not require fertilizer.

Care
Secure the vine to its support until established. Some gardeners train it into an espaliered form along an openwork fence. Don't let the mature plant get top-heavy, or the vine may topple its support. One way to manage its exuberant growth is to thin it annually in fall, after it blooms. Cut older, unkempt vines to the ground before spring growth emerges. Honeysuckle vine is generally pest free if well maintained. For general guidelines on managing common diseases, see page 248.

Companion Planting and Design
Nothing beats this vine's colorful blooms and lovely, almost blue-green foliage. It can stabilize a bank or create a lush and aromatic "wall" at the back of a hummingbird and butterfly garden, where winged creatures happily hover at the trumpetlike flowers. At its base, add other scarlet-bloomers, such as cape fuchsia or monarda. This vine's long season of colorful, fragrant blooms make it perfect for a carefree country garden.

We Recommend
The hybrid *Lonicera × heckrottii* 'Gold Flame' features sherbet blooms of pink and lemon. *L. × heckrottii* behaves better than *L. japonica*, Japanese honeysuckle, which grows to 30 feet and can engulf an old garage or shed. *L. japonica* 'Halliana' is ideal for stabilizing a slope.

Japanese Wisteria
Wisteria floribunda

Where, When, and How to Plant
Grow Japanese wisteria in spring or fall, planting it in fertile, moist, well-drained soil. Full sun or partial shade is fine, although like clematis, this vine prefers cool roots with the flowering portions exposed to sun. Site Japanese wisteria where it will be well supported; when mature, this very heavy vine can easily topple a flimsy fence or arbor. Plant the vine in a hole about 12 inches away from the supporting post to allow ample space for roots. Mulch to keep roots cool. For general information on planting vines, see page 233.

Growing Tips
Water Japanese wisteria regularly during the first season. This vine seems to thrive on neglect, requiring little to moderate irrigation once established. Fertilizing is generally not necessary.

Care
This vigorous, fast-growing vine responds best to consistent pruning. After planting, begin training the vine by cutting back the lead shoot (or multiple shoots) to about 3 feet above ground level. Loosely tie the side stems to the structure or fence, and remove any secondary shoots. To stimulate growth, groom or cut back the side stems to about one-third their length the first winter. Once the vine framework is in place, prune side branches into short spurs each winter, and groom again after flowering. Japanese wisteria is susceptible to aphids, scale insects, and mealy bugs. For general guidelines on managing common garden pests, see page 248.

Companion Planting and Design
Japanese wisteria commands a dominant place in your garden, especially during its blooming season. Give it center stage by creating a roomlike pavilion, arbor, or pergola that has 6- to 8-inch corner posts and sturdy beams above. Encourage the vine to engulf the top beams of a structure so its lovely blooms can form a fragrant canopy for those who walk or sit beneath it.

We Recommend
Choose from a wide array of bloom colors, including *Wisteria floribunda* 'Longissima Alba', a whitish pink selection. *W. f.* 'Plena' has double, deep blue-violet blooms.

Unparalleled for the romance and nostalgia it brings to a garden, Japanese wisteria is a deciduous, woody vine that may also be grown as a shrub or tree. With bright-green foliage composed of ten or more leaflets, it has a delicate appearance. But don't be fooled: This tough performer can take full sun and little to moderate water. The fanciful blue, white, lavender, or pink blooms arrive in spring, dripping beneath the foliage. Japanese wisteria is best appreciated from below; as you walk under an arbor or pergola, you'll be charmed by the numerous 12-inch (or longer) pealike flowers draped above your head. Careful pruning will establish a single trunk. The mature weight of this vine is considerable, so the plant requires substantial support.

Bloom Period and Seasonal Color
Late spring to early summer; purple, blue, white, and pink pendant blooms; soft-gold fall foliage

Mature Length
25 to 30 feet

Zones
5 to 9

Passion Flower
Passiflora species and cultivars

Passion flower hails from South America and evokes an exotic feeling, thanks to its unusual flowers and oval fruit. Up to 3 inches wide, the lavender, pink, or purple flowers signify for some the passion of Christ, thus its common name. Deciduous or semievergreen, passion flower climbs by tendrils. This vine is best appreciated at eye level, where the tropical appearance of the blooms wows onlookers. The flowers have an unusual form, with five distinct sepals and petals, a contrasting corona or "crown" of fringelike anthers, and three styles. While the blooms appear fragile, the vine is vigorous and will readily cover an unsightly structure or serve as a semitransparent screen on an openwork fence. Somewhat tender, the vine may suffer from frost in winter.

Bloom Period and Seasonal Color
Early to late summer; lavender, pink, or purple blooms

Mature Length
12 to 20 feet

Zones
6 to 9

Where, When, and How to Plant
Plant in spring or fall, in full or partial sun for optimum blooming. Protect from cold winds or exposure by situating it against a wall or beneath an overhang. Passion flower tolerates many soil types if drainage is adequate. When planting, top-dress with compost if necessary and mulch to protect the roots. A vigorous climber, passion flower requires good support. For general information on planting vines, see page 233.

Growing Tips
Passion flower does not adapt well to drought, preferring slightly moist soil and regular feeding, especially when blooming. Water deeply during extended dry periods.

Care
Secure the vine to its support until established. A vigorous grower that tends to tangle if not regularly maintained, passion flower requires regular pruning and thinning. Prune for shape in early spring to keep the vine tidy and prevent disease. Remove caterpillars by hand. Prune away any damaged sections immediately. Protect roots from freeze by mulching in late fall. A freeze may also cause vine dieback, which can be pruned away. Because this vine provides food for butterflies, use only organic amendments. For general guidelines on managing common garden pests and diseases, see page 248.

Companion Planting and Design
This vine can play a starring role in a tropical garden style. Hardy bananas, colorfully striped cannas, angel's trumpets, and giant gunneras welcome the exotic vibrant blooms of passion flower. The plum, pink, and ivory flowers look stunning against the vine's multilobed green foliage. Play up the hot purple and pink blooms with vibrant companion plants like cape fuchsia, dahlia, and rose.

We Recommend
Blue passion flower (*Passiflora caerulea*), a fast-growing climber, features bowl-shaped white and pink-tinged flowers. The hybrid *P. × caerulea-racemosa* offers stunning red-purple flowers. If you're growing this vine for its fruit, select a species bred for edible qualities, such as *P. edulis* and its cultivars, which produce unusual fruit with a deep-purple rind.

Purpleleaf Grape Vine

Vitis vinifera 'Purpurea'

Where, When, and How to Plant

Plant purpleleaf grape vine in spring or fall. This vine tolerates many soil types if given adequate drainage. Grown for its ornamental quality, purpleleaf grape vine should be situated in your garden's sunniest location to produce the best color show. Provide a sturdy support—whether arbor, wall, trellis, or tree. This slow starter eventually rewards you as its stems stretch out to display lovely burgundy and merlot foliage with a distinctive grape leaf shape. For general information on planting vines, see page 233.

Growing Tips

Water new plants regularly until established. Give them a deep watering twice a month during extended dry periods. Mature vines can resist drought if planted in well-drained soil. Feed once a year in spring with an organic fertilizer.

Care

This woody vine climbs by tendrils, requiring support against which it can grow. If you want the vine to blanket the surface of a trellis, you first need to coax the stems to grow where you want, tying a young vine with organic twine that will rot with time. Prune in midwinter and midsummer, as needed to control form and shape. Purpleleaf grape vine is generally free of pests and diseases.

Companion Planting and Design

This easy-to-grow vine won't take over your garden. Make design choices that take advantage of the impact created by purpleleaf grape vine's vibrant red-purple foliage. Plant the vine where it can provide a backdrop along the sunny wall of a courtyard, patio, or fence. Select gold-hued companions, such as golden deciduous trees, gold-formed conifers, or yellow perennials. With its classic foliage and form, this vine can be the star of a Mediterranean- or European-inspired garden.

We Recommend

In addition to purpleleaf grape vine, there are several other attractive ornamental vines in the grape family. *Vitis coignetiae* (crimson glory vine), a fast-growing deciduous climber with oversized heart-shaped foliage, turns bright-red in fall.

Oregon and Washington are known for their prolific wine regions, but if you don't have the room or inclination to grow grapes for winemaking or eating, consider an ornamental form of the common wine grape. There is nothing quite as stunning as a wall or trellis covered by the distinctive grape leaf foliage of a purpleleaf grape vine, especially when illuminated by late-afternoon sun or when climbing the trunk and branches of a golden deciduous tree. This woody, open-growing vine has green spring foliage with burgundy tinges and takes on deeper wine tones in the summer and autumn. The deep-purple foliage looks best in full sun. Purpleleaf grape vine produces clusters of dark-purple grapes, which enhance its beauty but probably won't ripen in our climate.

Bloom Period and Seasonal Color
Summer to fall; dramatic wine-colored foliage

Mature Length
15 to 30 feet

Zones
6 to 9

Variegated Kiwi

Actinidia kolomikta

If you're going for the exotic look in your garden landscape, variegated kiwi rewards you with a lush flamboyance. New growth on this twining deciduous vine emerges with tinges of purple, followed by splashy pink, cream, and dark-green variegated foliage. When grown in shade or dappled light, the 3- to 5-inch elongated heart-shaped leaves produce vibrant colors that become more prominent in mature vines. Most nurseries stock the male kiwi vine, which has interesting foliage that creates a lovely patterned effect against a trellis or arbor. The vine bears clusters of lightly fragrant cup-shaped flowers in early summer. You need to grow both male and female vines in order to produce small fruits. Variegated kiwi is a relative of the hardy fruiting kiwi (A. arguta).

Bloom Period and Seasonal Color
Spring through fall; dramatic variegated foliage

Mature Length
15 to 18 feet

Zones
4 to 8

Where, When, and How to Plant

Plant in spring or fall in moist, well-drained soil. Variegated kiwi can be situated in sun but performs best in partial sun or partial shade. Provide sturdy support, and shelter this plant from strong winds. As a twiner, it wraps itself around posts, railings, or the supporting beams of a trellis. To train it against a wall, provide a supporting grid to encourage the twining. For general information on planting vines, see page 233.

Growing Tips

Water new plants regularly until established. Give them a deep watering twice a month during extended dry periods. Don't allow the soil to dry out. Fertilize lightly upon planting, after which this vine requires little or no feeding.

Care

This energetic vine should be supported by a sturdy fence or arbor. Improve its appearance by pruning for shape in winter when the vine is dormant. Thin out tight clumps, or cut back shoots to train its form. All ornamental kiwi vines are susceptible to fungal diseases; avoid this problem by keeping your vine well pruned, clipping out dead or diseased shoots. Don't be alarmed if the leaves revert to green during their first few seasons in the landscape; the variegation becomes more apparent with maturity. For general guidelines on managing common garden pests and diseases, see page 248.

Companion Planting and Design

Foliage and color are variegated kiwi's strongest assets, so design accordingly. Plant where its pink- and cream-tinged foliage can create a big impact, providing a vibrant vertical element to a shade garden. Highlight the variegation by planting astilbes in varying pink tones or leafy cream-and-green variegated hostas in front of the vine. Create a colorful canopy overhead, and train variegated kiwi to cover an archway or dining pavilion.

We Recommend

Choose the male form for its dynamic foliage. Collectors may seek out unique cultivars, such as 'Adam' or 'Arctic Beauty', but retail nurseries generally carry the straight species.

Wintercreeper Euonymus

Euonymus fortunei

Where, When, and How to Plant

Plant in spring or fall. This plant tolerates most garden conditions, so it's a good choice for difficult spots. Some forms can be trained over rockeries and retaining walls; others are suitable for covering vertical structures. Situate the hole 6 to 12 inches away from the supporting structure to allow ample space for the roots. Ensure good drainage. For general information on planting vines, see page 233.

Growing Tips

Water new plants regularly until established. They prefer moderately moist soil. When grown in full sun, wintercreeper euonymus requires regular moisture. During extended dry periods, water deeply once a month. Feed in spring with a nitrogen formula.

Care

Pruning is rarely required, but tidy up its appearance by clipping errant stems. Wintercreeper euonymus may establish slowly, but will increase its vigor if given good support. Avoid pests and mildew by ensuring the area around the plant base is kept clean from debris and has good air circulation. Watch for scale, and remove damaged stems. Shelter from cold, drying winds by training the plant along east- or north-facing areas, or up a large evergreen trunk. For general guidelines on managing common garden pests and diseases, see page 248.

Companion Planting and Design

Take advantage of this plant's great features year-round; place wintercreeper euonymus where it will create an attractive backdrop pattern of evergreen or variegation along the wall of a courtyard or entry garden. Enjoy the vibrant orange arils of its late season fruit, and repeat the warm tones with copper- and gold-blooming perennials, such as crocosmia or rudbeckia.

We Recommend

Euonymus fortunei cultivars show up at nurseries more readily than the straight species. (Some nurseries still sell wintercreeper euonymus under the name *E. f.* var. *radicans*.) 'Gracilis' is a trailing variety; its dark-green leaves with white edges take on a pink tinge in winter. 'Coloratus', a purple-leaf wintercreeper, has deep-purple winter foliage with a sprawling habit that makes it a good ground cover.

Your garden will look vibrant in every season if you've found a place to grow wintercreeper euonymus. An evergreen creeping vine, with many shrub relatives in the genus, wintercreeper euonymus is a useful, hardy, easy-to-grow plant. Long stems anchor themselves to walls or arbors with aerial roots, covering any surface with a blanket of small, dark-green, oval leaves. Or choose a form with cream, gold, or white variegation—perfect to brighten up a dark spot or add winter interest (some actually redden when the temperatures drop). The vine produces insignificant greenish yellow flowers in summer, but fruit with dazzling orange arils follow through fall. Tolerant of shade and sun, as well as poor soils, wintercreeper euonymus is an invaluable plant for your landscape's tough spots.

Bloom Period and Seasonal Color

Summer; small greenish yellow blooms, followed by berries with orange arils; evergreen.

Mature Length

15 feet

Zones

5 to 9

Native Gardener's Guide

Each plant we gardeners bring into our landscapes is native somewhere on the planet, growing naturally in one region or another. Movements of plants and people around the world mean that it's not always easy to say which plants are precisely native; many common wildflowers like foxglove (*Digitalis* species) were introduced long ago and fool us into thinking they've always been here. Fortunately for Pacific Northwest gardeners, excellent studies identifying native plants for local garden conditions make choices easier. We're blessed with many useful, available native plants.

Native plants have some obvious advantages. Once adapted to the garden environment, they may require less summer irrigation and may be less susceptible to pest problems than exotic plants originating elsewhere. They also attract and feed birds and native animals, and they help create conditions supporting other native plants. Choosing native plants can be one strategy for environmentally friendly gardening.

Talk with nurseries, and walk in undeveloped areas looking at native plants. It's vital to understand the cultural needs of the plant and to be attracted to its qualities. Just as you would an exotic, you have to like the native plant! Native plants can be small herbaceous perennials, such as the native spring-blooming trillium (*Trillium ovatum*), midsized shrubs like red huckleberry (*Vaccinium parvifolium*), moderate-sized trees like vine maple (*Acer circinatum*), or huge trees like Douglas fir (*Pseudotsuga menziesii*) that aren't adaptable to small gardens.

A flowering shrub like oceanspray (*Holodiscus discolor*) grows naturally along meadow edges in sunny, dry locations. Its white summer blooms, named oceanspray for their frothy appearance, are familiar to travelers in western Washington and Oregon. Oceanspray won't grow well if it's tucked under the shade of a Douglas fir. But the native sword fern (*Polystichum munitum*) will thrive there. Use native plants in groupings that replicate their natural niches.

Before selecting a particular plant or group of plants, get acquainted with your own garden conditions. Native plants must be placed where they will grow best; just because it's native doesn't mean you can put a water-loving western cedar on a high, dry hilltop. Native plants will be no more capable than exotics of surviving in unsuitable locations. Think of this as selecting for "the right native in the right place." If your landscape already contains some native plants, look at the sunlight, available moisture, and soil conditions they're in. Use a good handbook (such as those listed below) to identify what's already growing, and seek plants that will join those conditions readily.

Whenever possible, select locally grown native plants. Many natives in Washington and Oregon grow in other locations—they're not exclusive to us. Red osier dogwood (*Cornus sericea*) grows in Maine, Alaska, and Southern California. Plants grown in other areas will not be as well adapted as locally produced ones, even though they may have the same botanical name.

The plant you choose may look different when grown with lots of tender loving garden care. Native plants respond to care by growing more vigorously, putting on more leaves, or blooming more. Nutrients and water will quite often alter the growth habit of a native plant. Keep their growth "lean" by using amendments sparingly.

Natives are adaptable and generally free of pests, though not resistant to all pest or disease problems. Slugs will chew trillium; Oregon grape (*Mahonia* species) may show powdery mildew. Such natural problems don't make these poor garden choices; they're simply one part of the plant's life.

Learning about and using native plants is a fine adventure, one that opens new worlds and helps us experience the beauty of our region in more depth. Native plant societies in Washington and Oregon can help you identify, locate, and grow these plants: Native Plant Society of Oregon, P.O. Box 902, Eugene, OR 97440, 503-248-9242, www.npsoregon.org; Washington Native Plant Society, 7400 Sand Point Way NE, Seattle, WA 98115, 206-527-3210, www.wnps.org. —MR

Other Useful Resources

Kruckeberg, Arthur. *Gardening with Native Plants of the Pacific Northwest.* University of Washington Press, 1982. (Use for both western and eastern regions.)

Pojar and MacKinnon. *Plants of Coastal British Columbia, Including Washington, Oregon, and Alaska.* BC Ministry of Forests, 1994.

Gardening on the Web

You have the wide world of gardening at your fingertips when you log onto a computer and type in a few key words. The horticultural community has embraced the Internet because it gives us a virtual introduction to an outstanding selection of plants, nurseries, gardening techniques, and design ideas. Check the Plant Resources chapter on page 256, to find the recommended retail and mail-order nurseries operate websites.

Here are some other great reference websites for Northwest gardeners:

Master Gardening Sites
Oregon: http://extension.oregonstate.edu/mg/
- Check this site for links to each county's Master Gardener program. You'll also find information about becoming a Master Gardener.

Oregon State University: http://eesc.orst.edu/
Extension & Experimentation Station Communications
- Click on "Gardening Information" and search hundreds of articles about everything from growing fruit to gardening for wildlife.
- Download or order dozens of gardening publications, such as "Maintaining a Healthy Lawn in Western Oregon" or "Controlling Diseases and Aphids on Your Roses."
- Learn what to do each month in the garden.

Washington: http://mastergardener.wsu.edu/
- This is the "master" site for Washington's Master Gardener program, which will link you to WSU Extension, each county's Master Gardener program, and the Master Gardener Foundation. You'll also find information about becoming a Master Gardener.

Washington State University: http://gardening.wsu.edu
- Read monthly gardening information for your region, do a "key word" search for plants or subjects, submit a question to "ask an expert," and follow links to specialty nurseries and native plant sources.

Plant Health Care Website: http://pep.wsu.edu/hortsense/
- Learn how to address pest problems with WSU's site devoted to Integrated Pest Management. Search the site by common cultural problems, diseases, and insects.

Plant Diagnostics. If you want to learn more about a plant's possible disease or pest problems, the Internet offers excellent tools. Use a search engine to type in your subject, such as "bark splitting mountain ash" and you'll soon see many website choices to visit. Cornell University's Plant Disease Diagnostic Clinic operates one excellent site at http://plantclinic.cornell.edu/. Here you can learn about plant diseases and suggested management strategies, see photographs and drawings, and download fact sheets.

Plants, Organizations and Societies
Great Plant Picks: www.greatplantpicks.com features more than 200 superior plants for gardens west of the Cascades. Experts from nurseries, arboretums, and horticulture education programs evaluate hundreds of plants each year in order to recommend the best for Northwest gardens.

Miller Horticultural Library: www.millerlibrary.org is a reference website maintained by staff and volunteers of the Elisabeth C. Miller Horticultural Society at the Center for Urban Horticulture in Seattle. Check this site for additions to the library's collection, links to plant sales, garden tours, and lectures. See the "Plant Answer Line" to email a question to reference librarians (or call Monday-Friday, 9 a.m. to 5 p.m., 206-897-5268 (206-UW-PLANT).

Native Plant Societies: Learn more about the native plants in your region.
- **Native Plant Society of Oregon:** www.npsoregon.org
- **Washington Native Plant Society:** www.wnps.org

Saving Water Program: www.savingwater.org
This is a service of Seattle Public Utilities and other area water/sewer districts to help you learn savvy ways to conserve water in the landscape. You'll find great tips for lawn care; natural pest, weed, and disease control; and water conservation.

—DP

Growing Them Right: Plant Health Care

Gardeners always want plants to thrive and grow without difficulties, adding relaxation to our landscapes by their easy-care performance. Success in growing plants starts with proper selection and care, which means choosing the plant to suit its location. Then we provide basic watering, fertilizing, and pruning—good care goes a long way toward preventing problems. Detailed growing directions in the individual Gardener's Guide plant profiles will give you a headstart on a healthy garden.

No matter how well selected the plants, problems will occur. For the long-term health of the garden and the environment, it's necessary to gather information about the plant problem and reach an appropriate solution. Doing this will prevent expensive mistakes that can possibly waste resources and certainly take time, without solving the problem.

Identify the plant. The first necessary step includes being sure you can identify the plant. Many plant problems are "host specific," meaning particular to certain plants. One example is the common fungal problem in western Washington and Oregon, brown rot, which affects bloom and leaves of ornamental cherries and other stone fruit such as peach, apricots, and plums. Knowing that the plant's in the stone fruit group will help you and others diagnose the difficulty properly. Without plant identification, it's impossible to diagnose the problem accurately.

Gather information. Observe the plant carefully. When did the problem begin? Is it getting worse? What part of the plant is affected? Having a list of questions and observations will help experts provide you with assistance. Even snapping some photos of the plant as the problem progresses may be helpful. Take your question to a full-service nursery or to garden advisors like the WSU and OSU Master Gardeners. When you do go for advice, take along, if possible, a part of the plant that looks normal as well as a sample of the affected part.

Quite often, the plant diagnostician will inform you that the difficulty's not caused by any pest—no disease or insect problems can be found—but the plant is suffering from problems caused by something related to how it's been grown. A beautiful winter-blooming shrub like sweetbox (*Sarcococca* species) will develop yellowed leaves if placed in too much light. Move it to a shadier spot, and the leaf color recovers. University Extension diagnosticians estimate that about two-thirds of problems brought into plant clinics are the result of cultural conditions rather than pests. This always surprises gardeners, but it's actually good news because it means the problem can often be dealt with by changing the way we're siting plants in gardens and taking care of them.

Collecting the plant's samples will also help you if you choose to search the Internet for plant problem identification. University web sites, particularly those connected with land-grant colleges, can be helpful. (See pages 247 for Internet sites.)

Tolerate some damage. I've been known to say that when I reach personal perfection, I'll expect it in my plants. Being alive, no matter where in the biology of the universe, means imperfection. Variations in growth and loss of some leaf surface to insects or diseases will occur, and often the best choice is to decide on a level of damage you can ignore, once you have identified the difficulty and know it won't be a long-term health problem for the plant. Often you will find that no action is needed: plants will often outgrow a problem, or the effect is relatively insignificant and won't harm the plant in its future growth.

Encourage birds and beneficial insects. By planting a variety of different plants, providing a water source, and limiting your use of toxic insecticides that target the good as well as the bad, you'll care for your best garden allies. Birds thrive on many types of insects. The beneficial insects, both the familiar such as lady beetles and the less known such as small parasitic wasps, will attack aphids, leafminers, and other plant damagers.

Watch for both predatory lady beetles (lady bugs) and their larvae, the alligator-shaped orange and black stage. Lady beetle larvae eat large quantities of aphids while bulking up for pupating. The surest way to have lady beetles stay in your own landscape is to have them born there, from a resident population of adults. Bags of purchased lady bugs will seldom remain in your garden; they respond to release by flying, exactly as they would at the end of a hibernation stage.

Choose a management strategy. Once you've identified the plant and the problem, choose the least toxic and most environmentally sensible control method. Check with the WSU website, Hortsense, for recommendations on specific problems (linked from gardening.wsu.edu). Or check with Oregon State University at http:/eesc.orst.edu/agcomwebfile/garden.

Management in the garden can often start with finding a pest-resistant substitute for the affected plant. For instance, rhododendrons in Washington and Oregon suffer from leaf edge chewing by root weevils, notching the margins. Because rhododendron leaves persist on the plants in the landscape and contribute to the year-round look of the plants, the notching bothers gardeners. By checking with nurseries, you can select rhododendrons resistant to that problem, including yellow 'Crest', white 'Dora Amateis', and pink 'Point Defiance'.

One good management approach would be to move the seriously chewed rhododendron to a more remote part of the garden. And place the new, resistant cultivar in a prominent spot such as next to the front door. Another useful technique is to avoid planting types of plants that recurrently and predictably suffer from disease or insect problems. Or if you plant them, recognize that they will require some extra work.

Despite its glorious beauty, the ornamental cherry is typically difficult to manage in western Washington. Mild, rainy spring days predispose ornamental and fruiting cherries to a fungal problem called "brown rot," aptly named for the damage that appears on leaves and blooms. Similarly, certain dogwood species succumb regularly to attacks of "dogwood anthracnose," which affects both the native western dogwood (*Cornus nutallii*) and the eastern dogwood (*Cornus florida*). You'll find that the *Washington & Oregon Gardener's Guide* recommends choosing Korean dogwood (*Cornus kousa*), which has elegant June blooms and considerable resistance to fungal disease. Working with your favorite nursery, you'll often find help in selecting plants that are not only beautiful, but sturdy and relatively trouble-free. Removing a plant because it's constantly afflicted with disease or insect problems can make the gardener's life easier. Remember, saying good-bye to a troublesome plant is no sin!

Read labels and keep records. No matter what the choice of garden chemicals, from the nontoxic to the more toxic, read the label carefully. Pesticide labels are technical, and not always user-friendly, but they are mandatory for using products properly. Read the label before purchasing it, before mixing it, before storing it, and before disposing of it. Look closely at the section on "Hazard to Humans and Domestic Animals" and at the "Environmental Hazards." Sometimes close reading of the label will lead you to choose a less-toxic product.

Wrap labels with wide, clear plastic package tape, including any detachable fold-out instructions. Keep all label information together with the product; you need all the instructions to correctly mix and use the product.

Keep a small notebook that indicates what you did, when, the plant's condition, and even weather, such as temperature when applied. Record the results after observing how the plant responds. Such records will save time and money later (and I've learned not to trust memory for such details!).

We can take our garden difficulties more calmly when we recognize that many are normal parts of the garden cycle. Two of the most common and determined problems Northwest gardeners face are aphids and our favorite mollusk, the slug. Here are some specific tips for dealing with their presence.

Aphids

Aphids, small oval-shaped sucking insects, damage plants by taking sap. They multiply prolifically, with many generations per summer. Encouraging the presence of birds and beneficial insects in your garden will help reduce their numbers. And gardeners can take some simple actions while waiting to see aphid populations decrease from predator activity. Put on a glove and "wipe or squish" them off stems. The "squish" method works well for small populations of aphids on growing tips of shrubs like roses. Washing the aphids off with a gentle spray of water also works but needs to be done frequently as the aphids multiply, every three days.

If you choose to use chemical controls for aphids, choose the least toxic. Think of your garden allies when selecting the pesticide! Insecticidal soaps have low toxicity. But avoid applying insecticidal soaps when hot sun is striking the plant, because it can burn the leaves then. Cover both sides of leaves, because aphids will be lurking everywhere. Another less toxic control, neem oil, also works against aphids.

Some gardeners choose to replace plants that are severely and regularly attacked by aphids (such as birch trees or herbaceous perennial lupine). Fortunately, our gardens will never be entirely aphid-free, because the food source is necessary to support beneficial insects and birds.

Slugs

Most gardeners will see both slugs and snails. Introduced European garden slugs have been joined by their snail relatives, mollusks with attitude as well as shells. Both types rummage through Northwest gardens for breakfast, lunch, dinner, and snacks. (The native slugs like the banana slug seldom damage gardens and should be protected as beneficial.)

Cold winter weather, especially with temperatures below freezing, reduces slug and snail activity but doesn't kill them during mild winters. Gardeners west of the Cascades should start checking as tender bulb shoots emerge in January to be sure they aren't being scooped hollow by mollusks.

These pests seek damp, protected places. They often tuck themselves against walls or stones, or hide under rock garden plants like candytuft. Look for and destroy their eggs—small, off-white, and round, resembling small heaps of pearls (40 to 120 per pile). Many dedicated Northwest gardeners hand-pick slugs from plants.

Controlling them means using traps and possibly baits in addition to hand-picking. Snails, like slugs, are attracted to saucers of beer freshly laid for them on the ground. Copper-strip barriers around raised wood bed edges and containers will repel them if the strip is at least 3 inches wide—wider than they can "bridge" by stretching. (Slugs, after all, give flexibility a whole new meaning.)

Slug baits, chemicals formulated to kill them, will work but should be used with caution. Remember that "baits" attract pests, and it's better to place the bait slightly away from the valuable plant, not directly around it! I once ringed a prize lily with slug bait and gathered in a splendid crop of slugs, which hadn't noticed it before that. A newer bait type containing iron (ferric) phosphate is far less toxic that the older metaldehyde baits, which can harm or even kill pets and wildlife that may eat them. Read and follow all label instructions on any pesticide you choose.

Don't rely on just one method of control; combine hand-picking, trapping, and other methods. You can manage, though never eliminate, snails and slugs. And think of the long silences in gardener conversation if they were gone!

—MR

Public Gardens

The Pacific Northwest has no shortage of superior display gardens to visit. These living laboratories offer an excellent introduction to uncommon and beloved plant collections. They show us the mature size of trees, shrubs, and conifers, not to mention design ideas for the residential landscape. Many feature docent-led tours, host symposia and workshops, and sell plants propagated from their collection. Please take the time to contact the gardens in advance to confirm days and times that they are open to the public. Some gardens are open by appointment only.

The gardens listed here—and numerous others worthy of your attention—are featured in *The Northwest Gardeners' Resource Directory*, 9th edition, for which Debra Prinzing served as editor (Sasquatch Books, 2002).

Oregon

Eugene

Mount Pisgah Arboretum
34901 Frank Parrish Rd.
Eugene, OR 97405
541-741-4110
www.efn.org/~mtpisgah

Mount Pisgah Arboretum is a 209-acre living tree museum. Its riverside trails, quiet paths through evergreen forests, water garden, wildflower meadows, and open views across oak savannas will introduce you to Oregon's natural and cultivated beauty. Species rhododendrons, woody plants, and native trees are a highlight.

Portland

Berry Botanic Garden
11505 S.W. Summerville Ave.
Portland, OR 97219
503-636-4112
www.berrybot.org

Visit to see an outstanding collection of perennials, ferns, shrubs, and trees. Berry Botanic Garden houses a seed bank for rare and endangered plants native to the Pacific Northwest.

Crystal Springs Rhododendron Garden
S.E. 28th and S.E. Woodstock Blvd.
Portland, OR 97286
503-771-8386
www.parks.ci.portland.or.us/Parks/CrysSpringRhodGar.htm

This 7-acre garden features more than 2,500 hybrid and species rhododendrons. Enjoy rhododendrons planted with companions including azaleas, magnolias, dogwoods, Japanese maples, and other ornamental trees and shrubs.

Hoyt Arboretum
4000 S.W. Fairview Blvd.
Portland, OR 97221
503-228-TREE (8733)
www.hoytarboretum.org

Portland's urban forest of 185 acres features 950 species of trees and shrubs and ten miles of hiking trails. A visit will introduce you to a wide range of woody plants, including collections of oaks, magnolias, and maples. Of special interest is a collection of Oregon's own Brewer's weeping spruce (*Picea breweriana*), which are very rare.

Leach Botanical Garden
6704 S.E. 122nd Ave.
Portland, OR 97236
503-823-9503
www.parks.ci.portland.or.us/Parks/LeachBotanicalGar.htm

This 25-year-old public garden is dedicated to the exhibition and botanical study of plants of the Pacific Northwest. Take note of the special collection of woodland beauties, including trillium. Ornamental shrubs to see include camellia, viburnum, and *Kalmiopsis leachiana*, which was introduced by founder Lilla Leach.

Portland Rose Gardens
400 S.W. Kingston Ave.
Portland, OR 97201
503-823-3636
www.parks.ci.portland.or.us/Parks/RoseGardens.htm
www.portlandrosesociety.org

Portland is home to one of the world's most famous rose gardens, the International Rose Test Garden. With spectacular views and more than 8,000 roses, this signature landmark features three terraces set on 4.5 acres. Peak bloom is June and July, but you can enjoy roses in bloom through October.

Silverton

The Oregon Garden
879 W. Main St.
Silverton, OR 97381
503-874-8100 or 877-674-2733
www.oregongarden.org

This garden showcases Oregon's best plants and design styles, including specialty displays representing many horticultural themes—from edible and children's gardens to a dazzling conifer garden and rose collection. Enjoy ongoing educational programs sponsored by some of Oregon's top growers and nurseries.

Washington

Bainbridge Island

Bloedel Reserve
7571 N.E. Dolphin Dr.
Bainbridge Island, WA 97110
206-842-7631
www.bloedelreserve.org

Visit the 150-acre reserve on the former estate of the Bloedel family. Here, surrounded by 84 acres of second-growth forest, is a series of established gardens designed by some of the Northwest's notable landscape architects. Japanese and European styles influence this amazing landscape. Enjoy the native woodland, bird refuge, rhododendrons, wildflower meadow, and lush moss garden, among other delightful scenes. This is an especially delightful garden to visit in late winter.

Bellevue

Bellevue Botanic Garden
12001 Main St.
Bellevue, WA 98005
425-452-2750
www.bellevuebotanical.org

In addition to the world-class Northwest Perennial Alliance perennial borders (12,000 square feet of mixed herbaceous plantings), the BBG features a water-wise demonstration garden with a diverse selection of plants that thrive in the Northwest's dry summer climate. An alpine rock garden, a fuchsia display, and a rhododendron garden are among the many points of interest in this 36-acre garden.

Everett

Evergreen Arboretum & Gardens
Legion Memorial Park, Alverson Avenue and West Marine View Drive
Everett, WA 98201
425-257-8300
www.evergreenarboretum.com

Planted with the Master Gardener Perennial border, Dahlia garden, Water Conservation garden, Japanese Maple grove, Woodland garden, and the Dwarf Conifer garden, the Arboretum offers ideas pertinent to today's home gardener and relaxed enjoyment of a peaceful, beautiful setting.

Federal Way

Rhododendron Species Botanical Garden
2525 S. 336th St.
Federal Way, WA 98003
253-838-4646
www.rhodygarden.org

A 22-acre woodland setting is home to one of the largest rhododendron collections in the world. Thousands of blooming rhododendrons make this garden a spectacular sight in March, April, and May. Complementing the rhododendrons are numerous companion plantings of ferns, primroses, iris, heathers, maples, magnolias, conifers, and many other exotic and unusual plants.

Mt. Vernon

Discovery Garden
Mt. Vernon/WSU Research & Extension Unit
16602 State Route 536 (Memorial Hwy.)
Mt. Vernon, WA 98273
360-428-4270
http://skagit.wsu.edu/mg/discovery-gardens.htm

Skagit County Master Gardeners have developed an extensive display garden with appealing themes, including a therapeutic "enabling garden," a "naturescaping garden" demonstrating yard-to-wildlife transitions, and an ethnobotany/herb garden focusing on historical plant uses. The ornamental area features a Cottage Garden, Japanese Garden, Shade Garden, Hot and Cool Color Borders, Fall and Winter Gardens, Heather Garden, Iris Garden, Fuchsia Garden, and Ground Cover Garden.

Seattle

Carl S. English Jr. Botanical Garden (at the Hiram M. Chittenden Locks)
3015 N.W. 54th St.
Seattle, WA 98107
206-783-7059

In a 7.5-acre site along the north side of the Chittenden Locks, this hidden treasure of a botanical garden is home to exotic trees, shrubs, and herbaceous plants (about 800 species). The garden is named after a leading horticulturist of the 20th century, who obtained plant material for this garden from around the Pacific Rim. Visit Seattle Fuchsia Society's demonstration garden in August and Puget Sound Daylily Society's demonstration garden throughout the summer.

Center for Urban Horticulture
3501 N.E. 41st St.
Seattle, WA 98195
206-543-8616
www.urbanhort.org

Home of the Miller Horticultural Library, the Center for Urban Horticulture is also an educational destination for hands-on gardening ideas, including the Orin and Althea Soest Herbaceous Display Garden. Planted in a circular display are eight pie-shaped beds featuring more that 250 plants in a variety of conditions (with soil, light, and water variables) so you can select plants to grow in similar conditions at home. When you visit, pick up a free brochure with site-specific plant lists.

Washington Park Arboretum
2300 Arboretum Dr. E.
Seattle, WA 98112
206-726-1954
www.arboretumfoundation.org

A Northwest treasure, the Arboretum is a 230-acre living museum of woody plants, with internationally renowned collections of oaks, conifers, camellias, Japanese maples, hollies, and other plants from the Pacific Northwest and nearly every temperate region of the world.

Shoreline

Kruckeberg Botanic Garden
20312 15th Ave. N.W.
Shoreline, WA 98177
206-542-4777
www.kruckeberg.org

Mareen and Arthur Kruckeberg amassed the garden's 4-acre plant collection over many years. It is rich in variety, both of native plants of the Pacific Northwest and exotic species from other lands.

Spokane

Finch Arboretum
3404 W. Woodland Blvd.
Spokane, WA 98
509-624-4832

Finch Arboretum is a 65-acre botanical garden with a collection of more than 2,000 ornamental, trees, shrubs, and perennials, representing more than 600 species.

Manito Park

S. Grand at 18th Ave.
Spokane, WA
509-625-6622
www.thefriendsofmanito.org

Founded in 1905, Manito Park is enjoying a renaissance among area gardeners. As Spokane's showcase of gardens, Manito Park includes Nishinomiya Japanese Garden, a rose garden, the French Renaissance-style Duncan Garden, and gardens featuring lilacs, perennials, and conservatory plants.

Tacoma

Pt. Defiance Park

5400 N. Pearl St.
Tacoma, W 98405
253-305-1070
www.metroparkstacoma.org/parks/point-defiance.view

Acres of gardens with sculptures, waterfalls, and thousands of flowers create beautiful displays throughout the city. Thematic gardens, including a Japanese Garden, Rose Garden, and Northwest Native Garden provide a wide variety of horticultural experiences for visitors.

Whidbey Island

Meerkerk Rhododendron Gardens

3531 Meerkerk Lane
Whidbey Island, WA 98253
360-678-1912
www.meerkerkgardens.org

Known as Whidbey Island's peaceful woodland garden, this 53-acre site was once home to Max and Ann Meerkerk. Plantings showcase more than 1,800 rhododendron varieties (species and hybrids) and include extensive displays of companion plants. This is a magical place with something delightful blooming every month of the year.

Wenatchee

Ohme Gardens

3327 Ohme Rd.
Wenatchee, WA 98801
509-662-5785
www.ohmegardens.com

A hidden gem of a garden, Ohme Gardens captivates visitors to this rocky bluff where flagstone paths, hidden grottos, and lush plantings transport them to an alpine paradise. Evergreen trees, alpine and rock garden plantings, and meadow plants make this a wonderful destination any time of the year.

Yakima

Yakima Area Arboretum & Botanical Garden

1401 Arboretum Drive
Yakima, Washington 98901
509-248-7337
www.ahtrees.org

Encompassing 46 acres, the Yakima Area Arboretum is a living museum and botanical garden. The semiarid climate of Central Washington (also known as the Columbia River Basin) provides unique conditions for the display and study of native and exotic species of woody plants. There are over 2,000 specimens in the Arboretum's collection.

—DP

Plant Sources for Washington & Oregon Gardeners

When it comes to choosing plants for your garden, there's nothing quite as satisfying as shopping at a local nursery or garden center where you can examine the health and vigor of a plant, compare different cultivars, and talk with experienced plant sellers. Other great sources for plants are the various plant sales staged in most counties by Master Gardener volunteers or by your local arboretum, botanical garden, or horticultural society. These events give you a chance to meet the growers and discover plants you may never before have seen. Take advantage of the local treasures in your own backyard.

As you experiment with the style of garden you're growing and as you begin expanding your own plant repertoire, you may begin relying on mail-order sources for plants and seeds. Many nurseries publish online catalogues that include fabulous color photography of the plants they sell. When you can't be gardening, either in the evening or during cold weather, you can learn a lot by reading catalogues and browsing the web (see page 247 for more website addresses).

—DP

A&D Nursery
P.O. Box 2338
Snohomish, WA 98291
360-668-9690 or 800-668-9290
www.adpeonies.com
Peonies, daylilies, and hostas

Adelman Peony Gardens
5690 Brooklake Road N.E.
Salem, OR 97305-9660
503-393-6185
www.peonyparadise.com
Herbaceous peonies

All Season Nursery
3829 Pleasant Hill Rd.
Kelso, WA 98626
360-577-7955
Full-service nursery

Antique Rose Farm
12220 Springhetti Rd.
Snohomish, WA 98296
360-568-1919
Old garden and modern roses

Bainbridge Gardens
9415 Miller Rd. N.E.
Bainbridge Island, WA 98110
206-842-5888
www.bainbridgegardens.com
Full-service nursery

B&D Lilies
P.O. Box 2007
Pt. Townsend, WA 98368
360-765-4341
www.bdlilies.com
Hybrid and species lilies

Barn Owl Nursery
22999 S.W. Newland Road
Wilsonville, OR 97070
503-638-0387
Herbs, including lavender and rosemary

Bassetti's Crooked Arbor Gardens
18512 N.E. 165th St.
Woodinville, WA 97072
425-788-6767
www.bassettisgardens.com
Dwarf conifers and alpines

Bosky Dell Natives
23111 S.W. Bosky Dell Lane
West Linn, OR 997068
503-638-5945
www.boskydellnatives.com
Oregon native plants

Christianson's Nursery & Greenhouse
15806 Best Rd.
Mt. Vernon, WA 98273
360-466-3821 or 800-585-8200
www.christiansonsnursery.com
Full-service nursery

Cistus Design Nursery
22711 N.W. Gillihan Rd.
Sauvie Island, OR 97231
503-621-2233
www.cistus.com
Asian, Mediterranean, and Northwest plants

Cooley's Gardens Inc.
11553 Silverton Rd. N.E.
Silverton, OR 97381
503-873-5463 or 800-225-5391
www.cooleysgardens.com
Bearded irises

Cornell Farm
8212 SW Barnes Rd.
Portland, OR 97225
503-292-9895
Perennials and annuals

Cultus Bay Nursery
7568 Cultus Bay Rd.
Clinton, WA 98236
360-579-2329
Perennials

DIG Floral & Garden
19028 Vashon Hwy. S.W.
Vashon, WA 98070
206-463-5096
Trees, shrubs, and perennials

Edmunds' Roses
6235 S.W. Kahle Rd.
Wilsonville, OR 97070
503-682-1476 or 888-481-7673
www.edmundsroses.com
Modern roses

Emery's Garden
2829 164th St. S.W.
Lynnwood, WA 98037
425-743-4555
www.emerysgarden.com
Full-service nursery

Fairie Perennial and Herb Gardens Nursery
6236 Elm St. S.E.
Tumwater, WA 97501
360-754-9249
www.fairiegardens.net
Herbs, perennials, and dwarf conifers

Fancy Fronds
P.O. Box 1090
Gold Bar, WA 98251
360-793-1472
www.fancyfronds.com
Ferns

Forestfarm
990 Tetherow Road
Williams, OR 97544-9599
541-846-7269
www.forestfarm.com
Northwest natives and ornamental trees, shrubs,
    vines, and perennials

Fremont Gardens
4001 Leary Way N.W.
Seattle, WA 98107
206-781-8283
www.fremontgardens.com
Perennials

Heaths and Heathers
502 E. Haskell Hill Rd.
Shelton, WA 98584
360-427-5318 or 800-294-3284
www.heathsandheathers.com
Heaths and heathers

Heronswood Nursery
7530 N.E. 288th St.
Kingston, WA 98346
360-297-4172
www.heronswood.com
Trees, shrubs, perennials, and hellebores

Gossler Farm Nursery
1200 Weaver Rd.
Springfield, OR 97478-9663
541-746-6611
Magnolias, ornamental trees, and shrubs

Greer Gardens
1280 Goodpasture Island Rd.
Eugene, OR 97401-1794
541-686-8266 or 800-548-0111
www.greergardens.com
Rhododendrons and Japanese maples

Wallace W. Hansen, Nursery & Gardens
2158 Bower Ct. S.E.
Salem, OR 997301
503-581-2638
www.nwplants.com
Northwest natives and wetland plants

Hedgerows Nursery
20165 S.W. Christenson Rd.
McMinnville, OR 97128
503-843-7522
Perennials, shrubs, and vines

Heirloom Roses
24062 Riverside Dr. N.E.
St. Paul, OR 97137
503-538-1576
www.heirloomroses.com
Roses

Joy Creek Nursery
20300 N.W. Watson Rd.
Scappoose, OR 97056
503-543-7474
www.joycreek.com
Perennials and clematis

McComb Road Nursery
751 McComb Rd.
Sequim, WA 98382
360-681-2827
www.mccombroadnursery.com
Full-service nursery

Molbak's Nursery
13625 N.E. 175th St.
Woodinville, WA 98072
425-483-5000
www.molbaks.com
Full-service nursery

Naylor Creek Nursery
2610 West Valley Rd.
Chimacum, WA 98325
360-732-4983
www.naylorcreek.com
Hostas and shade perennials

Nichols Garden Nursery
1190 Old Salem Rd.
Albany, OR 97321-4580
541-928-9280 or 800-422-3985
www.nicholsgardennursery.com
Seed source for herbs and vegetables

Northwest Garden Nursery
86813 Central Rd.
Eugene, OR 97402
541-935-3915
Perennials, vines, and shrubs

One Green World
28696 S. Cramer Rd.
Molalla, OR 97038-8576
503-651-3005 or 877-353-4028
www.onegreenworld.com
Edible fruit and ornamental trees

Piriformis
1051 N. 35th St.
Seattle, WA 98103
206-632-1760
www.piriformis.com
Drought-tolerant and low-maintenance plants

Portland Nursery
5050 S.E. Stark St.
Portland, OR 97215
503-231-5050
www.portlandnursery.com
Full-service nursery

Raintree Nursery
391 Butts Rd.
Morton, WA 98356
360-496-6400 or 888-496-8358.
www.raintreenursery.com
Edible and ornamental trees and shrubs

Ravenna Gardens
(check website for other locations)
2580 N.E. University Village
Seattle, WA 98105
206-729-7388
www.ravennagardens.com
Perennials, trees, and shrubs

Schreiner's Iris Gardens
3625 Quinaby Rd. N.E.
Salem, OR 97303
503-393-3232 or 800-525-2367
www.schreinersgardens.com
Bearded iris

Siskiyou Rare Plant Nursery
2825 Cummings Rd.
Medford, OR 97501
541-772-6846
www.siskiyourareplantnursery.com
Alpine and rockery plants

Sky Nursery
18528 Aurora Ave. N.
Shoreline, WA 98133
206-546-4851
www.skynursery.com
Full-service nursery; trees

Squaw Mountain Gardens
P.O. Box 946
Estacada, OR 97023
503-637-3585
www.squawmountaingardens.com
Sedums and succulents

Steamboat Island Nursery
8424 Steamboat Island Rd.
Olympia, WA 98502
360-866-2516
www.olywa.net/steamboat/
Trees, shrubs, perennials, and vines

Swan's Trail Gardens
7021 61st Ave. S.E.
Snohomish, WA 98290
425-334-4595
www.swanstrailgardens.com

Tower Perennials
4010 E. Jamieson Rd.
Spokane, WA 99223
509-448-6778
www.towerflower.com
Hostas and other perennials

Wells Medina Nursery
8300 N.E. 24th St.
Medina, WA 98039
425-454-1853
Trees, conifers, shrubs, vines, and perennials

Glossary

Alkaline soil: Soil with a pH greater than 7.0. It lacks acidity, often because it has limestone in it.

All-purpose fertilizer: Powdered, liquid, or granular fertilizer with a balanced proportion of the three key nutrients—nitrogen (N), phosphorus (P), and potassium (K). It is suitable for maintenance nutrition for most plants.

Annual: A plant that lives its entire life in one season. It is genetically determined to germinate, grow, flower, set seed, and die the same year.

Balled and burlapped: describes a tree or shrub grown in the field whose soilball was wrapped with protective material and twine when the plant was dug for sale.

Bare root: A plant without any soil around its roots, available in nurseries when dormant. (Young shrubs and trees purchased through the mail often arrive with their exposed roots covered with moist peat or sphagnum moss, sawdust, or similar material, and wrapped in plastic.)

Beneficial insects: Insects or their larvae that prey on pest organisms and their eggs. They may be flying insects, such as lady beetles, parasitic wasps, praying mantis, and soldier bugs; soil dwellers, such as predatory nematodes; or arachnids, such as spiders.

Berm: An area of added soil to provide a planting space, usually 1 to 3 feet high; or a narrow raised ring of soil around a tree, used to hold water so it will be directed to the root zone.

Bract: A modified leaf structure on a plant stem near its flower that resembles a petal. Often it is more colorful and visible than the actual flower, as in dogwood and poinsettia.

Bud union: The place where the top of a plant was grafted to the rootstock; usually refers to roses.

Canopy: The overhead branching area of a tree, usually referring to its total width including foliage.

Cold hardiness: The ability of a perennial plant to survive the lowest winter temperatures in a particular area.

Composite: A flower that is actually composed of many tiny flowers. Typically, they are flat clusters of tiny, tight florets, sometimes surrounded by wider petaled florets. Composite flowers are highly attractive to bees and beneficial insects.

Compost: Organic matter that has undergone progressive decomposition by microbial and macrobial activity Added to soil of any type, it improves the soil's ability to hold air and water and to drain well.

Corm: The swollen energy-storing structure, analogous to a bulb, at the base of the stem of plants such as crocus and gladiolus.

Crown: The base of a plant at, or just beneath, the surface of the soil where the roots meet the stems.

Cultivar: A CULTIvated VARiety. It is a naturally occurring form of a plant that has been purposely selected for propagation and production.

Deadhead: A pruning technique that removes faded flower heads from plants to improve their appearance, abort seed production, and stimulate further flowering.

Deciduous plants: Unlike conifers or broadleaf evergreens, these trees and shrubs lose their leaves in the fall.

Desiccation: The drying out of foliage tissues, usually due to drought or wind.

Division: Splitting perennial plants to create several smaller rooted segments. The practice is useful for controlling the plant's size and for acquiring more plants; it is also essential to the health and continued flowering of certain ones.

Dormancy: The period, usually the winter, when perennial plants temporarily cease active growth and rest. *Dormant* is the adjective form.

Established: The point at which a newly planted tree, shrub, or flower begins to produce new growth, either foliage or stems, when roots have recovered from transplant shock.

Evergreen: Perennial plants that do not lose their foliage annually with the onset of winter. Needled or broadleaf foliage persist and continue to function on a plant through one or more winters, aging and dropping in cycles of three or four years or more.

Foliar: Of or about foliage—usually refers to the practice of spraying foliage, as in fertilizing or treating with insecticide; leaf tissues absorb liquid directly for fast results.

Floret: A tiny flower, usually one of many forming a cluster, that comprises a single blossom.

Germinate: To sprout. Germination is a fertile seed's first stage of development.

Graft (union): The point on a woody plant where a stem from a highly ornamental plant is inserted so that it will join with it. Roses and tree peonies are often grafted.

Hardscape: The permanent, structural part of a landscape, such as walls, sheds, pools, patios, arbors, and walkways.

Herbaceous: Plants having stems that die back with frost; the opposite of woody.

Hybrid: A plant that is the result of intentional or natural cross-pollination between two or more plants of the same species or genus.

Low water demand: A plant's tolerance for dry soil for varying periods. Typically, such plants have succulent, hairy, or silvery-gray foliage and tuberous roots or taproots.

Mulch: A layer of material over bare soil to protect it from erosion and compaction by rain, and to discourage weeds. It may be inorganic (gravel, fabric) or organic (wood chips, bark, pine needles, chopped leaves).

Naturalize: *(a)* To plant seeds, bulbs, or plants in a random, informal pattern as they would appear in their natural habitat; *(b)* to adapt to and spread throughout adopted habitats.

Nectar: The sweet fluid produced by glands on flowers that attract pollinators, such as hummingbirds and honeybees, for whom it is a source of energy.

Organic material, organic matter: Any material or debris that is derived from plants. It is carbon-based material capable of undergoing decomposition and decay. We recommend finished compost over peat moss.

Perennial: A flowering plant that lives over two or more seasons. Many die back with frost, but their roots survive the winter and generate new growth in spring.

pH: A measurement of the relative acidity (low pH) or alkalinity (high pH) of soil or water based on a scale of 1 to 14, 7 being neutral. Individual plants require soil to be within a certain range so that nutrients are available to them.

Pinch: To remove tender stems or leaves (or both) by pressing them between thumb and forefinger. This pruning technique encourages branching, compactness, and flowering in plants.

Pollen: The yellow, powdery grains in the center of a flower. A plant's male sex cells, they are transferred to the female plant parts by means of wind or animal pollinators to fertilize them and create seeds.

Raceme: An arrangement of single-stalked flowers along an elongated, unbranched axis.

Rhizome: A swollen energy-storing stem structure, similar to a bulb, that lies horizontally in the soil, with roots emerging from its lower surface and growth shoots from a growing point, as in bearded iris.

Rootbound (or potbound): The condition of a plant that has been confined in a container too long, its roots having been forced to wrap around themselves and even swell out of the container. Successful transplanting or repotting requires untangling and trimming away matted roots.

Root flare: The transition at the base of a tree trunk where the bark tissue begins to differentiate and roots begin to form just before entering the soil. This area should not be covered with soil when planting a tree.

Self-seeding: The tendency of some plants to sow their seeds freely around the yard. It creates many seedlings the following season that may or may not be welcome.

Semievergreen: Tending to be evergreen in a mild climate but deciduous in a rigorous one.

Shear: The pruning technique whereby plant stems and branches are cut uniformly with long-bladed pruning shears (hedge shears) or powered hedge trimmers. It is used when creating and maintaining hedges and topiary.

Slow-acting fertilizer: Fertilizer that is water insoluble and therefore releases its nutrients gradually as a function of soil temperature, moisture, and related microbial activity. Typically granular, it may be organic or synthetic.

Succulent growth: The sometimes undesirable production of fleshy, water-storing leaves or stems that results from overfertilization or overwatering.

Sucker: A new growing shoot. Underground plant roots produce suckers to form new stems and spread by means of these suckering roots to form large plantings, or colonies. Some plants produce root suckers or branch suckers as a result of pruning or wounding.

Tuber: A type of underground storage structure in a plant stem, analogous to a bulb. It generates roots below and stems above ground (for example, dahlia or potato).

Variegated: Having various colors or color patterns. The term usually refers to plant foliage that is streaked, edged, blotched, or mottled with a contrasting color, often green with yellow, cream, or white.

Wings: *(a)* The corky tissue that forms edges along the twigs of some woody plants such as winged euonymus; *(b)* the flat, dried extension of tissue on some seeds, such as maple, that catch the wind and help them disseminate.

Bibliography

Armitage, Allan M. *Herbaceous Perennial Plants*. Athens, GA: Varsity Press, 1989.

Beck, Alison, and Marianne Binetti. *Annuals for Washington and Oregon*. Lone Pine Publishing, 2000.

Beck, Alison, and Marianne Binetti. *Perennials for Washington and Oregon*. Lone Pine Publishing, 2000.

Beck, Alison, and Marianne Binetti. *Tree & Shrub Gardening for Washington and Oregon*. Lone Pine Publishing, 2001.

Bloom, Adrian. *Gardening With Conifers*. Firefly Books Ltd, 2002.

Brenzel, Kathleen Norris, ed. *Sunset Western Garden Book*. Menlo Park, CA: Sunset Publishing Corp., 2001.

Brickell, Christopher, and Judith Zuk, eds. *The American Horticultural Society A-Z Encyclopedia of Garden Plants*. New York: DK Publishing, 1996.

Carter, George. *Herbs: A Garden Project Workbook*. Stewart, Tabori & Chang, 1997.

Cave, Yvonne. *Succulents for the Contemporary Garden*. Portland, OR: Timber Press, 2002.

Dirr, Michael A. *Dirr's Hardy Trees and Shrubs*. Portland, OR: Timber Press, 1997.

Dirr, Michael A. *Manual of Woody Landscape Plants*. Stipes Publishing, 1998.

DiSabato-Aust, Tracy. *The Well-Tended Perennial Garden*. Portland, OR: Timber Press, 1998.

Grant, John A., and Carol L. Grant. *Trees and Shrubs for Pacific Northwest Gardens*. Palo Alto, CA: Pacific Books, 1974 (first published 1943).

Hansen, Richard, and Friedrich Stahl. *Perennials and Their Garden Habitats*, Portland, OR: Timber Press, 1993.

Hart, Rhonda Massingham. *Northcoast Roses*. Seattle, WA: Sasquatch Books, 1993.

Heath, Brent, and Becky Heath. *Daffodils for American Gardens*. Washington, DC: Elliott & Clark Publishing, 1995.

Heath, Brent, and Becky Heath. *Tulips for North American Gardens*. Albany, TX: Bright Sky Press, 2001.

Hinkley, Dan. *Winter Ornamentals*. Seattle, WA: Sasquatch Books, 1993.

Hogan, Sean. *Flora: A Gardener's Encyclopedia*. Portland, OR: Timber Press, 2003.

Holmes, Roger, and Don Marshall. *Home Landscaping: Northwest Region Including Western British Columbia*. Upper Saddle River, NJ: Creative Homeowner, 2002.

Hume, Ed. *Gardening With Ed Hume*. Seattle, WA: Sasquatch Books, 2003.

Jacobson, Arthur Lee. *North American Landscape Trees*. Berkeley, CA: Ten Speed Press, 1996.

Jalbert, Brad, and Laura Peters. *Roses for Washington and Oregon*. Lone Pine Publishing, 2003.

Kruckeberg, Arthur. *Gardening With Native Plants of the Pacific Northwest*. Seattle, WA: Univ. of Wash. Press, 1982.

Link, Russell. *Landscaping for Wildlife in the Pacific Northwest*. Seattle, WA: Univ. of Wash. Press, 2003.

Mathew, Brian, and Philip Sweindeels. *The Complete Book of Bulbs, Corms, Tubers and Rhizomes*. Pleasantville, NY: Reader's Digest Association, 1994.

McNeilan, Ray, and Jan McNeilan. *The Pacific Northwest Gardener's Books of Lists*. Dallas, TX: Taylor Publishing Co., 1997.

Ondra, Nancy J. *Grasses: Versatile Partners for Uncommon Garden Design*. Storey Publishing, 2002.

Preus, Mary. *The Northwest Herb Lover's Handbook*. Seattle, WA: Sasquatch Books, 2000.

Schenk, George. *The Complete Shade Gardener*. Boston: Houghton Mifflin Company, 1984.

Smittle, Delilah (general ed.). *Carefree Plants*. Pleasantville, NY: Reader's Digest Association, Inc., 2002.

Still, Steven M. *Manual of Herbaceous Ornamental Plants*. Stipes Publishing, 1994.

Thomas, Graham Stuart. *Perennial Garden Plants*. Portland, OR: Timber Press, 1994 (first published 1976).

Thomas, Graham Stuart. *Ornamental Shrubs, Climbers, and Bamboo*. Portland, OR: Timber Press, 1994.

Thomas, Graham Stuart. *The Rose Book*. Portland, OR: Timber Press, 1994.

Turnbull, Cass. *Guide to Pruning*. Seattle, WA: Sasquatch Books, 2004.

Winterrowd, Wayne. *Annuals and Tender Plants for North American Gardens*. NY: Random House, 2004.

Oregon State University and Washington State University Extension Publications:

Cogger, Dr. Craig. "Soil Management in Yards and Gardens," EB 1102, WSU Extension, 1994.

Cook, Dr. Tom. "Maintaining a Healthy Lawn in Western Oregon," EC1521, OSU Extension, 2000.

Hunter, Raymond. "Establishing a Lawn in Eastern Washington," EB1153, WSU Extension, 2000.

Fitzgerald, Tonie. "Landscaping With Native Plants in the Inland Northwest," MISC 0267, WSU Extension, 2000. Revised 2003.

Maleike, Dr. Ray, and George Pinyuh. "Fertilizing Landscape Trees and Shrubs," EB 1034, WSU Extension, 1991.

McNeilan, Ray, and Ann Marie VanDer Zanden. "Plant Materials for Landscaping: A List of Plants for the Pacific NW," PNW 0500, OSU Extension, 1998.

Stahnke, Dr. Gwen. "Home Lawns," EB 0482, WSU Extension, rev. 2004.

Stahnke, Dr. Gwen, et al. "Watering Home Garden and Landscape Plants," EB 1090, WSU Extension, 1994.

Photography Credits

Thomas Eltzroth: pages 13, 19, 23, 24, 25, 27, 30, 31, 33, 34, 35, 36, 37, 38, 40, 41, 42, 45, 46, 49, 50, 51, 53, 56, 57, 60, 63, 65, 66, 68, 69, 72, 75, 78, 79, 80, 81, 82, 83, 84, 87, 88, 90, 92, 94, 96, 97, 98, 99, 100, 101, 103, 106, 107, 108, 109, 111, 113, 114, 115, 120, 121, 122, 124, 125, 126, 128, 129, 131, 132, 133, 134, 136, 140, 143, 146, 147, 148, 150, 151, 153, 157, 158, 159, 160, 164, 165, 166, 167, 168, 169, 170, 173, 177, 178, 179, 182, 186, 187, 188, 189, 190, 194, 195, 197, 199, 203, 206, 207, 208, 216, 220, 231, 232, 245, and the first, third, and fourth photos on the back cover

Jerry Pavia: pages 15, 26, 29, 32, 59, 73, 74, 85, 91, 93, 110, 112, 137, 139, 144, 145, 149, 155, 161, 162, 171, 172, 176, 180, 181, 183, 184, 191, 196, 200, 202, 212, 221, 222, 224, 229, 230, 233

Liz Ball and Rick Ray: pages 22, 39, 44, 58, 61, 76, 95, 135, 141, 204, 205, 209, 211, 213, 214, 215, 217, 218, 219, 225, 227, 237, 241, and the second photo on the back cover

Charles Mann: pages 43, 48, 55, 70, 123, 185, 192, 223, 240

Felder Rushing: pages 16, 64, 89, 127, 198, 238

Mark Turner/Turner Photographics®: the front cover, and pages 8, 62, 142, 156, 226

Dr. Mike Dirr: pages 71, 210, 243, 244

Pam Harper: pages 67, 175, 201, 228

André Viette: pages 130, 234, 235, 236

William (Bill) Adams: pages 10, 11, 86

Dency Kane: pages 116, 138, 242

The Netherlands Flower Bulb Information Center: pages 47, 54

Cathy Barash: page 154

Laura Coit: page 77

Lorenzo Gunn: page 174

Dr. Bob Lyons: page 239

Mary Robson: page 193

Ralph Snodsmith: pages 52

David Winger: page 152

William Wright Photography: page 272 (both photos)

Bill Kersey: all illustrations

Authors' Caution: Gardening is a joyful and rewarding practice; however, we urge you to approach the use of any tools or amendments with responsibility. Educate yourself on the proper use of sharp tools before you begin digging, cutting, or cultivating areas of the garden. Wear appropriate clothing that will protect you from scrapes, cuts, or exposure to plants that are potentially poisonous or toxic. Gloves and sturdy footwear are recommended whenever you're gardening. You should consider using protective eyewear to avoid irritants. Read all labels on gardening products and/or amendments and follow the directions provided. In other words, the more you educate yourself, the more you'll succeed at gardening!

Index

Featured plant selections are indicated in **boldface**.

Sorbus aria, 223
Sorbus hupehensis, 223
Sorbus scopulina, 223
Sorbus species, 223
sorrel tree, 229
sourwood, 229
Spanish
  fir, 68
  lavender, 143
spirea, 196, 213
  bridal wreath, 196
  false, 122
Spirea japonica, 196
Spirea species and cultivars, 196
Spirea × vanhouttei, 196
spurge, 156
  Allegheny, 94
  cushion, 156
  donkey-tail, 156
  Japanese, 94, 95
St. Augustine, 101
stachys, 61
staghorn sumac, 198
stewartia
  Japanese, 219
  Korean, 219
  tall, 219
Stewartia koreana, 219
Stewartia monadelpha, 219
Stewartia pseudocamellia, 219
stonecrop, 87, 153
strawberry
  geranium, 98
  tree, 179, **197**
    Killarney, 197
styrax, 218
Styrax japonicus, 218
Styrax obassia, 218
sumac, 195, **198**
  Chinese, 198
  flameleaf, 198
  smooth, 198
  staghorn, 198
  tree, 68
sunflower, 30, 42, **43**, 113, 126, 158
  golden, 43
Sutera cordata, 26
swamp maple, 226
sweet
  box, 179, 186, **199**
    Himalayan, 199
  pea, 44
  potato vine, 45, 128
  woodruff, 76, 127
Swiss mountain pine, 69
switch grass, 109, 113
sword fern, 123, **157**, 174, 179, 199
Syringa patula, 185
Syringa species, 185
Tagetes erecta, 38
Tagetes patula, 38
Tagetes species and cultivars, 38
Tagetes tenuifolia, 38
tall stewartia, 219
tam juniper, 72, 96
tamarack, 74
Taxus brevifolia, 77
Taxus × media species and cultivars, 77
tea rose, 168, 170

Teucrium chamaedrys, 134
Teucrium fruticans, 134
thistle, globe, 152
three-flowered maple, 224
thrift, sea, 146
Thuja occidentalis species and
  cultivars, 66
Thuja plicata, 75
thyme
  common, 88
  creeping, 88, 146
  elfin, 88
  prostrate, 88
  red, 88
  woolly, 88
Thymus praecox articus, 88
Thymus pseudolanuginosus, 88
Thymus serphyllum ssp., 88
Thymus vulgaris, 88
tickseed, 158, 159
tobacco, flowering, 33, 40
tomato, 40
torch lily, 150
trillium, 58, 76
Trillium ovatum, 127
Tropaeolum majus, 39
trumpet lily, 60
Tsuga canadensis, 73
Tsuga heterophylla, 73
Tsuga mertensiana, 73
tuberous begonia, 27
tulip, 56, 58, 59, **63**, 74, 127, 136, 139,
  142, 185, 194, 212
  tree, 227
Tulipa fosteriana, 63
Tulipa species and hybrids, 63
Tulipa tarda, 63
turf-type tall fescue, 101
Vaccinium ovatum, 179
Vancouveria chrysantha, 137
Vancouveria hexandra, 137
Vancouveria planipelata, 137
Vancouveria species, 137
variegated kiwi, 244
Verbena bonariensis, 31
Verbena × hybrida, 31
verbena
  Brazilian, 31
  garden, 31
viburnum, 200
  Burkwood, 200
  cranberry bush, 200
  dwarf, 213
  Korean spice, 200
Viburnum × bodnantense, 200
Viburnum × burkwoodii, 200
Viburnum carlesii, 200
Viburnum opulus, 200
Viburnum plicatum f. *tomentosum*, 200
Viburnum × rhytidophyllum, 200
Viburnum species and cultivars, 200
vinca, 52, **99**
Vinca major, 99
Vinca minor, 99
Vinca minor f. *alba*, 99
Vinca species, 99
vine maple, 68, **230**
  cut leaf, 230
viola, 168

violet, 142
Vitis coignetiae, 243
  'Purpurea', 243
Vitis vinifera, 243
wall germander, 134
wax
  begonia, 27
  myrtle, 123, 138, 188
    Pacific, 188, 189
weeping
  Japanese larch, 74
  willow, Babylon, 231
western
  azalea, 175
  cedar, 77
  hemlock, 73
  larch, 74
  native yew, 77
  red cedar, 73, **75**, 94
  white pine, 76
  yellow pine, 70
white
  cedar, 66
  goddess flowering cherry, 212
  pine, 76
    eastern, 76, 226
    western, 76
  rockrose, 194
  sage, 120
  striped bamboo, dwarf, 89
  willow, 231
whitebeam ash, 223
wild
  lilac, 96
  rose, 166
willow, 74, **231**
  Babylon weeping, 231
  creeping, 231
  purple osier, 231
  ringleaf, 231
  white, 231
windflower, Grecian, 140
wintercreeper euonymus, 245
winter heather, 91
Wisteria floribunda, 241
wisteria, Japanese, 241
witch
  alder, dwarf, 180
  hazel, 97, 180, **201**
    Chinese, 125
woodruff, sweet, 76, 127
woolly thyme, 88
wormwood, 120
yarrow, 111, 112, 120, 126, 158, **159**
yellow
  foxglove, 133
  pine, 70
  pine, western, 70
yew, 77, 188, 193
  western native, 77
Zabel's laurel, 174
Zantedeschia aethiopica and cultivars, 50
zinnia, 38
zonal geranium, 31, 32, 41, 90
zoysia, 101

Meet Debra Prinzing &
Mary Robson

Debra Prinzing

Debra Prinzing is an experienced Seattle-based writer who writes about and styles gardens, interiors, and floral design projects. Prinzing previously covered home and garden topics for *The Everett Herald*. She currently writes about home design topics for *The Seattle Times* and is the Pacific-Northwest Regional columnist for *Gardening How-To* magazine. Prinzing is a contributor-at-large for *Romantic Homes*, covers interior design and retail trends for *Home Décor Buyer*, and has been published in *Fine Gardening, Sunset, Better Homes & Gardens* special interest titles, and a range of other publications.

In addition, Prinzing is an established author and editor of several books. These include *Northwest Gardeners' Resource Directory, Gardening in the Northwest*, and *The Northwest Survival Guide*. Debra also fits in a busy lecture schedule with appearances on HGTV "Outer Spaces" and other television and radio programs. This is Prinzing's first book for Cool Springs Press.

Prinzing credits the preparation of her background—a degree in textiles and design and many years as a business reporter—for her success. Debra and her husband, Bruce Brooks, and their children live in Seattle, Washington. Both sons, Benjamin and Alexander, are avid gardeners and also enjoy learning botanical names for plants.

Mary Robson

Mary Robson loves gardening. An experienced Washington-based horticulturalist, Robson worked with Washington State University Extension from 1987 through 2004. During that time, she headed the Master Gardener program of King County, teaching gardening skills to thousands of eager students, and served as Horticulture faculty member in western Washington.

Robson is well known for her speaking and writing abilities, as well as her teaching expertise. She answers gardening questions in her regularly published column in *The Seattle Times*, "The Practical Gardener", as well as contributing articles to other local and national publications. In 2002, Robson received an award from the National Association of County Agriculture Agents in recognition of her writing skills.

Robson learned gardening from her devoted mother and grandmother, and has dedicated herself to the "green world" since she helped move trilliums threatened by development at the age of 9. Her greatest satisfaction comes from learning, teaching, and responding to the world's beauty. Robson lives near Discovery Bay, Washington, where she enjoys sharing her world with birds, deer, the mountains, and clouds.